'Hewitt writes with a quiet magnificence, a warm and very detailed knowledge, of an artistic tradition which includes Sir John Lavery, AE, Paul Henry, William Conor, F.E. McWilliam, William Scott, Tom Carr, Gerard Dillon, Colin Middleton and T.P. Flanagan.' Tom Paulin, *Times Literary Supplement*

'John Hewitt's writing on art is rather like John Betjeman's on sculpture – urbane, deeply knowledgeable, unpedantic.' Brian Fallon, *Irish Times*

Drawing on a lifetime's gallery work and art criticism, John Hewitt presents a richly detailed and fascinating survey of four hundred years of art in Ulster – including the eighteenth-century portraiture of Joseph Wilson and Philip Hussey; AE, John Campbell and the Celtic revival; the 'timeless motifs' of Paul Henry; William Conor's pioneering representations of urban life and the eclectic experimentation of Colin Middleton and John Luke.

Here are oil paintings, watercolours, woodcuts, sculpture, cartoons, all presenting the growth and development of Ulster art, accompanied by an incisive text that firmly sets the artists and their work within the context of the social framework and prevailing artistic influences of their times, vividly capturing shifts and changes in fashion and aesthetics.

Infused with characteristic enthusiasm and good humour, Hewitt's authoritative study of Ulster art and its deep involvement with Ulster life and Irish landscape is complemented by over one hundred biographical sketches by the art critic Theo Snoddy, making *Art in Ulster 1: 1557–1957* an indispensable guide to the 'emerging cultural regional consciousness' of a province, its artists and craftsmen.

Front cover painting: *The Rehearsal* by John Luke.
Reproduced with kind permission of the Trustees of the Ulster Museum.
Courtesy of Mrs S. McKee.
Back cover painting: *A Bank of Flowers with a View of Bray, Co. Wicklow* by Andrew Nicholl.
Reproduced with kind permission of the Trustees of the Ulster Museum.

ART IN ULSTER 1
1557 – 1957

JOHN HEWITT

with biographies of the artists by
THEO SNODDY

THE
BLACKSTAFF PRESS
BELFAST

First published in 1977 by
The Blackstaff Press Limited
in association with
The Arts Council of Northern Ireland

This new edition published in 1991 by
The Blackstaff Press Limited
3 Galway Park, Dundonald, Belfast BT16 0AN, Northern Ireland

This edition has received financial assistance under the Cultural Traditions Programme which aims to encourage acceptance and understanding of cultural diversity.

Printed in Northern Ireland by Nicholson and Bass Limited

ISBN 0-85640-128-5

CONTENTS

ILLUSTRATIONS

COLOUR PLATES

BLACK AND WHITE ILLUSTRATIONS

ACKNOWLEDGEMENTS

This book would not have been written without the help of many persons. My thanks are therefore due to the following:

Brian Ferran, director of art and film of the Arts Council of Northern Ireland and to Brian Ballard, exhibitions officer, for their assistance, particularly in making visits to various provincial centres comfortable and expeditious, and to the young ladies of the typing pool who strove so bravely with my crabbed calligraphy:

To Ted Hickey of the art department of the Ulster Museum and to Martyn Anglesea and Eileen Black for making easy my access to the Museum's reserve collections:

To Roger Weatherup of the Armagh County Museum for similar co-operation:

To James Vitty of the Linen Hall Library and Ronald Adams for making available the resources of their shelves, for drawing my attention to a number of rare publications, and for allowing me to examine the Conor material deposited there:

To the courteous and cheerful young ladies of the Reference Department of the Belfast Public Library:

and to my nephew Dr John Keith Millar for clarifying a technical point of which I was ignorant:

and to those artists whose memories confirmed or extended mine:

H Echlin Neill, Padraic Woods and Rowel Friers.

INTRODUCTION

In presenting this account of the course of painting, sculpture and the graphic arts in Northern Ireland, the most difficult problem has been with the inclusions and exclusions of names from the compendious files so carefully compiled by Theo Snoddy. As, on the one hand, only a very few Ulster-born artists have achieved any recognition or notice across the water, and, on the other, since consideration of everyone who has painted, drawn, or modelled, and shown their work in public, would have had only the temporary significance of a directory of names, I have been compelled to apply subjective standards of quality, or have attempted to assess influence on the work of others, or relative popularity in the community, or remark the human interest in persons who once lived and worked here in these fields of activity. The area from which the names I have noticed have come, has been taken as the historical province of Ulster, if the artists were born before 1921. After that date, we have taken only those who were born and were active in the six counties of the State of Northern Ireland, or those born here whose working careers lay outside, but who retained some evidence or acknowledgment of their regional origin. It has been impossible simply to confine my comments to those born in the Province, since artists from elsewhere, who resided here for periods of varying length, have, in many instances, influenced their local contemporaries, or have been popular with local picture-buyers, and have therefore been part of the scene.

Of the living or recently deceased, I have considered those who, by 1957, were at least thirty years old, as, by that age, the sessions of pupilage were over and their work had been remarked in public exhibitions. There is to be another volume by another, younger hand, dealing with the art of the last two decades here, so I have set my limit at that year when I left Belfast, where, from 1930 I had been on the staff of the Belfast Museum and Art Gallery (now the Ulster Museum), and, from its establishment in 1943, a member of the Art advisory committee of the Council for the Encouragement of Music and the Arts, (CEMA, now the Arts Council of Northern Ireland). Also from 1953 to 1957, I had been critic of the *Belfast Telegraph* and reported on northern exhibitions for the *Irish Times*. So, for the second quarter of the century, I can put a face to every name I mention, and I have been privileged to talk or listen to old men whose memories went back to George Trobridge and John Vinycomb.

This survey covers a restricted area and a small population at some distance from the art centres of Europe, so I have necessarily been modest about claiming any great aesthetic significance for the works mentioned in my narrative; but as a chapter too frequently disregarded in local history, I believe that it possesses some interest.

John Hewitt

CHAPTER 1

Generalisations, particularly about peoples or nations, are notoriously suspect. Nevertheless, it can be asserted with some assurance that Ireland which has given to English and, some among them, to world literature and drama, such names as Swift, Goldsmith, Sheridan, Wilde, Shaw, Yeats, Synge, Joyce, O'Casey, Beckett, has, whether for geographical, historical, economic or even psychological reasons, made no comparable contribution to the visual arts. Yet Scotland, not greatly dissimilar in area, population or in its placing on the earth's surface, can claim an honourable muster of painters, Ramsay, Raeburn, Geddes, Wilkie, MacTaggart, though both have been markedly deficient in sculpture.

Noting this, we are simply accepting the fact that Ireland has not been among the greater painting nations like the Italians, the Flemish, the Dutch, the French. *The Oxford Companion of Art* has entries for Islamic, Indian and Italian art, but none for Irish. This has stood in relation to English work, itself not one of the great master-schools, perhaps as Portugal has stood to Spain.

When we write of painting and sculpture in the North of Ireland, we are writing of a small area and a small population; and that small area, which can be crossed east to west or south to north in a day's car drive, is also part of an island on the westernmost edge of Europe, two seas away from the great historic centres of European art. So that any ripples or pulsations from those centres which may have reached it, have, by necessity, taken some time to arrive and have suffered varying degrees of dilution.

The North of Ireland, given the name of Ulster when the whole island was divided into its four provinces, has had a history with its own peculiar differences, remaining for a long time much less affected by attempts at conquest from the larger sister island of Great Britain after Agricola, with his Roman legions, glimpsed it across the grey waters. The Vikings established a port at Dublin, but their hurried incursions to the North have left us no more than a place-name or two, Carlingford, Strangford. Their Dublin port became the Anglo-Norman point of entry, bridge-head, base for expansion, but their influence in the north was confined to a few coastal forts such as Dundrum, Ardglass, Carrickfergus, Dunluce, on the rim of a land of forests and broadwaters.

Before the Norsemen's long ships, there had been a flowering of Celtic Christianity in Ireland, and the north of the country had been the chief territory of Patrick's missionary travels. But time and the Vikings wrought their havoc, and, of physical evidence of that epoch, have left only scant remains, a sprinkle of monastic sites, of round towers such as those at Antrim, at Devenish, of high sculptured crosses such as Tynan and Arboe. And of the characteristic arts of calligraphy and illumination of manuscripts, no more than one document, the Latin copy of the New Testament and the life of St Patrick, known as the *Book of Armagh* (c AD 807), preserves the name of a northern scribe, Ferdomnach, who, according to the *Annals of Ulster*, died in 845 AD.

The art and craft of working metal into significant shapes, or delicately decorated surfaces, the carving of figures and designs in stone, suffered the same eclipse. Only in stone-carving in the Lough Erne basin did any trace of the earlier preoccupations persist beyond the great Early Christian and Romanesque periods, 5th to 12th centuries, and this was in a remote pocket among trees and waters, not much subject to the influx of invading peoples until the seventeenth century. Helen Hickey, in her recent study, *Images of Stone* (1976) has sought to demonstrate the survival of this in a rudimentary, unsophisticated form, until the third quarter of the nineteenth century.

Though from remote times, because of its proximity to Scotland, the north-east had penetrations, these had been to and fro movements. Not until the later sixteenth century did any marked immigration in historic times, in this instance from the Lowlands of Scotland, have its effect on north and east Down, and, from the western Scottish seaboard, on east Antrim. But with the defeat of the northern Irish clans and the resultant Flight of the Earls in 1609, the centre and west of the Province was laid open to the new Plantation of English and Scots settlers which inevitably changed the balance of populations. As a consequence of this, we have no old cities or towns in Ulster, nothing so redolent of its historic past as Kilkenny with its churches and their recumbent effigies, its capacious merchants' dwellings. Apart from St Nicholas' church and its castle, the past of Carrickfergus is only now being laid bare.

On the continent of Europe the great schools of painting and sculpture seem in the past to have required, besides the existence of talented persons, wealthy ecclesiastical establishments, the authority of a royal or ducal court, or the bustle of towns of commerce and trade, to give purpose and sustenance to the practice of the arts. The influential patrons were princes, aristocratic landowners or rich merchants.

In a land beset by tribal or clan warfare, complicated by the intruders from England struggling to establish their sovereignty, with an economy which had its basis in cattle-raising, there was little domestic architecture on a large scale save within the Pale. And the churches were too often pillaged, to permit the accumulation of rich decorative embellishment or equipment.

The influence of the Renaissance, slow in reaching Great Britain with its own ruling class meshed in the Wars of the Roses, was even slower in touching our northern shores. Only that strange Italianate *loggia* incorporated in the jumble of Dunluce Castle symbolises its tardy coming.

Apart from the squat conventional figures carved in relief on the high crosses or the much sculptured knights on their tombs, the first convincing representation of natives of the island seems to have been Albrecht Dürer's drawings taken in 1521, of a gang of wandering mercenary soldiers encountered somewhere on the edge of the landmass of Europe.

During the Elizabethan wars of subjugation a few of the English made scribbles and crude sketches of their strange and exotic enemies. But John Derricke's *The Image of Irelande* (1581) provides a remarkable record of the appliances and equipment of those engaged in one of these campaigns. This book, a rhyming poem on the warring Irish, and their defeat by the Lord Deputy, Sir Henry Sidney, is illustrated with a dozen large woodcuts: these appear, by variations in style and execution, to have come from three separate hands, two of the artists signing their wood-blocks with the initials I.D., or F.D., the first likely to have been John Derricke himself, the second his brother Francis; the third, less skilful, anonymous. Of these illustrations, two have specifically Ulster themes; Plate III of the chief of the MacSweeneys of Donegal, seated with companions at an *al fresco* lunch, surrounded by servants cutting up an animal carcase, cooking the meat, or apparently warming their backsides at a little fire, while a harper plays his instrument and a bard entertains the company with song or recitation. Of this, Derricke remarks that the scene comes 'Out of the North — whose usages I beheld after the fashion there sette downe'. Plate XII represents the submission of Tourlough Luineach O'Neill in 1578 to the Lord Deputy, the tribal chief and his bareheaded henchmen kneeling before the English commander who is seated in his tent, surrounded by his standing officers. In the background, a later stage in the submission is depicted; Sidney has come out of his tent and stoops to embrace the Irish chief very cordially. This second illustration is much more accomplished in composition and detail, and must be given its early place in the Imperialist Gallery, an ikon fit to rank with that oil painting by Jones Barker, now in the National Portrait Gallery, of Queen Victoria presenting a bible, in the audience chamber at Windsor, to a turbaned black man, copies, or unacknowledged versions of which have billowed on the banners of many an Orange Lodge.

The Planters, the new settlers in the north, though they kept to a class-structure rooted in the terms of their conditions of land tenure, were, in effect, frontiersmen living uneasily beside the natives, clearing the woods, tilling the largely virgin soil, and, as in the rather fiercer settlement in North America, it was some time before any call went out for painting or sculpture. Muskets, axes, spades and sickles were more eagerly grasped than pencils or brushes, bibles and maps more urgently needed than sketching pads or canvasses.

In Dublin, the seat of the Vice-regal court, and of the apparatus of law and administration, some urge to patronage, to the employment of artists, was emerging; likenesses to be taken, visual commemorations to be made, memorials to be erected. But in Ulster, with the rising of the dispossessed Irish in 1641, the Plantation underwent its most serious challenge, so that not until the Cromwellian campaign, and its resultant plantations outside the north, did a period of some stability ensue, which lasted until the Williamite wars thirty years later. Among the great landowning families, paintings begin to be mentioned in the household inventories. English and foreign artists seem to have arrived in Dublin, hearing of, and hoping for the chance of work.

And, often, there was a demand for portraits of King William and Queen Mary, to certify the loyalty of those who found or had placed themselves on the winning side and had walls capacious enough to hang them on. Bishop Walker, the famous defender of the beseiged Londonderry, and Duke Schomberg, killed at the Battle of the Boyne, were also popular subjects among northern aristocratic families.

Of many of these, a cursory glance would suggest that the canvasses had been produced with the half-length torsos already painted, and the heads supplied when the purchasers' preferences were expressed.

In time, a few Irish-born artists appear, those most talented to cross over to London, to follow the calling in the busier, more profitable market, or to further their professional studies on the continent. But not until the next century were any of the great Georgian houses built, and with the new security, the wealth and prestige of the aristocracy, required works of art to embellish the spacious buildings which no longer needed to be fortified by other than demesne walls against the resentful natives whom the Penal Laws kept in check. This circumstance drew in more painters from England, but, at that time, to quote Sir Kenneth Clark, 'The first twenty-five years of the eighteenth century saw English painting at its lowest ebb.' So that those who could not find a footing in London or the English provinces and sought employment in Ireland, were not among the most highly skilled, or else, for non-aesthetic reasons, found the voyage necessary.

By mid-century the foundation of the Dublin Society's schools would indicate that the profession of painting had established itself in the country, and the urge for the better equipped to seek and hold recognised status among the artists in London was confirmed by the migration of two of the best of the Irish born, Nathaniel Hone (1718-1784) and George Barrett (1728-1784), both of whom ultimately became members of the newly-founded Royal Academy.

In the same period we find the first painter from the north holding his own among his Dublin contemporaries: Robert Hunter became the leading portraitist there for thirty years, described as 'a mild, amiable man, liberal in communicating what he knew, and generous in estimating the works of his brother artists'. He was born probably around 1730, and, likely, trained at the Dublin Society's schools, but we know nothing of his birthplace, or how long he had spent in his native province before going south.

The traffic of visiting English artists continued, and a few of these made their way north as the owners of the newly built large country-houses began to offer commissions, and as a more secure and prosperous middle class began to merge with the growth of Belfast.

Although its charter had been granted as far back as 1613, this had simply been a device to increase parliamentary representation and to strengthen the King's party, and Belfast, for a long time, remained a small market town with an unimpressive little castle, a church, a market-house, a huddle of thatched cottages and the Long Bridge across the tidal waters of the Lagan estuary.

Then, in the second half of the eighteenth century, it began to develop as a port and a place of commerce; ships sailing to France, to Holland and the Baltic, and, across the Atlantic, to Philadelphia, Boston, and the West Indies, carrying out cargoes of linen, butter, hides, bringing in hardware, steel, sugar, tobacco and wine. But an attempt to bring it into line with Liverpool and Bristol, by joining in the Slave Trade, was challenged and rebuffed.

As the town prospered and leases were lengthened, handsome houses were built for the merchants round Donegall Place and Donegall Square where the Marquess of Donegall, Chichester's descendant, had his town dwelling, his large house was out at Ormeau. Anglican churches from 1776, and, for Dissenters from 1783, were erected. The Exchange and assembly rooms (1763, the Brown Linen Hall (1773), the White Linen Hall (1785), the Poor House (1774), signalised vastly increased importance. The Belfast Academy, the Reading Society extended to become the Society for Promoting Knowledge (1788), a theatre, and local newspapers, were required to meet the developing demands of the prospering middle class. By 1800 the population stood at 20,000. Painters' names began to appear in the press.

The first that we know of was Joseph Wilson who had previously worked in Dublin. So we are not sure if he was one of the travelling artists who settled in Belfast or whether he was native to the north. Wealthy Belfast merchants had had family portraits painted before this, very likely going up to Dublin for the occasion, as, perhaps, when Philip Hussey (1713-1783) painted the Batesons in 1763. But Wilson found customers

1 JOSEPH WILSON
Captain William Dawson
n d; oil; 76.5 x 63.6 cms;
Ulster Museum collection

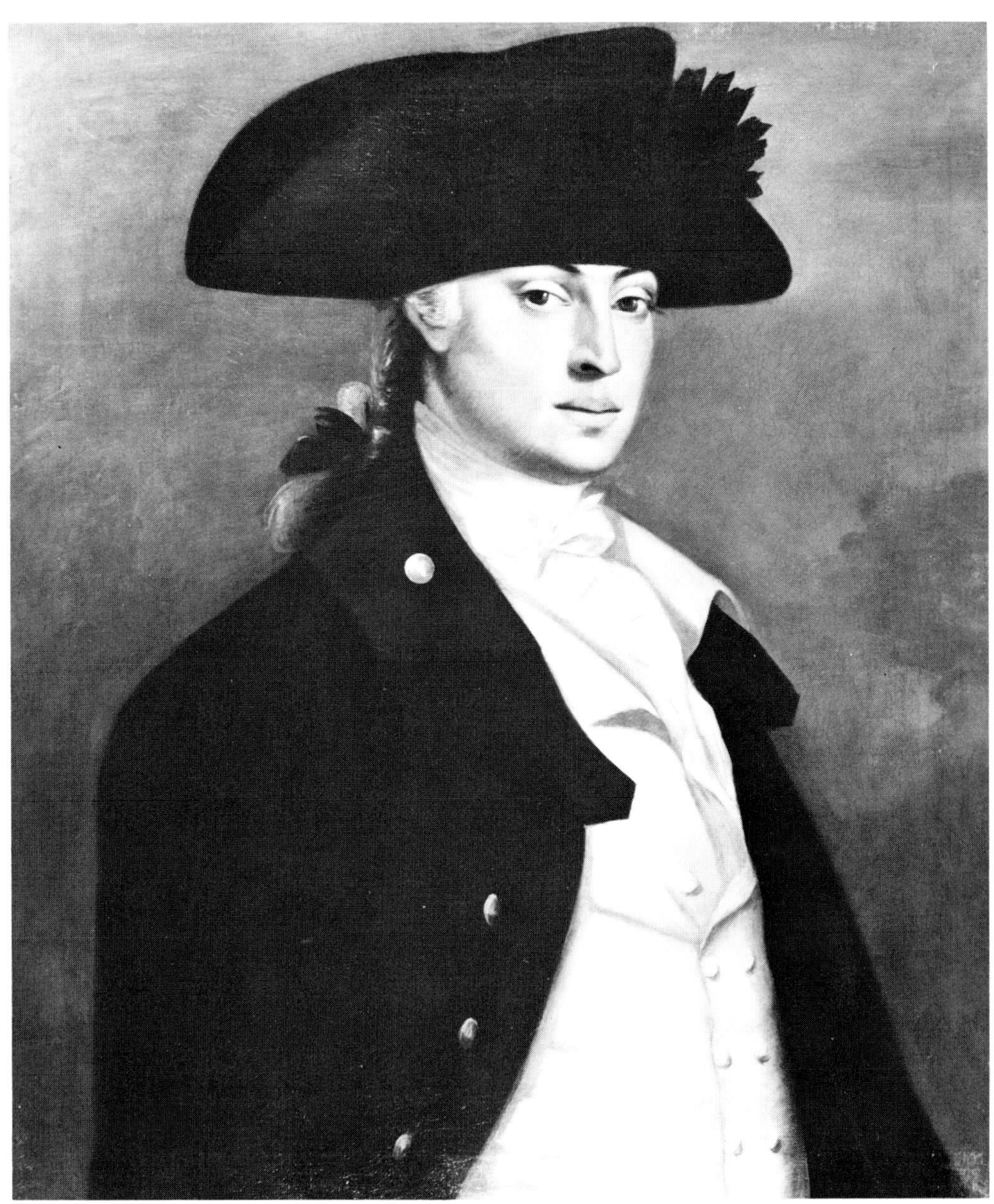

to hand, his most interesting sitter being David Manson who ran a rather experimental school. Yet, as with so many who made their living by likeness-catching. Wilson dreamed of competing with the great masters who handled great subjects and tremendous themes. In 1782 he painted a large composition 'Daniel interpreting to Belshazzar the writing on the Wall', that event Rembrandt had tackled so dramatically. There was an advertisement in the *News Letter* giving the details of the raffle the artist had organised to dispose of it. In the same journal of 15 March 1793, his death is reported: 'Died on Wednesday, at Echlinvale, Co Down, Mr Joseph Wilson long a portrait painter and landscape painter in this town, and a very worthy man.' From the portraits surviving, he seems to have been an honest journeyman of the brush, a little unsophisticated but not a primitive, frequently having a kind of affectionate regard for his sitter.

'A travelling portrait painter stopping at Belfast to take the likenesses of a few persons he had brought letters to' was John Williams, who engaged also in the career of polemical and satirical journalist under the pseudonym of 'Anthony Pasquin', met Amyas Griffith, surveyor of Excise, a vain, crooked-legged writer of verses and miscellaneous tracts, who was also, perhaps, under-cover editor of *The Belfast Mercury or Freeman's Chronicle*. Griffith introduced him to the little centre to which he belonged.

Shortly after, Williams painted the conversation piece, *The Adelphi Club*. The ten men represented include, besides Griffith and Williams himself, three local merchants, a couple of actors, the then celebrated comedian Richard Cox Rowe, Michael Atkins, owner and manager of the Belfast Theatre, and an unidentified person. Some books lie on the table, with a decanter of rum and glasses, and a tankard of ale is in Griffith's fist.

Griffith had arrived in Belfast only a year or two earlier, became involved in politics and, as a consequence, lost his job, and had to leave the town in 1785. In the *Belfast Mercury* of 13th January of the next year, there is an advertisement of an engraving of Griffith's 'excellent likeness', 'from an original drawing by Joseph Wilson, of Belfast, portrait painter', which had been first published in the *Gentleman and London Magazine* the month before, and was now available from all the booksellers in Belfast, Lisburn, Newry, Armagh, Strabane, Derry, Coleraine and Downpatrick.

Another more numerous, and otherwise very different, gathering of folk was the subject of a watercolour by William Miller, the inventive Lurgan Quaker, who seems to have been a woollen draper. John Wesley, on his preaching tour of 1763, visited him and inspected his 'speaking clock' which announced the hours, and on his next visit, eleven years later, found that he had adapted the clock 'not only to speak but sing hymns alternately with an articulate voice'. Miller also painted flowers and portraits on glass, and an angel pointing to a text in *Revelations*, in the little Methodist meeting-house, behind the preaching dais.

The great Methodist Revival also provided the theme for Miller's surviving picture, now in the

2 JOHN WILLIAMS
The Adelphi Club
1782/1783; oil; size not known (photographic copy); Linen Hall Library collection

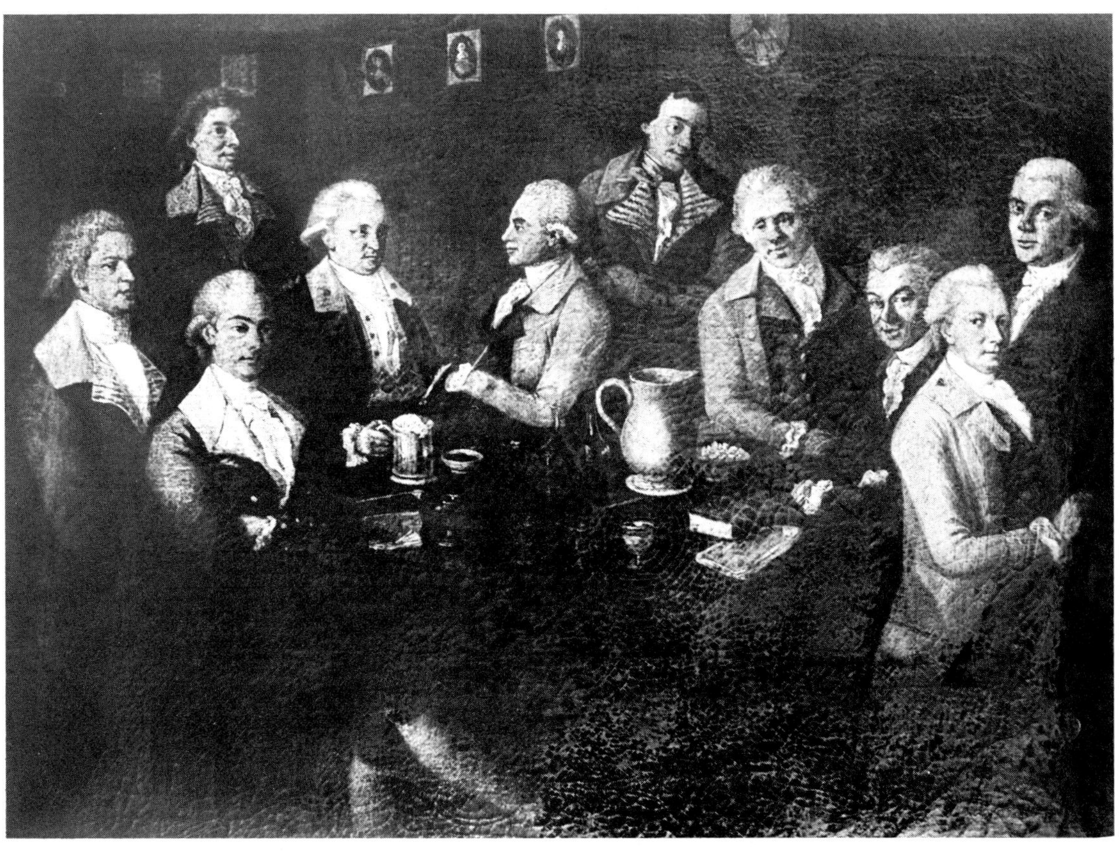

Ulster Museum, which represents George Whitefield preaching in a timber-yard in Lurgan in July 1751. The watercolour which reminds one of New England work, is naive, obviously not by a trained professional, with abrupt changes of scale — Whitefield, of a much more ample build, with wig, Geneva bands and squinting eyes, towers over a jostle of some scores of rather grotesque, bonnetted women and bare-headed men, facing disconcertingly in all directions. The sky-line is punctuated by the massive preacher's upper body, slender trees, and leaning buildings, and, above, ragged cloud-like areas are inscribed with a somewhat Miltonic set of blank verses in a minute calligraphy. Here and there, the ingenious artist has, with a sharp knife or razor, cut around various heads, to give the composition something of the appearance of a three-dimensional *collage*.

George Whitefield, the supreme orator of the Revival, was the pioneer of field or open air

3 WILLIAM MILLER
George Whitefield preaching in the timber yard at Lurgan, 12 July 1751
n d; watercolour; 33 x 43.5 cms; Ulster Museum collection

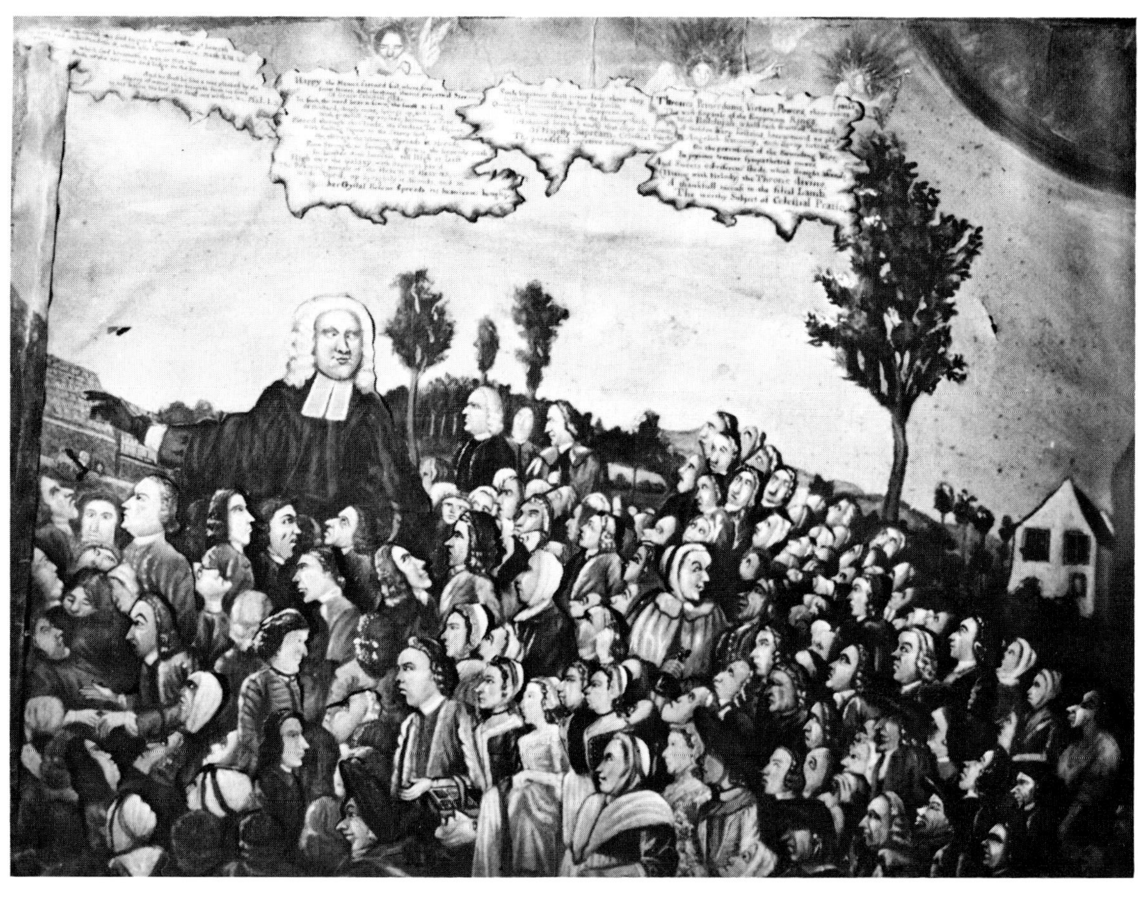

preaching. John Richard Green, in his once popular *Short History of the English People* (1874) has described the effect of that eloquence which 'was such as England had never heard before..., extravagant, often commonplace, but hushing all criticism with its intense reality, its earnestness of belief, its deep tremulous sympathy with the sin and sorrow of mankind'. It was no common enthusiast who could wring gold from the close-fisted Franklin and admiration from the fastidious Horace Walpole, or who could look down from a green knoll at Kingswood on twenty thousand colliers, from their Bristol coal-pits, and see as he preached the cross 'marking white channels down their blackened cheeks'.

But, largely because of his associations, the most

interesting of the travelling painters was Thomas Robinson of Windermere, a pupil of Romney, after whom he called his son. Dublin had been his point of entry, where that son, Thomas Romney Robinson, was born in 1793. Shortly after, he came north to Lawrencetown, County Down, to paint portraits for Captain Thomas Dawson Lawrence, the local squire.

Lawrence, a schoolfellow of Oliver Goldsmith, and a veteran of Minden, had in 1789, dedicated his volume of conventional verse to his neighbour, Thomas Percy, Bishop of Dromore. The famous Bishop, who had edited *Reliques of Ancient English Poetry* in 1765, had been one of Samuel Johnson's circle, and had had his portrait painted by Sir Joshua Reynolds, when he came to Dromore, was, by far, the most celebrated and prestigious man-of-letters and general culture to take up his residence in the north.

His Palace, which was, in fact, a newlybuilt, spacious, but not remarkable house, became a great centre for those with like tastes to the Bishop, and for visiting celebrities. Very soon Robinson became a frequent caller with various tasks to fulfil — to repaint the face in one of Percy's portraits, to colour the obelisk and the plaster busts set up in the extended garden. The boy, Thomas Romney, became a favourite of the Bishop's, since his precocity made him of some interest, composing rhymes by the age of three, and a bright listener to Percy's literary anecdotes. By the time he entered Trinity College, Dublin, at the age of thirteen, his single volume of verse was brought out in 1806. *Juvenile Poems* was, of course, dedicated to Percy, and had as a frontispiece a drawing of the lad by his father. The list of subscribers runs to over 1,800 names, an amazing roll-call of national and local notabilities, and must have been the result of a massive public relations exercise, lent prestige and authority by the Bishop's support. Among these names we find 'Signior Fabbrini', the Italian drawing-master at the Belfast Academy, which the boy-poet attended, and 'Mr Thomson, painter' — Thomas Clement Thompson, who was later to establish himself in London.

Thomas Robinson had earlier provided the original drawing for the aquatint-frontispiece to *Ardglass or the Ruined Castles* (1802) by the Rev Samuel Burdy, whose association with Percy had had its ups and downs. In a prefatory note, Burdy apologises for having to raise the price of his little book from three shillings and threepence to four shillings and fourpence; 'when he promised in his conditions to subscribers that an elegant Print of the Ruined Castles, accurately engraved, should be prefixed, he understood that he could get it executed in this country in the style proposed, at a very small expense. But at the express desire of the artist, who had volunteered to take the drawing required, he was obliged to send it to London to be engraved in *aqua tinta*.'

Robinson also painted the *Giant's Causeway*, the canvas passing into Percy's possession, but he was primarily a portrait painter, moving to Lisburn and to Belfast, to attract commissions. Of his Belfast portraits, one of the best is that of William Ritchie, the Scots shipbuilder, who had transferred his business from Saltcoats, Ayrshire, to the Lagan in 1791. That year he constructed the first Graving Dock, and the next successfully launched a vessel of 300 tons. The boy-poet saluted him in his couplet verses, *The Triumph*

4 THOMAS ROBINSON
William Ritchie
n d; oil; 93.7 x 74.6 cms;
Ulster Museum collection

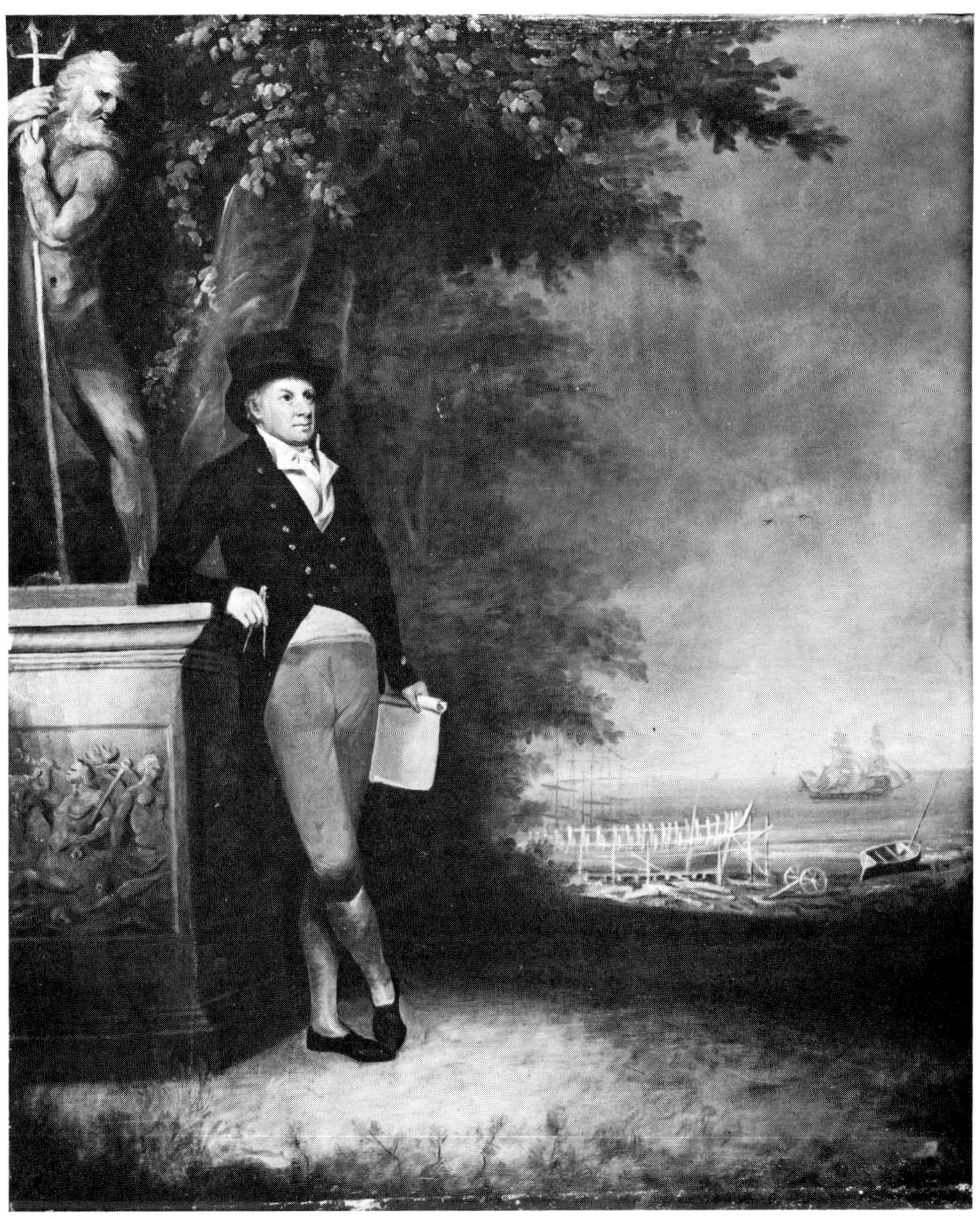

5 THOMAS ROBINSON
aquatint; illustration from *Ardglass or the Ruined Castles*... by Rev Samuel Burdy, Dublin 1802

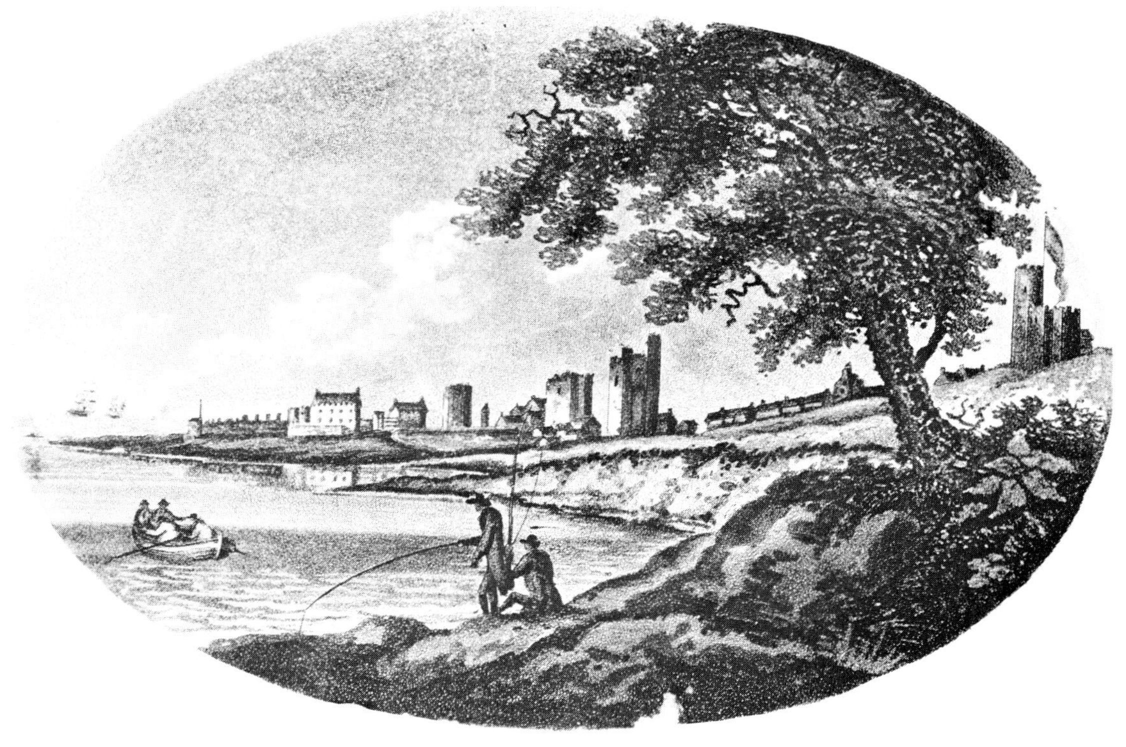

of Commerce, written in his ninth year:

> Ingenious Ritchie! Commerce now may smile,
> And shed her blessings o'er Hibernia's Isle,
> Go, teach her sons to raise the ship on high,
> The pointed mast, high towering to the sky...

Robinson's best known tribute to Percy and his friends may be seen in his *Group at Dromore* (1807) now at Castleward. The occasion depicted was the reading by Thomas Stott, bleaching master of Dromore and once target of Byron's satire, of his elegy on the Bishop's recently deceased wife. Beside Percy, seated with bowed head on the left, we have the Rev Henry Boyd, first English translator of Dante, a clutch of noble gentlemen, involving Castlereagh, an Irish harper, the painter himself and his tall son.

Like most other ambitious artists of the period, he tried his hand at large compositions, in one notable instance, at history painting; *The Battle of Ballinahinch* (1798), one of the very few commemorations of a local historical event. Based to some degree on Benjamin West's *Death of General Wolfe*, it represents the death of the adjutant of the Monaghan Militia in the battle between the Crown forces and the United Irishmen, which was the most serious encounter in the north during the famous Ninety-eight Rebellion. The landscape behind and beyond the battle-smoke is carefully recorded. From an advertisement for its public exhibition, the artist asserts that the 'Picture contains many original portraits and is a faithful representation of the field of Battle and its events'. The admission charge to the showing was 'one British shilling'. A raffle for its possession was organised, with tickets at one guinea; ticket holders being admitted free.

A second large work (1804) had, for its first title, *Review of the Belfast Volunteers*, later *Military Procession in honour of Lord Nelson*, and, finally, *The Entry of Lord Hardwick into Belfast, as Lord Lieutenant, 27th August 1804*. The architectural background is entirely fictitious, with classical columns and a statue of Nelson on a high plinth — there was no public statue in the town for another fifty years. The painting was not disposed of, and remained in the artist's family until, in 1852, the boy-poet, by this time Dr T R Robinson, Astronomer at Armagh, brought it to Belfast for exhibition in the museum, on the occasion of the meeting of the British Association. Seeing the impressive plans for the new Harbour Office, then in course of construction, he presented it to the Board for display in the completed building, where it now hangs. A numbered key identifies most of the participating crowd which included many of those later subscribers to *Juvenile Poems*; over forty of them.

Robinson left Belfast in 1808, and died in Dublin two years later. A contemporary described him as 'an interesting, sensible man, of great simplicity and very poor': His work has little painterly quality, seldom rising above mediocrity, but because many of his subjects have local historical interest, we are grateful for his efforts.

Thomas Clement Thompson, whose portrait appears among the admiring crowd in Robinson's *Review* and who was subscriber to the book of verse, seems to have been a local man. In 1796 he entered the Dublin Society's schools, and later carried on his craft as miniaturist there and in Belfast, before taking up oilpainting, and, in 1817, crossing over to London. An original member of the RHA in 1823, he is remembered for his drawings which were the bases for the prints of *A View of the Lagan from Ormeau Park*, 'which shows the Marquess of Donegall alighting from a pleasure boat', and *A View of Old Paper Mills on the edge of the Blackstaff river*, and for a couple of portraits more fully realised than Robinson's.

Miniatures had their place for those who could not afford anything larger, and, certainly, from their size and cost made handy presents, so itinerant makers of these visited Belfast often. In the first half of 1800 we find George Madden begging 'leave to inform his Friends in Belfast that he intends residing among them for *a short time* in his Professional capacity, at Mr Williamson's, opposite the Donegall Arms', and Miss Higginson, 'from Dublin, the only pupil of the celebrated Hone', who intended staying for

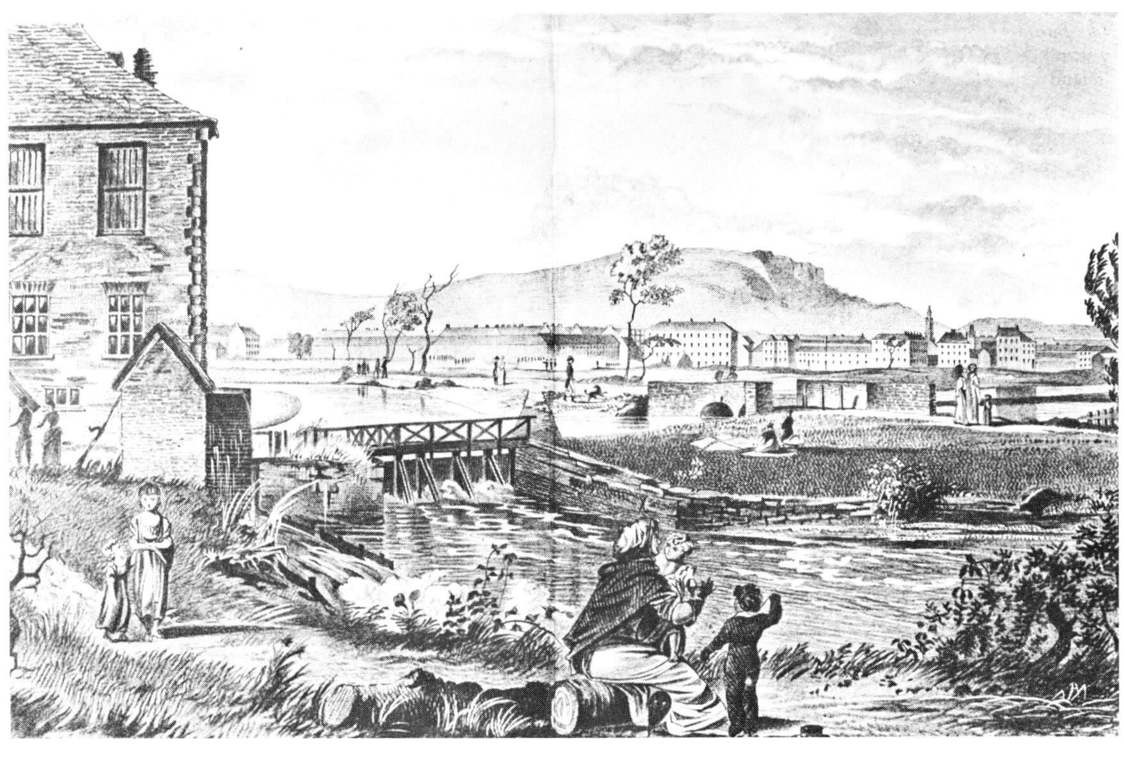

6 THOMAS CLEMENT THOMPSON
View of Belfast from the Old Paper Mill in 1805
From a reproduction in *The History of the Belfast Library* (Linen Hall Library) by John Anderson, Belfast 1888

some time 'at Mr Orr's, High Street, where she will be happy to execute the commands of such Ladies and Gentlemen as may favour with theirs. Hours of attendance, from 10 to 4. She hopes that on inspection her paintings will appear to be executed in a superior stile.'

Richard William Dyke 'little Dyke', he was called, who had been a medal-winning pupil of the Dublin Society schools, had been living in Belfast for about a decade, producing 'striking likenesses in crayons and watercolours at a guinea apiece'. He also taught figure, landscape and flower drawing, ran an evening school 'for the tuition of young gentlemen'; and gave lessons on the flute: a member of the Anacreontic Society, he kept a music shop for a short time. But he seems to have found the competition severe, for, by April, the *News Letter* carries the announcement 'Mr Dyke miniature painter, from Belfast, presents his respects to the polite inhabitants of Armagh, and its vicinity, and informs them, that in the course of a few days he intends to pay his respects to them, in the line of his profession. As his engagements in Belfast will not admit of his making any long stay in that city, he will be proud to receive the commands of such Ladies and Gentlemen, who may do him

I THOMAS ROBINSON
The Battle of Ballynahinch
n d; oil; National Gallery of Ireland

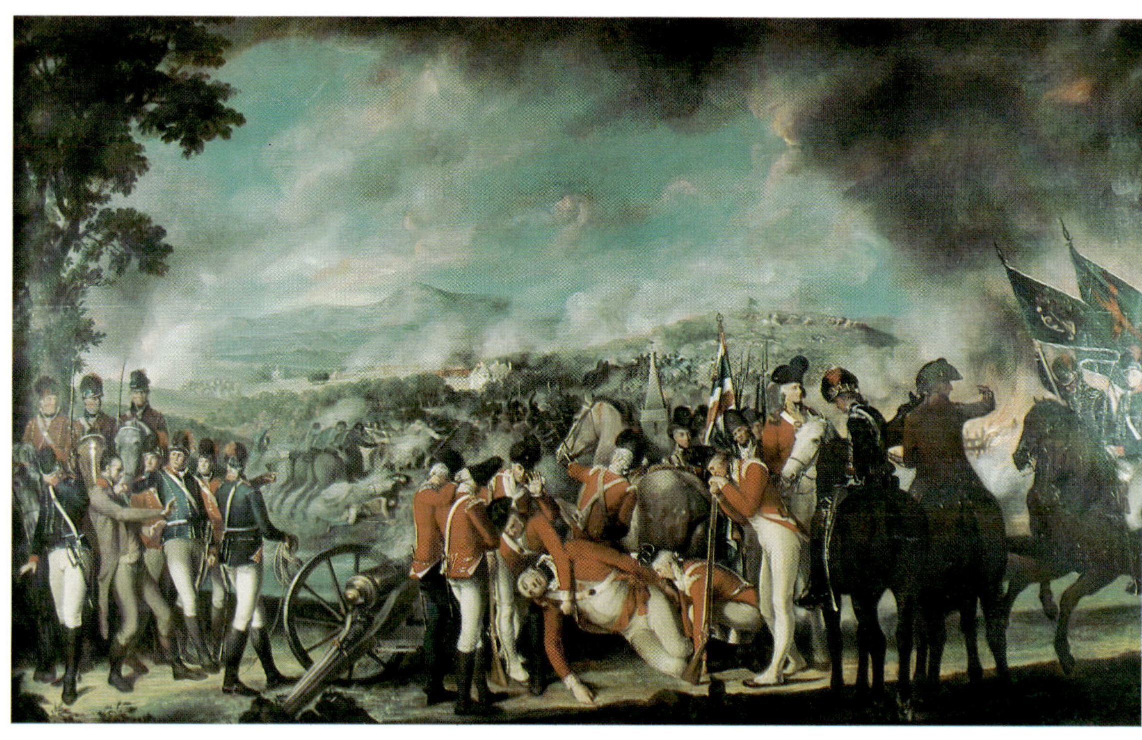

facing page 16

the honour of employing him as soon as possible.' (18 April 1800).

At the same time, Mr Herbert, while acting in the local theatre, acquainted 'those Ladies and Gentlemen who intend sitting to him for their Portraits, that he has begun, and *will continue* to paint for the *short time* he intends remaining in Belfast'. While acting and making his miniatures he also found vacant hours to paint figures for the scenery for which Michael Atkins, the manager, provided the landscapes, and Mr Atkins junior, the architectural portions for the play *Pizarro* which comprised, act by act, 'the magnificent tent and pavilion of *Pizarro* with a distant view of the Peruvian camp, the temple of the sun,' a rocky Caskade down a precipice and the falling bridge'. The whole production proved so expensive that 'nothing under full price can be taken'. Then, later, he requested that, after his benefit on the 16th May, 'Those Ladies and Gentlemen whose Portraits he has begun... will favour him with an opportunity of finishing the pictures to the 25th instant, as his engagement in England will oblige them to leave Belfast that day.'

Mr Hilmer, who played Motley to Mr Herbert's Earl Desmond in *The Castle Spectre*, spent his daylight hours giving lessons in 'Figure, Landscape and Ornamental Drawing', as well as painting watercolour and oil designs on silk and satin.

Topographical or landscape work was slow in emerging in the British Isles. The first exponents were from farther east. Perhaps the most influential was the Bohemian, Wenceslaus Hollar (1607-1677), who was first brought over to England by a patron in 1636, and came back after seeking refuge from the Civil War. He made watercolour drawings, many of them to be used for his later engravings. Then there was the Flemish Jan Siberechts (1627-1703) who arrived in England in 1672 and remained until his death.

The making of paintings or drawings of places not faces had an even more uncertain and later start in Ireland. The first of the visiting artists to make drawings of Irish scenes was probably the English amateur, Francis Place (1647-1728), who had been a pupil of Hollar. Arriving in 1698, he visited Drogheda, Dublin and Kilkenny, and produced a number of fine drawings, the pioneer of the many Irish Tours to be undertaken later. Before him, and for some time after, topographical work in Ireland was of a map-like kind, of forts, seiges, battle-sites, and, later, of estates or towns taken from a elevated viewpoint.

But it was the young noblemen or gentlemen returning after the Grand Tour whose taste determined landscape art, coming back with their visual imaginations stimulated by the vistas of the Roman Campagna and memories of the paintings of Claude, Salvatore Rosa, and Gaspard Poussin. The term Picturesque seems to have been used for the first time in 1784, and, during the eighteenth century, travellers became increasingly responsive to castles, ruins, mountains, lakes, meandering rivers, as items with pictorial resonance.

The history of landscape painting is closely related to the appearance of topographical verse,

7 DONALD STEWART
Benmore Head
before 1810; sepia; Armagh Museum collection

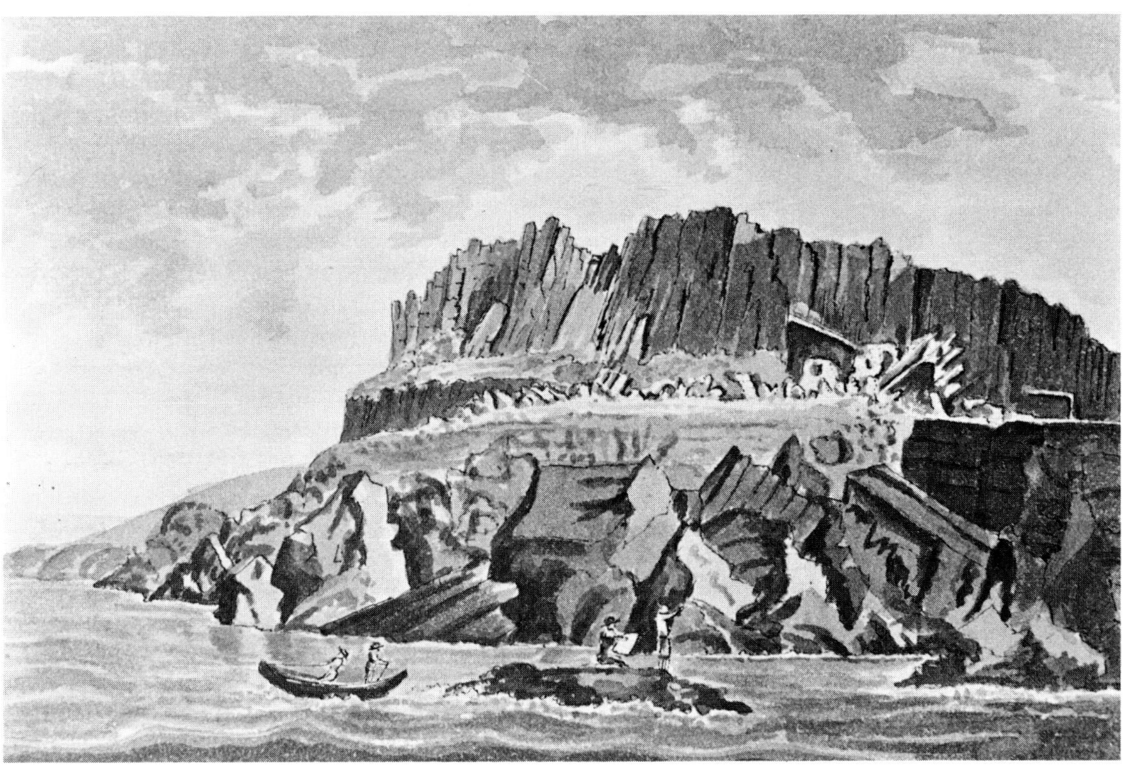

what are often called Prospect Poems. John Dyer's *Grongar Hill* is a good example, for Dyer was both a poet and a painter. English poetry has a host of examples: from Jago's *Edge Hill* (1767) every county has its solid batch of blank verse. But, here too, Ireland made a slower and much more muted response. John Ward's *Phoenix Park* (1718) was followed very infrequently. In Ulster, those that came were much later.

Our best example is William Carr's *Rosstrevor* (1810), since W H Drummond's *Giant's Causeway* (1811) is more of a treatise in geological theory than an authentic landscape prospect, though the Causeway had been, since the first half of the eighteenth century, a famous example of the Sublime and the Beautiful. But Drummond's couplets have the advantage of the relevant illustrations by Donald Stewart, engraved from the original wash drawings now in the Armagh County Museum.

A foreign landscape painter working in Ireland was Johann Van der Hagen (flourished 1715-1745), who found interesting subjects in the

South but ventured as far north as Londonderry, which he made the subject of a study which contains identifiable architectural details, and includes himself sketching in the foreground.

With the building of great houses outside Dublin arose a demand from the proprietors for records of their new, prestige-conferring dwellings. So we have a number of Ulster houses, throughout the eighteenth century, depicted by unnamed hands, Castleward, Shane's Castle, Glenarm Castle, Castle Dillon, Crom Castle, Rosemount, Greyabbey. Several towns were also painted, Coleraine, Enniskillen, in this instance attributed to the Cork artist, John Butts (1727-1765), and, with the interest which was becoming fashionable, attention shifted to romantic motifs, ruins, archaeological remains, like Dunluce, Devenish. The Giant's Causeway, which had been accepted as one of the wonders of the world, was the most attractive subject for those seeking the astonishing and impressive. In an early Account of the *Giant's Causeway in the North of Ireland* by Dr Samuel Foley, in the philosophical Transactions of the Royal Society, there is an illustration, 'A Draught of the Gyant's Causeway which lyes near Pengore Head in the County of Antrim' by C Cole, 'a collector of those parts'. In a subsequent communication to the society, it was declared that the representation was inadequate, 'being done by one who was no extraordinary artist, though the best that could be had'. But, by 1740, the first awards made by the Dublin Society went to Susanna Drury for her watercolours of the subject. Engravings of these proved popular: the originals are now in the Ulster Museum.

Many landscape drawings were made to be engraved and multiplied. An Englishman, John Nixon, visited the north frequently between 1785 and 1799, and his prints after these circulated widely, particularly that of Belfast with the oddly rural foreground.

But for an oil-landscape of an Ulster subject by an artist of outstanding quality, we have to take *A View of Castleward from the Doric Temple* (1785) by William Ashford (1746-1824). Ashford, an Englishman, lived in Ireland for many years, becoming the first president of the RHA. It is only in the last decade or two that his reputation has been renewed. One of the most interesting in this field is *Armagh* (1810) by a James Black. As has already been noted, Robinson had made a few landscape essays, and T C Thompson had moved from miniatures in that direction, but it was not until the first third of the nineteenth century that the northern countryside and towns were painted or drawn by known Ulster artists. This is related to the rise in prosperity of the middleclass, now seeking the small oilpainting, the watercolour, or the engraved view, to decorate their drawing-rooms. The premier example on this head was the publication of *Belfast Scenery in Thirty Views* (1832) engraved by Edward K Proctor in aquatint from drawings by Joseph Molloy. This was a late provincial descendant of the kind of publication inaugurated by a book such as *Britannia Illustrata* (1714) which contained 'Views of several of the Queen's Palaces, as also of the Principal Seats of Nobility and Gentry curiously engraved on 80 copper plates'.

The *Thirty Views* book was dedicated to the Marchioness of Donegall, and had as its subjects the houses of local gentry, mostly of fairly recent

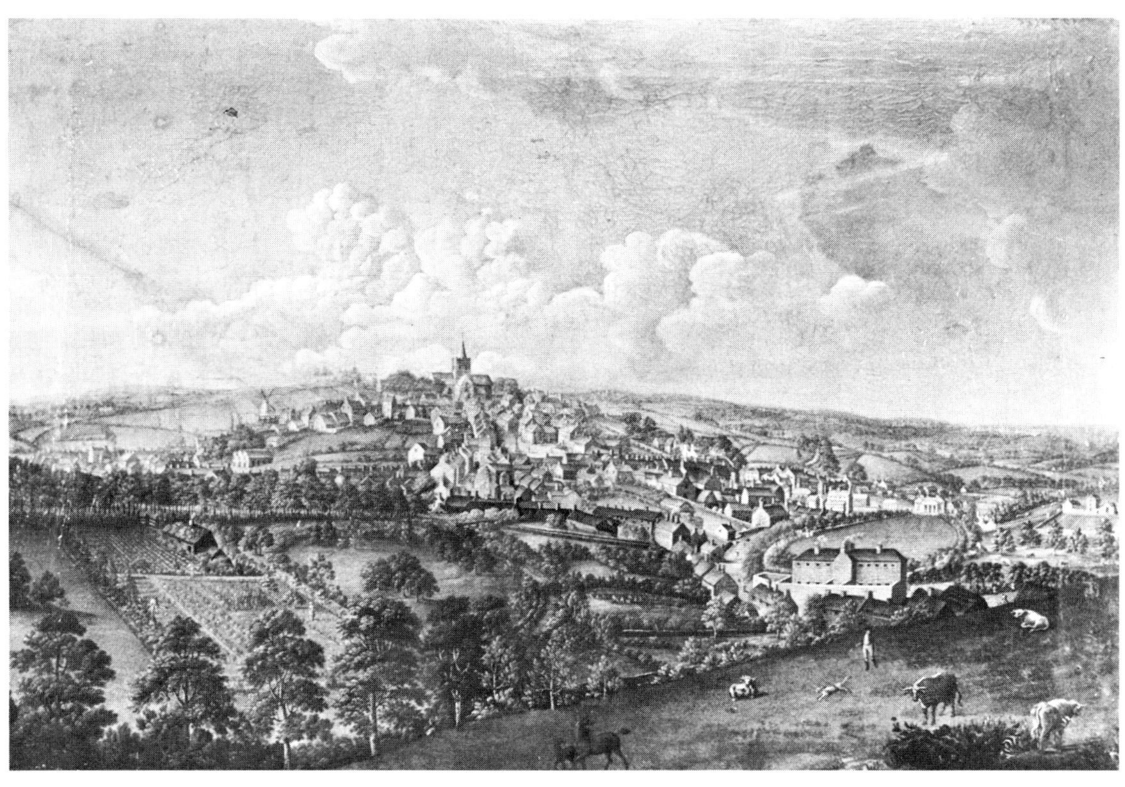

8 JAMES BLACK
Armagh
1810; oil; 91.5 x 132.1 cms;
Armagh Museum collection

date and of modest proportions, set in their suburban or country estates, along the Lagan Valley or on the shores of Belfast Lough, Cultra, Crawfordsburn, Bangor, Merville, Whitehouse. A bad period for architecture, none had the style or grace of the Palladian mansions of the previous age, plain structures with only, here and there, any evidence of the Gothick style pointing its doorways and windows, as in the Donegall's house at Ormeau, or the house of that generous patron of the arts, Narcissus Batt at Purdysburn. Most of the sepia drawings are now in the Ulster Museum, rather faded and ghostly, some foxed, but giving evidence that the engraver has taken no great liberties with the artist's statements.

There has been a habit for how long I do not know, for owners of sets of the prints to have them hand-coloured, and, in that condition, they have achieved a lasting popularity. The drawings follow a conventional form; the building, being of little interest, is usually placed well back in the middle-distance, some rather far away, or thrust to one side and obscured by foliage. Taller trees to left and right normally frame the composition, and bands of flowing

9 JOSEPH MOLLOY
aquatint; *Purdys Burn [the seat of Narcissus Batt, Esq]* engraved by F K Proctor, London, from *Belfast Scenery in Thirty Views*, London and Belfast 1832

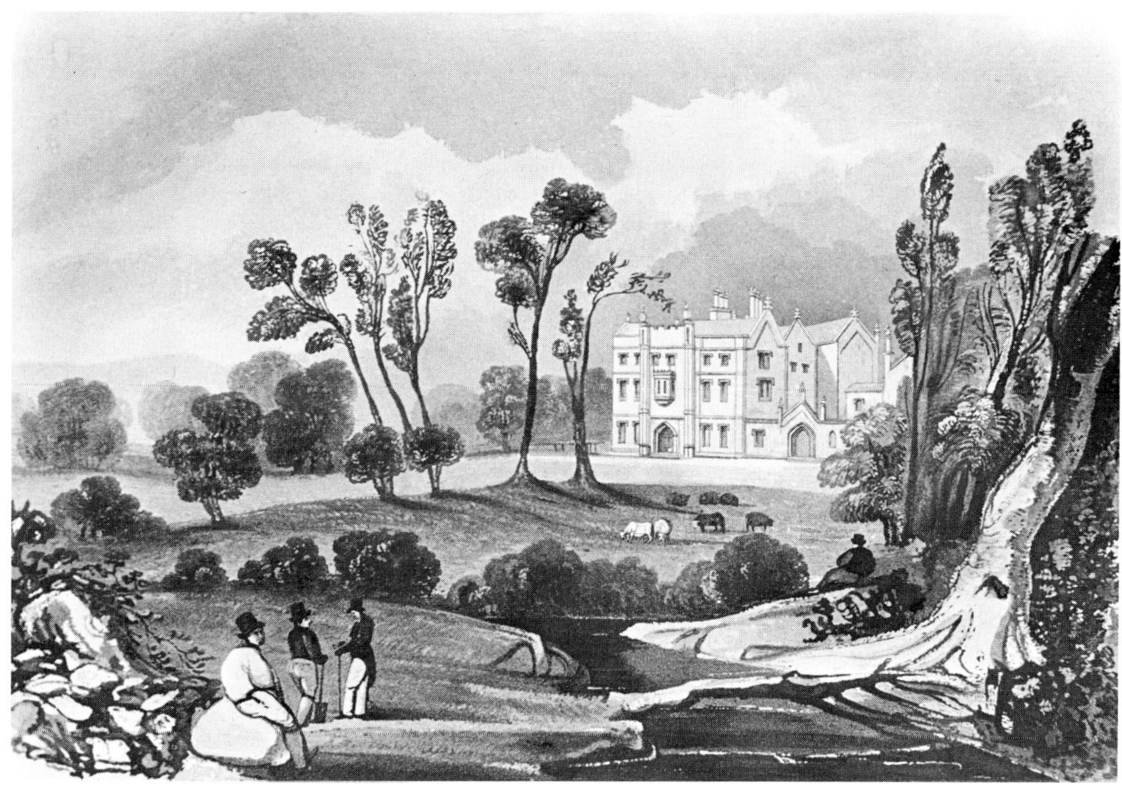

water supply a steady, horizontal element. Figures, clumsily drawn, are placed in the foreground, often seated on a fallen tree, a log, or a rock, the seated man reading, or sketching, or admiring the prospect. Provincial, derivative work certainly, but there is a good-natured innocence in the conception and the detail, which are handled with some grace, that raises them beyond the plodding pedestrianism of mere journeyman work.

Molloy was drawing master of the Academical Institution, 'a little quiet unassuming man. He never passed as an art critic or gave expression to opinion injurious to others, but contented himself with showing you the way he went about landscape work', as Robert Young, the architect, remembered him. He was more various and accomplished than his *Views* suggest; the Ulster Museum's collection includes a sound portrait and a small oil painting of *Tilbury Fort*, which have more strength than might have been guessed from these quiet, half-hidden houses and the smooth water flowing past.

A few years before the publication of Molloy's *Views*, the anonymous *Northern Athens, or Life in the Emerald Isle, a serio-comico-ludicro-satirical poem* (1826) was printed by F D Finlay for its author. Among the many prose footnotes, one runs 'The art of painting is pretty much cultivated among amateurs; whilst the classic city has given birth to several celebrated artists — Messrs Thomas Warrington; James Atkins; Samuel Hawksett; Dyke, etc.' It should be Robert, not Thomas, Warrington, an established miniaturist and painter of small portraits, and Dyke, Richard William Dyke, was not a native of the town but born in Dublin where he returned to spend his last years. Samuel Hawksett, now that T C Thompson was living in London, was the leading portraitist in the north. A competent painter, he made individual use of colour difficult to define but recognisably his own. James Atkins was the son of a painter of coaches, military colours, drums, and signs, with painting lofts in Anne Street. So the boy grew up among pigments and varnishes. He was a pupil of Gaetano Fabbrini at the Belfast Academy, and later, sustained by the patronage of Narcissus Batt, and other local benefactors, he went to Italy to study. The rest of his life seems to have been spent there, in Greece and the Eastern Mediterranean, for he died of fever at Malta while still a young man in his early thirties. After his death, many of his paintings, original work or copies after the old Masters, were brought home. The Ulster Museum has, among other items, the copy of Titian's *Lavinia*, a Roman landscape, and a small painting of a young woman in white which possesses a certain delicacy and charm, and in the great hall of Queen's University there hangs his copy of the large *Martyrdom of St Peter*, the original of which was destroyed by fire, later in the century.

We may take it then, that this handful of names fairly represented those accepted as giving some credit to the town at that time. The author of *Northern Athens*, in both stanza and footnotes, expressed another opinion which, very likely, was held among the more educated townsfolk, which deplored the absence of any public 'monument either to living talent or deceased worth'

> ''Tis very strange, nor more strange than true,
> No statue Athens' Eminence adorns...
> Has there no worth in weeping Erin shone?
> Is there no living talent to regard?
> Are *Grattan, Drennan, Sheridan*, unknown?
> Is there no virtuous *Brownlow* to reward?

It is the same lack which we have already remarked that Thomas Robinson was conscious of, when he inserted a statue into his many-titled *Volunteers Review* over twenty years earlier.

In these years the printing shop of F D Finlay gave work to a talented apprentice, Andrew Nicholl, born in Church Lane. The lad's skill, encouraged and instructed by his elder brother, William, himself a highly competent amateur, was such that he, in turn, gave drawing lessons in his spare hours. And, in time, as Robert Young recalled, on his way to or from school, 'at the corner of Corn Market there were generally to be seen three or four of his powerful studies in one of McComb's windows'. Stationer and bookseller, William McComb was an indefatigable if rather tedious poet, saluted then or later as 'The Laureate of Presbyterianism', friend and staunch supporter of Henry Cooke, and who, in the Reform Bill election of 1832, voted for James

Emerson Tennent the recently-turned Tory candidate.

By about 1830, Nicholl, befriended by the dependable Narcissus Batt, crossed to London, where he copied paintings hanging in the Dulwich College Gallery, and became influenced by the great Turner of the sunsets and the radiant skies, and, to a lesser degree, by the popular Peter De Wint and Copley Fielding. After two years he came back to Ireland, to Dublin this time, where he had pictures hung in the RHA and sent several to the RA in London. Just founded, the *Dublin Penny Journal* carried illustrations after some of his drawings, and he supplied thirteen others for Robert Clayton's engravings for *Views of the Dublin and Kingstown Railway* in 1835, very early demonstrations of Irish Locomotive history.

The same year saw the publication of *Picturesque sketches of some of the finest landscape and coastal scenery of Ireland* in Dublin. For this set of aquatints Nicholl provided seven drawings, three of these of northern subjects; the remaining eighteen came from drawings by George Petrie and Henry O'Neill, work which placed him with the leaders of topographical illustration of the period. Andrew and his brother William figure among the members of the Belfast Association of Artists which mounted the first of its three annual exhibitions in 1836. This was the year before the accession of the young Victoria, when the town's population stood at 50,000, and there were artists numerous enough in the prospering community, to meet the increased demand for portraits, miniatures, landscapes, or to teach drawing to the young ladies of the professional or commercial families.

By good fortune, catalogues of the first and third exhibitions have been preserved in the Linen Hall Library, and from these we can learn a great deal of interest about the state of art in and its relation to the northern community. At its foundation, the Association's members were Hugh Frazer, then ARHA, the President, a landscape painter from Dromore, the Treasurer was Samuel Hawksett, the town's leading portrait painter, not long before commissioned to paint King William the Fourth, by the Governors of the Academical Institution, Nicholas J Crowley ARHA was the Secretary, a young Dublin artist whose work included portraits, conversation pieces, and 'fancy subjects', who had recently came north. Besides the two Nicholls, other rank-and-file members were Robert Warrington, Joseph Molloy, and Fortuné La Moile, French master at Inst; an excitable man, much beset by financial trouble — four years later he was to write to the school governors asking for three or four weeks' leave of absence, as he was then in the debtor's prison in Dublin, and sometime after, he assaulted a colleague in the staff-room, and his resignation forestalled his dismissal. Thereafter he disappears from the records. J W Miller, architect, was also a member. To these were added a couple of Associates, Henry Maguire, a painter of town and country scenes, and Edward McCormick, of whom I know nothing.

The founding members had nominated three Honorary members; Martin Cregan, PRHA, Thomas Kirk, Professor of Sculpture at the Academy, and Gaetano Fabbrini, whom we first met as subscriber to *Juvenile Poems* thirty years before. He had been drawing master and Italian teacher at Inst; the first had involved 'Figure

10 HUGH FRAZER
View of Belfast
1820; oil; Belfast Harbour Commissioners' collection

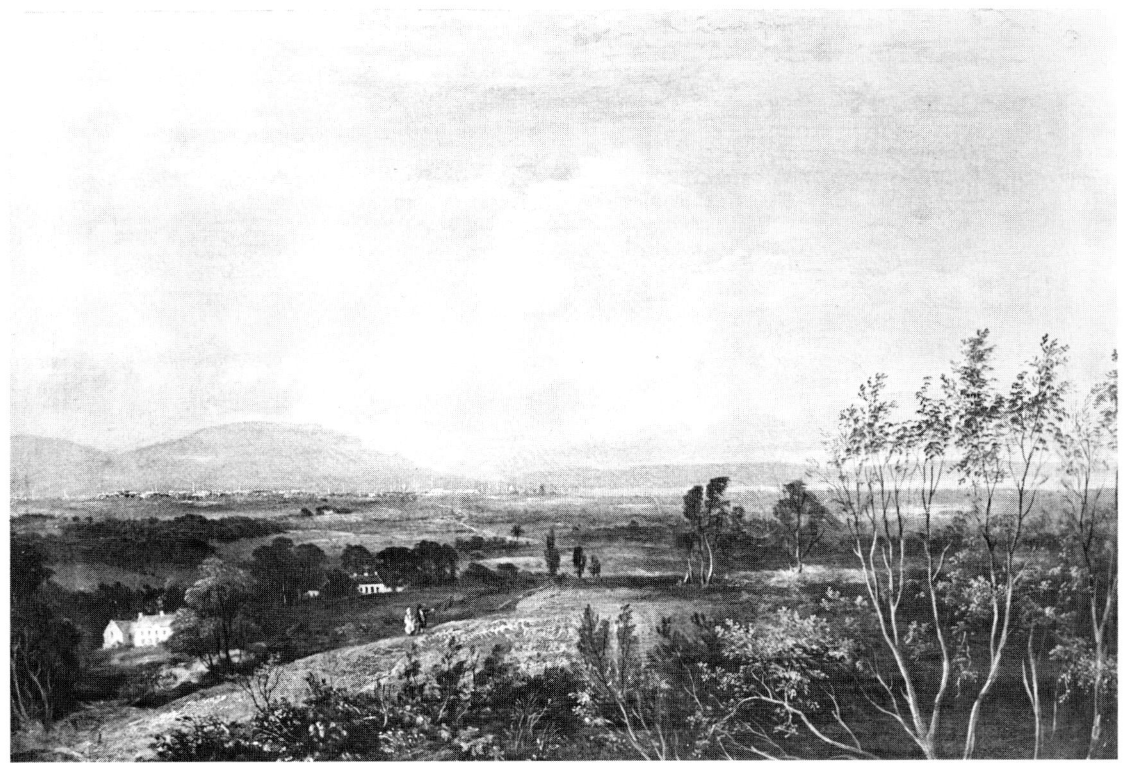

drawing, ornamental drawing and oilpainting on Grecian models and in the style of the Florentine Academy'; for the second, Italian was to be 'spoken and read with the Tuscan accent'. Even more troublesome than his French colleague, he was dismissed in 1816, following an attack on the tall and bulky Henry Montgomery, headmaster of the English school, and compounded by a series of criticisms and complaints against other staff members. Befriended by powerful persons such as Lady Londonderry and the Marchioness of Downshire; for many years his campaign against Inst, was sustained by angry pamphlets and stormy meetings of shareholders, till as late as 1845. As a painter he had exhibited at the RHA, in 1834 and 1835.

Incidentally, Fabbrini was succeeded at Inst by Ferdinand Besaucle who taught his native language, Spanish, instead of Italian, until 1830, when he was followed by Molloy who held the drawing-master's post for forty years.

The Association described it as the 'first Exhibition of Modern Art'; true enough at the time, but, with the passing of the years, a sober warning that meanings are as mortal as those who use them, and that it would be more accurate for a longer time to say 'contemporary'. The regulations were just and generous; 'All artists in the United Kingdom are invited to become Exhibitors, if their Works be original. No picture can be exhibited without a frame... No commission shall be charged for Sales... Quotations and descriptions to be subject to the approbation of the committee...' and so on. The catalogue was prefaced with an 'Address to the Public' signed by the President, and dated 5 September 1836. The following passages from it give the tone and intention very worthily.

> 'The backward state of the Arts in Ireland, and more particularly in the North, compared with other parts of the empire, has been remarked, with regret, by those who take comprehensive views of their capabilities, when cultivated with an enlightened spirit, in refining public taste, and in adding beauty and harmony to the ornamental branches of manufacturers.
>
> 'Taking into consideration the limited demand for productions in the higher departments of Art, and the humble position they hold in artistical attainment, when compared with other incorporated Societies of British Artists, the Belfast Association submit their first Exhibition of Modern Art to the Northern public, in the hope that their exertions will meet that approbation and support, which will enable them to furnish an annual display, at least equal to the present one.
>
> 'They trust they will not be thought presuming too much on their own position, in appealing to a liberal and enlightened public, for their co-operation in raising a fund, by subscription, for the purpose of erecting an appropriate building for an Institution of Fine Arts in the Northern metropolis, to which object the surplus proceeds of the present Exhibition are to be devoted.
>
> 'The present Exhibition must be considered as an experiment, in regard to the measure of support and encouragement which the public may concede to this mode of advancing native Art, also, how far the resident Artists would be enabled to sustain an Annual Exhibition. Calculating on an increased diffusion of taste for Art, which a public Exhibition tends to produce, and, consequently, an increased demand for the productions of Artists, the result, as regards the latter, has been most favourable.
>
> 'It is the earnest wish of the Belfast Association to open a general market for British Art; but, in the first instance, the appropriation of the Funds will, until a building be accomplished, prevent them paying the carriage of contributions from distant places.'

The exhibition was held in 'the great hall' of the Museum, College Square North, by courtesy of the Natural History and Philosophical Society, and ran to 217 items, four of them sculpture, three by Kirk, and a bust by Fabbrini of the late David Legge, whose house at Malone, above Shaw's Bridge, had been one of Molloy's subjects for *Belfast Views*. (Even now, a few old people refer to the steep slope down to the bridge as 'Legge's Brae'.) Frazer contributed twenty-five landscapes of Irish, English and

Welsh scenes, with two continental subjects. Crowley had eight portraits; Hawksett twenty-five, including that of King William the Fourth, and one of James Emerson Tennent MP; Warrington had eight. The Nicholls, between them, had thirty landscapes, most probably watercolours, but that is not specified; La Moile had twenty-five; Maguire two pieces. The architect, Miller, had a perspective view of the new Presbyterian Church in Rosemary Street. This church had been completed in 1831, and after the air raids of 1941, when it was destroyed, it was discovered that the four Doric columns of the porch were, in fact, of cast iron. He also had a design for Gosford Castle, and several other drawings, including a view of the Entrance Hall for the proposed Ulster Gallery of Fine Arts, and a view of *a Park Entrance in the Grecian style, about to be erected at The Lodge, the residence of James Emerson Tennent.*

Among exhibitors who were not members of the Association, the principal figure was James Arthur O'Connor, the nowadays highly regarded Irish landscape painter, then resident in London, with eleven items. W C Nixon, who, by 1838, was to become a member, had a couple of portraits. But two of the non-members were represented posthumously 'the late Thomas Robinson', with, appropriately, a portrait of Thomas Percy, Bishop of Dromore, and James Atkins, not long dead, with thirteen works, among them a Greek Girl, an Albanian figure set in a landscape by Frazer, and a portrait of John Gibson the celebrated sculptor who worked in Rome. Atkins had died in 1833, and a cargo of his canvasses had been shipped back for an auction in 1835.

There were four landscapes by Donald Stewart, very likely the D Stewart who illustrated Drummond's *Giant's Causeway* (1811), and made the drawing of Ritchies' Dock (c 1805), for the aquatint which is set in a mirror-frame in the Ulster Museum Collection. But some of the exhibitors are never likely to be traced, living, as they do, under the most impenetrable of titles such as An Amateur, A Lady, A Young Lady. From the locations given, most of the members seem to have lived in the vicinity of the newer part of the town, Fountain Street, Fisherwick Place, College Street and College Square.

The catalogue for the third and, as it proved, the last exhibition of the Association, in 1838, shows some changes in the membership. Frazer, still President, is now RHA, and Professor of Painting of that Academy. Miller is now Secretary, William Nicholl, with his business experience, Treasurer. Molloy, and, not surprisingly, La Moile, have dropped out, replaced only by Henry McManus ARHA, now with an Armagh address. W C Nixon, the portrait painter, is an Associate member. And, for additional Honorary Member, is added Patrick MacDowell, the Belfast-born sculptor, by this time making a name for himself in London and deserving some local recognition.

The forty-nine exhibitors present 240 items. And, perhaps to broaden the interest, members with Dublin links are joined by several others, Charles Grey, Bernard Mulrenin, T J and G F Mulvany, as well as J A O'Connor once again. To the same intention we may ascribe the inclusion of the English watercolourists, J C Bentley, David Cox, and Samuel Prout. Frazer, from an address in Kennedy's Place, Shankill

11 ELISH LAMONT
Illustration from *Christmas Rhymes or Three Nights' Revelry* by Frances and Elish Lamont, Belfast, 1846

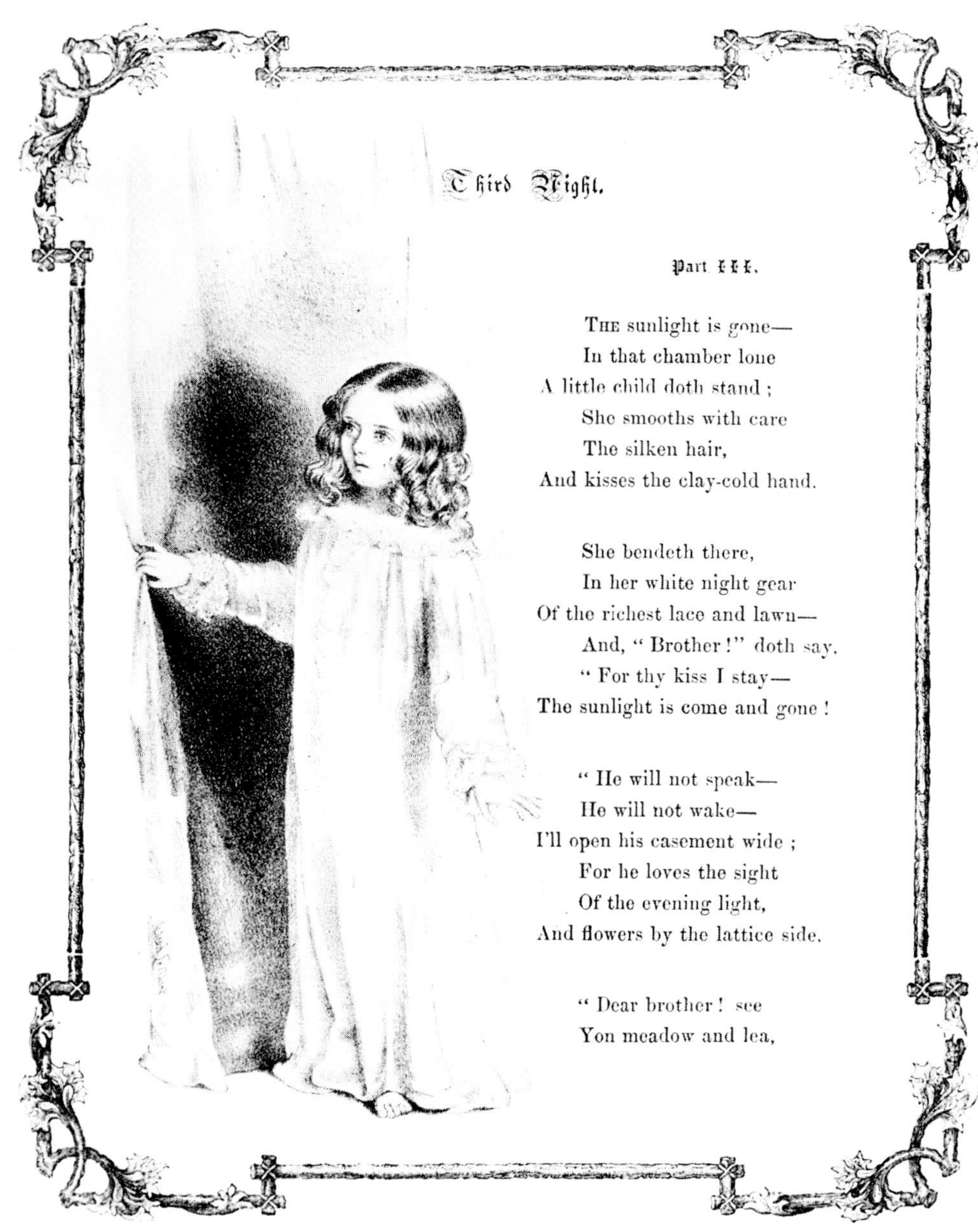

Third Night.

Part III.

THE sunlight is gone—
In that chamber lone
A little child doth stand;
She smooths with care
The silken hair,
And kisses the clay-cold hand.

She bendeth there,
In her white night gear
Of the richest lace and lawn—
And, "Brother!" doth say,
"For thy kiss I stay—
The sunlight is come and gone!

"He will not speak—
He will not wake—
I'll open his casement wide;
For he loves the sight
Of the evening light,
And flowers by the lattice side.

"Dear brother! see
Yon meadow and lea,

Road, has, in addition to landscapes, a *Faction Fight*, of which 'all the leading incidents... came under the painter's personal observation'. Crowley, from a London address, has, among his varied exhibits, a portrait of Francis McCracken, brother of Henry Joy McCracken executed after the Battle of Antrim in 1798. His sister Mary Ann had been a model for the fortune-teller in another painting by Crowley. Hawksett, in his eleven portraits, has one of the Lord Mayor of Dublin, and has recruited younger members of his family to join him in exhibiting. Warrington has ten portraits. Fabbrini, more versatile than ever, has a portrait of the Marchioness of Londonderry, a landscape, a sketch for an Altar-piece, and a 'medallion, in Alto-relievo, of the late Mrs Bond, done from recollection after her death'. The late James Atkins' stock has been the source of more original works and of copies after Titian, Rubens, and Sir Thomas Lawrence. T C Thompson, from London, is represented by the portrait of a clergyman, and the Rev Dr Henry Cooke has had his likeness taken by W Stevenson.

Watercolours and Miniatures are listed under a separate heading. In this section, Andrew Nicholl, now RHA, is prominent with ten pictures of Irish and Scottish scenes, his brother's seven range from Loch Lomond to the Coal Quay, Belfast. A new name, that of Miss Lamont, who must have been Elish Lamont, daughter of a well-known Belfast family — her mother had written a book of *Poems and Tales in Verse* (1818) — has a batch of miniatures, A Gentleman, A Lady and Child, A Lady, A Child, A Family Group. In 1846 Elish and her sister Frances composed, and Elish illustrated a romantic set of *Christmas Rhymes*. She later achieved reputation across the water, Dickens and Ruskin being among admirers of her work.

The public response seems to have been insufficient for the continuance of the Association or for the furtherance of its object of promoting 'an appropriate building for an Institute of Fine Art' a project which took the most of a century to make more than a hope. With the break-up of the membership, Nicholl left for London, Miller for New Zealand.

The demand for portraiture persisted, though its utility was soon to be threatened by photography. Hawksett, Warrington and Nixon carried on their craft, and Felice Piccioni, an Italian who had come to work for the firm of Marcus Ward, found his charcoal drawings very popular. These were joined, in a decade, by Richard Hooke, a country lad from the Banbridge district, who became Hawksett's successor as the leading portraitist. Not nearly so interesting a painter, but a far more representative of the newly emergent clientele, the new industrialists, self-made men with no sort of cultural tradition, admiring themselves, who sought to have their features perpetuated in a no-nonsense style. So photography was extensively used by Hooke as a basis and support for his pedestrian productions, exactly to the simple taste of his patrons. Exhibiting at the RHA, for a long time, he was never elected to Academic status. Ultimately he married a rich widow and retired to Manchester. Another portrait painter, William Foy of Londonderry, had his own localised following; and, from his, later, London base, he returned at intervals to fulfil commissions.

Between 1835 and 1850 the population of

II ANDREW NICHOLL
McArt's Fort
1830; watercolour; 24.4 x 35.5 cms; Ulster Museum collection

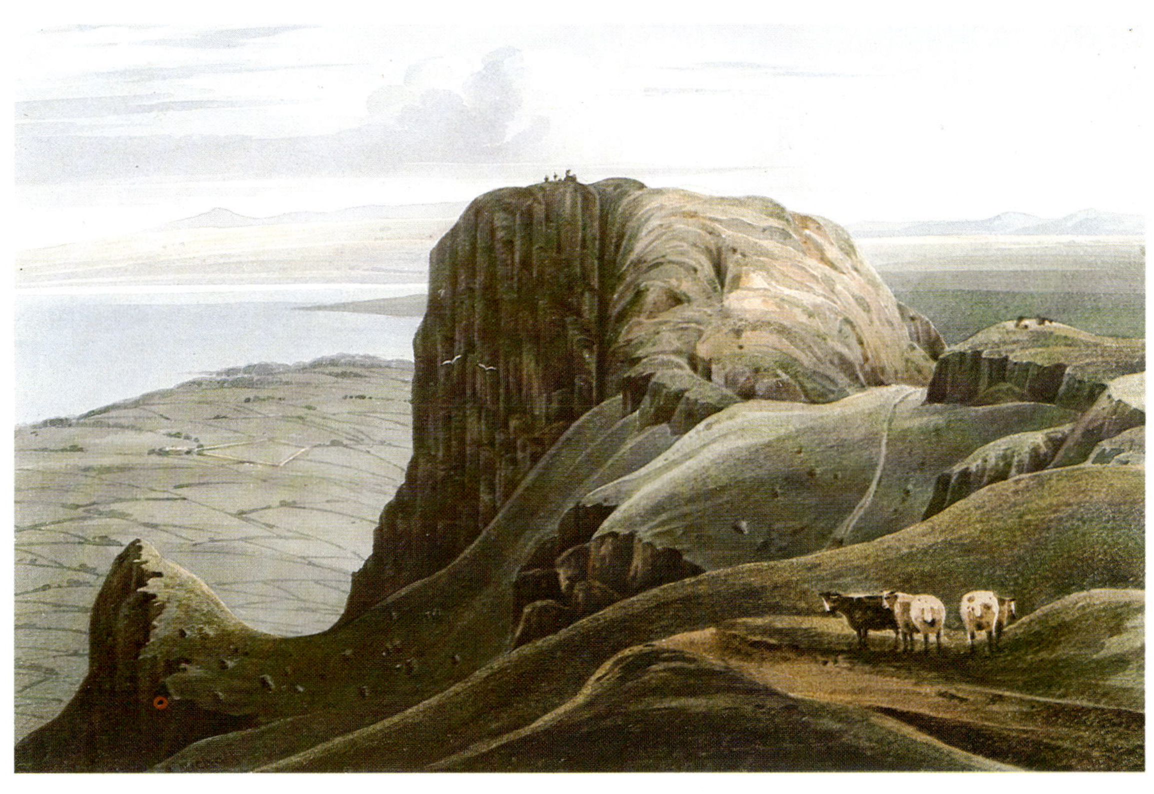

facing page 28

Belfast rose to 90,000, but half that number were under twenty years of age, and the average expectation of life was only nine, for, though industry and commerce expanded rapidly, as the tall mill chimneys rose in the western parts of the town and the port grew in importance as the new Authority, The Harbour Commission, was set up, the Blackstaff river stank, and the alleys and tenements round Smithfield and Peter's Hill were vulnerable to epidemics of typhoid and cholera.

But the old Long Bridge over the tidal mud-flats of the Lagan, so often depicted by artists like Andrew Nicholl, was replaced by the Queen's Bridge in 1842, and the residential area south of High Street was passing over to commercial use, as the well-to-do moved out along the fields on the Malone Road, a dry and airy ridge above the noisome and readily-flooded Bog Meadows. The Workhouse was built in 1841, and the Queen's College opened in 1849, and the railway trains now ran to Portadown, Ballymena, and Holywood.

In the Belfast Directory of 1852, in the professional pages under the heading of Portrait and Landscape, among fewer than a dozen names we find Nursery and Raimbach, the first and second masters of the newly established School of Design, as well as Hooke, who lived in Chichester Street, not many doors from Dr James Moore, Miss Lamont in Castle Street, and James Howard Burgess in Donegall Place.

While in London, Nicholl exhibited at the RA and sent work over to Dublin, to the RHA but he probably maintained himself by giving private lessons. Then, in 1846, he was appointed to teach landscape drawing, painting and design, at the Academy in Colombo, Ceylon. A couple of watercolours in the Ulster Museum drew their subjects from the voyage. The Colonial Secretary of the administration on the island was none other than James Emerson Tennent, and when he was writing his descriptive volumes, he engaged Nicholl to sketch local subjects for use as illustrations. With Tennent, Nicholl, in 1848, went on tour for these. Later, in the *Dublin University Magazine* in 1852, his own account of the journey, 'a sketching tour of four weeks in the forests of Ceylon', was published.

We cannot say how long his Singhalese sojourn lasted; when he returned to these islands, he lived at various addresses in London, in Dublin, and in Belfast, where he taught landscape painting privately. In 1860 he was elected an RHA. A prolific artist, often for teaching-purposes making versions of earlier themes, seldom dating his sketches, it is difficult, if not impossible, to plot any line of development in his middle and later years, for he was an uneven worker. He was fond of dramatic effects, of ruins, rugged cliffs and rough seas, of the arches of caves looking seaward. His colours were restricted to browns, russets, keen in his slighter sketches to use pencil with flecks of chinese white on a darker paper. His statement of human figures or cattle was always inexpert. Apart from his watercolours of the Antrim Coast of 1828-1830, those which impressed so much the boy, Robert Young, 'his sketches of Irish scenery have great fascination for me... particularly those of the Antrim Coast', with their broader washes and bolder patterning, his originality appears most strongly in the few odd pieces with a landscape of distant hills, fore-

12 FELICE PICCIONI
Portrait of Andrew Nicholl
c1840; charcoal; 38.4 x 25.7 cms; Ulster Museum collection

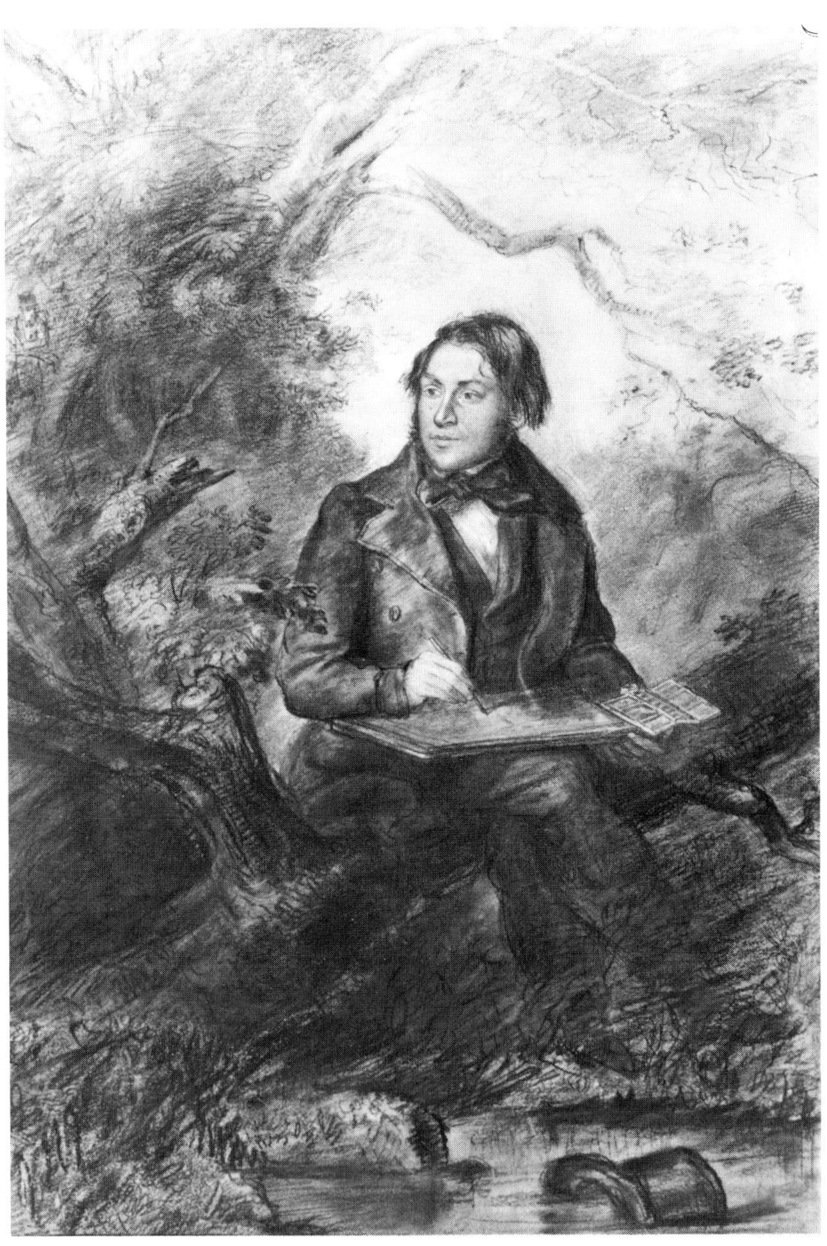

13 ANDREW NICHOLL
A Bank of flowers with view of Bray
n d; watercolour; 35.1 x 52.1 cms; Ulster Museum collection

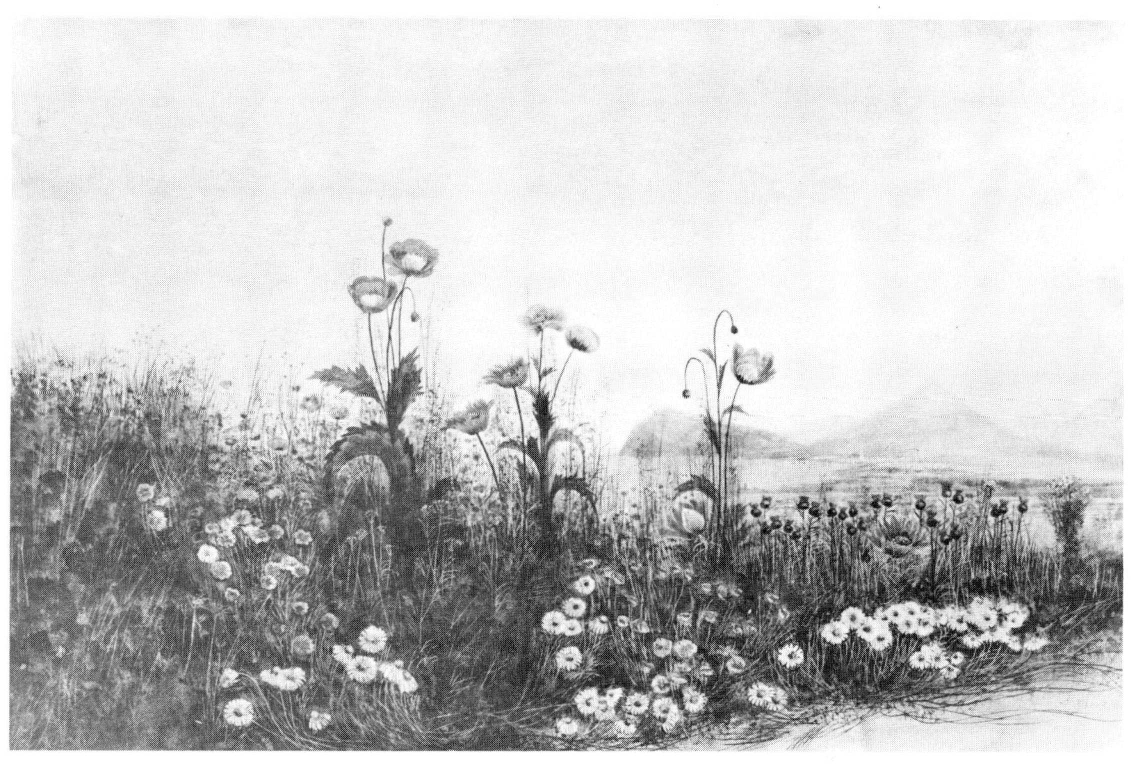

grounded by a wedge or bank of roadside wild-flowers. By scratch and scrape of the surface of his paper, a device which served well in other drawings, for the spray-frayed tips of breaking waves, he gave his flowers and grasses an illusory precision and finish.

He died at his London house in 1886, at the advanced age of eighty-two, and a large exhibition of nearly 300 works was speedily displayed at 55 Donegall Place, in his native town, its intention 'to vindicate the reputation of the late Mr Nicholl as an artist of no mean order'. From this, many of his watercolours must have passed into local hands, for they can still be seen at the walls of the homes of older families, or come up often in the auction rooms.

As a topographical artist, Nicholl's principal rival was a younger man, James Howard Burgess. They both provided drawings for the Hall's *Ireland*, and, sometime in the eighteen-forties, Burgess supplied the twenty drawings for Marcus Ward's *Illustrations of the North of Ireland and guide to the Giant's Causeway*. He was a firmer, more skilful and accurate draughtsman, but as a watercolourist in his later studies of the Mourne mountains, of Scotland and Wales, instead of

14 JAMES HOWARD BURGESS
Queen's Bridge, 1858
1858; oil; 66.7 x 94.0 cms; Belfast Harbour Commissioners' collection

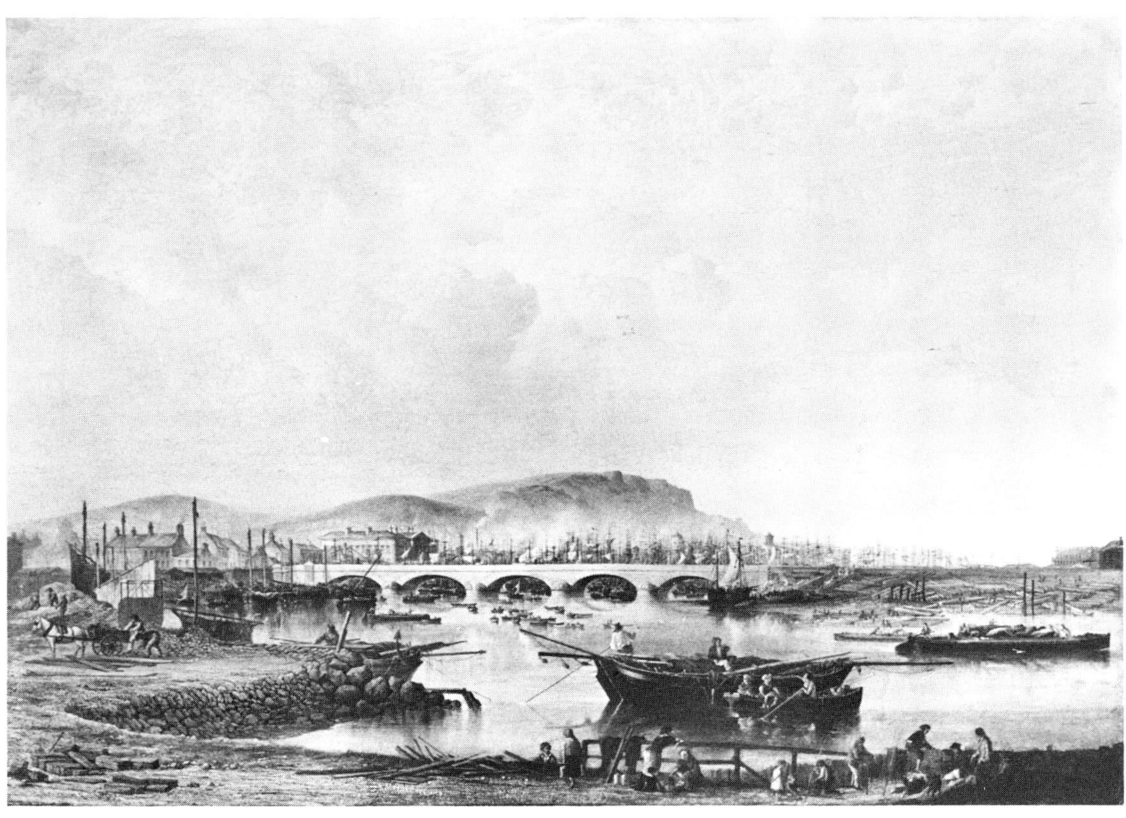

washes of colour, he used opaque pigment, chinese-white and body-colour, as if striving to give his forms the strength and solidity of oil paint. His work has very seldom anything approaching the lyricism of Nicholl's, and, though often he deals with the same romantic subjects, Dunluce, The Giant's Causeway, Nicholl's emphasis on gloom of rocky headland, or glow of setting sun, gives a poetical quality to his less well-drawn and less sharply detailed forms.

The most various and best of the town's watercolourists was the amateur, Dr James Moore. Son of a retired naval surgeon who had come to live in Belfast, he entered the medical school at Edinburgh when he was eighteen years old and graduated after five years' study. Pupil and friend of the professor of clinical surgery, he provided the illustrations for a text-book written by the latter. While in Edinburgh he became acquainted with the active school of Scottish painters, and particularly intimate with the highly popular Sam Bough (1822-1878). Moore's earliest sketch is inscribed and dated 'Portpatrick about 1836 or 7', very likely made while passing

15 JAMES HOWARD BURGESS
Greencastle, Inishowen
1869; watercolour; 49.5 x 73.5 cms; Ulster Museum collection

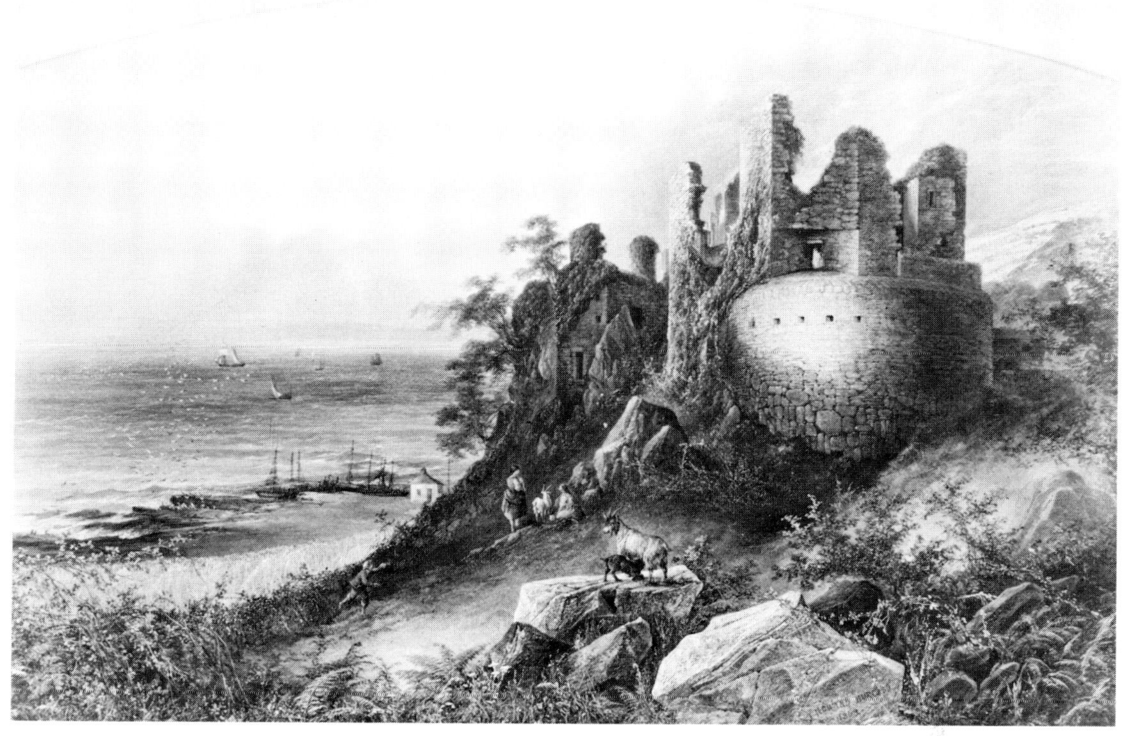

between Belfast and Edinburgh.

Settling in Belfast to a busy and useful career, he became consultant surgeon to the General Hospital. For many years he went abroad on holiday, visiting France, Holland, Belgium, and Germany repeatedly, and on these journeys he made a vast number of brisk watercolour and pen sketches. A compulsive note-taker, for example, at railway stations or race meetings, his quick memoranda record a host of corners or occasions. Besides his sketches, Moore, once in a while, enlarged some subjects to a high degree of finish and submitted these to the RHA. The accomplished quality of these exhibits resulted in his election as an Honorary Academician in 1868.

Slieve Bernagh from the Trassy Bog is, unfortunately, the only example of this in a public collection. In this, he can be seen as a very good practitioner of the contemporary style of British Watercolour; but it is in the unexhibited, rapid sketches that his uniqueness is demonstrated. His *Coleraine Regatta* (1847) and the *Sham Fight at Scarva* which brings to mind the vision

16 JAMES MOORE
Slieve Bernagh from the Trassy Bog, Mourne Mountains
n d; watercolour; 57.2 x 77.4 cms; Ulster Museum collection

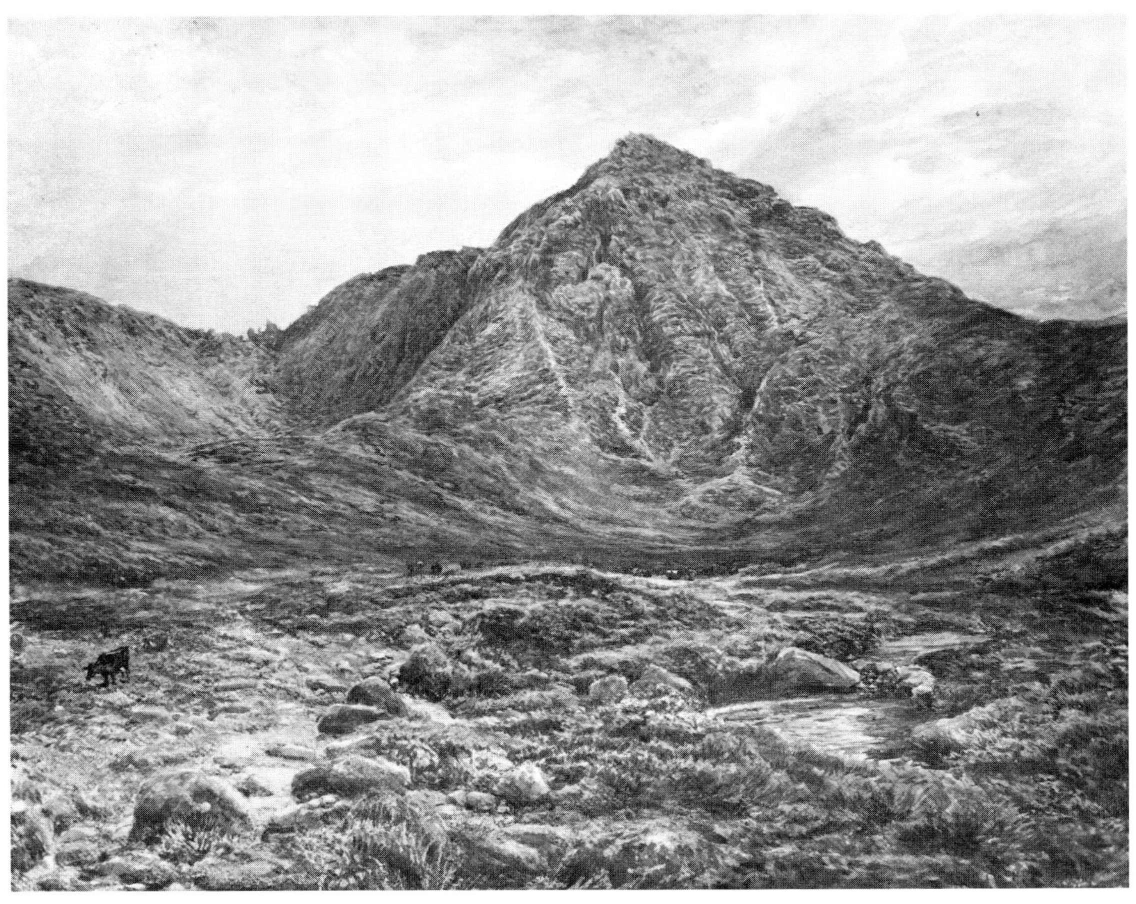

of Jack B Yeats, could readily pass for Impressionist work from the School of Paris much later. It has only been since the exhibition in 1977 at the Ulster Museum of over one hundred of his sketches out of the Museum's holding of 400, that his vivid creativeness can be assessed.

On one of Moore's sketches of the Mournes, he inscribed 'with Lynn'. This must have been William Henry Lynn, brother of the sculptor Samual Ferres Lynn, and partner of Lanyon, most eminent of local architects. Lynn was vice-chairman of the Board of Managers of the Government School of Art, to which Moore also belonged. He was a very good draughtsman, and some of his designs, such as the project for the *Carlisle Bridge, Dublin*, are impressive.

There were, of course, other amateurs of the brush and pen, busy in their secluded corners,

17 JAMES MOORE
Sham Fight at Scarva
n d; watercolour; 18 x 26 cms; Ulster Museum collection

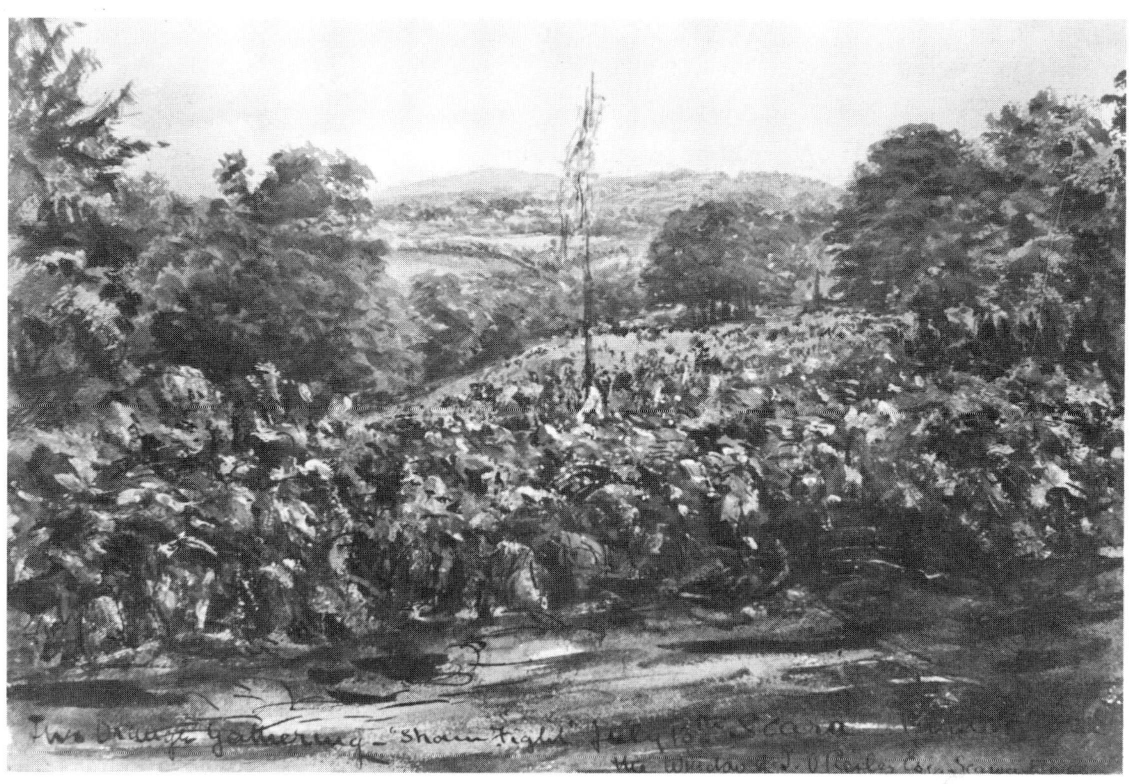

Samuel Ferguson, for example. Known as public servant and antiquarian in his life-time, he now is accepted as one of the founding fathers of Anglo-Irish literature, saluted by Yeats who longed 'to be accounted one With Mangan, Davis, Ferguson'.

Born in Belfast, at his maternal grandparents' house in High Street, with a somewhat unsettled home-life, with a spendthrift father and a resolute mother, he lived in the town or its environs while attending the Belfast Academy and, later, Inst. And it was in Belfast, that, with his friends, George Fox and John O'Hagan, he formed a little class for the study of the Irish language. But it was while at TCD that his interest in Irish archaeology became a passion, and, in this study, his facility for sketching found a utilitarian direction. In his correspondence with George Petrie, that significant archaeologist, fine draughtsman, and inspiring guide, we find Petrie telling him of a certain ancient church, and urging him to 'see it and tell me and draw me all about it'; and, on another occasion, Petrie wrote: 'When I give a few lessons in foliage, you will be a first rate sketcher as well as antiquary.' When attending to his law studies in London in 1832, Ferguson met George Cruikshank, the celebrated graphic artist, who showed his drawings and demonstrated 'the process of etching on copper'.

In 1846 Ferguson was commissioned by a publisher to write and illustrate a book describing a journey in the footsteps of the early Irish Saints, missionaries to Continental Europe. When he had collected his advance payment, essential to a law student dependent on his journalistic work for *The Dublin University Magazine*, Petrie gave him a letter of introduction to John Hogan, the Irish sculptor, then living in Rome, presenting him as a brother artist. He visited France, Germany, Austria, Switzerland and Italy; but the book never got written, and paying back the publisher's advance remained a drag for years on the earnings of the newly married and struggling barrister. Many of the sketches he made on this continental tour are in the archives of the Linen Hall Library.

His dutiful widow, in her jumbled but invaluable biography of him, recorded that 'he drew and etched with accuracy, and had a fine eye for colour but lacked technical instruction. His sketches from nature were full of feeling, revealing his sense of her loveliness and charm.' But just as Standish O'Grady later discovered that Ferguson did not parade his achievement in poetry, so his practice of drawing was kept a rather private matter.

Another amateur who did little to share his gift with the public was Frederick Blackwood, Lord Dufferin. Handy with watercolour in a rather old-fashioned manner, he used only a few sketches and drawings he made for the illustrations to his account of that interesting voyage, recounted in the popular *Letters from High Latitudes* (1856).

John Ward, son of Marcus Ward, who had attended the School of Design, was another amateur who sketched assiduously on his Mediterranean vacations; but his involvement in local art had rather to do with his work with the firm, and with the foundation and running of the Government School of Art.

Though Nicholl, Burgess and Moore were working well and would each continue for many years, perhaps the most interesting painter briefly at mid century was John Glen Wilson. Date and place of his birth are unknown, but, for folk skilled in guessing a great deal from names shown, that name sounds like one of Ulster Planter stock. At any rate, his *Emigrant Ship* (Ulster Museum) is an important document, and, in its own right, one of the better paintings of life in this place at anytime. On a smaller scale, but still a fine oil painting. *The Harbour Steps* (1851) now in the Harbour Office, makes us regret that so few of Glen Wilson's pictures of Belfast are extant.

In 1835 a select committee had been set up 'to inquire into the best means of extending a knowledge of the arts and of the principles of design, among the people (especially the manufacturing population) of the country; also to inquire into the constitution, management, and effects of institutions connected with the arts'.

18 JOHN GLEN WILSON
Belfast Harbour Ferry Steps, Donegall Quay
1851; oil; 47.6 x 60 cms; Belfast Harbour Commissioners collection

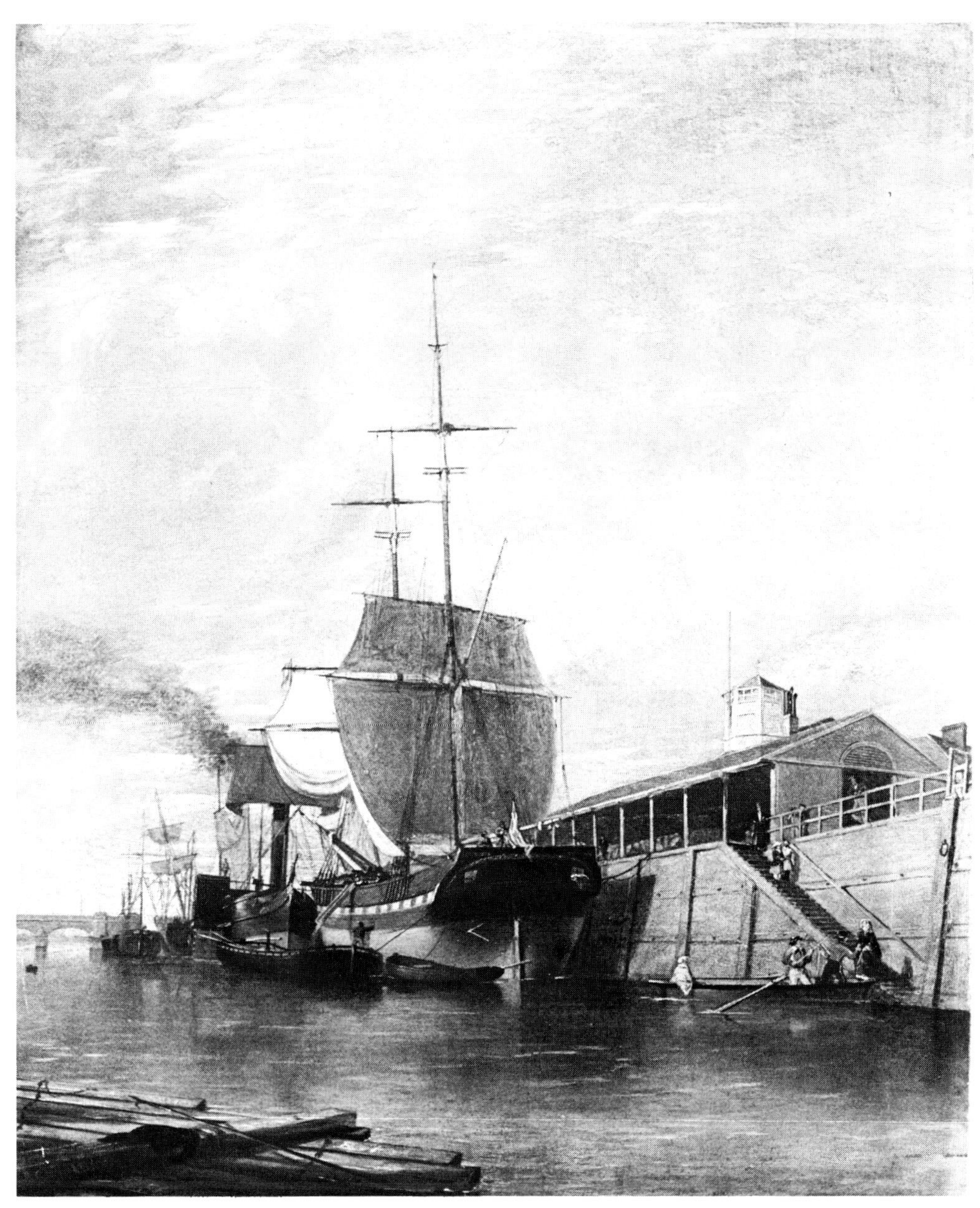

The next year, the Committee reported and the Government voted financial aid to have a School of Design established in London as a pilot-project. With five years' experience of this, it was decided to authorise a sum of £10,000 towards the establishment of similar schools of design in large towns in the United Kingdom. So, in 1849, through the influence of the Viceroy, Belfast received an offer of £500 per annum, dependent upon proportionate local support. The premises selected were in the north wing of the Academical Institution, and a headmaster, Claude Lorraine Nursery and a second master were appointed. After delays, the school was opened in April 1850, Lord Dufferin, the president of the controlling committee, giving an inaugural address. At the first prize distribution in March 1851, the Earl of Belfast, the son of the Marquess of Donegall, and a cultivated, public-spirited young man, advocated 'the building of an Atheneum, Sculpture and Art Gallery' on much the same lines as those enunciated by Hugh Frazer fifteen years before. Referring to the school, his Lordship said: 'Artistic talent is among the brightest qualities with which the national mind has been endowed. It has often flashed out from the gloom, but we may now expect that its radiance... will ere long cheer the workshop of the toiler and shed a cheerful glow on his hearth. How desirable it is that the eye of the workman should be taught to seek refreshment in forms of beauty; how the artist and the manufacturer shall henceforth join hands, and, labouring together for the industrial weal, shall promote at once the prosperity and glory of this country...' And, from what we may judge of his character, as evidenced in his activities, he believed every word of it. But his concluding sentence strikes a more rhetorical note; 'I have sought to show how, by the establishment of schools of this nature, the finer but hitherto undecorated pillar of Irish Commerce has received the Corinthian capital, and has been transformed from a column of rude solidity into a support no less solid, though more refined and graceful.' That column of rude solidity might well have stood later in the bizarre world of Amanda McKittrick Ros.

But in spite of the inspiration of the Great Exhibition, as in many other industrial towns, local manufacturers indifferent to the value and significance of good design, proved unco-operative, and, by 1853, the Government, realising that its policy would have to be drastically revised, reduced its grant and stopped paying the appointed teachers. Nursery and Raimbach resigned, and the school limped to a close within a year. But in the five years of its existence several talented artists passed through its doors, men like Samuel McCloy, Ebenezer Crawford, Samuel Ferres Lynn, and the Fitzpatrick brothers, too, who, if they were not remarkable artists, were good men in their generation.

Samuel McCloy, a Lisburn lad, left Belfast for South Kensington, but shortly was appointed master in charge of the Waterford school, where he remained for nearly twenty-five years. He came back to Belfast for a decade, but spent his last years in London. Though a skilful watercolourist, as the study of pieces of armour on a bench, in the Ulster Museum, shows, and a painter in oils, usually on a small scale, while, from time to time, he exhibited with local groups, he only touches the edge of our story, with nothing specifically beyond technical competence to contribute to it. Crawford, who became a pupil of the Academician E M Ward, followed his master in the painting of historical costume subjects. One of these, of *The Plague of London* was popular and was reproduced widely. He had other successes at the RA and a couple of his pictures were of County Antrim subjects, *The Smithy, Red Bay Cave* and *Interior of an Irish Cabin*, shown in 1860, but he died before fulfilling the highest expression of his evident skill.

Another man of much the same generation, not, this time, a student of the School of Design, who had little or no local impact, John O'Connor followed a strange career for a Londonderry lad. Becoming a call-boy at the Belfast Theatre, he drifted or was conscribed into scenery-painting. In his teens, good at his trade, he crossed to London, to work at Drury Lane, and, after at the Haymarket Theatre. Successful and popular, he took up easel-painting in oil and watercolour. Before he was thirty, he had landscapes accepted by the RA and thereafter exhibited frequently, as well as becoming a founder-member of the New Watercolour Society, his subjects usually drawing upon his visits abroad. He also gained some reputation for his paintings of Royal occasions such as the *Jubilee Service at Westminster in 1887* which were consistent with the ceremonial, decorative quality of his theatrical experience. This Derry boy travelled so far from his native ground as to share a house in Leicester Square with Lord Ronald Gower, the amateur sculptor who designed the Shakespeare statue which stands, or sits, before the Memorial Theatre at Stratford-on-Avon.

A Society for the Advancement of the Fine Arts was, it seems, founded in Belfast in 1843, the members meeting to read papers on relevant subjects and to pass around their sketches for discussion and criticism. I am not sure if this was the same as, or another name for, the Society for the Promotion of the Fine Arts of that decade, of which Lord Dufferin was President, and, among the lengthy list of names of its Vice-Presidents, that of James Emerson Tennent appears. Of its committee we may cite five, the brusque but benevolent Dr James Moore, the ubiquitous architect Charles Lanyon, the two shadowy masters of the school of Design, Nursery and Raimbach and Francis McCracken. The last was nephew of that other Francis 'the last of the Irish Volunteers', and of Mary Ann, the kindly and fearless. Their brother John, his father, had been a successful cotton manufacturer, partner in the first steamship line to Glasgow, an eager yachtsman, frequenter of regattas round the Irish coast and the Clyde. Francis, his third son, was a ships' broker and wine-importer, whose financial dealings with Dante Gabriel Rossetti provoked that poet-painter to much malicious gossip, and that sonnet parodying Tennyson's *Kraken*, which begins

> 'Getting his pictures, like his supper cheap,
> Far, far away in Belfast by the sea
> His watchful one-eyed uninvaded sleep
> MacCracken keepeth...'

McCracken had, in fact, invited him to come over to Belfast for a visit, but, as the artist wrote to a friend, 'I have no idea of going.' They did eventually meet in London, which McCracken visited on business and to see the RA exhibition, and, one evening, they called at William Allingham's lodgings, only to find the Donegal poet out. In Allingham's *Diary*, however, we note that in March 1857, when visiting Belfast, he called on the art collector, and must have had some good and lively talk about the London artists they knew.

McCracken was one of the early patrons of the Pre-Raphaelite Brotherhood, besides Rossetti's, acquiring works by Holman Hunt, Millais, Ford Madox Brown and Arthur Hughes. His sending of a Rossetti drawing to Ruskin, for that master-critic's opinion, led to Ruskin calling on the artist for the first time, and all that followed from the momentous encounter. He was one of the three collectors to whom Rossetti separately promised his painting, *Found*. His first Rossetti purchase, *Ecce Ancilia Domini* [*The Annunciation*] — 'I have got rid of my white painting to an Irish maniac', Rossetti wrote — now hangs in The Tate Gallery, and his Holman Hunt, *Valentine rescuing Sylvia from Proteus* or, otherwise, *Two Gentlemen of Verona*, which he had seen praised in a newspaper and bought sight unseen, is in the Birmingham City Art Gallery. A knowledgeable visitor from this side of the Irish Sea might be forgiven for regretting a little that these fine works are not now hanging in the Ulster Museum. But even more strongly, descendants of the tenantry of the Marquess of Hereford from round Lisburn might have cause to covet the wealth of the Wallace Collection, gathered by the Marquess and his elegant son, Sir Richard Wallace, for a good proportion of those French and other masterpieces must have been paid for out of our countrymen's hard-wrought rents.

The Society, whether for Advancement or Promotion, put on exhibitions in Belfast, of 224 pictures in 1852, of 334 in 1854, of 402 in 1859, but no catalogues survive to show if any of McCracken's adventures, in what was then the most outrageous kind of paintings, were included.

Incidentally, in the Armagh County Museum, there is a marble bust by Shakspere Wood, of Coventry Patmore, author of that best-selling Victorian poem, *The Angel in the House*, and, behind his back, known as 'The Viper' among the lively tongued Pre-Raphaelites. It was Patmore, then employed in the British Museum, who took Allingham first to Rossetti's studio. How such a strange object should have travelled so far, would be interesting to discover. For instance, had it been in Wood's luggage when he came to Belfast?

CHAPTER 2

When the School of Design was opened in 1850, Molloy lost most of his pupils to it, those left numbering only nine, and, as at Inst, masters were paid on a capitation basis, this was a serious circumstance. But he also took pupils privately, for this was the period when the unmarried daughters of the well-to-do dabbled in drawing and watercolours as genteel hobbies. Queen Victoria herself had had her own drawing-masters. Among Molloy's young ladies were the two daughters of Professor James Thomson, mathematics master at Inst, sisters of William, later Lord Kelvin. But with the failure of the School, Molloy's position recovered.

By 1870, old Joseph Molloy was getting due for retirement, and the Governors' generous offer of a pension of fifty pounds a year made this easier, since there had, just then, been a movement afoot to establish a new School of Art in accordance with the schemes and regulations of the Department of Science and Design. When a constitution had been drafted, a board of managers was set up. Among the thirty names, which included Edward Harland the shipbuilder, the busy Lanyon, now Sir Charles, his partner W H Lynn, we find Thomas Fitzpatrick, pupil of the old School of Design, Dr James Moore, John Ward and John Vinycomb of the booming firm of Marcus Ward, Robert Young, early admirer of Nicholl's work, Vere Foster the industrious philanthropist, and William Gray, District Surveyor of the Board of Works, and unparalleled cultural agitator, who spent a life-time trying to bring educational facilities to the town.

The north wing of Inst was again leased, this time for thirty years, at a rent of £100 a year, paid for its full term by a local benefactor. The Honorary Secretary of the Board, John Carlisle, was also headmaster of Inst, which facilitated Molloy's retirement and pension. A building grant was forthcoming from the Government to adapt the premises. Among the local subscribers were listed the Fitzpatrick brothers, the indomitable William Gray, John Ward, and, of course, the kindly Vere Foster, who, in addition, personally guaranteed the headmaster's salary. And, from an art exhibition at the Workingman's Association, another fifty pounds was raised.

So the Government School of Art was opened in October 1870, with T M Lindsay as headmaster, a post he was to hold for the next ten years. At the inauguration Lindsay gave a key note address, and, since in such an ideological climate as the industrialists and manufacturers of Victorian Belfast dominated, his emphasis was necessarily severely utilitarian.

'We especially invite the cunning artificer in brass and iron; we shall be disappointed if we do not meet the young mason, cabinet maker, upholsterer, joiner, carver and gilder, house-painter and decorator in our classes; we have no hesitation in saying that we can impart instruction of practical value to the operative no matter by which craft he earns his daily bread... They cannot expect that the acquisition of the art of drawing and of the principles upon which all constructive soundness must be based, and those, too, of which all elegance and beauty are the expression — that such an acquisition can be made without prolonged and self sacrificing attention.' An interesting rhetorical period-piece: 'the cunning artificer in brass and iron' gives the proper archaic solemnity, sustained by the slow iambic cadence of 'no matter by what craft he earns his daily bread'. Authority pompously asserted, the edict enjoins 'prolonged and self sacrificing attention' upon 'the operative' — a pernicious word: an operative is part of an operation, implying something mechanical, dehumanised. A nod in the direction of 'beauty' and 'elegance': not a hint of self-expression, imagination, or creativity, no respect or affection for textures or any other qualities of materials which we might expect in an artist, and, hence, in a School of Art. Even the use of the word, 'acquisition' is a giveaway, not an understanding of, or an enthusiasm for, not even training in, but instead, the grasping signal of an acquisitive society.

By 1872 the success of the school seemed assured. To celebrate this, the managers organised a Grand Conversazione on the premises, with an exhibition of 4,000 drawings, including 'designs for damask, printed goods, embroideries, linen ornaments, metal work, architecture'. In addition to this students' display, a local exhibition was also put on show. Lord Dufferin handed out the prizes awarded by the Department of Science and Art. The band of the 78th Regiment played, and 'suitable refreshments' were provided.

Parallel with, and, in some measure contributory to the establishment of the Government School of Art, was the increased activity of the firm of Marcus Ward. The original Marcus had set up a stationer's and lithographic business, in 1843, in the Cornmarket, Belfast. Expanding his interests, the firm of Marcus Ward and Company was brought into being with the three sons as partners, William, Francis Davis, and John, the amateur watercolourist, whose vigorous interest, until he retired in 1876, gave much of the distinctive character to the company. The firm developed its stock-in-trade: paper, inkwells, pencils, blotters, diaries, illuminated addresses, fine printing, chromolithography, book-binding and book publishing. At one stage, with a London office, and more extensive premises in Belfast, where the Royal Ulster Works was opened in Ormeau Avenue in 1873, 150 book titles had been produced.

Vere Foster, dedicated to the improvement of educational facilities in the whole country, and particularly distressed by the low standard of handwriting in the schools, in 1865, inaugurated his first series of Writing Copy Books, sold for one penny, or, superior, for twopence. Having made the acquaintance of John Ward, he arranged for the firm to take over all further production. It was this circumstance which occasioned Foster to settle in Belfast, where he was given a room in the firm's building from whence his personal supervision of the undertaking operated. Under John's influence, Foster, in 1868, devised his series of Drawing Copy Books and, later, the Watercolour Copy Books, which made use of the chromolithographic resources at hand. But, owing to the cost of production and Foster's earnest concern to keep prices low, this last venture was not a financial success.

By 1870, Foster launched his first annual 'Competition in Writing, Lettering, Drawing and Painting open to pupils of either Public or Private Schools. Prizes from five pounds to half-a-crown, throughout the British Empire.' Within two years' time, over 2,000 competitors in Ireland submitted work.

Once, when Foster learned of a young Cork girl prize-winner, whose father's death had left the family in straitened circumstances, he arranged for examples of her skill to be sent in, and she found a place in the illuminating department of the firm. Ultimately, she married John Vinycomb, the chief designer, and, in due course, a baby daughter was christened Vera in honour of the good man.

The expansion of Marcus Ward and Sons, by now, was offering employment to young people of an artistic bent, and, while John Ward organised art classes out of working hours, superintended by Vinycomb, the Government School of Art and the firm together stimulated a great deal of activity for native talent. I can remember old men who still sketched or painted, who were proud to say that they had been employed in Marcus Ward's in their youth.

However, in spite of the agitation of William Gray and others, for the first twenty years of its existence, the Art School received no municipal support, although, with its pressing difficulties, it continued to achieve useful results in national examinations, and in gaining scholarships to the Royal College of Art, South Kensington, and to the Dublin Metropolitan School of Art.

In 1880 Lindsay was succeeded by George Trobridge as headmaster, and until the school was finally taken over by the civic authorities at the beginning of the new century, practically every man or woman with talent within the province enrolled as a student. Trobridge, a gentle bearded vegetarian, and an admirer and author of a book on Swedenborg, was a good watercolourist whose clean and fluent style of handling his medium was a recognisable influence on the practice of several of his pupils almost to the middle of the twentieth century.

In 1864, half a dozen employees of Marcus Ward's, Vinycomb among them, formed themselves into the Belfast Sketching Club, but the membership never rose beyond sixteen, and in a couple of years, the club disintegrated. However, with the coming into being of the School of Art, circumstances became more propitious. In 1872 a group of women students started a ladies' sketching club. Two years later evening students followed suit, and, in 1879, the Marcus Ward staff formed the Ramblers' Sketching Club, with Vinycomb as president, meeting in the same Rainbow Tavern where the first club had foregathered. In 1881, the first annual exhibition was held in a church hall in Botanic Avenue. Three years later the Ramblers and the Ladies joined forces. When the Public Library, designed by W H Lynn, was opened in 1888, another long overdue civic undertaking for which William Gray had campaigned for years, the Ramblers provided 190 works as their share in a loan exhibition held on the upper floor. And, in 1890, the title of the organisation was changed to the Belfast Art Society.

One night in November 1883, when the *Manx Queen* steamed out of Belfast for Barrow, there were three young men on board whose names we remember; Albert Morrow, Arthur D McCormick, Hugh Thomson. The last of these was born in Church Street Coleraine, in 1860. McCormick too had been born in the same street in the very same year. Morrow was one of the remarkable company of brothers whose family was in the painting and decorating business in Clifton Street, Belfast, all but one of the eight becoming an artist of some kind. But to go back.

Thomson left school to become apprenticed to a local linen firm, but his hobby, his whole interest, had been in drawing, devoted to copying illustrations in books and such publications as the *Dublin Penny Journal* which he found lying around in the attic. When his talent became public in the making of an illuminated address for a schoolmaster's retirement, he secured a job in Belfast with Marcus Ward and Sons in 1877, his Coleraine employers allowing him to break his apprenticeship with them. With Marcus Ward's he found Vinycomb a generous mentor, and made friends with his workmates, especially with J W Carey, who was, for many years, a highly popular watercolourist. But, just at this time, there was little scope for original work with the firm, since the designers most favoured were in the London office. So, having on only a half a dozen occasions sat at a drawing-board in the Art School, he continued his own drawings at home in the evenings, with Vinycomb's encouragement. When he had made a set of illustrations for Thackeray's *Vanity Fair*, Vinycomb showed this work to John Ward whose taste largely determined the firm's policy; the latter merely glanced at and dismissed the drawings. So, since working hours were long, from 8.30 to 6.45, with a Saturday halfday, the pay at the end of six years only two pounds ten shillings

19 HUGH THOMSON
The Church
Illustration from *Highways and Byways in Donegal and Antrim* by Stephen Gwynn, Macmillan, London, 1899

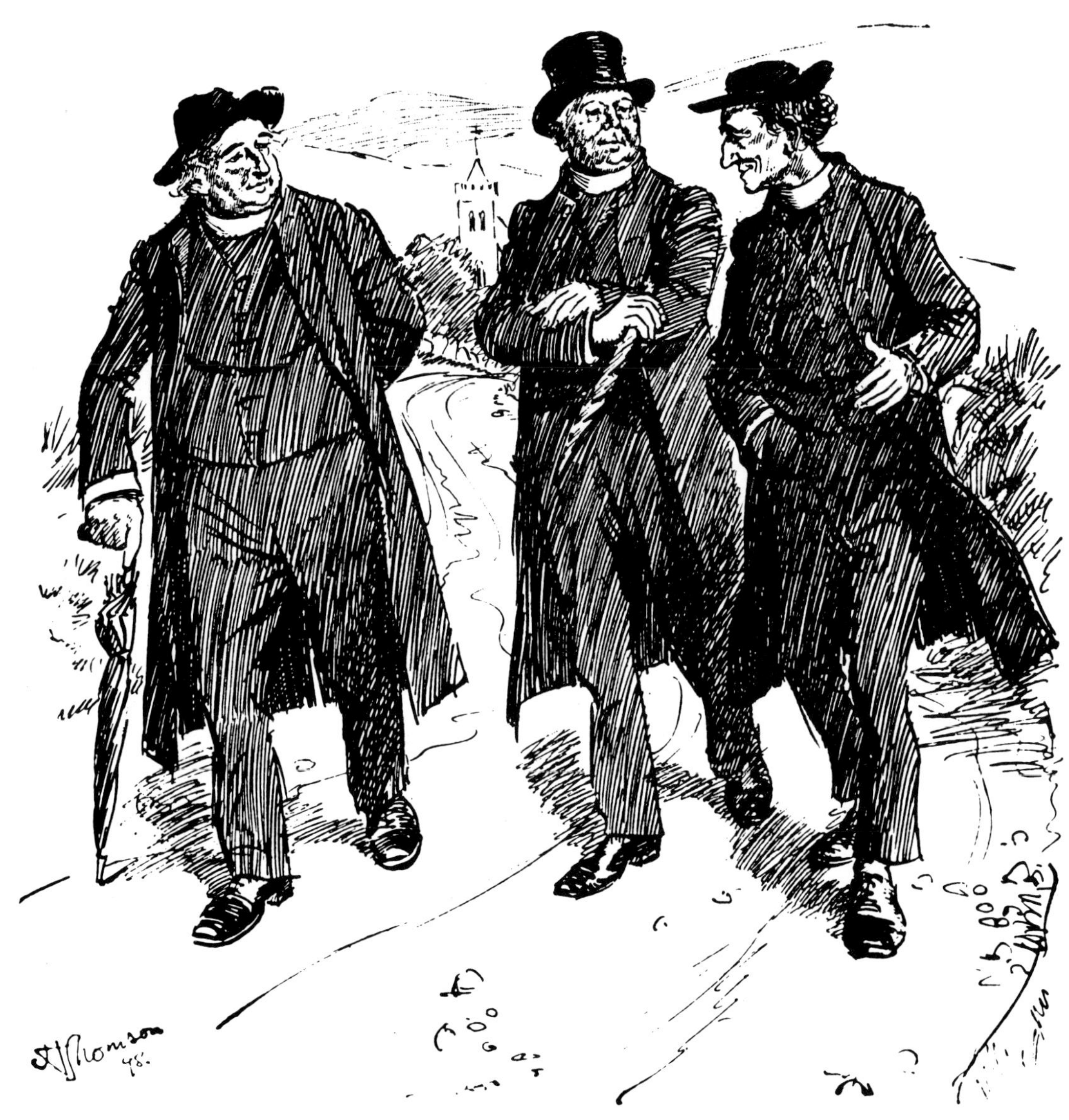

The Church.

a week, and the work tedious, Thomson decided to try his luck at free-lancing in London.

It was there that he was able fairly soon to find the pages of the *English Illustrated Magazine* hospitable to his kind of work. In the prospectus of that journal for the year 1887-88 we read that 'The Editor has also secured the continued and exclusive services of Mr Hugh Thomson, a young artist whose talent is well known... and whose charming illustrations to *Sir Roger de Coverley* serve to place him high in the rank of original designers in black and white.' His special interest was in 'old world scenes... recreated with an accurate representation of all the period accessories of architecture, costume and furniture'. This accuracy he based on long hours of attention to the collections in the Victoria and Albert Museum, an experience not available back in Belfast, where the unquenchable William Gray was still battling for a municipal museum.

At this time, the older process of reproduction by means of woodcut gave way to the line-block, the photographically produced line-block, which suited Thomson's pen drawing admirably, and, by its reduction of the size of the original, gave it an apparently sharper fineness of line and detail. It was in April 1886 that the *English Illustrated Magazine* had first reproduced his work by the new method.

Thereafter Thomson's future career was secure until his death in 1920. From *Coaching Days and Coaching Ways. The Ballad of Beau Brocade,* to *The Vicar of Wakefield*, and *Pride and Prejudice*, his mastery was clear, and in the Highway and Byway series, his contributions to *Devon and Cornwall, Middlesex, Surrey*, etc, show that his interests were not narrowly antiquarian, and his ninety drawings for Stephen Gwynn's *Highways and Byways in Donegal and Antrim* (1899) are emphatic evidence that he had not severed the tap-roots of his early affections, among the flounces and buckled shoes, for cattledrovers, creel-laden asses, and unlicenced anglers, as well as the little stone-bridges and the mountain roads of his native north. Today, the ecumenical amity of the frontispiece, with the Presbyterian minister, the Church of Ireland clergymen and the Roman Catholic parish priest stepping together, is, for all the good nature of the penwork, a serious tract for the times.

Almost immediately, both Albert Morrow and Arthur D McCormick were contributing drawings or designs to the *English Illustrated Magazine*. But, though he became popular in two distinct areas of artwork, McCormick has left us little evidence of any local kinship. As deviser of the once widely recognised naval emblem for Player's cigarettes and the painter of the large canvasses of seamen and buccaneers which, as colourful and richly conceived posters, served a like purpose, he was more prolific in his illustrations for books on mountaineering, for example, in *From the Alps to the Andes Climbing and Exploration in the Karakorum Himalayas*, and his own account of *An Artist in the Mimalayas*, all of which was a long climb out of Church Street, Coleraine. It is worthwhile noting that most of these were based on photographs.

Albert Morrow too, became a well known poster artist, many of his, not simply transfers from oil-paintings on a larger scale, but worked-out in the flat patterns, decorative forms and bold, simpler colours of the great pioneers of poster-

20 HUGH THOMSON
Bringing Him to the Point
1898; pen and watercolour; 38.2 x 53.8 cms; Ulster Museum collection

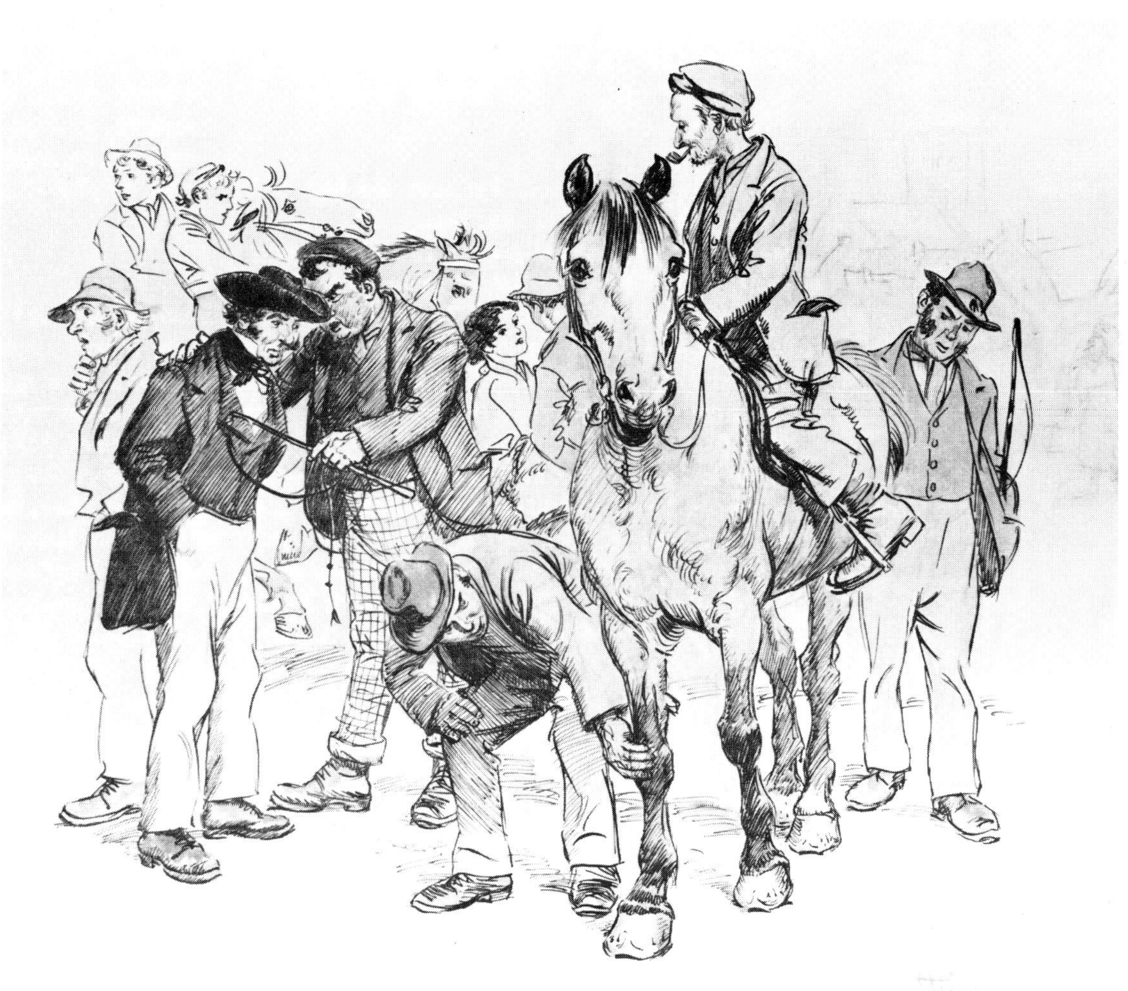

making. One of these, of the actress, Sarah Bernhardt, is still remembered, out of what, by its nature and use, has proved a flutter of ephemera.

Albert's brother, George, has been the best and longest remembered of that family. His nimble but scholarly drawings guying historical events and legends were familiar in humourous journals, especially in *Punch*, and Norman's sketches in *Ulad*, the short-lived magazine of the Ulster Literary Theatre, November 1904 to September 1905, are part of our stage tradition.

Of the students who attended the Government School of Art in its last years, it was the Morrow brothers who seemed to dominate. Contemporaries have told me how their boisterous good humour and practical jokes found a ready target in the gentle George Trobridge. And, though, none of them, for all their talents, achieved any lasting success in serious art, their zest for life was a healthy and necessary challenge to the staid conventional non-conformism of the province. It was very much through their influence and example that a drama group flowered out of the School of Art Sketching Club, and, when the Government School of Art closed in 1904, to be metamorphosed into the municipal institution it was to become, the group joined the young men who had formed what they had daringly called the Ulster Branch of the Irish Literary Theatre a year or two earlier. As Harry Morrow, who became a playwright under the pen name of Gerald MacNamara, has stated:

> 'These men and women (they were all out of their teens) joined the Ulster Literary Theatre *en masse*... There were no authors among them, but they had played before large audiences... Being occupied in artistic professions outside acting, they were capable of painting scenery, making props, drawing posters, designing cosutumes and other things which were helpful to the Theatre.'

Thomson and his fellow passengers were but part of the steady stream of artists travelling out of the province in search of themselves. The most widely known was John Lavery, born in North Queen Street, Belfast, in March 1856. Orphaned at the age of three, he was given a home by an uncle with whom he spent the years of childhood on a farm between Soldierstown and Moira, attending Magheralin National School. Sent, at the age of ten, to live with a kinsman in Saltcoats, Ayrshire, he was unhappy and ran away to Glasgow, but destitution in that great city drove him back to his uncle's where he worked on the farm for a further two years. Then he returned to Glasgow, a common haven for the landless Irish, and found work on the railway, before being apprenticed to a photographer where he learned to touch up and colour prints, for, in the days before colour-photography, hand-tinted enlargements were popular among the working-class.

With growing interest in drawing and painting, he found time to attend early morning and evening sessions at the Haldane School of Art. His first picture was painted in 1876. Two years later, he hired a studio and went free-lance, working for the trade, and engaged in some portraiture from live sitters. In 1879 his studio was gutted by fire, but, with £300 compensation from the insurance company, he took himself to

21 DAVID WILSON
Sir John Lavery RA
n d; pen; National Gallery of Ireland collection

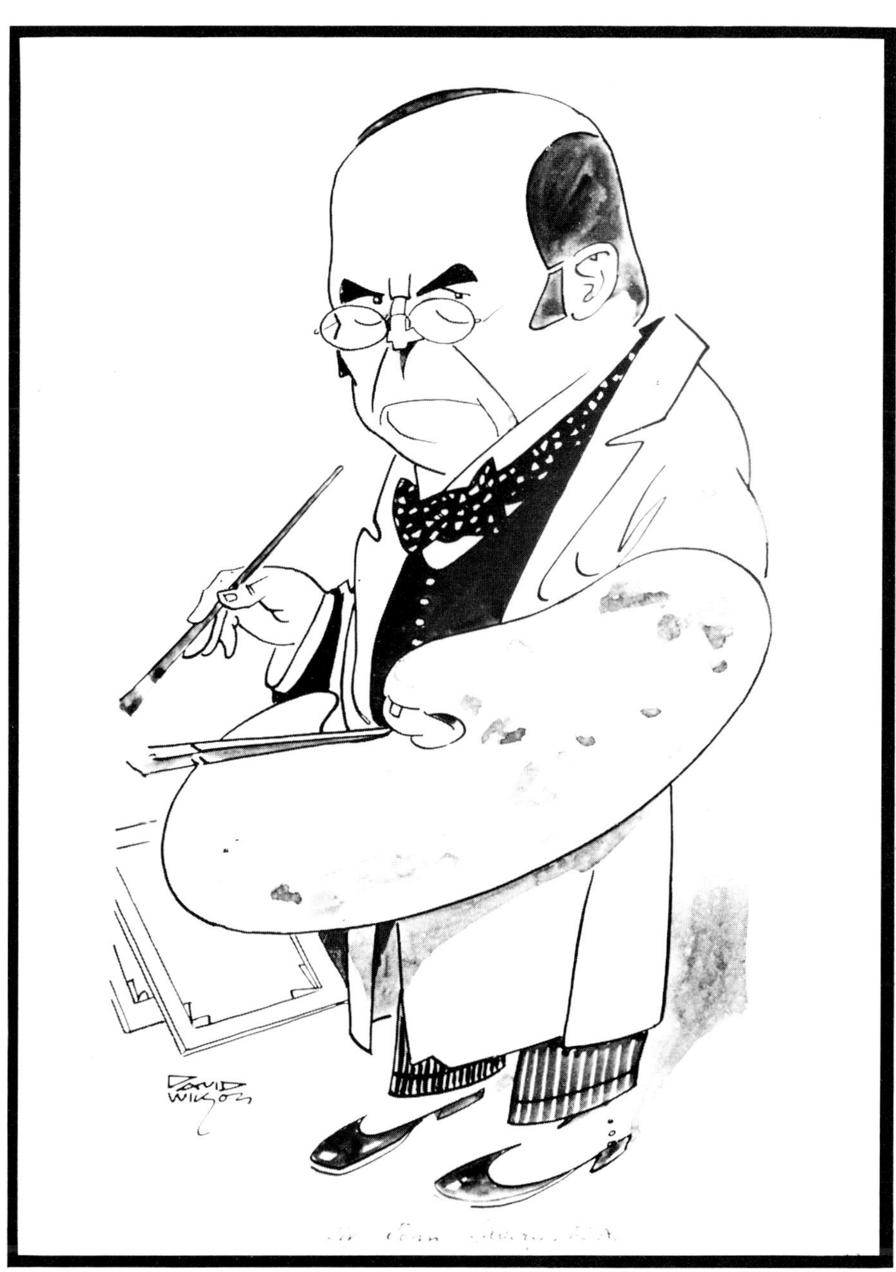

London, and attended Heatherley's Art School for a year. He then crossed to Paris, where he studied at Julian's academy: By 1883 he was exhibiting at the Paris Salon, and had joined the artists' colony at Grés-sur-Loing, where he first practised painting in the open-air, and executed his first notable works.

The strongest influence in Grés was that of the French painter Bastien Lepage with his open air realism; and in *The Cherry Tree* (1884) Lavery worked in this manner, peasant figures in a rural setting, with a cool diffused light. Returning to Glasgow in 1885, he soon gained recognition as one of the soon celebrated Glasgow School of painters, a group influenced by French painting, which included James Guthrie who had also worked at Grés. Three years later, Lavery's first official commission was to paint *Queen Victoria's visit to the Glasgow Exhibition*.

Making a reputation as a portrait painter, he moved to London and was able to travel on the Continent and North Africa. Friendly with James McNeill Whistler, his painting of both life and landscape began to show that influence by the first decade of the new century, and, as he had paid attention in his visits to foreign galleries to the work of Goya, Hals, Manet, and Velasquez, he soon, from hints from these, formed a style of his own for portraiture. The landscapes began to evidence awareness of Impressionism in its concern with the elimination of detail, and with broader handling and the growing response to the effects of sunlight, as can be seen in his *Bridge at Grés*.

His subsequent career was a matter of becoming a member of the academies of these islands, of having his paintings hung in galleries throughout the civilised world, an official war-artist, a knight. His drawing of his second wife, an American lady, much taller than he, appeared in the design of the paper money of the Irish Free State. Altogether, for his last years he was an Establishment figure, beyond politics, painting James Maxton the Glasgow socialist and the dead Michael Collins, giving lessons to Winston Churchill. Queen's University gave him an honorary doctorate; Belfast, the freedom of the City. Yet he was a small, gentle, courteous man who dressed in a rather Edwardian fashion.

But, though his working life and his holidays kept him away from Belfast, he retained an interest in his native town, painted a triptych in St Patrick's RC Church where he had been baptised, and when it was opened at Stranmillis, presented a collection of his work to the Museum and Art Gallery, many of the portraits of religious and political leaders specially painted, other subjects representative of various phases in his development.

While each has its interest, two of them, the portrait of *Cardinal Logue*, a very honest unflattering statement, and *The Twelfth of July, Portadown*, a colourful evocation of our premier folk-festival, show him to have been a good painter and a good Ulsterman.

Another man from the north who achieved his high reputation outside his native province was George William Russell, perhaps better known as AE. On his well known Dublin home, a plaque bears these words 'Poet, Painter, Econo-

22 SIR JOHN LAVERY
Michael, Cardinal Logue, Hiberniae Totius Primas Armachanus Archiepiscopus
1920; oil; 79.1 x 64.1 cms;
Ulster Museum collection

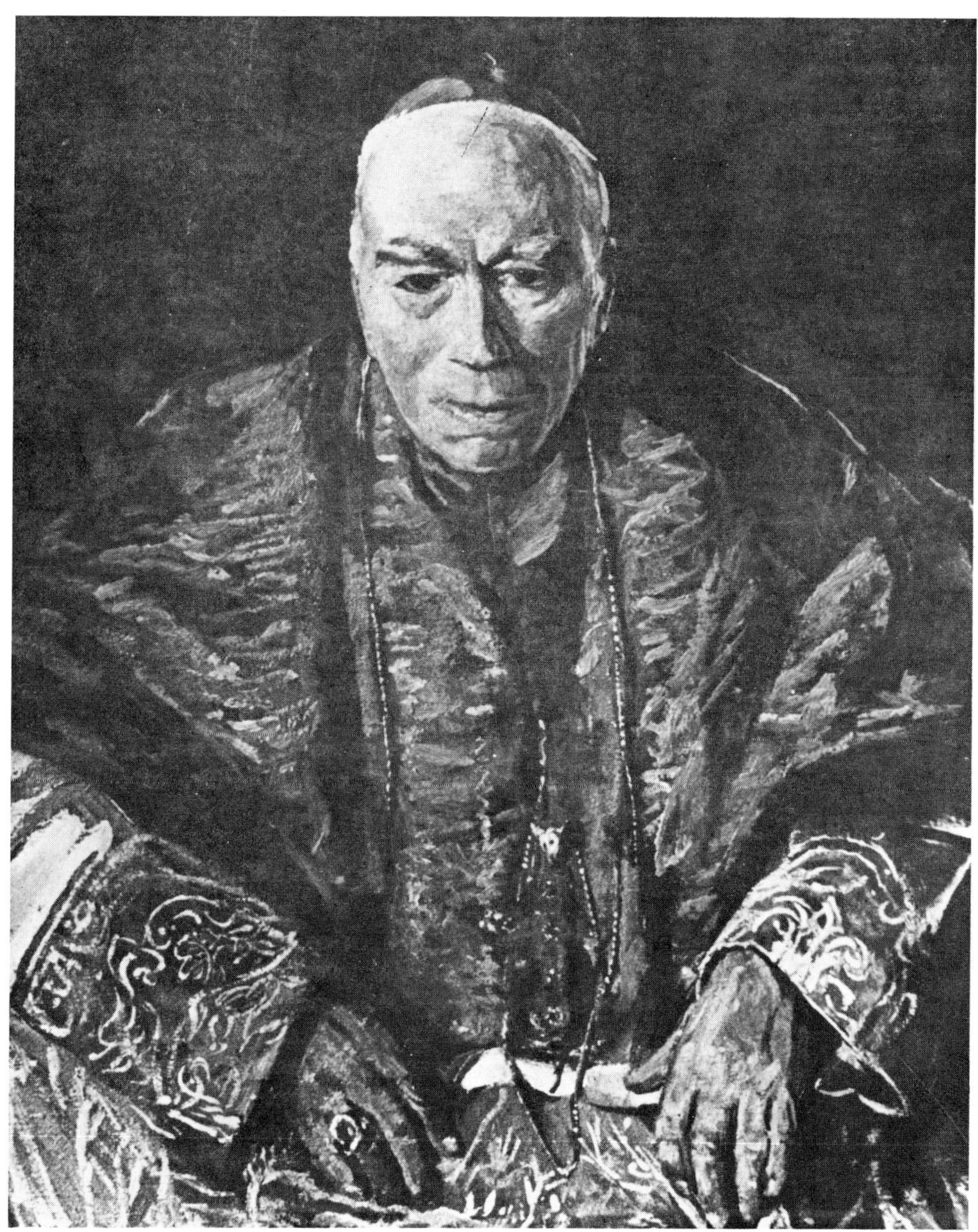

23 GEORGE RUSSELL (AE)
In County Donegal
n d; oil; 52.7 x 81.3 cms;
Armagh Museum collection

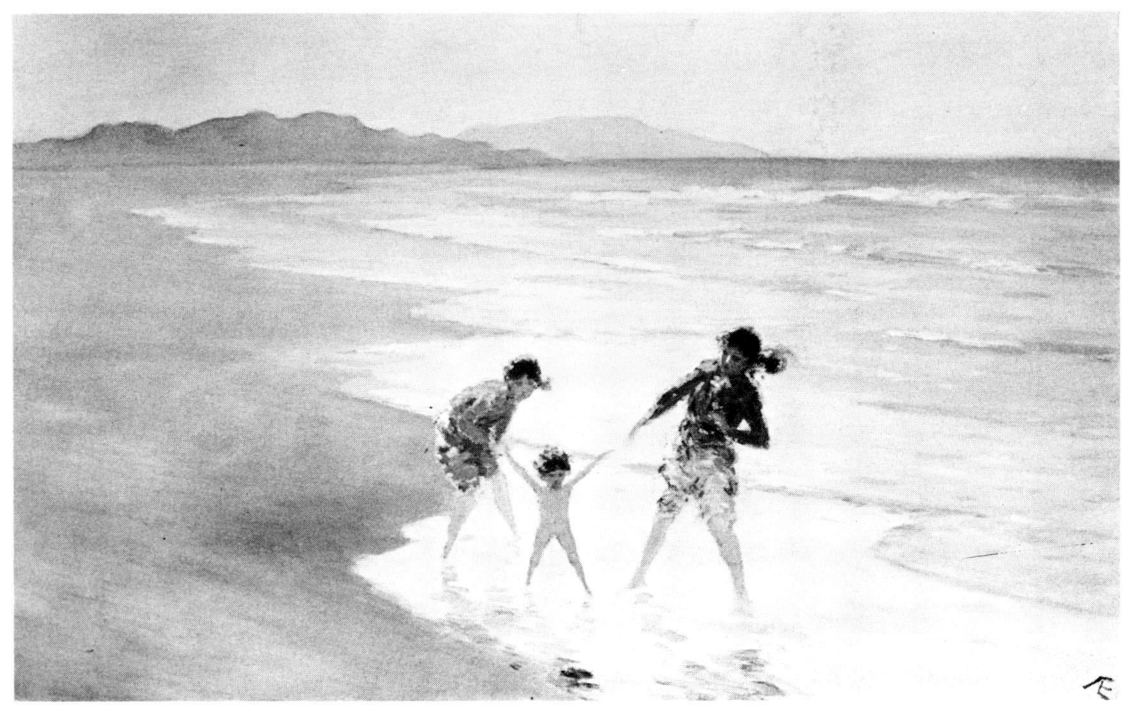

mist, Mystic, George William Russell lived in this house 1911-1933', a brief reminder of a great and many-gifted man.

He was born in Lurgan in 1867. When he was eleven the family moved to Dublin, with his father's change of job. After some years at school, he went to the Metropolitan Art School for three months in 1880, and, for periods in 1883-4, to the RHA School, to develop his drawing and painting. In these years he became friendly with John Hughes who modelled a bust of him as a youth, Oliver Sheppard who carved that great head in his Olympian maturity, and W B Yeats. Though he wrote later: 'Painting was the only thing I have any delight in doing. Nature intended me to be a painter', family resources were unable to maintain him in his preparations for that career.

When, a draper's clerk, he joined the Theosophists, besides discovering himself as a poet, he painted appropriate murals in the house he shared with fellow-heretics. He also made pastel drawings on esoteric themes. These murals have been preserved and restored and are now in the National Gallery in Dublin; and, on the strength of them, James White, the Gallery's Director, has claimed that 'he must be considered as an important and interesting symbolist of the period 1890-1920'. These compositions represent the journey of the pilgrim soul, matching the

III SIR JOHN LAVERY
The Twelfth of July in Portadown
1928; oil; 63.8 x 76.4 cms;
Ulster Museum collection

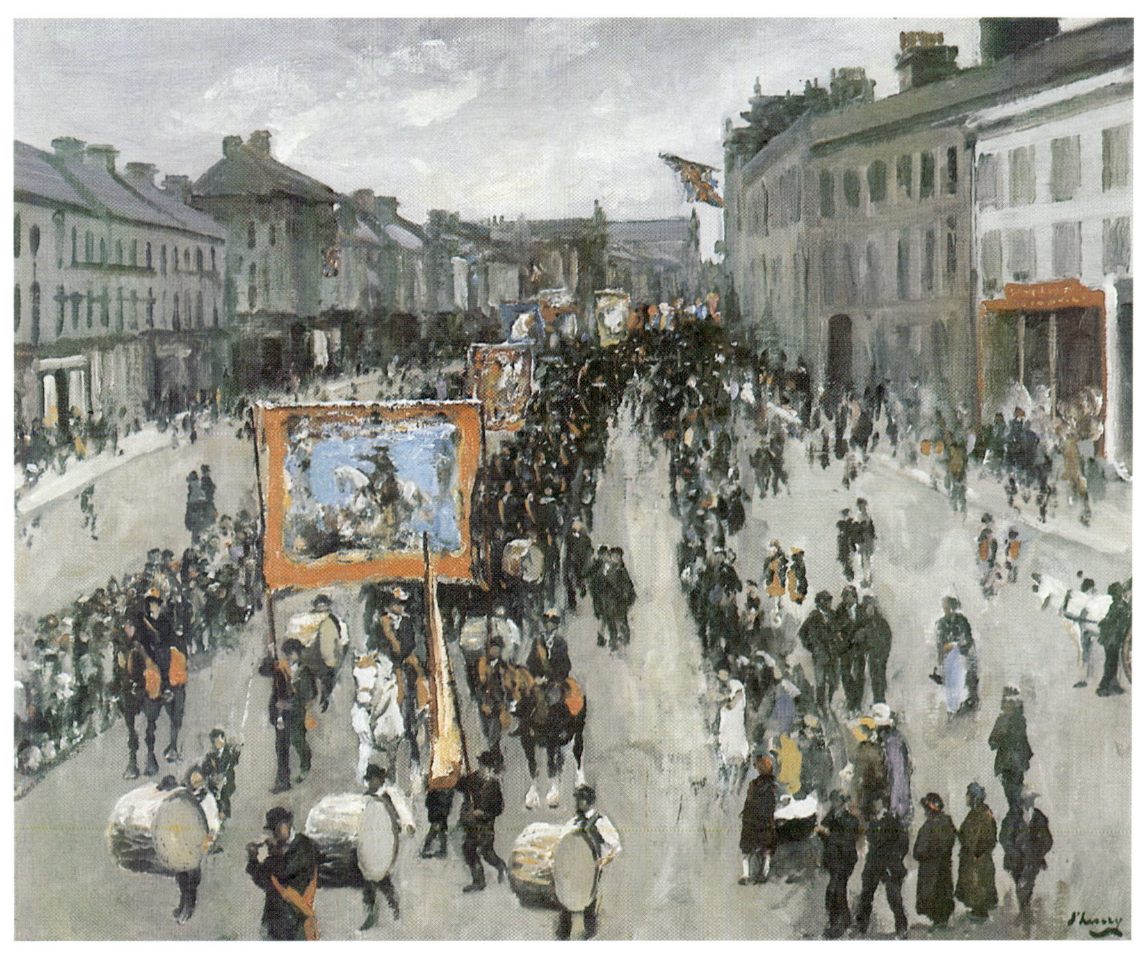

facing page 52

title of his first book of verse; *Homeward, Songs by the Way* (1904). Influenced in these by Puvis de Chavannes, by Corot, by Monticelli, examples of whose work Hugh Lane, the art dealer and collector, had brought to Dublin, he took to easel painting more systematically, not merely depicting visionary gods and super-natural forms, but carrying out a number of competent portraits, like the *Ella Young* and the *Self Portrait* in the Armagh County Museum, and that of *Sir Horace Plunkett*, the founder of the Irish Agricultural Organisation Society, by whom he was engaged, in 1897, to organise farmers' banks. By 1902 he had given up mystical subjects.

He was persuaded to exhibit with Constance Markiewicz and her Polish husband in 1904, and, thereafter, for more than a decade he showed his work every year, with other painters such as Paul Henry, Dermot O'Brien, Walter Osborne, but always priced his canvasses modestly; so much so that other, professional artists complained, and he stopped exhibiting. The blurred figures, lacking detail or definition, and the colour, 'lilacs and violet melting into dove-grey and silver', were coherently consistent with the aesthetic atmosphere of the Celtic Twilight, the literary and cultural movement in which he was, with W B Yeats, one of the leaders.

With the country travelling and field-work for the IAOS, and the office-desk occupation as editor of the *Irish Homestead* and, later, *The Irish Statesmen*, in his middle years he became, literally, a Sunday painter. There is an apocryphal story of his once counting the canvasses stacked against the walls of his room, and saying, 'Forty-nine-Fifty-Fifty-one', and, as he leafed through again, 'Forty-eight, Forty-nine-Fifty. Fifty-one. There's one missing...' Every year he spent his holidays painting at Marble Hill, near Dunfanaghy, where, to quote John Eglinton 'He came to think of this corner of Donegal as his own peculiar spiritual kingdom, and it supplied the themes of his pictures.' These were of sand-dunes and beaches with children vaguely at play, of sombre bogland and hillsides with gleams of light on the dark pools, and shadowy girls in the twilight. The sketches he made there, 'between the lights' — to use that charming and characteristic Glens of Antrim phrase — he worked up into full sized canvasses during the weekends at home for the rest of the year.

After his death in 1935, his reputation as a poet and painter declined quickly, but in the last four or five years, his paintings, his landscapes, have become eagerly sought after by collectors, willing to pay prices which he would have thought absurd. The Armagh County Museum is the fortunate repository of a representative selection of his work. Among the items there, a pastel, *The Stolen Child*, delicately indicates his mysticial phase, his oil *Self Portrait*, and, more colourful, that of *Ella Young* whose verses he had presented in his anthology of young Irish writers, *New Poems* (1904), as well as the stark *Potato Gatherers*, and a group of sand-dune landscapes, display his remarkable versatility.

We have had our recurrent difficulty with definitions and demarcations, but if one who was born in Lurgan, and painted his best pictures on Donegal scenes, cannot be claimed as an Ulster artist, who can?

In 1893 a loan exhibition was put on in the Free Public Library. The main part of this showed locally owned works by the expected artists of the town's past, from Thomas Robinson with his *Volunteers Review* from the Harbour Office, to James Howard Burgess. Only McCloy, Vinycomb and Stannus represented the living. A smaller section, given the description of Modern, consisted of minor Victorians also in local hands; as possession of these did not imply any sense of obligation to the past, but presented the collectors' contemporary taste, it is not surprising that the best known painters were Benjamin Leader and Hubert Herkomer, not yet a knight. John A Lomax, too, was among them, who, for a long time after, remained popular with the prosperous unsophisticated for his refectory groups of jovial monks. A number of these works by now forgotten painters were lent by Sir Robert Lloyd Patterson, giving a hint of the quality of his collection later bequeathed to the city.

The prosperity of the city, its population now 300,000, found its peak expression in the building of the new City Hall (1897-1907). And this also signalised a serious disruption in the visual awareness of the town and its past, the clearing of the site which necessitated the demolition of the White Linen Hall, so long the structure which represented the centre and symbol of the town's significance. It had, of course, fallen into disrepair as the economic emphases had changed with the years. Its function outlived, it can best be recalled in old prints such as that by Howard Burgess, and by a stanza from that poem, *Northern Athens* published three quarters of a century before it disappeared:

> Its fine green foliage throws a rich deep shade
> Where bales on bales of linen overtop;
> At once a storehouse and a fairy glade,
> The green Arcadia and a weaver's shop
> Where lone Retirement, *urbs in rure*, roams
> 'Midst vistas, alcoves, treddles, webs and
> thrums.

The old building had, among its many uses, housed the library of the Society for Promoting Knowledge, and, now, new premises had to be found for this, which moved to a warehouse across the road, taking its familiar name with it. So, in May, 1900, the new rooms were opened with a batch of exhibitions and lectures. One of the latter on The Desirability of Establishing a MacDowell Sculpture Gallery in Belfast, would indicate dissatisfaction with the failure of the civic authorities in erecting the Free Public Library so reluctantly, with no adequate provision for the visual arts, leaving the hopes of Frazer and his associates, and of the Earl of Belfast and so many others, unfulfilled. An exhibition of *Works of Deceased Local Artists* offers an interesting check on which artists were thought worth remembering at the century's close, by the best informed citizens, and what works were then extant. Of the 114 exhibits, Andrew Nicholl had, not surprisingly, thirty-two; his brother William four; Burgess fourteen, and Dr Moore seven. James Atkins' seven included *The Sultan*. Dyke, Warrington, Maguire, Frazer and Joseph Wilson had one item each. Hawksetts' single contribution was a portrait of William McComb; Thomas Robinson's *The Blind Harper*, Arthur O'Neill, who appears at the side of his *Group at Dromore*. Crawford had three oil paintings, one of them a costume-piece, *Ben Jonson's Meeting with Drummond of Hawthorden*, and a watercolour of a *Cottage Interior, Antrim Coast*, perhaps one which has already been mentioned. Patrick MacDowell had a relief in wax of a family group, and a plaster-cast of the head of Dr Henry Cooke; S F Lynn, that bust of P S Henry, first president of Queen's College, still at the University. Piccioni, misspelt as Piccisini, had the charcoal of Dr James Moore. Elish Lamont, described as Elise La Monte, had a miniature on ivory and a crayon portrait. Unascribed, *The Adelphi Club* lent 'by the trustees of the late J C Pinkerton'; reminds us that, when Griffith, faced by financial disaster, was forced to sell it, that other member of the group took it off his hands. A useful appendix to the catalogue deals with the identification of these and the other participants. Of artists not so far considered, portraits by Richard Rothwell remind us of that sad figure who trundled, disgruntled, over Europe, never quite fulfilling his early promise, and whose only link with the town was that he married the daughter of an eminent doctor whose portrait still hangs in the Royal Victoria Hospital. Besides portraits, the Ulster Museum also holds several copies he made in Italian galleries. Several other names waken no echoes... W Kelly, W O'Brien, or John Q Lane, although he was represented by a portrait of that interesting and eccentric man *Canon William MacIlwaine*, and a *Landscape View near Larne*. Among those who were lenders, Robert Young, with seven Andrew Nicholls, shows that his loyalties were steadfast.

Other exhibits were of rare books lent by Lord Dufferin and notable local collectors, but that most relevant to our purpose consisted of *Books illustrated by local artists*, some 140 items. Hugh Thomson with pencil drawings and printed volumes, these mostly lent by John Vinycomb; A D McCormick with work in wash, line, or charcoal, and books on his Alpine or Himalayan subjects; George Morrow with drawings in magazines, not yet from *Punch*, his brother Albert with issues of the *English Illustrated Magazine*, lent by George Trobridge.

Another artist, so far not mentioned, was David Wilson, Tyrone-born son of a Presbyterian minister. First employed as a bank clerk, his talent for black and white work prompted him to quit the counting-house for Fleet Street, where he became a successful illustrator and caricaturist. One of his drawings in this show was of *The Queen in Ireland, 1900*, published in *The Magpie*, a local journal. Among the books he later illustrated was *A Song of the Open Road and other verses* (n d) by Louis J McQuilland (1880-1951), a Donegal man who also found himself in Fleet Street after a spell on *The Irish News*. Apart from the drawing of the author with pipe and book, the best of the three decorative drawings, *The King's Bride*, is highly romantic, from the gentler pastures of the Beardsley country, elaborate in the flowered garments, the wild flower-studded headland and star-speckled sky. This book came out about 1916 or 1917; much later Wilson worked in watercolour, producing flower-pieces of bold colour and southern English landscapes, within the conventions of medium and period well observed and executed. John Carey, brother of J W, Thomson's friend at Marcus Ward's, who had black and white drawings from *The Jarvey*, was also represented by watercolours in a rather Victorian manner, of a *Galway Peasant Girl*, *An*

Irish Colleen, A squadron of Hussars, etc — he was much praised for his studies of horses, whereas his brother tended to eschew all living forms.

That book of *Christmas Rhymes* illustrated by Elish Lamont in 1846 was one of the few items of any age, and John Vinycomb included a set of book-plates for the making of which he was justly celebrated, as it accorded with his skill and scholarship in heraldry, and original designs for the covers of *The Irish Naturalist* and *The Ulster Journal of Archaeology*.

Perhaps the most surprising, since now long-forgotten, exhibits, their memory blotted out by the vast popularity of her work in another art, were the illustrations for *An Alphabet Book*, for *A Visit to Babyland*, both published by Marcus Ward, and *The Adventures of the Three Bold Babes*, from a London publisher, by Miss S Rosamund Praeger. A student at the Slade where the French sculptor Lanteri was her principal instructor, she took up modelling her single figures and groups in rather sentimental postures, which made her, for her long life, one of our most popular and representative artists. A tall stately lady of great dignity, I still recall her rebuke, when, once, I failed to mention her friend, Wilhelmina Geddes, the stained-glass designer, who had been, she claimed, the greatest creative artist to have come out of the province. But, alas, the Geddes windows in Rosemary Street Church were destroyed in an air raid, and the few examples of her work in the Ulster Museum's collection have not been seen for some time, so that, even now, I cannot make amends. Still, it is worth remarking that Evie Hone, greatest of Irish stained-glass workers, received much help and kindness in her early years from Wilhelmina Geddes.

The year 1900 saw the passing at Westminster of the Agriculture and Technical Instruction Act, and this no longer made it possible for the Belfast Corporation to evade its responsibility, so the Government School of Art, after thirty years, was reconstituted, George Trobridge's services terminated, and one R A Dawson appointed as principal, and plans for the building of the Municipal Technical Institute drawn up. This structure, not of local material to William Gray's disgust, partially obscured the front of the Academical Institution with huge dull indifference, but when the Art School, moving from temporary premises in North Street, took over the top floor, it was no more than a stone's drop from that old north wing of Inst which had served both the Design School of 1850 and the Government School of 1870.

Marcus Ward's dominant position in the field of reproductive design had gone into swift decline, largely due to business differences between the brothers, and the firm of McCaw, Stevenson and Orr succeeded to much of the work, while David Allen and Sons, designers and producers of theatrical and stage posters, came into prominence, and it was with these, particularly the latter, that many local artists underwent apprenticeship and training in graphic work for many years, from William Conor to Frank McKelvey to Rowel Friers.

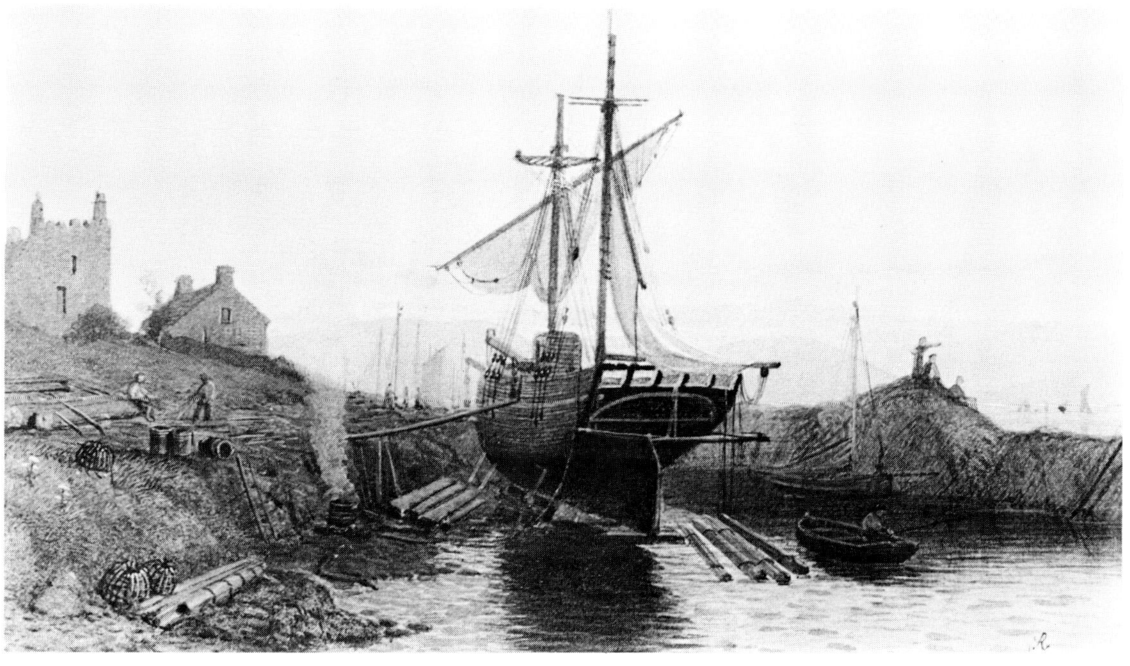

24 A C STANNUS
A Quiet Evening at Bangor
n d; watercolour; 14.3 x 24.1 cms; North Down District Council collection at the Castle, Bangor

The leading painters, those prominent locally then, were W G MacKenzie, Miss S M Thompson and A C Stannus. The third of these, a survivor of the old School of Design, tried his hand at most media, portraiture, oil-landscape and watercolour, and was active in the town's art societies, becoming president of the reorganised Ramblers' Sketching Club which, as the Belfast Art Society, became in 1930 the Ulster Academy of Arts, and in 1950 received permission to incorporate the prefix Royal. Stannus was a dull painter, as works in the Ulster Museum stores and in the Harbour Office show. Only a small watercolour in the civic offices housed in Bangor Castle has more than antiquarian interest. Miss S M Thompson, later Madame Christen after her marriage to a Swiss artist, student at the Government School of Art, was also active with exhibiting groups, becoming for a time secretary of the Art Society. Her portrait of *Samuel Alexander Stewart*, curator of the Old Museum and an eminent botanist, is a work of some character and strength. W G MacKenzie, the best painter here of his period, had been at the Government School of Art, had gone on to London and to Paris. Showing at the Royal Academy, his *The New Shoes* is evidence of that, for it was favourably noticed, and remains a well-painted Victorian picture, he was brought back home with the promise of numerous portrait commissions, few of which materialised. This was a grudge he bore forever after; though he did receive a couple of official orders. In the years of his prime, the most prestigious tasks

25 WILLIAM GIBBS MACKENZIE
My New Shoes
n d; oil; 120 x 79 cms;
Ulster Museum collection

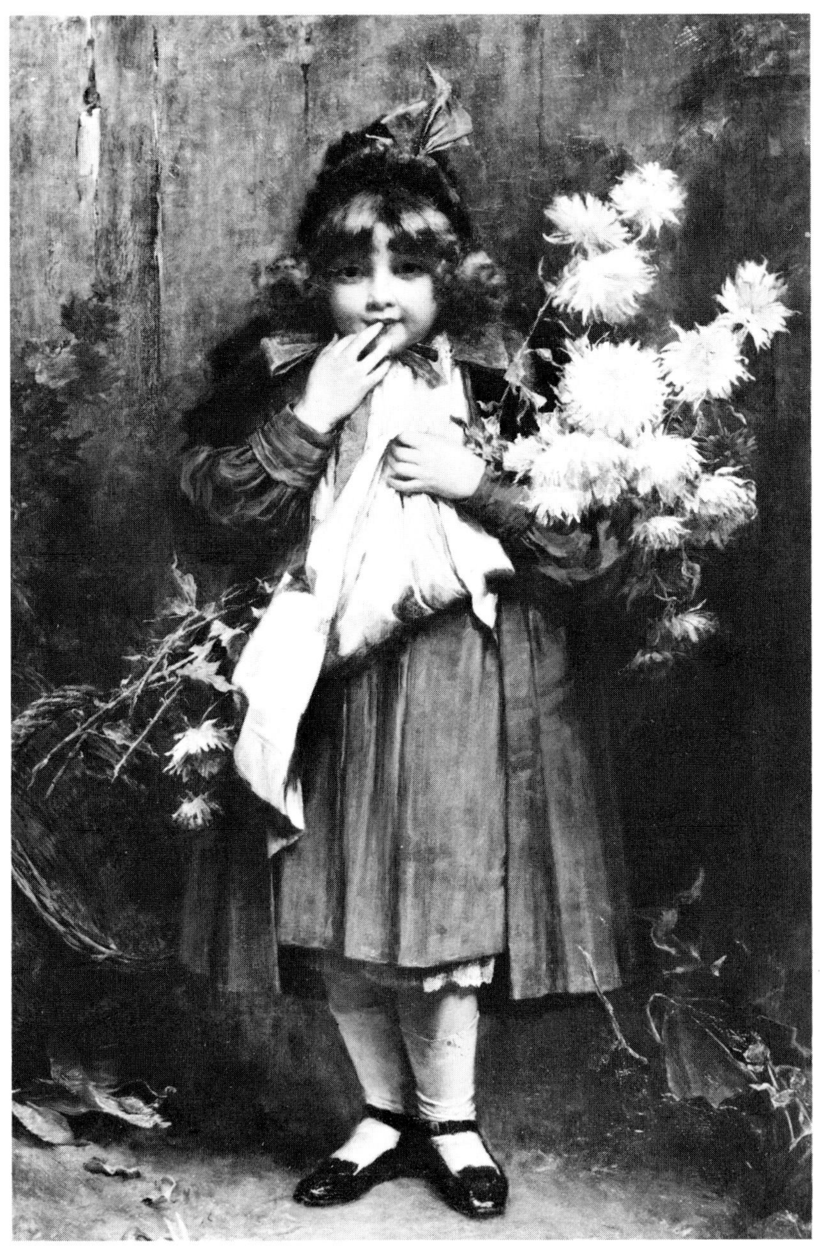

were taken up by an English woman, Henrietta Rae, who, for several months each year, hired a studio in Wellington Place, to paint her richly smouldering, slightly blurred images. Her *Marquess of Dufferin and Ava*, in naval uniform, perhaps the most successful of these, exists in several versions. By contrast, MacKenzie's *William Gray*, which should have its place along with Seamus Stoupe's bronze of the old campaigner's head, in the entrance hall of the Ulster Museum, is honest and unpretentious. MacKenzie painted landscapes, usually of the country round Belfast and of the Lagan Valley, in sombre autumnal colours, a certain sadness pervading the scene. Life had its griefs for him, as when, a small fellow working at a portrait in some big country house, he had the ill-luck to fall in love with his employer's young daughter, and, in consequence, lost both the girl and the commission.

Early in the century a rival portraitist, the Englishman Ernest E Taylor — the very man who executed the pleasant likeness of *John Vinycomb* (Ulster Museum) — was commissioned to represent the *Reading of the Proclamation* of Edward the Seventh as King. Tragically, before this large canvas was completed, Taylor, called home to see his dying father, caught some infection, and died himself; MacKenzie was recruited to finish the job, and it is a nice exercise in discrimination to allocate the parts to their makers. Set before the Old Town Hall in Victoria Street, Sir Daniel Dixon reads the document — Sir Daniel's own speeches were written for him by his private secretary, the poet, James H Cousins. With the Lord Mayor in the middle, he is backed by raised tiers of about 120 notabilities, some still identifiable. There used to a story current that you could have had your face included by paying a stipulated sum, whether to the artist, the Lord Mayor or some *entrepreneur*. Below the crowded tiers, a bugle party stands flanked by tophatted, uniformed mace-bearers. The foreground which looks more like MacKenzie's work, is crammed, the common multitude greeting the proclamation with raised arms and huzzas. These being merely backviews, there must have been nothing to pay. Another less entertaining painting in the City Hall is that of the temporary cenotaph set up after the First World War; a soldier stands with arms reversed, and, to the left, among a group of civilians may be detected the artist himself, if you are old enough to remember which is he.

Born a year after MacKenzie, A Marjorie Robinson, at Vere Foster's suggestion, was found a place under Vinycomb's tutelage at Marcus Ward's, and became a skilled illuminator. A prize-winning student at the Government School of Art, she went free-lance for a time, but in 1907 went to London to practice as a miniaturist, where she remained till the war started. So, for that period, she played little part locally. Her last decade in Belfast restored that, and now her versatility is represented in the Ulster Museum with a batch of miniatures, a straightforward *Self Portrait* in oil, and a triptych on the life of *St Bridget*, a brave attempt to state a Celtic theme in a rather derivative Pre-Raphaelite manner.

Apart from scattered survivals from antiquity such as the Lough Erne figures in relief, the eleventh century crucifixion in Maghera Old Church and the fourteenth century O Cahan Tomb in the Augustinian Priory, Dungiven, there was little sculpture to be seen until the Chichester monument in St Nicholas Church, Carrickfergus, was erected early in the seventeenth, that tomb recalled by Louis MacNeice in the well known lines:

'The Chichesters knelt in marble at the end of a transept
With ruffs about their necks, their portion sure.'

This, the work of an unknown sculptor, was almost certainly not made locally. Indeed, from this period and long after, monuments were ordered from London workshops and brought over for installation. Works by well known sculptors such as Rysbrach (1720), Roubiliac (1752), Chantrey (1826) in Armagh Cathedral, by Nollekens in Hillsborough, and Flaxman (1816) in Antrim Parish Church, were probably the best of these. Since there was not a great enough demand for such relatively expensive objects to keep skilled craftsmen in work, these had to be imported, and were to be found only in episcopal churches, for, with so many Dissenters among the population not sympathetic to sculptured effigies, and the Catholics not rich enough, until money began to flow back from the American emigrants, most places of worship remained unadorned.

The first Belfast-born sculptor we can name was Peter Turnerelli (b 1776), son of an Italian carver whose name he changed into a more pronounceable form. He had really little to do with this place, learning his craft in London, and, in due course, becoming amazingly popular with half the royal families of Europe. Perhaps his best known piece is not of a king but a poet, the statue of Robert Burns at Dumfries. He also executed a few portrait busts of eminent Irishmen, that of Daniel O'Connell, reproduced in miniature form, most widely diffused, 10,000 copies being sold in Ireland.

Patrick MacDowell (b 1790), another townsman, left his birthplace at an early age, and, like Turnerelli, learned his craft in London, where he lodged with a sculptor and attended the Royal Academy Schools. He spent nearly a year in Italy. At that time any serious artist, above all, any sculptor, felt obliged to study in Rome where there was so much classical sculpture to be admired. Some never returned home but sold their work to tourists. MacDowell came back to London, made pieces on classical subjects, for example, *Bacchus and a Satyr* or on poetical themes, for example, *The Loves of the Angels*. He became an R A, and was one of the sculptors engaged on the elaborate Albert Memorial in Hyde Park, being responsible for the group of figures symbolising Europe, Europa on her bull, England, France, Holland, Germany. He also made statues of Chatham and Pitt for St Stephen's, Westminster.

But his Belfast connexion was recognised; a good example is the rather Byronic marble bust of James Emerson Tennent in the City Hall, his subject looking every inch the idealist, who, with his cousin, had gone to fight in the struggle for Greek independence. Of even more interest is his bronze statue of Frederick Richard, the Earl of Belfast, which has found its resting-place just across the floor from the Emerson Tennent bust,

26 PATRICK MACDOWELL
Sir James Emerson Tennent
n d; marble; Belfast City Council collection at the City Hall

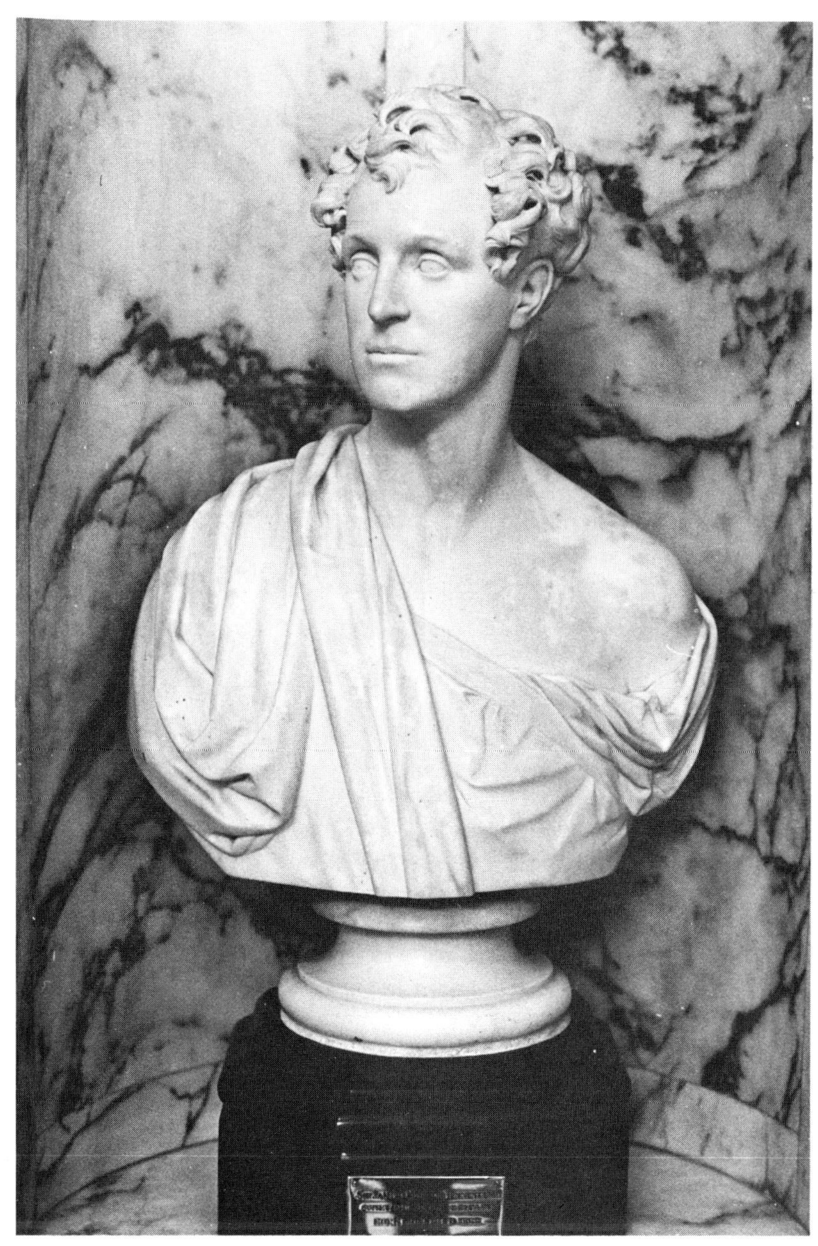

27 PATRICK MACDOWELL
Memorial to the Earl of Belfast
n d; marble; at the Chapel, Belfast Castle

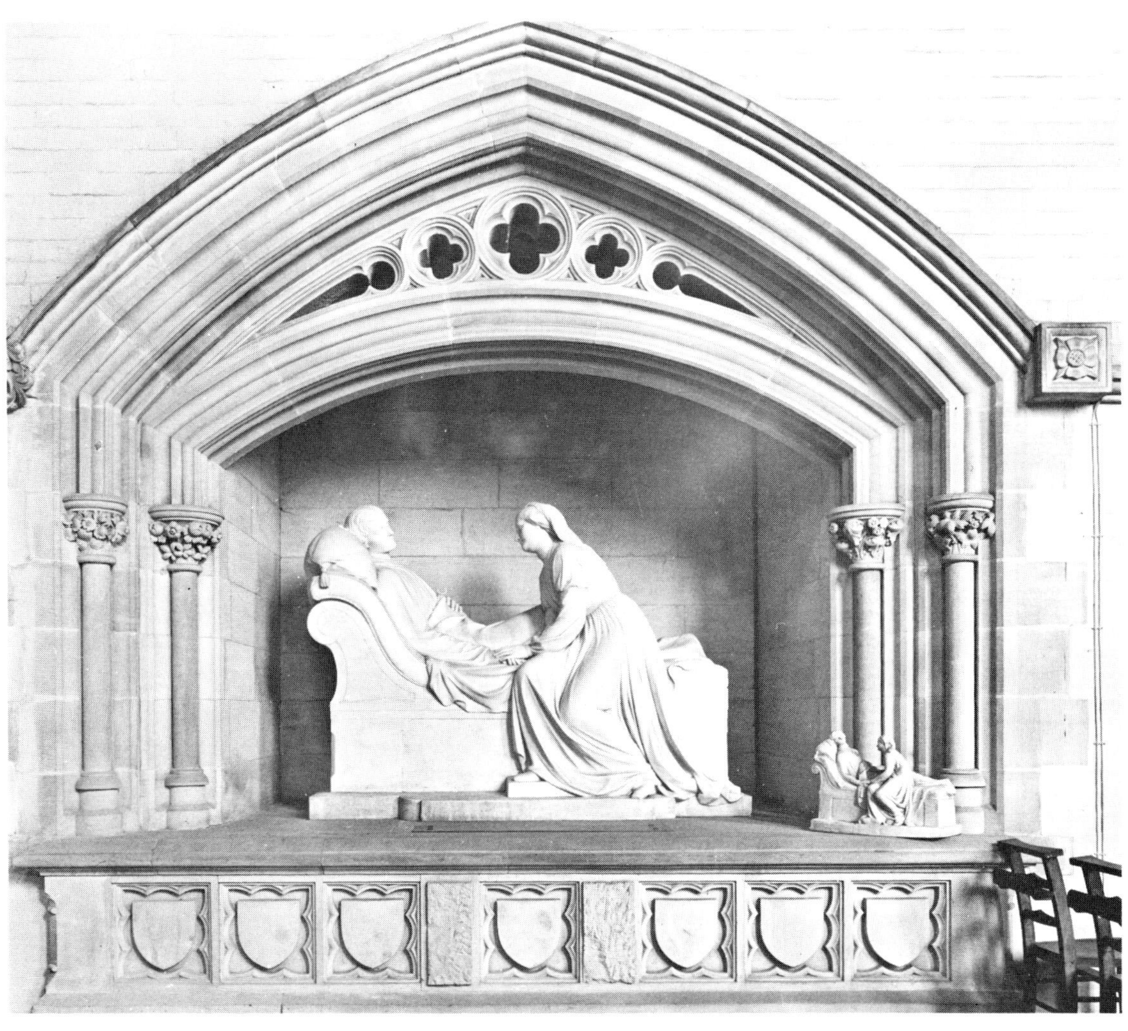

at the top of the stair-well under the dome.

The Earl, a young man with literary interests and a strong sense of social responsibility, in 1852 delivered a series of lectures on the English poets of the nineteenth century, in the Music Hall, May Street, for the benefit of the Library Fund of the local Working Classes Association, which were published in book form. He composed several songs and had them printed and sold for Famine Relief. He wrote a novel, not a very good one, in six weeks. Ill-health drove him, like John

Keats, of whose work he held a high opinion, to Italy. Landing at Naples, then under a very reactionary dictatorship, he was detained for a while, on suspicion of being 'one of the English liberal lords'. He died in 1853, and his body was brought home for ultimate burial in the specially built Chapel of the Resurrection at Belfast Castle, designed for its purpose by W H Lynn, where it now lies under a very handsome group of statuary of the dying young man being comforted by his sister. This seldom-seen work is MacDowell's masterpiece, and is an outstanding example of Victorian sculpture.

So great was the general sorrow and regret at the young earl's sad end, that, by popular demand, a public statue of him was commissioned from the same sculptor. This, erected in College Square East, in front of the Academical Institution, was the first work of its kind to be set up in the town. The ceremonial unveiling by the Lord-Lieutenant in November 1855 was further signalised by the publication of an ode written for the occasion by the fashionable Dublin poet, Denis Florence McCarthy; this, too, was sold, at half a crown, to benefit the same fund as the earl's book of lectures. Chagrinned, perhaps, by the task having been given to an outsider, the town's most prominent poet, Francis Davis, 'The Belfast man' (1810-86), produced his own tribute in sonorous verse, *Belfast, The City and The Man*. In this, the poet challenges 'The Fair City of the ancient ford' with the question

Ah! thou of many masts and spires,
Shall arch and column scale thy skies
And genius shed her holiest fires
Unnoted 'midst your merchandise?

This was the same question posed nearly thirty years before, in that anonymous *Northern Athens*, but now the answer was at hand. The poet suggested that the 'Vice-ruler of Thine isle', ie the Lord Lieutenant, had come to pay the nation's tribute of grief:

'And lo! the form that saints this shrine
Was chiselled by a child of mine!'

But this last line shows the poet betrayed by alliteration, for, while 'child of mine' was certainly true of MacDowell, the statue was, in fact, bronze, first modelled in clay and then cast in metal, not stone, not carved or chiselled. It has been said, on what authority I do not know, that the figure was lacquered or painted black at some time so that it became known to the public as The Black Man. It is more likely that the brown *patina* gave rise to the nickname, by the analogy of coffee without milk being called 'black'.

In 1876 the Earl's statue was removed and replaced by another, that of Rev Dr Henry Cooke (1788-1867), whose vast repute as the champion of religious orthodoxy and conservative party-politics made him altogether more representative of the town's dominant beliefs than the philanthropic and literary young lord. The insistence on this site, rather than in the grounds of his own Assembly College, was provocative, since he had been a bitter critic of that very institution to which his back is now turned. Dressed in clerical and academic attire, and in bronze with a green *patina*, this, too, has succeeded to the popular title, Black Man.

Cooke's sculptor was Samuel Ferres Lynn,

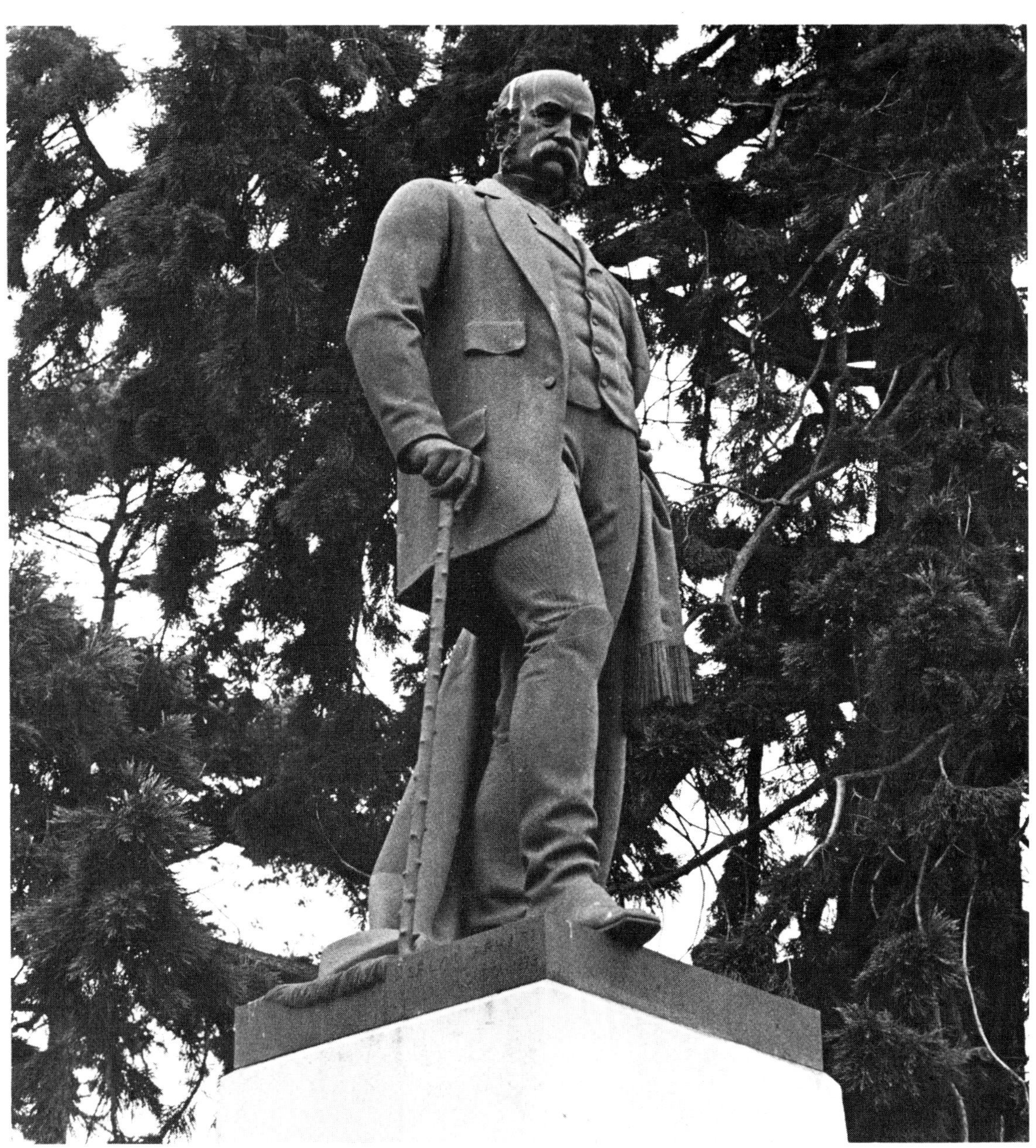

28 SAMUEL FERRES LYNN
The Marquess of Downshire
n d; bronze; at Hillsborough

ARHA, brother of W H Lynn the architect. Not, like him, born in County Down, but in the South of Ireland, he came to Belfast in his youth and assisted his brother at the drawing-board and attended classes at the old School of Design. When he went to London, he enrolled at the Royal Academy Schools, and worked in the studios of MacDowell and that other Irish sculptor, John Henry Foley. Lynn also designed, in 1855, and the Fitzpatricks carved, the figures on the east front of the Customs House, the tympanum with Britannia flanked by Neptune and Mercury, and the spandrels with Manufacture, Peace, Commerce, Industry. The figure of the Prince Consort on the Albert Memorial clock tower (1869) was his also, though the architect was W J Barre and not his brother's firm, Lynn and Lanyon, who had tried hard to secure the job. The statue of the fourth Marquess of Downshire with the shawl and black-thorn stick in Hillsborough was his, too. There are busts by him in the Harbour Office and in the entrance hall of Queen's University, the first, of John Clarke considered a good likeness, and the second, of Professor P S Henry wrapped in a toga or bath-robe.

The Fitzpatricks were very likely the carvers of the heads of the Red Indian and the Chinaman on the warehouse in Victoria Street, and modelled or carved the delightful series on the building at the corner of Linen Hall Street and Donegall Square south, whose named subjects constitute a Victorian provincial survey of world culture, including, as they do, Newton, Humboldt, Jacquard, Peace, Flora, Stevenson (this should be George Stephenson, or did they intend the lighthouse builder, ancestor of RLS?), Moore, Watt, M Angelo, Columbus, Washington, Mercury, Minerva, Shakespeare, Schiller, Homer.

Another public statute of a robust Presbyterian minister, the Rev Hugh Hanna, 'Roaring Hugh', immortalised in *Punch* by a parody of Tennyson's *Oriana*, was set up at Carlisle Circus, but the sculptor was an Englishman of little critical importance. Similarly, the King William, Prince of Orange, above the Orange Hall, Clifton Street, our only equestrian statue, came from the busy workshop of one, Harry Hems, who also fathered the row of indistinguishable heads affixed to the cliff-face of Robinson and Cleaver's establishment, facing the City Hall. But the statue of William Thompson, Lord Kelvin, placed in the Botanic Gardens in 1912, was the work of a Dublin-born member of an old Belfast family, Albert Bruce-Joy. He too had attended the Royal Academy Schools, worked under Foley and studied in Rome.

When the City Hall was built and statues were called for, to embellish the surrounding garden, these were designed by Academicians from England, at a period when British sculpture was at a low ebb. These stone-men in frockcoats or mayoral robes, only one of whom, Sir Edward Harland the shipbuilder, of any significance in the city's development, have no aesthetic merit and merely minor sociological interest. Only the grand commemoration of the Marquess of Dufferin and Ava makes its emphatic point as a superb expression of Imperialism at its zenith. The Marquess, flanked by a seated Sikh warrior with sabre and shield and a Canadian trapper with appropriate equipment — for he was Viceroy of India and Governor-General of the Dominion — is set under an elaborate canopy with pillars and a small dome surmounted by a symbolical figure of a victory or some such abstraction. As with other much less flamboyant City Hall statues, the sculpture was by F W Pomeroy, RA, but the architectural shrine was by Sir Brummell Thomas, architect of the City Hall itself, who had to sue the Corporation for his fee.

Another example of artistic collaboration which has attracted attention is the Crozier Memorial (1861) in Banbridge; the Newry-born architect, W J Barre and the Irish sculptor J B Kirk, RHA (1821-84) combining to celebrate the Arctic explorer, Francis Rawdon Crozier, RN, FRS (1796-1846), set on his pillar and supported by four polar bears slithering down flying buttresses. Kirk has other statues in Londonderry and Castlecaulfield, but none so pleasant.

Portrait busts, too, given some sort of architectural setting, have served as memorials, such as the two-tiered slender steeple in the new cemetery, Ballymena, which canopies the bust of David Herbison, the Bard of Dunclug (1800-80), longest lived of the Rhyming Weavers. A more interesting head, that of Andrew James McKenna (1833-74), is by one, John Loughlin, in the Friar's Bush graveyard at Stranmillis. MacKenna too, besides being an editor, wrote verse.

At this period, the English sculptor Shakspere Wood, had for a time, a busy practice round Belfast, his subjects being largely professional men and their wives, like Sir William and Lady McCormick, now in the Ulster Museum. In the University entrance hall his more vigorous George Lillie Craik (1789-1866), first professor of English Literature and History at Queen's, author of *The Pursuit of Knowledge Under Difficulties* and dozens of other volumes, practical friend of Francis Davis and other local poets, contrasts with Lynn's P S Henry on the same window-sill. The *Dictionary of National Biography* does not mention Wood's Belfast visit, concentrating on his years in Rome, but while here he also gave help to the project for launching the Government School of Art in 1870.

Parallel with the foundation of the Ulster Literary Theatre, sharing many of the same members, certainly part of the same cultural quickening, the Ulster Arts Club had its first meeting in November 1902, renting its premises in a terrace in Fisherwick Place. Its entirely male membership consisted of those most keenly active and interested in the visual arts, artists, art teachers, designers in damask, embroidery, stained glass. Its first president, inevitably, was John Vinycomb, one of its vice-presidents H C Morrow, one of the two honorary secretaries, another player, W R Gordon, who was to remain a member for over forty years, and when they elected Honorary Members, these were Lavery, McCormick, Trobridge, Albert Morrow and, of course, William Gray. The club organised lectures, ran exhibitons, the first of these had work by every member, including Lavery, Trobridge and six of the Morrow brothers. At that time, a broad non-political, non-sectarian interest in Celtic ideas, language and imagery was in the air. The annual dinner was held on St Patrick's Day. Some of the members gave an

29 SEAMUS STOUPE
William Gray
n d; bronze; at the Arts Club, Belfast

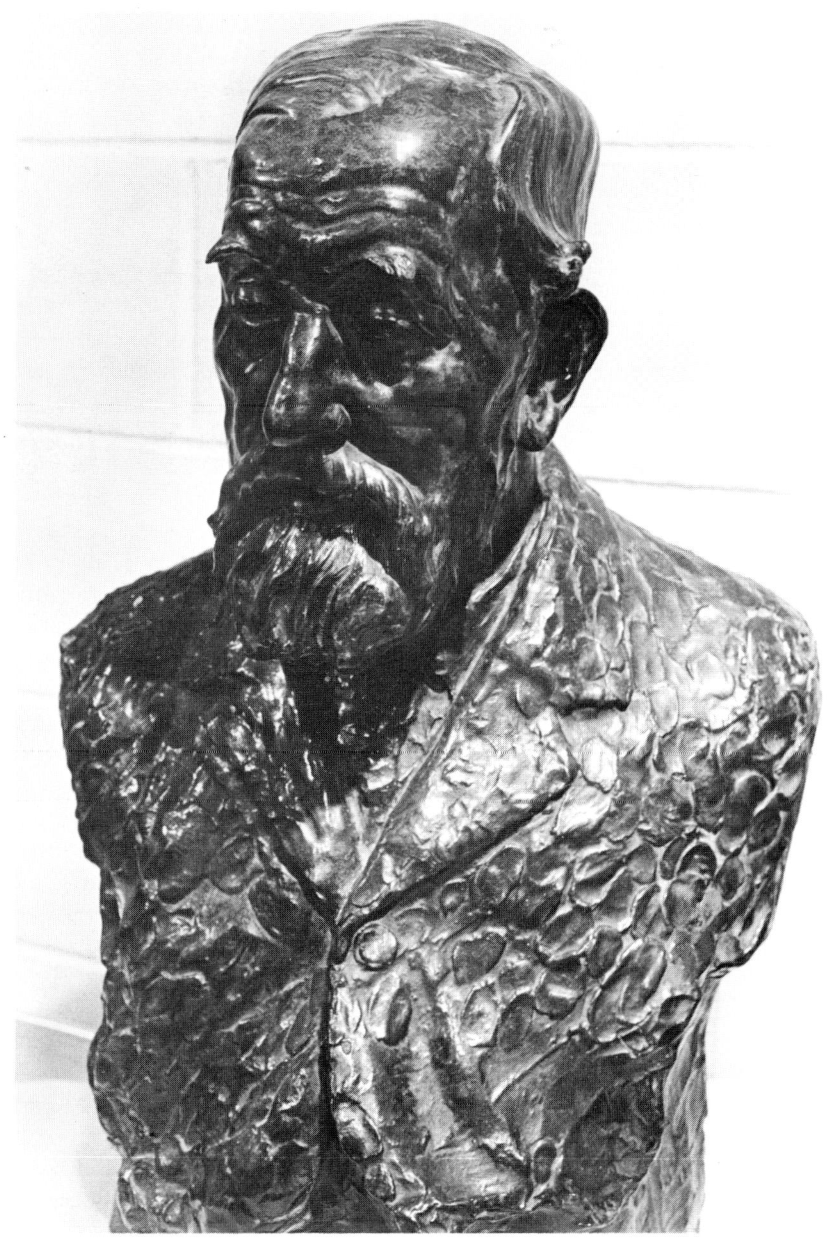

Irish form to their first names, thus James became Seamus Stoupe and Joseph and John Campbell were given forms more comprehensively metamorphosed. Ulster artists living elsewhere were given some display, Hugh Thomson in 1906, Paul Henry and his wife Grace in 1907, and Albert Morrow in 1908. The club led the agitation against the inadequacies of the Public Library and its failure to organise exhibitions of importance, to let the community experience what was afoot elsewhere. As a consequence of this, Hugh Lane, the collector and dealer, now an Honorary Member, was put in charge, and, in the spring of 1906, the *First Exhibition of Modern Paintings* was sponsored by a joint committee with the Arts Society and the Ulster Society of Architects. With forty-five paintings chiefly British, from Lane's own collection, and almost a hundred lent by dealers in Paris, the top floor of the Public Library housed what by any standard must be considered the greatest art display the city ever saw; with Burne Jones and Whistler, Corot and Daumier, with the masters of Impressionism from Manet to Pissarro. But although a couple of score were for sale at prices which would seem derisory to us, the city fathers, despite Lane's public appeal, made no response, and the well-meaning efforts of a couple of ladies gathered subscriptions large enough only to secure an Orpen canvas and another by Henri de Sidaner, that not very exciting Frenchman.

But even before that Seamus Stoupe with another colleague from the Art School had had a holiday in France and brought back report of Impressionism and the colour in shadows, and students such as John McBurney, with his scholarship to South Kensington, could talk of the New English Art Club and Wilson Steer and George Clausen, then considered adventurous painters.

Among the designers, some came from England, and farther afield. Hans Iten, for instance, a Swiss, arrived in 1904, equipped also with highly professional skills as a painter of landscapes and flower-pieces, skills he had learnt of the French like his friend Montezin. And Charles Middleton, designer, from the north of England, with a passion for painting the sea and ships in the new way, had come to town two or three years before the Arts Club was founded. Years later, but not many, he was to shoulder his little son, Colin, down to the docks, on Sunday mornings, to see the steamers idle by the quayside, experience not forgotten when that son had grown up.

Hans Iten, John, to his friends, a sturdy bearded man, was the Arts Club's most respected painter, his flower studies and the landscapes, snowscenes, ploughed fields, bluebell glades and the woods at Belvoir or by the Lagan, soon sought after by the small band of earnest collectors. You would come upon his work in doctors' houses. E M O'Rorke Dickey once told me that, when he was a lad, he longed to be able to paint like Hans Iten. His work always had the authority of a professional, though, in fact, in his bread and butter calling, he ranked highly among the designers and possessed an uncanny familiarity with the forms of rare plants, and could turn that knowledge to instant use, as when, once he was called upon to decorate the menu-card for a dinner for the All Blacks, the New Zealand rugby visitors, without a reference book to hand.

Influenced by Iten, Frederick W Hull followed

30 HANS ITEN
Le Moulin de Monthuley
n d; oil; 62.2 x 80 cms;
private collection

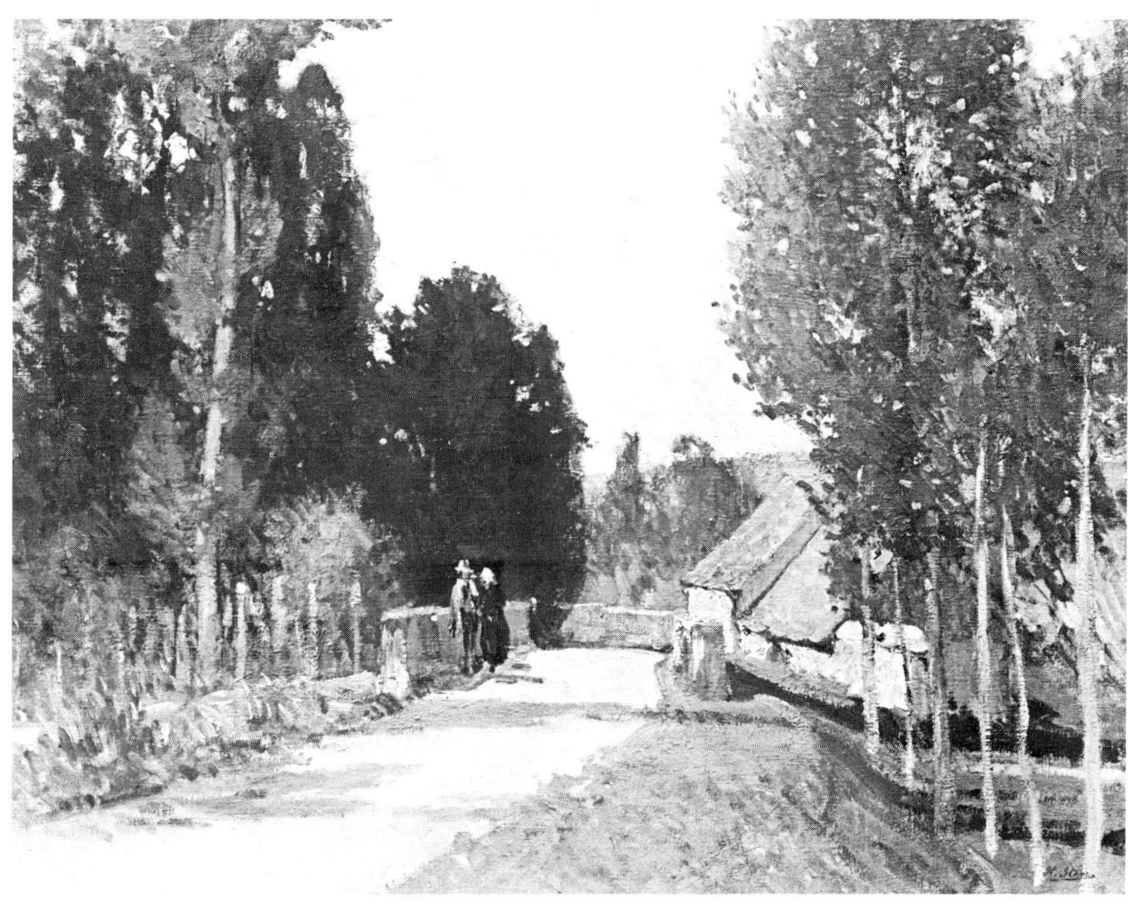

his own line consistently; a commercial traveller, he could frequently be encountered on the town's early closing day, heading for the Lagan with his box of paints, the little panels slotted neatly in place, upon which he made his swift transcripts of towpath and timber, of tall dry grasses by the water, of the brown, reflection-broken, water drifting past. He had a barrel full of these boards at home, to be worked up on larger canvas when time allowed.

Another Club member of influence, John McBurney, never very robust, died early; but, with a burning interest in Art and Theatre, his lively wit stimulated discussion of the newest trends. Now a couple of landscapes and a *Self portrait*, with beard and tilted hat, in the Ulster Museum, and a little book, entitled *Unknown Immortals* (1917) by Herbert Moore Pim, with McBurney's black and white illustrations of the Whelk Woman and other Smithfield Market

31 GEORGE MACDOWELL KANE
John Whaley
1912; plaster painted brown;
53.3 x 20.3 x 27.3 cms;
Ulster Museum collection

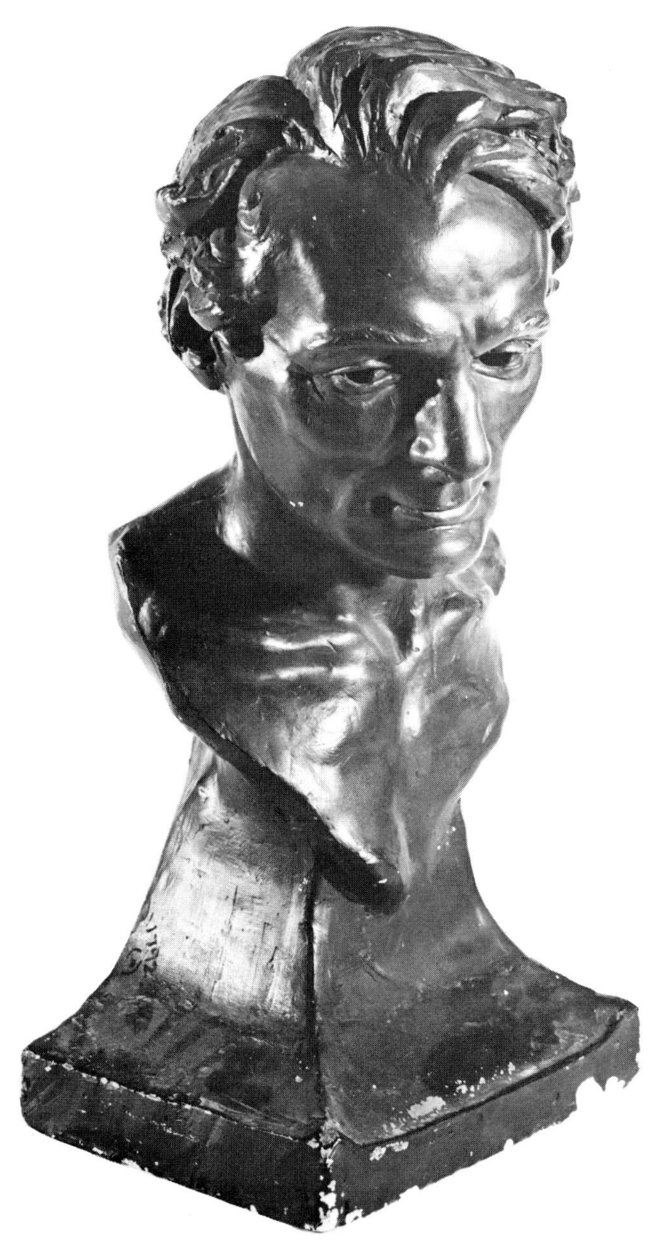

characters, is all we have left of that vigorous mind.

George Kane, too, had a short working life, since not his physical strength but his mind surrendered to enduring lethargy. He left a fine drawing of *Forrest Reid*, the novelist, who was also a Club member, a lithographed *Self portrait*, and the finely modelled head of John Whaley, now in the Ulster Museum, his promise of becoming our best sculptor unfilfilled. The only really comparable sculpture is that of *William Gray*, by Seamus Stoupe, which was commissioned by, and still is in the Arts Club, through all its migrations from address to address. Stoupe, modelling master at the Art School, saw very little of his work translated into bronze, and turned to painting in oil and watercolour in later years. Both his *William Gray* and George Kane's *John Whaley* belong to the period when Rodin's bold and vivid fingering influenced the reaction to the stolid Victorian imitations of the Romans, which, for so long, had been the accepted convention.

The Celtic Revival had a more significant effect on the poets, musicians and men of the theatre than on the visual arts. However, when *Ulad*, a literary and critical magazine was launched, as organ of the Ulster Theatre, in November 1904, it carried a decorative cover of an armed warrior with a torch-bearing companion which, with the interlaced ornamentation and heroic symbolism, announced its immediate allegiance to the Celtic past; even the advertisements for The Celtic Harp Company in Donegall Street, and the Irish Decorative Art Association, Garfield Chambers, fall into line.

The fourth and final issue came out in September 1905, but in its brief career it represented an interesting *cul de sac* worth visiting. The verse, though it included poems by Alice Milligan and Joseph Campbell, and the prose, apart from two articles, one by Forrest Reid and the other by H C Morrow, lie outside our purpose. Reid's essay on The R H A Exhibition is chiefly notable for its description and evocation of a painting by George Russell, *The Waders*, a very characteristic subject. Morrow on 'The Decoration of the Villa' gives some hint of contemporary advance in taste. But the illustrations enlist three of the Morrows; George for the loose page inserted of 'The Isle of Laughing', a group of medieval peasants laughing at a warrior; Edwin, for a wash drawing of a seated *Saint Brigid*; Norman for near-caricatures of players in that pioneer Ulster drama, *The Enthusiast*, one of them recognisably of W R Gordon. The chief contributor was John P Campbell, brother of the poet. In addition to the cover-design, his distinctive style, more determinedly Celtic, can be seen in the illustration to 'The Deluge', a poem by Bulmer Hobson, in *Manannan MacLir* the ancient sea-god surrounded by the faggots for his fabulous fire; in the highly decorative illustration of a woman kneeling by a stream which companions a poem by Padraic Colum; in the closely-wrought figure of *MacCrimmon, The Scottish piper*; and in the wash drawing for his brother's poem, 'The Women at their Doors', which takes the form of a horizontal triptych, and is more simplified in its treatment.

In his cover design for *The Lane of the Thrushes* (1905) — a book of verse by Cathal O'Byrne and

32 GEORGE MORROW
The Isle of Laughing
Illustration from *Ulad*, Vol 1
No 2, February 1905

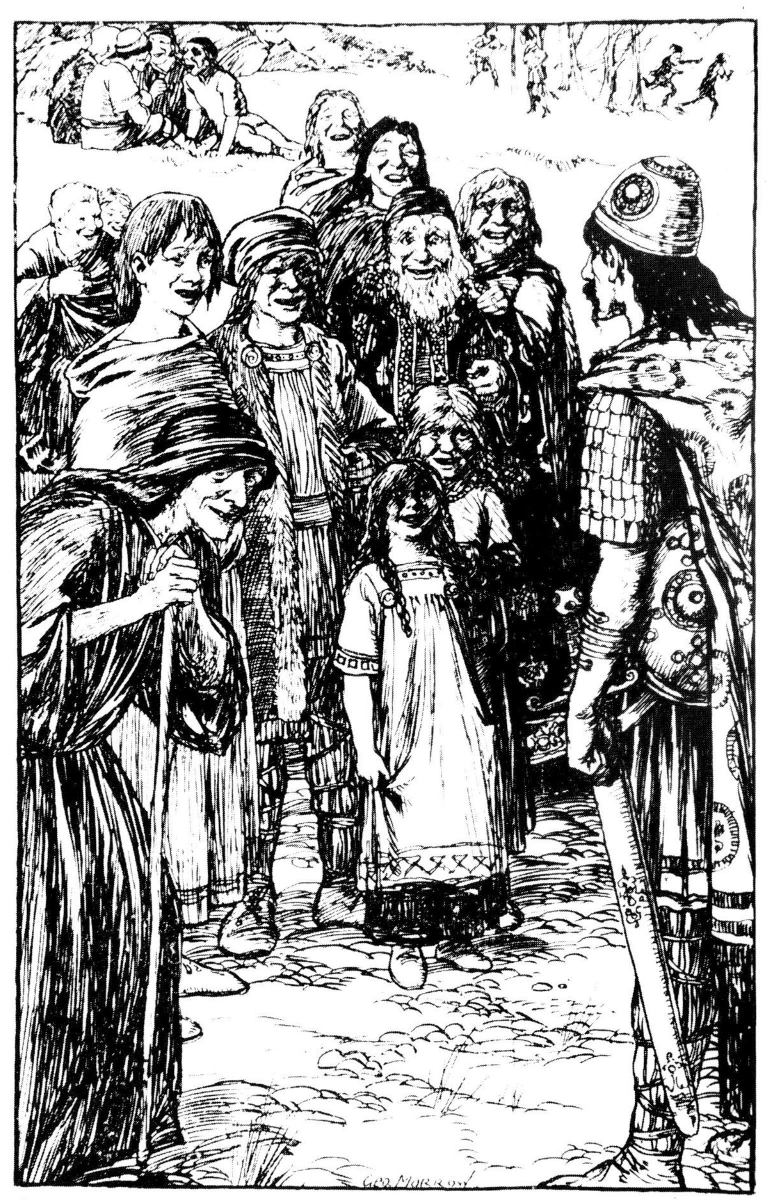

33 NORMAN MORROW
W R Gordon as William John McKinstry in 'The Enthusiast by Lewis Purcell
Illustration from *Ulad*, Vol 1 No 4, September 1905

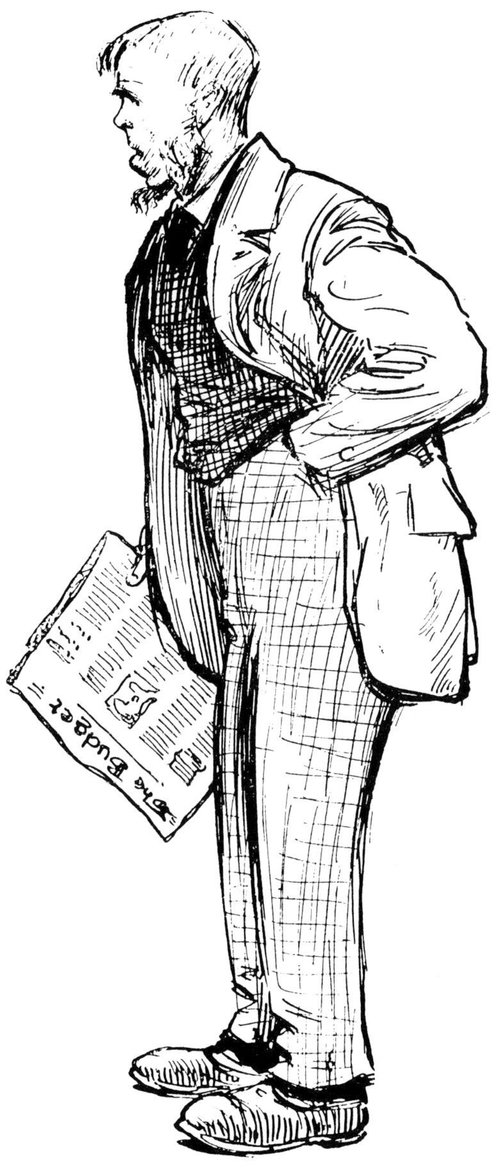

Cahir Healey — of a blind fiddler and his companion with her basket, listening beneath a tree, he utilised the same complications to convey textures, but has shed the direct quotation of interlacing which has threatened to become obsessively mannered. And in his drawings for *Four Irish Songs* (n d) by C Milligan Fox, the more spacious page seems better suited to, by making less crowded and dense, his detailed surfaces. These employ a strong rhythm, in the procession of the heavily cloaked warriors and their women, following their lord's bier, in the travelling man stepping the hill-track, and in the great sweep of the hill over the horizon.

The Gaelic name for the Province occurs again in an attractive act of collaboration, *Songs of Ulad* (1904), something we should be proud to claim as our own beyond challenge. The title-page tells us that the songs had been collected and arranged by Padraig Mac Aodh O'Neill, otherwise Herbert Hughes, with words by Joseph Campbell and illustrations by his brother John, both spelt out in their idiosyncratic Irish form, and a note insists that the songs were picked up in Donegal, the words written and the illustrative designs made 'by three Belfast youths', the printing and making of the blocks in Belfast, the paper from Ballyclare; so that the work was therefore inevitably a home production.

Several of the songs and their accompanying words have passed back into the anonymity of the folk: The Ninepenny Fiddle, My Lagan Love, The Gartan Mother's Lullaby, The Blue Hills of Antrim; the first with a drawing of a wee leprechaun playing a fiddle as one would a cello, with an astonished country girl listening; the second with a girl bearing a bundle of sticks beside a

34 JOHN CAMPBELL
Beauty Forsaken
Illustration from *Ulad*, Vol 1
No 2, February 1905

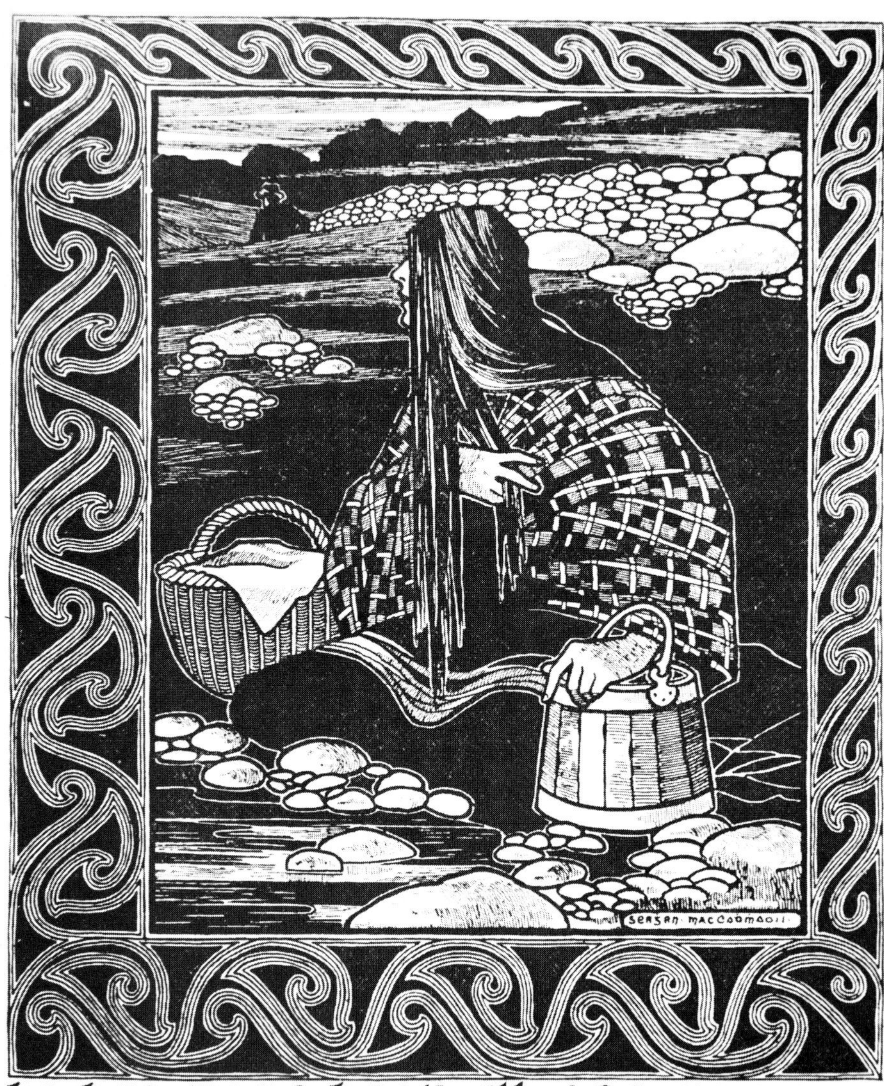

he·has·gone·back·I'll·see·no·more
mine·image·in·his·deep'ning·eyes
I'll·lean·me·here·across·this·well·
and·in·my·beauty·peace·will·rise

35 JOHN CAMPBELL
The Women at their Doors
Illustration from *Ulad*, Vol 1
No 4, September 1905

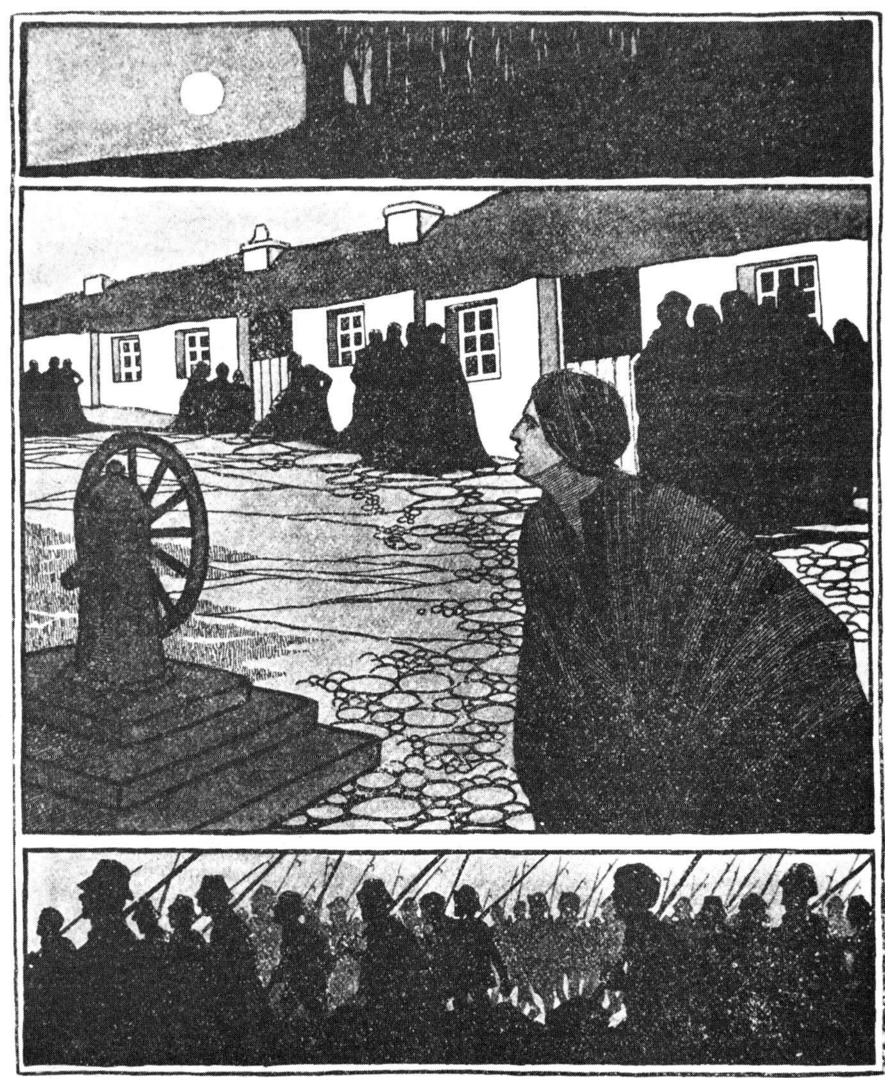

THEN · THE · MOON · ROSE · OVER · THE · VALLEY
AND · THE · CHEERING · DIED · AWAY · · · ·
AND · THE · WOMEN · WENT · WITHIN · THEIR · DOORS
AT · THE · MOUTH · OF · THE · SUMMER · DAY

lake in a wooded landscape; the third with a shawled woman and her nestling baby before an open hearth with a pot crook swung across it; the last a landscape with a foreground of hedge, tree and fence, and, beyond, a rim of hills recalling Tierebullagh or Lurigedan. There are fifteen other drawings, all in bold black and white, rather in the manner Jack B Yeats used for his little Irish Readers or Phrase-books: a period-piece of the peasant-saluting, folklore-gathering, place-name-weighted, arts-and-crafts emphasis of the Anglo-Irish Revival.

Certainly, Seaghan MacCathmhaiol, as he signed himself, forged an individual style, but found no followers, his work evidencing only a period quality and charm; and when Padraig Marrinan, about 1950, painted his *Aengus Og*, it owed more to John Luke's *Madonna and Child* than to Campbell, in the flowing draperies and formalised bushes. But Celtic interlacery survived, more appropriately, in illuminated addresses and similar calligraphic exercises, and it was, I believe, for his skill in this that Charles Braithwaite, art master of the Methodist College, Belfast, became an ARHA, for the few landscapes from his brush that I have seen would hardly have warranted it.

George Trobridge, who, in his twenty years as principal of the Government School of Art, had, among other advances, introduced the use of nude models in its life classes, and had seen his students achieve excellent results till, in 1900, sixteen awards, including a gold medal, were gained in the national competition, retired in that year, and the headship of the school, now fully under municipal control, was taken over by R A Dawson who superintended the removal to premises in North Street, till, six years later, it was housed on the top floor of the Technical Institute.

CHAPTER 3

The long agitation of William Gray had only achieved partial success in the establishment of the Free Public Library by the city council, with no adequate provision for museum or art gallery within its walls. But with the added support of the Arts Club and educated opinion, and the pressure of the bequest of Canon Grainger's antiquities collection to the city and the need to house it, circumstances changed. Arthur Deane who had learned something of his business in the Warrington museum, was appointed curator to look after museum and art gallery development. An annex at the back gave a roof to Grainger's benefactions. The Belfast Natural History and Philosophical Society offered the contents, gathered over the years in the Old Museum, College Square North, where the Belfast Association of Artists had exhibited so long ago, on condition that a purpose-built structure be erected, at the city's charge, in the Botanic Gardens, Stranmillis, which had come into civic ownership.

By 1911 a competition had been held and an architect's design for the new building had been accepted. But, with the City Council's customary lack of urgency and the outbreak of the war, nothing was done until the demand for public works in the years of industrial depression after the war, forced the project up the agenda. So, in 1929, erected to a plan already eighteen years old and its architect gone to Japan, two-fifths of his original conception was opened, as the Belfast Museum and Art Gallery, resembling, as someone declared, 'a Board of Works' money box', with stone figure-heads on its fractional facade.

The curator's coming had made a difference. The Canon's full length portrait by Stannus was given a place. The Egyptian mummy, saluted so long ago in a poem by Francis Davis, was brought over from the old Museum, to fascinate generations of little boys every day of the week except Sunday, whereas before, it had been the traditional Easter Monday treat.

It was under Arthur Deane's guidance that visitors to the top floor in Royal Avenue had a chance to see examples of Brangwyn, Sickert, and the rest of those British artists then acclaimed, when occasion arose. Lane lent works from his own collection. Exhibitions from the Contemporary Art Society and by the local Arts Club and Art Society were shown. After the war an important display of Nathaniel Hone's paintings introduced the best of Irish landscape men to the northern public, and a memorable exhibition of Austrian children's work from the celebrated Professor Cizek's classes brought attention to the significance of child art in a pioneer effort. The colourful exhibits would now seem pretty and rather conventional to generations accustomed to more spontaneous juvenile pictorial experiments. And in 1927 a *Loan Exhibition of Irish Portraits by Ulster Artists* which assembled canvasses from Joseph Wilson to Frank McKelvey, including many mentioned in the foregoing pages, was a valuable exercise in regional realisation. In that year, too, a *British Artists' Exhibition*, sponsored by Sir Joseph Duveen to give the unknown or little-known the chance to show their work to the provincial public, was organised for Belfast. Of its 291 exhibits as many as sixty one were purchased, but these did not include an L S Lowry priced at twenty pounds. A series of public lectures on the appreciation of modern art, Frank Rutter, then a popular critic, gave one of them, stimulated the lively controversy which filled the letter pages of the local press. Still a student, I added my polemic on behalf of the new.

Sir Robert Lloyd Patterson had bequeathed his collection to the city, with £5,000 to ensure that it be adequately displayed. Unfortunately, the pictures were Victorian rubbish, some of them imitations of well known works, some with titles like *The Favourite of the Harem*. Among those represented, only one, Val Prinsep, by name, would now be recognised by the most painstaking scholar of their period. So, Rutter, being at hand, the curator shrewdly had him commissioned to report on the collection's artistic value. Rutter's report was tactful, but just; the collection was not appropriate for showing in the new gallery then being built. It would have done no credit to the benefactor's memory, and should be disposed of. Any monies accruing from its sale, added to the £5,000, could be used to buy more fitting works.

Sir Robert's executors accepted Rutter's estimate. The will was legally adjusted, the collection to be sold and new works purchased to the aggregated amount. But here the executors, making a fair assessment of the good taste of the city's aldermen and councillors, stipulated that the substituted paintings should be acquired for the gallery, by the Contemporary Art Society in London, and not by the Libraries, Museum and Art Gallery Committee of the Corporation. So, Belfast came to have a collection representing British painting of the period, Augustus John, Walter Sickert, Wilson Steer, Paul and John Nash, Edward Wadsworth, Mark Gertler,

William Roberts, Stanley and Gilbert Spencer, and those familiars of the C A S, Vanessa Bell, Roger Fry and Duncan Grant. The modernity of these had reluctantly to be accepted by the committee, one councillor blaming it all on what he called The Contemptible Art Society. There was, however, one regrettable event. One of the paintings, *Mother and Child*, by Wilson Steer, was of a plump naked woman with her off-spring, which, when put on show, became the target for criticism of several elderly ladies, powerful among them, the wife of the Town Clerk. Its removal was demanded. The curator, at this point, lost his nerve. He might have taken the picture off exhibition and stored it safely till the fuss and the critics had died away. The C A S refused to take it back, for it was a fine painting, but some willing London dealer effected the required exchange to a safe uncontroversial landscape. By coincidence, Steer's *Mother and Child* which had passed after the exchange into the highly reputable possession of Sir Michael Sadler, briefly returned to the gallery walls when the Lewinter Frankl Collection was shown there in 1958.

Another committee decision might be recalled as giving some hint of the level of civic taste a few years later. The Haverty Trust had the function of buying works by living Irish artists and presenting them to public galleries in the country. When it was realised that Belfast did not have a painting by Jack B Yeats, the Haverty Trustees purchased a good-sized canvas, *Morning in the City*, specifically to remedy Belfast's lack. Offered as a gift, from the source of other fine works the gallery had already accepted, it was rejected, and returned to Dublin; where it now hangs in the National Gallery.

But though members of the Arts Club brought back some awareness of what had been happening in the arts abroad, triumphantly supported by Lane's great Exhibition of 1906, the chief carrier of continental usages, the painter who opened the path to the twentieth century was, most certainly, Paul Henry, and for that influence and for the vigour with which he created his vision of Irish landscape and fixed an individual convention on the seeing of a generation, he must be accepted and saluted as one of our half dozen authoritative painters.

Born in Belfast in 1876, son of a Baptist pastor, in his teens he had drawing lessons from Tom Bond Walker, an Englishman who gave private tuition, was apprenticed to damask designing, at the Government Art School was strongly influenced by the teaching of Harry Morrow. By the generosity of a kinsman, he was enabled to spend a year in Paris, attending Julian's academy, and in Whistler's studio, when he came back to London, he had some success as a draughtsman with his figure studies. But his Paris sojourn had introduced him to the forceful painting of Van Gogh, and gave him a fondness for the peasant honesty of 'Millet, influences which took him time to digest and become the basis of his work. So that, when he exhibited with the younger progressives of the Allied Art Association in 1910, it was with drawings mainly.

In 1912 he visited Achill Island, was excited by the look of it, and stayed in the west for the next seven years, exhibiting his paintings with those of his first wife, Grace, in Dublin and Belfast. His first Irish subjects were of peasants working in hilly little fields, digging potatoes, Millet-like

36 PAUL HENRY
Cliffs at Ballintoy
1934; oil painting original for Northern Ireland Tourist Development Association poster; 70 x 116 cms; Northern Ireland Tourist Board collection

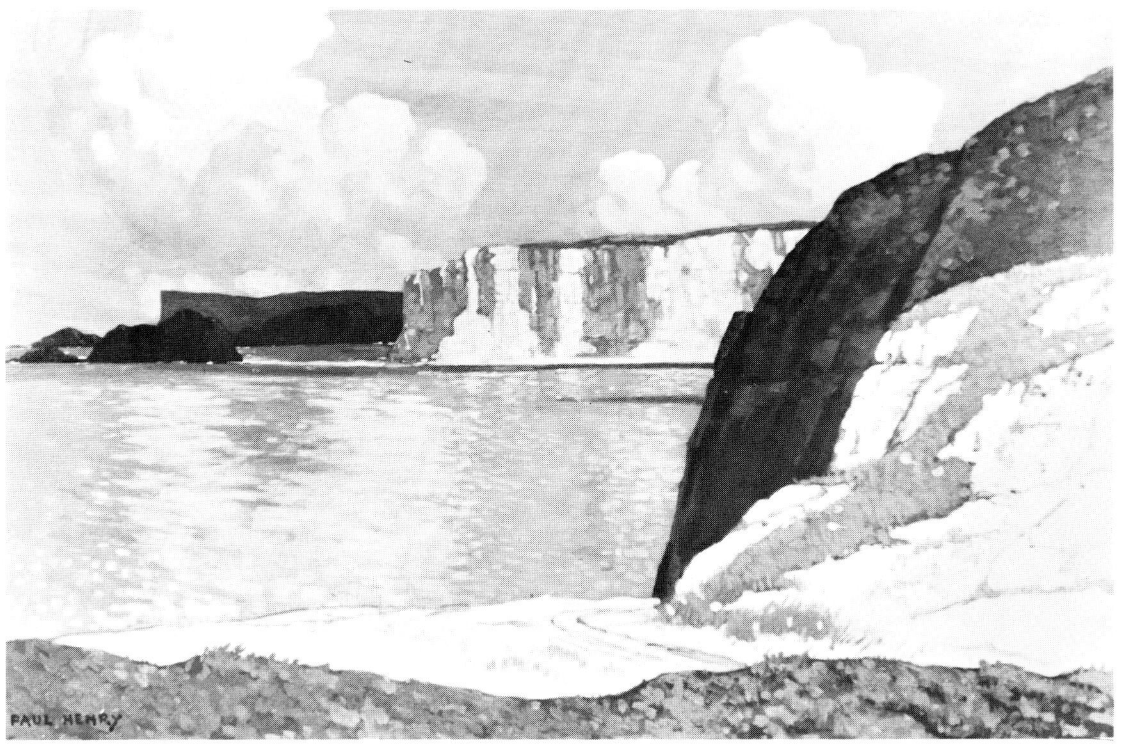

groups with a Van Gogh richness and strength of colour, or of small parties of country folk seated in dark cottage interiors, but he was moving towards a concentration on landscape, first misty mountains and still inland waters, turfstacks and bogland with a Whistlerian quiet. Then, by the time he had returned to Dublin, he moved into his characteristic vein, the great billowing cloudscape above the blue mountains with snug white cottages leaning on the lower slopes across or behind the reflecting foreground of a lonely lake. From this period he derived his series of posters for the London Midland and Scottish Railway, about 1925; one of these, *Connemara Landscape* had far larger sales and wider distribution than any other LMS poster. It was this which fixed the form and colour of the archetypal Paul Henry in the public imagination. By now, gallery-goers were able to recognise one of his pictures like a pleasurable known brand.

Back in Dublin he exhibited with a group which he and Grace had formed, called the Dublin Painters, which included local artists like Mainie Jellett, Laetitia Hamilton and Harry Clark, joined by northerners, Charles Lamb who had come from Portadown and E M O'R Dickey from Belfast. By now, many of his compositions of Connemara were painted from sketches or from memory, and it may be that this gave a greater

37 CHARLES LAMB
Bringing in Lobster Pots
1947; oil; 50.8 x 61 cms;
Armagh Museum collection

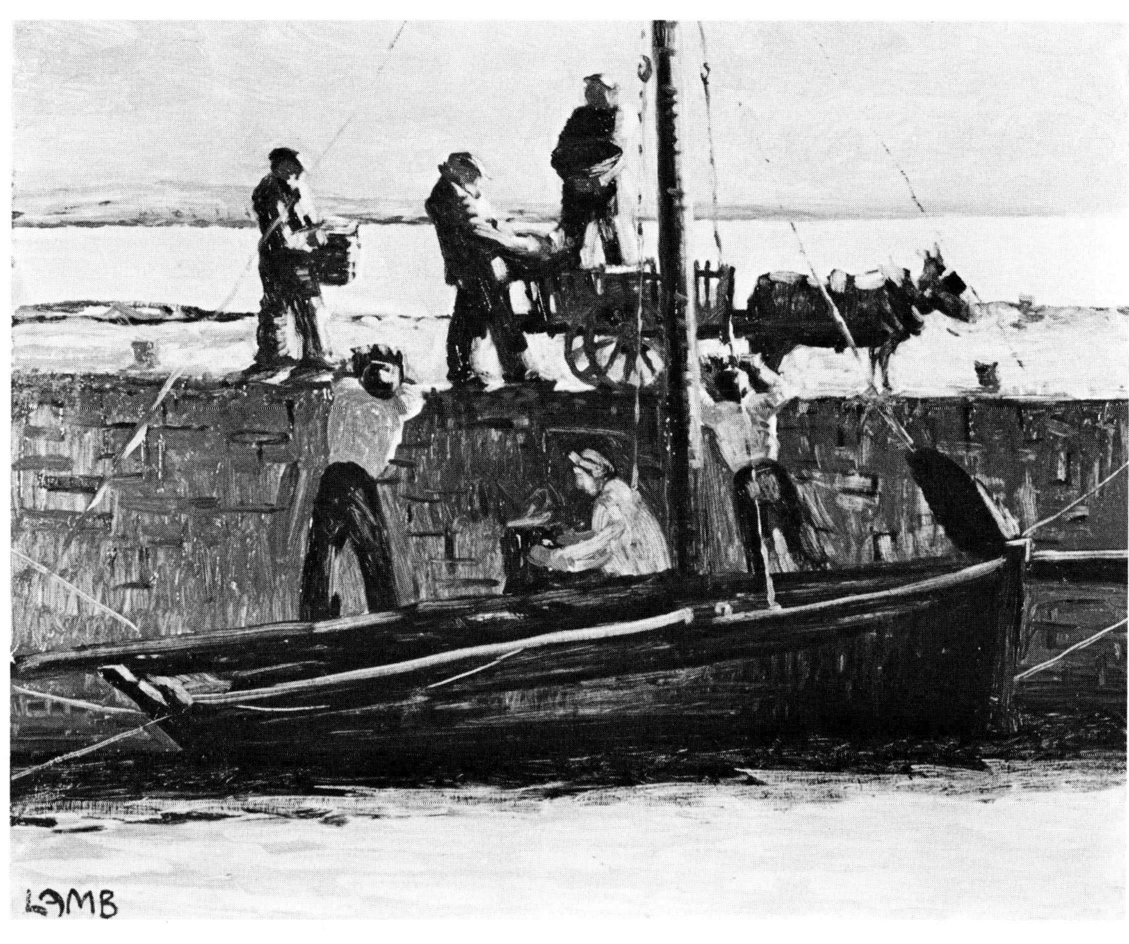

degree of abstraction to his paintings, to his large patterning, by the elimination of detail, making more conclusive and immediate response. Henry very seldom dated his paintings, but, once established, his personal style was so marked that actual dating is neither important or relevant; a leafless, twisted thorn-bush leaning athwart a rough dry-stone wall is a timeless motif.

He made drawings of well known people, such as the head of Cosgrave, the Free State Prime Minister, or the sketch after death of Arthur Griffith, but a late, unusual for him, oil painting of his brother, R M Henry, Professor of Latin, which hangs in the Great Hall of Queen's University, has painterly qualities which lift it above the dull formality of the presentation piece, if, for me, it fails somewhat to communicate the intellectual strength and integrity of that scholarly and indomitable man; but has portraiture ever been able to convey so much, except from the hands of the greatest masters?

It has been disclosed that Paul Henry suffered from red-green colour blindness, but what effect this had is not apparent to most of us. Near-blind and then, blind in his last years, when I met him for the first time, he was a burly, pink-faced man of medium height, with a wide-brimmed black hat that recalled artists of an older generation.

Charles Lamb, a younger, tiny man with a long beard, gingerish, if my memory serves, who had been, with the Henrys, a member of the Dublin Painters, followed his example, and made the west his home-ground. He, too, was successful in his studies of the folk who lived there. *A Quaint Couple*, of an elderly man and his shawled wife, is well composed and cleanly painted; but his *Lough Neagh Fisherman*, now in the Ulster Museum, though painted with sensitivity, I find, somehow, at odds with its title. But Sean Keating rather than Henry was the greater influence on his work.

Sometimes one may discover a social circumstance or report of an occasion or event, which offers a kind of measuring rod by which one may assess the relative significance of its artists in a community at a given time. One such occasion was when, in 1917, a petition was addressed to Lloyd George, the British Premier, begging him to find a way by which Hugh Lane's wishes, in the unsigned codicil to his will, might be given effect. This was signed by 150 artists and writers of Ireland, and included G B Shaw, W B Yeats, and many southern writers and artists; but from the north, our writers with names presumed to carry weight were Robert Lynd, St John Ervine, Forrest Reid, Rutherford Mayne, Joseph Campbell and Shan F Bullock, and our artists were John Lavery now ARA, RSA, Paul Henry, W G MacKenzie, S Rosamund Praeger, J W Carey, J S Sleator, Seamus Stoupe, George and Jack Morrow and R A Dawson, there because he was head master of the Art School — his opposite number of the Dublin Metropolitan School was included. Sleator was making a reputation as Orpen's potential successor. Paul Henry and George Morrow were, by now, household names. Stoupe probably represented the Belfast Arts Club with Forrest Reid. I have no notion what Jack Morrow stood for, but clearly the three artists who represented the arts as they were followed in the north at that date, were Miss S R Praeger, W G MacKenzie and J W Carey.

Henry's going to the west to find inspiration, and the successful outcome, naturally prompted others to follow. James Humbert Craig (born 1878) was a popular, and, at his best, an individual painter of landscape, whose subjects frequently had a marked geographical affinity with his. A close contemporary of Henry, like him, born in Belfast, his father a businessman, his mother Swiss, he grew up in Bangor, was keen on drawing, but attended the Art School for less than a term. Becoming a tea-traveller, he developed his hobby, went abroad, to his

38 JAMES HUMBERT CRAIG
Glendun, near Cushendun
n d; oil; 54.6 x 74.9 cms; North Down District Council collection at the Castle, Bangor

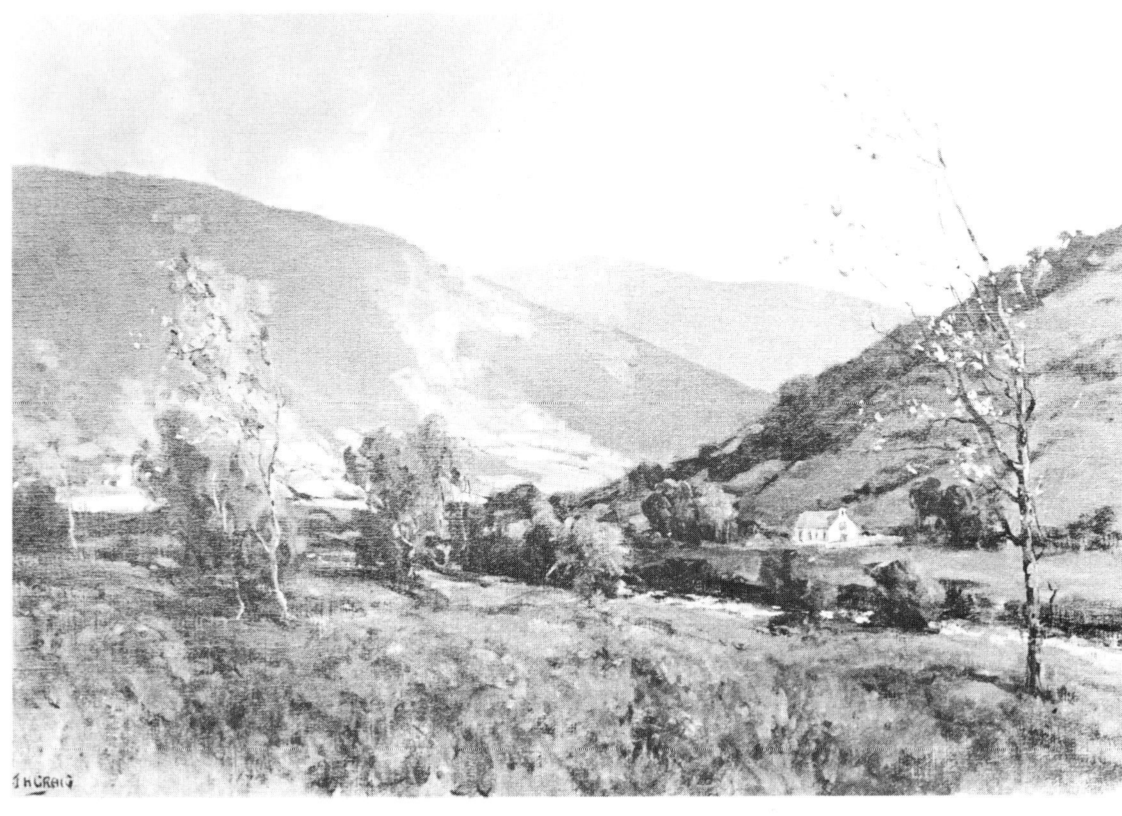

mother's country, to the south of France and the north of Spain on visits. His earlier paintings were of snow scenes or of dark bogland, though some of his Mediterranean sketches had fuller colour. Then, when he took up painting as a profession, he found his style in impressionism, not Impressionism of 'the divided touch', the broken colour, 'the rainbow palette', but of the swift notation of the insistent effect, the momentary flicker, the flash of light, the passing shadow. Craig was a life-long angler, and I have sometimes thought that his kind of seeing was compounded of the long hours of tranquil watching and the quick eye for the telltale ripple, the suddenly-troubled surface.

Exhibiting in the Bond Street galleries, at the Royal Academy, the Glasgow Institute, but more frequently and consistently at the R H A, of which he became a member, his work popular in reproduction — those doctors who had their Itens had Craigs too; the less prosperous, Craig-reproductions — he became accepted as the premier landscape painter of the north, for, after about 1920 or so, Paul Henry's work was seldom seen in Belfast, only the railway posters sustaining his local fame.

Though making his sketching tours of Connemara and Donegal, Craig found so much stimulus in the scenery of the Glens of Antrim, that he acquired a cottage at Cushendun and added to it and built a studio, becoming closely identified with the middle Glens thereafter. 'Even on his last journey to paint in Donegal, he could not rest until he was back again in the Glens,' Stanley Prosser, the watercolourist, his brother-in-law, has told us in his brief but sense-packed essay.

The Glens had been popular since the beginning of the century when the first Feis was held at Waterfoot, since the publication of the poems of 'Moira O'Neill' — her real name Nesta Higginson, she lived at Rockport House, Cushendun — *Songs of the Glens of Antrim* (1900), which fixed place-names like 'the long blue head of Garron', Loughaveema, the Brabla Burn, 'Waters o' Moyle', 'lone Glendun', like burrs in the memories of the many who, travelling the coast-road, had come to love the Nine Glens, for those level fifty miles led them into a roughly modelled landscape inhabited by what seemed to the city folk a romantic race of fishermen and sheepfarmers of an older, more Gaelic culture than theirs. The success and wide popularity of Craig's subject-matter and style of treatment established something of an expected convention for Ulster landscape, and, among those who bought his pictures, created a lasting demand for work of that nature. Craig himself felt the pressure of this, and, at one period, seemed to be eager to fall in with his public's taste. At that time, seeing canvas after canvas in which clouds billowed from the top left hand corner diagonally across a blue sky, with patches of bright sunlight on the broad moorland slopes, with a scatter of grazing sheep, I was critical of the convention. But one morning, walking on the road along the Fair Hill out of Cushendall, thinking of other things, I glanced up at the sky and across Glencorp to Trostan and Tievebulliagh, and suddenly recognised that nature was imitating art, and presenting me with an authentic Craig-view; and, thereafter, I respected him for the accuracy of his vision. But so firmly had he fixed his style, colour and subject-matter on the manner in which, by which a generation or two saw our landscape, that he was followed by waves of disciples working within the same limits.

One of those who, because he was much more than that, is worth mentioning is Maurice C Wilks (born 1910), at the Art School a very good draughtsman of the life-model — the figure was never Craig's strength — with an interesting *Clarendon Dock* painting in the Harbour Office, and with watercolours and portraits outside Craig's range, appeared to be the heir apparent, since for a time he lived in the same village and often chose the same mountains, glens, headlands, for subject, which, after all, were the fabric of that landscape. Painters, if they are not, as so many nowadays are, art teachers, must live by their work, and this circumstance, I believe, while not limiting the general popularity of the painting, has, in Wilks' instance, unduly restricted the full development of an undoubtedly versatile gift. A fine painting, *Morning Light, Hoorn*, and a few others, the results of a visit to Holland in 1956, seemed to suggest an entirely new terrain, called up an unexpected sensitivity and resource.

39 MAURICE WILKS
Portrait of J Humbert Craig
n d; drawing; 40.6 x 26.3 cms; North Down District Council collection at the Castle, Bangor

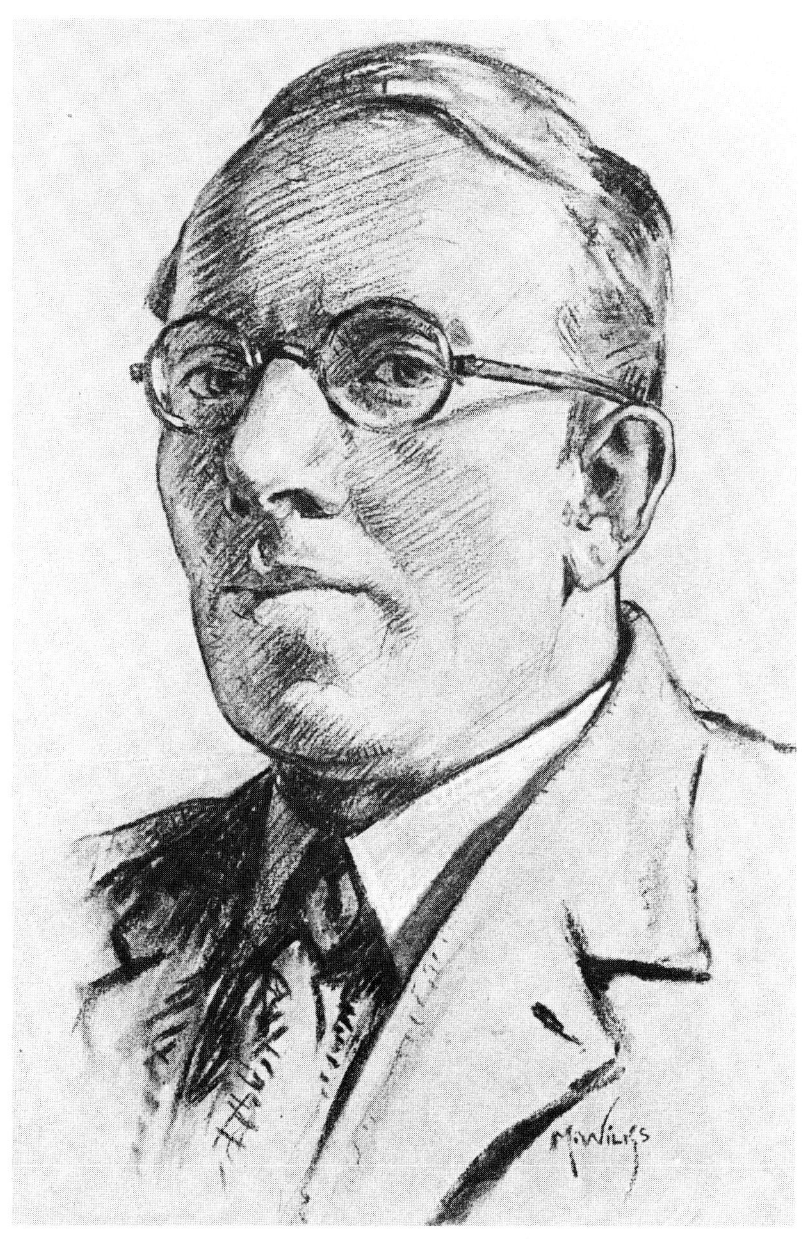

When Craig is master it would be invidious to list his derivatives. Their pictures can be seen in exhibitions or art shop windows in any Ulster town, as fresh as paint, though Craig has been dead for a third of a century.

Although James Humbert Craig established and represented the popular convention for, and the style to be used in, Ulster landscape painting, it was the work and not the man that was taken as representative, for Craig was, in no sense, a figure in the public mythology. With his long jaw, hat with brim turned down all round, and loose Donegal tweeds, he might have passed for a kindly comfortable farmer. For the middle decades of the century William Conor was the representative artist.

When, in 1957, CEMA organised a large retrospective exhibition of his work in the Museum and Art gallery, consisting of 147 oil paintings, watercolours, crayons and drawings, I wrote the foreword to the catalogue for it, which ran:-

> 'A little late in the day, perhaps, William Conor is paid the tribute of a retrospective exhibition. For those of us who have grown up in the past half-century always knowing him as the artist, he has been as surely part of the background as the Albert Clock. And just because he has been an institution we have rather taken him for granted, seldom considering or attempting to assess his true worth. We have mentioned him to visitors eager for word of "our cultural heritage". We have put his name in the handbooks along with the names of field-marshals and famous industrialists, claiming him as one of our representative men. But, till this exhibition, few can have realised how representative he has been, how broadly typical of our best moods and impulses.
>
> 'In the art history of Ireland, William Conor must be placed with Paul Henry and Jack B Yeats, as one of the first to record the life of the people in painterly terms, without the trappings of stage-Irishry, and by himself, the pioneer in taking his subjects from town — rather than country — folk. Paul Henry's studies of the peasants and islanders of the West paralleled the work of John Millington Synge in drama; similarly William Conor was the first exponent of the same kind of material Sean O'Casey used in his *Juno* period; without the political passion or the tragic sense, but with as warm a humanity and as kindly an eye.
>
> 'The inhabitants of Conor's little streets belong to the old economy before the Welfare State, to Belfast of the Twenties, with its shawled millgirls, its "old clo'es man", its "delph-woman", and its tramcars. Yet it was by no means unrelievedly a grim or a drab world, for it was shot through with snatches of laughter and badinage. It was the Belfast period of Conor's work which established his reputation, and, because of this circumstance, has been allowed, quite uncritically, to overshadow his much richer variety and far more extensive range.
>
> 'In the last twenty five years Conor has turned to country life, to the hunt, the *ceilidhe*, the cattle auction, the market in the square, the

40 WILLIAM CONOR
Gossiping
1910; conté crayon; 35.6 x 27.3 cms; Ulster Folk Museum collection

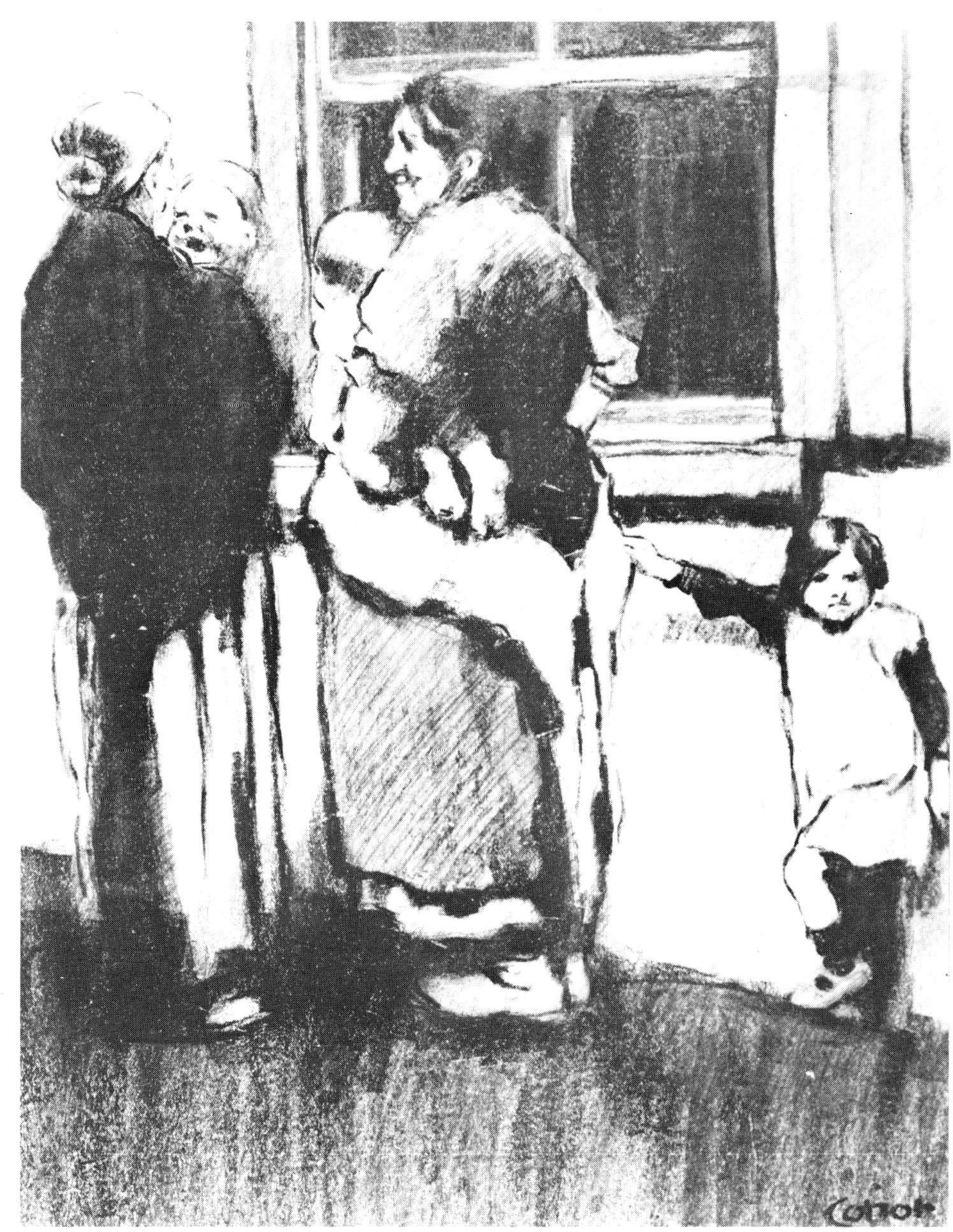

labour in the fields and the traffic on the rough roads; and here too, his abundant humanity has been evident. For, in an epoch in which art has been much concerned with abstraction and fantasy, Conor has kept to the representation of human life and movement as "the main region of his song".

'This is not the place to emphasise his so-widely-unrealised technical virtuosity; his vivid draughtsmanship, his adept use of water-colour, his skilful portraiture in many styles, his few but original essays in landscape. But it can safely be asserted that this display of his work will show him to be the most considerable painter that this province has yet produced, and a very special kind of representative man.'

Now, twenty years later, I would hardly change a word of it. But that temperate eulogy should be given a little more sinew and a sharper edge.

William Conor was born into a family of the skilled working-class in Belfast in 1881. He attended a national school not far uphill from the quiet respectable street to which the family moved. One of his close kin became a trades union official. William was apprenticed to David Allen and Sons, the poster firm. He certainly was with them in 1903, and he attended the Art School on the top floor of the Technical Institute. But it was probably at Allen's that he learned to use the greasy crayons, which, when scraped and rubbed, were so effective in his coloured drawings. But the years after are difficult to chart. There have been stories of his study in Paris and Venice and London; but a note which gives no date, simply records that after 'a short sojourn' in Paris he went to London. We do know that when he visited Paul Henry's studio there, he was already, by the evidence of that fine study of a young coloured woman, a good painter, and it was then, too, that he, very likely, became friendly with John Lavery and Augustus John. As he very seldom dated his paintings, any accurate line of his development is impossible to identify.

The Linen Hall Library has the comprehensive hoard of drawings and papers which he bequeathed, and in this, besides letters, drafts of letters, albums of photographs of the artist and his paintings, catalogues, there are hundreds of pencil drawings of people, with pages of details of feet, hands, heads, as well as of horses, and a few sketches of landscape, mostly of the Lagan. By good fortune, some carry dates, the earliest being 1904, with the bulk of those dated coming in the period 1906 to 1910. These drawings, made in the city markets and parks, or at race meetings (Lisnalinchy Races 1910), vary in quality and kind, some simple notes, others carefully executed, but all displaying an abundant skill for catching a required posture, feature of face or body. Not on drawing-paper of good texture, but small pieces, as if torn from a jotter, they could well be those he made behind a folded newspaper, not to disconcert his subjects, as he wandered round the streets.

Scrutinising them, it becomes clear that he made, kept, and used them to provide hints, suggestions, fuller information towards making many of his future paintings or coloured drawings, a bank upon which he could draw at any time. By costume, detail, and by a few dates, this hoard could be judged as Edwardian, and it

41 WILLIAM CONOR
The Twelfth
1918; oil; 69.9 x 91.4 cms; Ulster Folk Museum collection

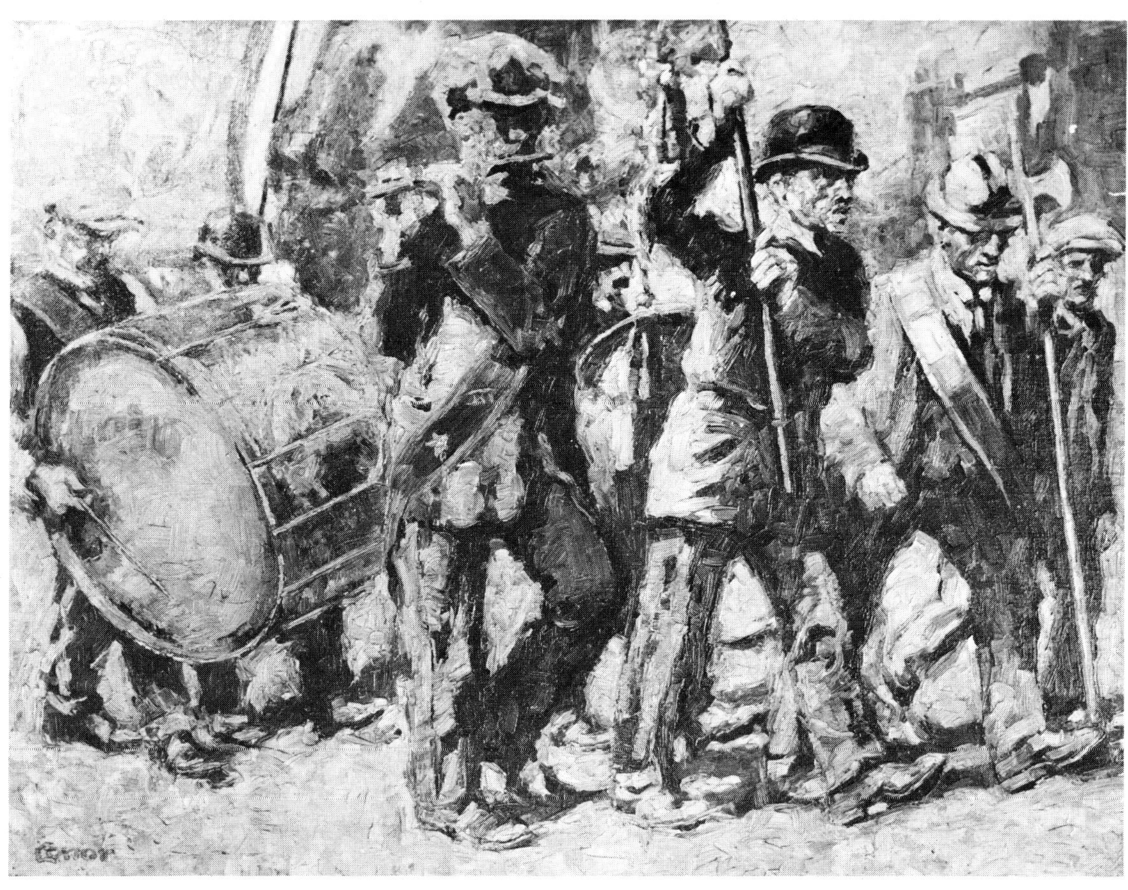

might well be that this has made paintings so derived, of earlier inspiration and origin than might have appeared from the actual exhibited works.

Sometime in that period, he must have modified the spelling of his surname, Connor becoming Conor, in sympathy with the trend among local artists and writers to find names more in keeping with the ideals of the Celtic Revival. This is supported by the fact that perhaps half a dozen drawings were signed *Liam*, the Irish translation of William, but this fuller commitment was quickly disregarded, and, thereafter, it was William Conor. Though, later, for a CEMA exhibition of *Recent Paintings and Drawings* in November 1950, he insisted on being announced simply as Conor, since Picasso and others found a single word described them adequately.

Some drawings of soldiers in uniform, and details of rifles or puttees, would have been made after 1914, but the manner of the drawings are of working-class women, young and old, a decade earlier. Among the yellowing sheets of flimsy paper, the drawing of a wooden chair on the reverse of an invitation to an exhibition with the printed date, 1956, displays no alteration of style of half a century before. Many of the drawings are of working-class woman, young and old, selling in the market, carrying babies, but none that I have seen of the shawled figures which he made so familiar, and which fixed his first generally recognised *métier* in the Nineteen Twenties, being greeted in the *Westminster Gazette* for 11 February 1922, as 'the delineator of Ulster industrialism'.

Where catalogues survive, even if the listed exhibits are not themselves dated, these do set down fixed points, so that, for example, we find that in 1916, a collection of watercolours and drawings of soldiers was displayed for auction in the Belfast City Hall, to benefit the fund for limbless ex-service men, and that in 1920 Conor held his first Dublin show, and in 1926 he went to New York with a collection of his paintings. It was during this American tour that John Lavery once dropped in, bought two, and presented them to the Brooklyn Art Gallery.

In 1932 Sir Robert Baird, proprietor of the *Belfast Evening Telegraph*, commissioned, very probably through Arthur Deane's persuasion, for he was a good friend to Conor, a painting entitled, with a comfortable vagueness, *Ulster Past and Present*, large enough to cover a long wall in the antiquities gallery in the Museum. Though this was not a true mural, but a canvas on a stretcher carried out with flat, unreflecting pigments, it was, with some carelessness, referred to as a *Fresco* in the programme for its presentation. The costume-designs Conor made that year for The Pageant of St Patrick, written by his friend Richard Rowley, to celebrate the 1,500th anniversary of the saint's coming to Ireland, and held at Audley's Castle, Strangford, are related to the group in 'the fresco', of Irish warriors marching downhill to the left of the central Dolmen; the company of shipyard and factory workers coming forward to the right was more consistent with the artist's usual mode.

Versatile professional painters often look to the practice of portraiture as a useful economic support. Though he tried hard, Conor never became the north's most popular provider of

42 WILLIAM CONOR
The Joke
crayon drawing; reproduced from *The Tree* published by the Ulster Society for the Prevention of Cruelty to Animals, Belfast, 1936.

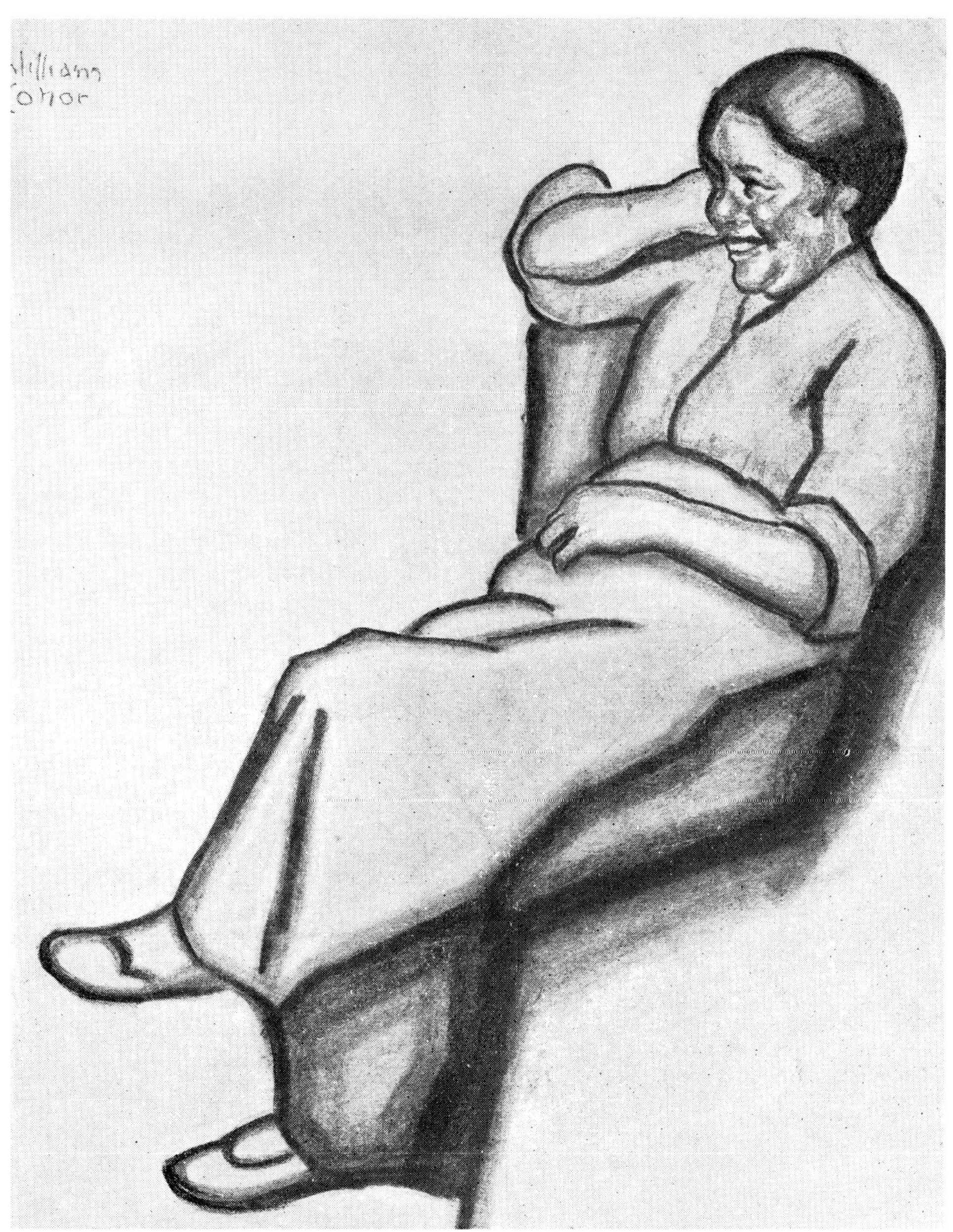

43 FRANK McKELVEY
Evening, Ballycastle
c1924; oil; 76.5 x 102 cms;
Ulster Museum collection

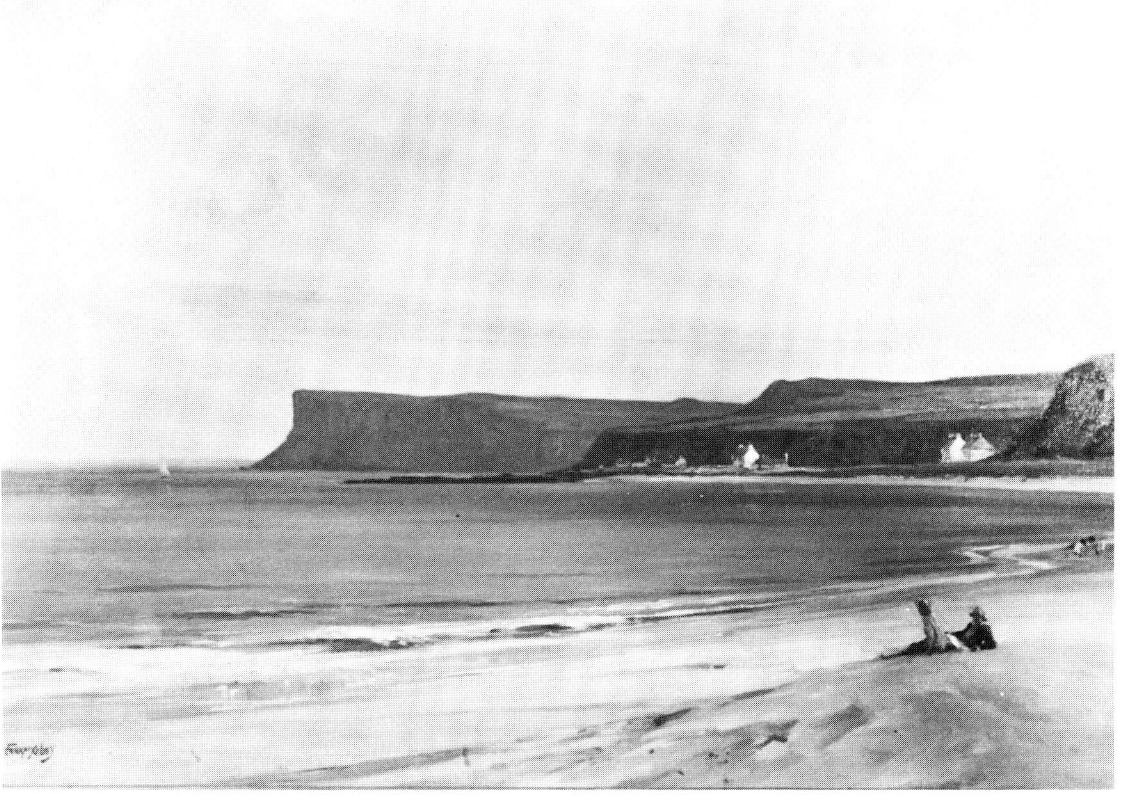

likenesses. Local commissions for portraits of Lord Mayors for the City Hall, or of Presidents of the Medical Society, more frequently went to Frank McKelvey RHA, or, at various times, to laborious journeymen like Harry R Douglas, as when he set the then Town Clerk, Sir Robert Meyer, behind an enormous desk stacked with addressed notepaper and a formidable telephone which had as much presence as the ostensible subject. The more prestigious orders were secured by visiting artists such as Henrietta Rae, daubing her rather unctuous, out-of-focus canvasses. With her rich use of pigment, she could communicate a sense of grandeur to noblemen, or confer it on lesser mortals, but she could never have painted a stuffed fish in a glass case with any of the uncanny realism of the knickerbockered Douglas, who, with the passion of an angler, several times produced paintings indistinguishable from the fish in the glass case on the wall.

Two other contemporaries of Conor, James S Sleator, who learned much in Sir William Orpen's studio, and ended his career as President of the Royal Hibernian Academy, the only Ulsterman to reach that position, and Miss Sarah Cecilia Harrison from Holywood, County Down, whose entire painting career was spent in Dublin, reached and more consistently maintained the academic standards this craft required; but each of them painted at least one portrait of local significance.

Conor always insisted that his failure was due to his portrait of Richard Rowley, linen manufacturer and poet, his friend for many years. This half-length of the grey-haired man with his left hand on his hip, against a dark background, was executed in thick pigment with the abrupt broad-ribbed strokes of the coarse hog's hair brush, in 1920; not the smooth surface of the academic portrait. His painting of the *Marquess of Londonderry* in peer's robes, the chance to carry out which he solicited, did not give satisfaction to the sitter, or his wife; he refused to buy it and regretted that the canvas was among those Conor took to New York.

Later, the artist developed a method which used thinner paint, and secured a few commissions, the most satisfactory being Alderman J A Doran, Chairman of the Libraries and Museum Committee, which was a good likeness and an honest evocation of the old man. Another commission, for University College, Dublin, of Douglas Hyde, first President of the Republic, was a kindly statement, not complicated by the fact that the heavily-moustached, bulky, aged man kept falling asleep during the progress of the work. Keeping his hand in by painting his friends, Robert Lynd, the essayist, and St John Ervine, novelist and playwright, Conor somehow failed to give much illusion of body to his subjects, the Lynd in particular being stubbornly two-dimensional. Much more successful was the smaller head of Lynn Doyle, the humorous writer, worked with a palette knife in bright segments of colour. Among his other records of local literary figures, the drawing of Thomas Carnduff, the shipyard poet, sensitively observed, make us regret that he did not leave us more records of this kind.

In his landscape paintings Conor seems deliberately to have avoided the Craig-McKelvey style, but as he presents them, as in *Strangford*, the observed parts seem not to cohere, to achieve a unity of place. In the smaller study of a red coat huntsman on horseback jogging along the towpath in *On the Lagan*, the unity seems, not of place, but of moment, and, in that, succeeds. His paintings of buildings are much happier than those of countryside; *Downpatrick* with its climbing streets, and *The City Hall in Winter*, the latter taken from his studio window in Wellington Place, are examples of this. His watercolours of the Lagan mouth, *York Dock*, and others, suggest that this was a medium too meagrely utilised by him.

But, for a long time to come, it will be as the 'delineator of Ulster industrialism' that he will be remembered. In this phase from the Twenties, he caught the shabbiness and the good humour, albeit clumsily at times, of those who laboured in the factories and shipyards, and inhabited the back streets of the town, but without tragedy or anger, with, sometimes, a touch of sentimentality, yet with genuine acceptance, a

44 JAMES S SLEATOR
Self Portrait
n d; oil; 58.4 x 43.2 cms;
Armagh Museum

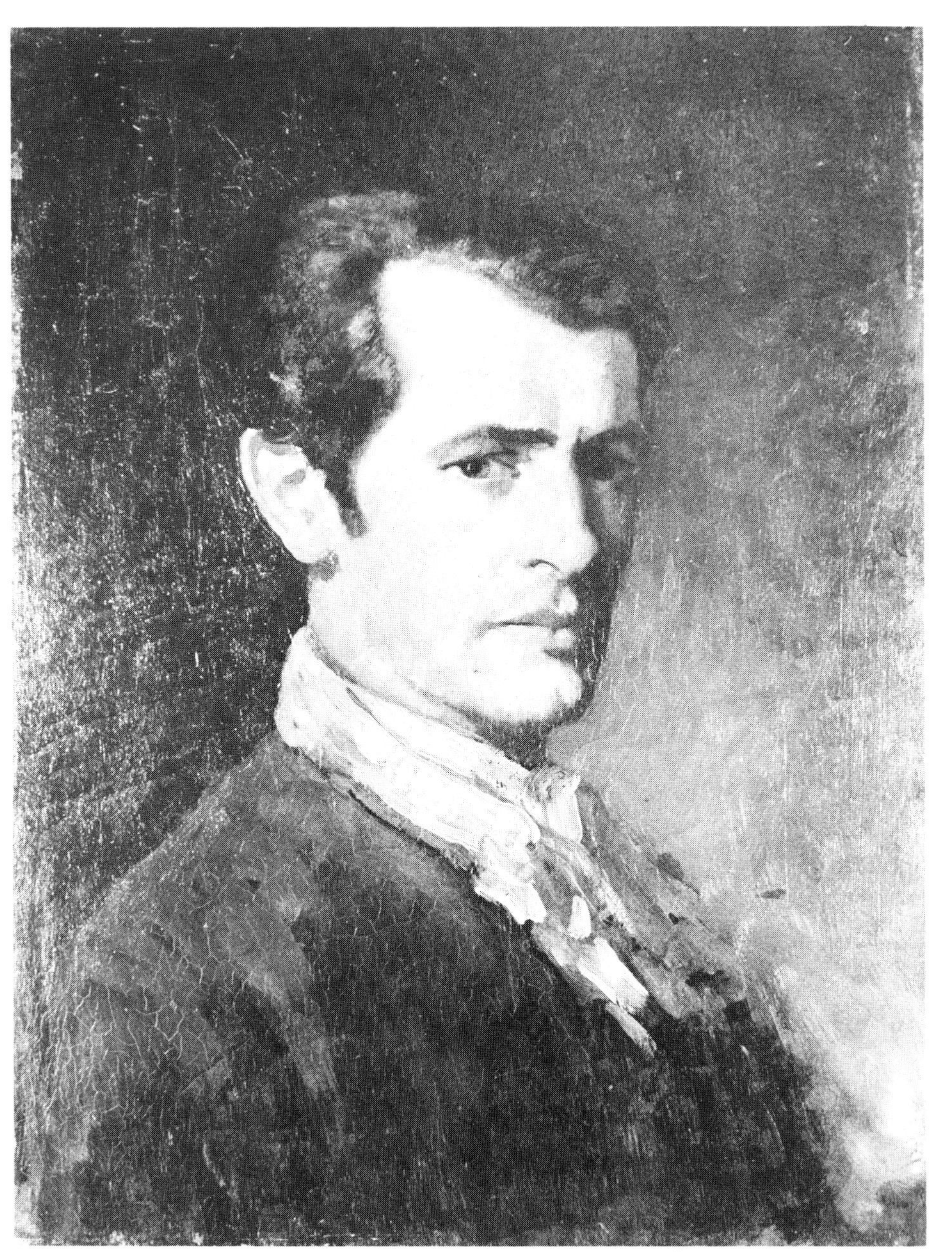

proletarian painter without protest.

Of a younger generation than Craig or Conor, Frank McKelvey (born 1895) caught up with them in reaching the level of local recognition by 1925. A student at the art school, he found employment and further training with David Allen's. He tackled any artwork that was offered, and, when engaged by a local businessman to produce a series of Old Belfast views for presentation to the Art Gallery, he translated faded photographs into effective watercolours which speedily became popular exhibits. Another commission from the same benefactor, of United States Presidents of Ulster origin, based on old prints or photographs, transformed into pencil drawings tinted with washes of colour, ran to fourteen items, a more optimistic muster than firm evidence would support. His resource and the versatility of his professionalism was remarked once, when a local shirt manufacturer informed me that McKelvey was the best artist we had, for 'no one else could make as good a drawing of a new collar, so as to bring out its advantages'.

He applied himself to the field of portraiture, and became the accepted provider of presentation canvasses skilfully painted, accurately observed and straightforwardly composed, but with little aesthetic excitement, a risk which the painter of boardroom portraits always runs. But it was in landscape that he made a reputation outside his native province, before he was thirty years old, becoming an Associate, and, in 1930, a full member of the RHA. Craig had been fifty when he attained the same distinction.

In landscape his work harked back to an older tradition than Craig, to quieter colour, to a kind of Constable-impressionism, with, maybe a hint of MacKenzie, most effective in its rendering of evening light, over level estuary-plains, out of a lowering sky, or mist coming in from the sea and the water flooding across the sands, or perhaps, on a smaller scale, children in bright dresses beside the little lake in a city park. He is not represented at his best in the Ulster Museum, with his *Fair Head, Ballycastle*, which might have made an attractive poster.

McKelvey was a regular exhibitor with the Ulster Academy from the days when it was the Belfast Art Society, and his pictures could be seen in Magee's Gallery in small numbers; when a one-man show was proposed for the Art Gallery, where Craig's memorial exhibition was held in 1944, a sudden reluctance, after initial interest, on the part of the artist, prevented its realisation, and so there never has been an opportunity for serious critical assessment based on a representative body of his work, which is a pity, for, of the three, Conor, Craig and McKelvey, the last was the most skilful, technically, and the most versatile, although, unfortunately, he lacked any originality and, indeed, much aesthetic awareness or curiosity.

Sometime in the Nineteen Twenties, about the middle of the decade, Robert Ponsonby Staples had an exhibition of *Drawings and Paintings* in the Alpine Club, Savile Row, London. This comprised 290 pictures, but the catalogue did not indicate which were oil paintings, watercolours, or drawings in whatever medium. They ranged in time from a self-portrait dated 1869 to a *Belfast Girl* 1924, and varied in subject from *Spider eating a blue bottle* to *Police Raid on an Anarchists' Club, Charlotte Street, February 1894*, with many sketches of artists such as John or Epstein, and Irish politicians like John Redmond and T M Healy. But, with at least fifty pictures of Ulster landscape from the Giant's Causeway to the Mourne Mountains, with titles like *Marble fountain at Sir William Whitla's Lennoxvale*, or *Sir Samuel Kelly's Coal wharves, Belfast*, and with *Sir James Craig* (1911) and the *Opening of the North of Ireland Parliament by Their Majesties The King and Queen, showing the last Portrait of Viscount Pirrie on the extreme left*, as well as *A Cookstown Mill-hand* and *A Belfast Bar Maid* he certainly was an artist who made abundant use of local material.

His lengthy introduction bristles with sharp opinions and spiky comments. He regrets the disappearance of his painting of Swinburne, and that he cannot locate the owner of a collection of 'sixty portraits of minor celebrities' by him. He recalls his emotion at seeing a drawing of his in the National Portrait gallery which he left 'trembling and in tears'. He recounts briefly the story of his triptych illustrative of the shipbuilding of Belfast and how it took twenty years before the Library and Arts committee got round to having it properly framed, and ends this episode, 'An artist in Belfast is held but little higher than a shoeblack, but certainly beneath the serious consideration of their busy merchant princes.' Having for the last twenty-five years lived in Lissan House, County Tyrone, in his family's possession since 1610, he 'executed a considerable number of works of very diverse types, [for] this residence aloof from the artistic camaraderie of London, Paris or Brussels, has thrown me back upon my own resources, and like the bears in winter, I have had to feed upon my own fat, and not had time even to read art reviews'. He does not mention that his *Australia v England, 1887*, hangs, perhaps it did not then hang, in the Pavilion at Lord's cricket ground, or make any reference to the portrait-frontispiece of the author, Herbert Moore Pim, of *Songs from a Ulster Valley* (1920), another of whose books was illustrated by John McBurney.

Listing his recreations in *Who's Who*, as 'argument, historical and metaphysical reading, plenty of fresh air, and early barefoot walking', at eighty he succeeded to the family baronetcy. I remember him as a large elderly man with a big mustache, but only heard that he enjoyed walking on the tramlines, barefoot, his boots slung over his shoulder by their tied laces, since he believed, it was averred, that electricity was good for the system; which another ten years of life made no insubstantial claim. Ponsonby Staples' introduction ends with a reference to 'my illustration of Victory and Death, which had the distinguished honour of being considered too dangerous for publication by the late Irish Government in Dublin Castle. Perhaps they were right, but I think in the work of imagination I have reached the highest level I have yet attained.' We may judge the force of this, since *Victory and Death* is illustrated at the back of the catalogue. To the right stands an Irish High Cross, at its foot the heaped bodies of dead with shawled mourning women crouching among and over them. In the middle distance a stream of wispy spirits or banshees floats off the ground behind the cross. In the distant centre can be recognised Nelson's Pillar. To its left the facade of the Dublin GPO with the tricolour hoisted aloft. The left half of the design is filled with an ornate shape based on a Celtic initial letter, which, below, is transformed into two skeletal legs. In the space in the middle of the strange shape, a skull with a laurel wreath round its brow peers out, while the upper extremities of the latter terminate in two hands clutching a torch, its flame bearing the legend A Nation Once Again. The whole design clearly satirises the Easter Rebellion of 1916, the Celtic letter-figure symbolising the Irish Myth which ends in the Cross of sacrifice and the mound of dead, and the retreating spirits of illusion; certainly a vigorous comment, an apocalyptic conception which immediately brings to mind the strange dreams and imagining of another contemporary artist, John Langtry Lynas.

Lynas, born at Greenock, came to Belfast as a child, attended a national school in the east of the town, where he had a school-mate whom he disliked cordially, the future playwright St John Ervine. At an early age he was admitted to the Government School of Art in George Trobridge's time, when the Morrow brothers set the boisterous tone of the institution. The years after are obscure, crammed with sign writing — painting ducal crests on buckets in London mews, travelling, letter-cutting in stone, managing a quarry somewhere. All the while, the tiny man was possessed by grandiose dreams. He painted portraits, some still life — flowerpieces usually bathed in the gloom of a darkened Old Master — made a few dry-point etchings, one of himself, an excellent likeness, constructed a scale model for a hypothetical Temple of Destiny crammed with relief sculptures, modelled terra cotta busts, and executed a large number of red chalk or sanguine drawings on religious themes. Some of these he published in two volumes. The first *Psychological Satyr or the Hounds of Hell* (1928) was dedicated to G F Watts, the Victorian painter, whose vision did much to condition and shape Lynas' own. It consisted of lively drawings of hypocrites, artists of Hell and art connoisseurs. It would seem that the word Satyr was a mistake for Satire. The second, entitled *Why?* (1935) was dedicated to his 'unseen friends Christ, Savonarole, Socrates, and Paracelsus' with reproduced pastels telling the story of Creation from the Void to the Resurrection, and, as an appendix, a number of plates reproduce Lynas' portraits of *Alexander Irvine* and the *Rev T M Johnson*, full length, and a drawing of a frieze of horses intended for his Temple of Destiny. The colour-frontispiece, *Melody*, is dedicated to his 'unseen friends Beethoven and Schubert'. When, after a stroke, he made a drawing in coloured chalks, with his left hand, of a view from his studio window, and I suggested that he should rightly be content with similar studies, short of the monumental, he replied, 'If I cannot rank with the greatest, I don't want to rank at all,' and when he was encountered at an exhibition of another artist, he was asked, 'Come to criticise, John?' his terse *riposte* was, 'I never criticise. I condemn.' The two or three small oil paintings in the Ulster Museum must fail to do any sort of justice to such a man.

Among those recruited to the staff of the Art School in the first decades after the city authorities took it over, none was more remarkable than Newton Penprase, another man of small physical stature, but with enormous and varied skills. A Cornishman, he studied at the Redruth School of Mines and Art, winning many awards; nine sheets of his designs and studies were acquired by the Victoria and Albert Museum. He came to Belfast in 1911 into the employment of the Art School at £120 *per annum*, and remained for forty-two years, enlarging the range of crafts he already possessed: wood-turning, metal-casting, designing a vertical loom when he had mastered the technique of damask weaving; a superlative instructor in the science of perspective. With the students he was a popular and inspiring teacher, Colin Middleton, for one, recalled his debt with gratitude. Besides his work in the Art school, Penprase also painted and made sculptures, exhibiting with the Arts Club and the Ulster Academy, though not frequently. In contrast to his practical gifts and the meticulous accuracy of his drawings, many of his paintings and sculptures went far beyond the confines of observed appearance. One large canvas, for instance, its title, *Progression*, was a rendering of the legendary Hercules and Hydra duel, the many-headed monster belching out, not only smoke and flame, but bats and lizards, the foreground and background rich with symbolical shapes; an unexpected amalgam of G F Watts and his Victorian rhetoric with the more recent conventions of Superman. In his sculpture the same grotesque inventiveness gave such a piece as *The Mystic*, a gaunt, emaciated mask with shut lids and a single eye staring from the middle of a high bald forehead. But undoubtedly his most complicated and original work was the house which he spent his leisure building, 'Bendhu', perched on a cliff-top at Ballintoy, on the north coast of County Antrim, started in 1936. With infrequent help from friends and students in the vacations, and only occasionally with local labour, he carried out the work himself. Adding room to room till it achieved the effect of a fragmented honeycomb or the appearance of a Turkish fort assaulted by a cubist task-force, the ingenious interior became an idiosyncratic essay in the arts and crafts of the pre-plastic age. A raw pile of concrete boxes, concealing any logic of its apartments, the interior wood panelling and carving, the relief-decorated or painted ceilings, the stained glass inserts in many of the windows, all gave scope and occasion for the artist's passion for Greek mythology.

With Conor, Craig, and McKelvey accepted as the north of Ireland's most prominent painters, a position they held until the late Thirties, there had been a growing awareness of our comparative isolation from the main trends of the century elsewhere. The British painters represented in the re-formed Lloyd Patterson Collection at Stranmillis seemed, to the uninformed, so outrageously modern; and a collection of paintings and sculptures from a country as far away as Yugo-Slavia showed that we were very far behind.

After the setting-up of the State of Northern Ireland with its own administration, which included a Ministry of Education, very much through the efforts of John F Hunter, the newly appointed Art Inspector, the extent and quality of art education in the schools was tackled as a serious problem, to bring the secondary, or, as we should now call them, grammar schools, into line with those very few which already had art teachers, like W R Gordon of Inst and Charles Braithwaite at Methodist College, Belfast.

45 LADY MABEL ANNESLEY
Wood cut illustration from *County Down Songs and Poems* by Richard Rowley Duckworth, London, 1924

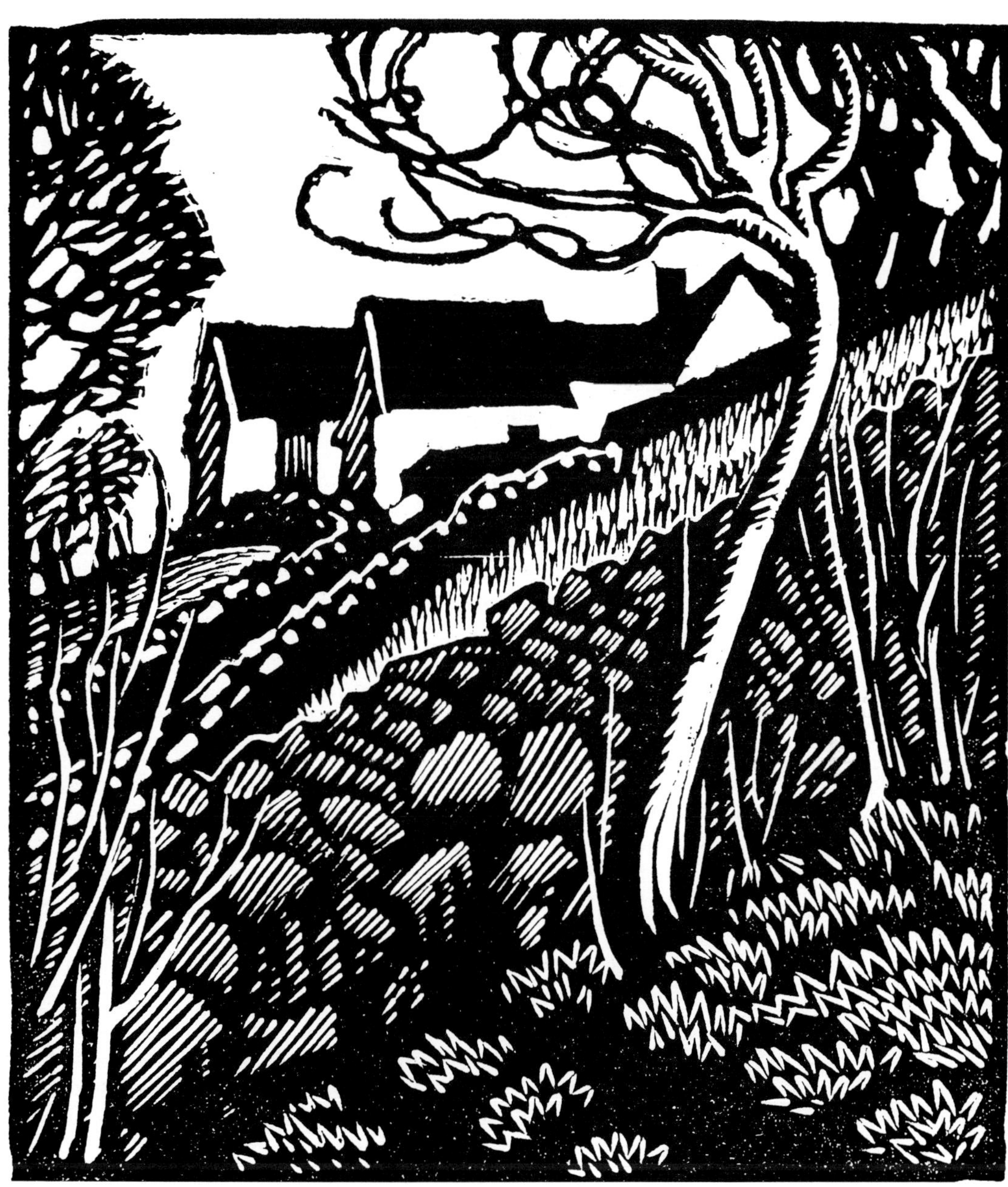

John Hunter had studied at the Metropolitan School in Dublin and the Royal College of Art in London, which had persuaded him, a vigorous painter and an accomplished wood engraver, of the value of training somewhere away from home. So, in time, scholarships to the Slade and the R C A became more readily accessible and more numerous, and students of the Belfast College of Art crossed the channel to return afterwards to teach in Ulster.

As I wrote in the introduction to my essay on Colin Middleton, 'The return of the scholarship holders gave the province a much larger number of teachers and practising artists no longer penalised by the disadvantages of the traditional "time-lag". A group of these, reinforced by three or four older but progressive artists, and a couple of members of the staff of the local College of Art, came together in the winter of 1934, under the title of the Ulster Unit. This title was a perhaps naive tribute to Unit One, a London group formed earlier that year, and given the authority of a volume of reproductions and manifestoes edited by Herbert Read. The exhibition, in December, of the Ulster Unit was the first to consist of avowedly and demonstrably modern work by artists living in the North of Ireland.' When I wrote that I had not seen that reference by Hugh Frazer to the Belfast Association of Artists nearly a century before, about what he denominated as their 'First Exhibition of Modern Art'.

The catalogue, its cover decorated with a wood engraving by Colin Middleton, contained statements by the artists of their principles and intentions, an unusual feature for any group of local artists at that time, since the nature of art had long been assumed with a minimum of verbalisation. In the preface, which as secretary, I wrote '... Since the Great War and partly consequently upon it acceleration of social change has narrowed the gap between Ulster and Europe. In this Unit, Ulster has for the first time a body of artists alert to continental influence while that influence is still real, and vital...'

Held in a hall belonging to a café, used for dances and receptions, the exhibition consisted of about eighty items, oil paintings, watercolours, prints and drawings, sculpture and pottery. Of the participants, four would two years later have pictures reproduced in *The Tree*, a commemorative volume to which reference will be made: Lady Mabel Annesley, W R Gordon, Charles Harvey and John Hunter. Gordon, with two oilpaintings, one of them a *Girl Reading*, a portrait of his daughter, Maeve, had also three watercolours of Cushendun. Charles Harvey, London-born, had come to Belfast with his parents in 1906 at the age of eleven. A student at the Art School, he worked as a textile designer, and was a member of the Arts Club. Two years before this exhibition he had been appointed to the staff of St Mary's Training College, and later became head of the Art Department of St Joseph's. He exhibited infrequently in Arts Club shows, but his fine sombre landscapes, as I recall them, were much concerned with the recession of flat bogland and the depth of the straight cuttings in it, below the dark surface-textures a kind of Cubist structure. With the years, long after the Unit exhibition, his palette lightened and his work became more decorative, his few flower-pieces chastely presented. A serious student of aesthetics, he had a fine and discriminating awareness of the develop-

IV COLIN MIDDLETON
Jacob Wrestling with the Angel
1948; oil on canvas; 75 x 65 cms; private collection

facing page 100

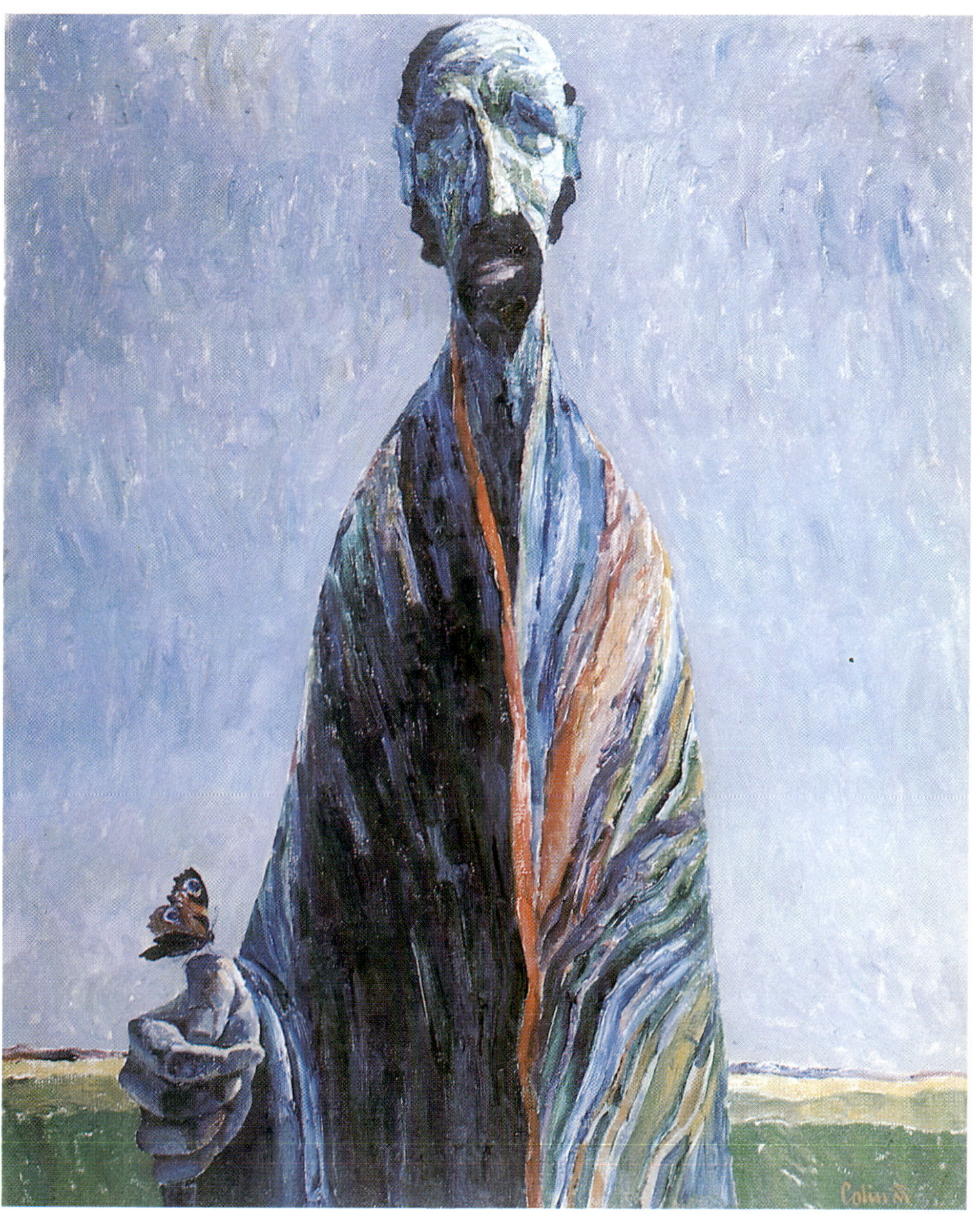

ments of his period. Lady Mabel Annesley, represented by three brightly coloured watercolours of County Down, her home county, was a first-rate exponent of woodcut and wood-engraving. For this was the heyday of the black and white print in Great Britain. In 1939 she presented a collection of about 100 prints to the Belfast Art Gallery, twenty of them her own work, others by leaders of the craft, John Farleigh, Robert Gibbings, Eric Gill, Gertrude Hermes. E M O'R Dickey, a Belfastman, had five prints in this collection. John Hunter, in the Unit exhibition, had four linocuts of Derry subjects; he too belonged to the highly-skilled body of printmakers. As art inspector travelling round the Six Counties, he introduced the linocut as a technique into many a remote corner. One instance worth remembering, was to Tullygrawley public elementary school, where the principal of that two-teacher establishment, R L Russell, an inspiring force, led his pupils on to remarkable results. Russell's fine book, *The Child and his Pencil* (1935), though it nowhere mentions Hunter's name, remains the embodiment of a heartening phenomenon, a harvest John Hunter's passing seeded. Though Crawford Mitchell, whose scholarship had taken him to the RCA, was represented, not by wood-engravings, but by etchings, he continued throughout his career as a good printmaker with a number of fine engravings like the sharply observed *Chrysanthemums*; in his last years he made attractive colour linocuts of the kind of subject which interested Andrew Nicholl a century before, old church or abbey ruins. But printmaking had few followers into the years ahead, apart from Mitchell, and R G Sellar of a slightly younger generation with consistent essays maintaining the standards of Lady Mabel, whose woodcuts so firmly companion the verses in Richard Rowley's *County Down Songs* (1924) making it one of the most successful marriages of picture and word to have come out of the north; the nearest parallel being Dickey's for the same poet's volume, *Workers* (1923). A good painter also, Dickey's career took him across the water into educational administration, which inevitably reduced his direct impact on the local scene.

Of other members of the Ulster Unit, John Luke and Colin Middleton afterwards became important painters in their divergent ways. The first, John Luke, left the Belfast Art School for the Slade where he shared a studio with the sculptor F E McWilliam. After the Slade and a year at the Westminster School of Art, the economic depression drove him home in 1931, where his first commission, for a derisory sum, and since he had expressed interest in the medium, was for a landscape in tempera, at that time given the title *County Down*, as the imaginary composition used the drumlin countours and mountains of that county. This was shown with three oilpaintings, the earth-coloured *MacArt's Fort* and *The Lustre Jug*, one of his two or three flowerpieces, and the large *Connswater*, in which the map-like blobs of the mud-banks assisted the flat pattern of the composition. Luke had, too, not surprisingly, a couple of linocuts, *The Dead Tree* and the more elaborate *Shaw's Bridge*. In the years after, he was to intensify his studies of, and research into technique and material and develop a more decorative style, highly rhythmical and imaginative.

Colin Middleton already had given evidence of his progressive awareness with a few paintings shown with the Ulster Academy of Arts, with two small paintings, each entitled *Composition*, offered, if memory serves me right, essays rather in the manner of Paul Klee, with George MacCann's similarly named items comprising the few really modern exhibits; for, generally, what seemed modern here, were well within modes and manners current in Great Britain. Middleton, too, followed the printmaking practice with linocut and wood engraving.

Kathleen Bridle, with four oilpaintings and two watercolours, all of Fermanagh subjects, and a linocut, had not usually displayed this variety of media; watercolour of a freshness and strength, marked her work out from the more restrained styles then current. Trained at the Metropolitan School of Art and a scholarship-and-prizewinner at the RCA, in 1926, she had come to Enniskillen to begin a long teaching career in that area, in various schools and colleges, and as County art organiser. Among her best known pupils were William Scott and T P Flanagan, a circumstance which was commemorated years later by a Three-person Show organised by the Arts Council of Northern Ireland. This later exhibition included her oil sketch of Scott and pencil drawing of Flanagan when she taught them.

Romeo Toogood with two oilpaintings, took his place among his forward-looking companions, but perhaps realised himself more fully when, as a member of the staff at the College of Art, he deeply influenced the Blackshaw-Flanagan wave of students, for, an infrequent exhibitor, as painter he is very probably known only for his two paintings in the Ulster Museum, *Dan Nancy's Brae* and *Barges at Edenderry*.

In the Sculpture and Pottery section the few small sculptures by Elizabeth Clements in a variety of materials, wood, lead, ceramic and alabaster, and the pots and pottery figures by Jean MacGregor, showed that their modernity of form had an easier passage to appreciation, and, with none of them priced at more than three guineas, sold best. George MacCann's *Stone Mask* was emphatically in the style of Henry Moore, low-browed, flat-nosed, for Moore had been his instructor at the RCA.

Just as the Belfast Association of Artists had had its sympathetic architect, Miller, so the Unit also displayed a handful of architectural drawings from the drawing-board of Denis O'D Hanna, illustrating his fervent advocacy of a rejuvenated Irish Romanesque style in church building. Shortly he was to focus attention on certain characteristics in our regional building tradition and the necessity of identifying and preserving examples of these, as a forerunner of the Ulster Architectural Heritage Society. His book *The Face of Ulster* (1952) which has the qualities of his buoyant enthusiasm, popularised those valuable labels, Barn Church, Planter's Gothic, Post Regency.

Financed by its exhibitors' subscriptions, with the sale of cheaply priced items, the show did little more than pay for itself when the rent of the hall, the advertising, and the printer's bill were settled; soon after the group dissolved amicably.

The Belfast News Letter's art critic had declared that the exhibition contained 'a good deal that is startling and even bizarre ... many of the exhibits crude ... a certain amount must be dis-

46 J W CAREY
Kilkeel
1936; watercolour; reproduced from *The Tree*, published by the Ulster Society for the Prevention of Cruelty to Animals, Belfast, 1936

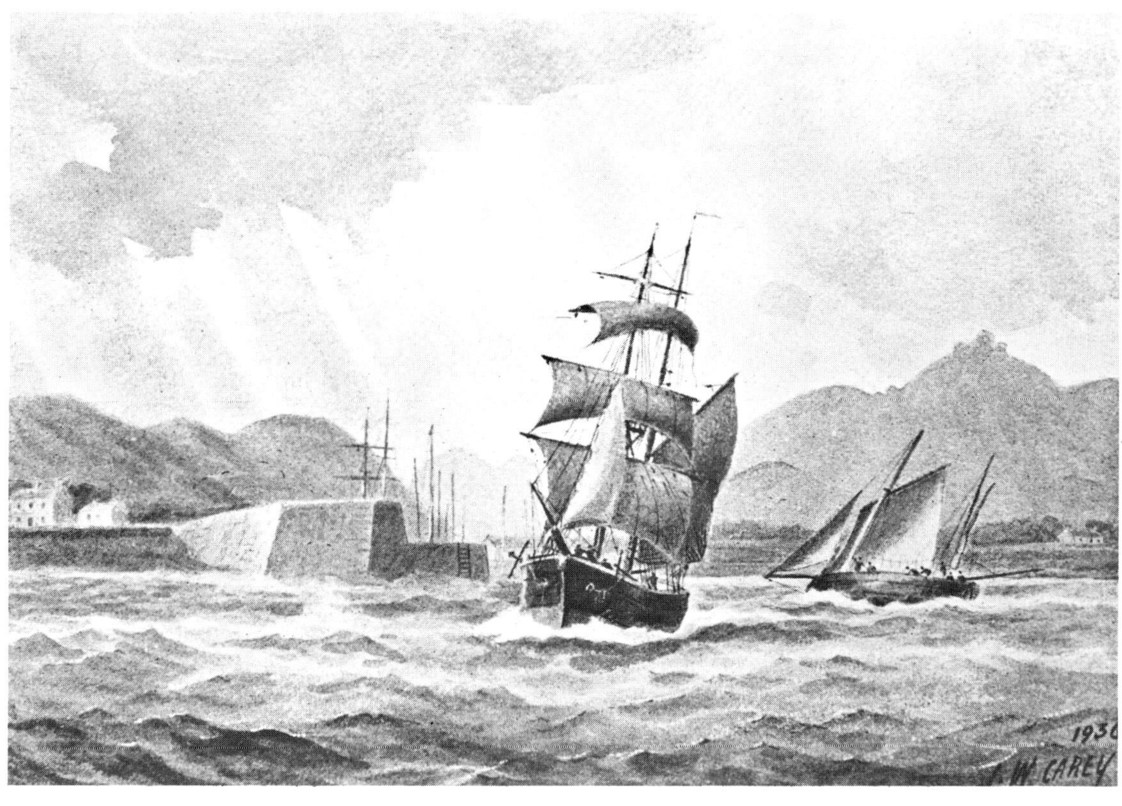

missed as hocus-pocus ... yet even the most unreal things in it represent honest and worthy experiment'.

The Ulster Society for the Prevention of Cruelty to Animals in 1936 produced a souvenir centenary volume; this consisted of invited contributions by writers, and musicians, with reproductions of pictures, the bulk of the material being of Ulster origin. While not designedly a definitive anthology of the best in these fields, it does provide a useful check-list of those then locally held in high esteem. Prose and verse by writers such as Robert Lynd, St John Ervine, Lynn Doyle, Helen Waddell, Alice Milligan and others not now so well remembered, Padraic Gregory, Cahal O'Byrne, Thomas Carnduff. Musical compositions by Hamilton Harty, Herbert Hughes, Carl Hardebeck, are interspersed with reproductions after the expected names of Sir John Lavery with a scene from a race-course weighing-room, one of the many he depicted, Craig by a drawing of a road in Donegal, McKelvey by an Irish Fair in a village street, full of beasts and people — he was better at figures than Craig — Conor by bold crayon of a smiling women, J W Carey who first worked in Marcus Ward's, by a watercolour of *Kilkeel* with a fishing smack, dated that very year but in a style rather earlier, John Carey with an illustration which was shown in the Linen Hall Library exhibition of 1900, George Morrow with a typical *Challenge*, a mounted knight confronting a cheerful dragon, and Miss Rosamund Praeger with an affectionate *Study of Children*.

Of those we might have anticipated, only Paul Henry is absent. More surprisingly, W R Gordon has a watercolour of *Downpatrick*, of the steep street and the cathedral on its wooded hill; Lady Mabel Annesley has a woodcut, *Farm at Drumdrinagh*; John Hunter, too, has another woodcut, his well known, fully-peopled map, *A Corner of Ulster*, and Charles Harvey *Interior of a Fisherman's Hut*, a still life arrangement of barrel, ropes and anchor.

More relevant to the Society's interest, David Bond Walker's *Cara, an Irish Wolfhound*; a son of Tom Bond Walker, Paul Henry's early mentor, he too was a portrait painter; A P Jury's *An Irish Setter* — Miss Jury, daughter of Belfast's *art nouveau* architect — this study does not show her at her best; she was later to become one of the staunchest supporters of the Ulster Academy, sturdily maintaining its defensible standards.

A couple of items, an etching of *Donegall Place* by R Creswell Boak, and *An Elizabethan Galleon* by Kenneth Shoesmith, are not by Ulstermen. Boak, I remember as one whose coloured etchings of local scenes were once highly popular in the local art shops — I once saw him seated on the low wall of Queen's Elms, sketching the Hamilton Tower which then stood in front of the University. Shoesmith (1890-1939) well-known for his shipping posters, had married a Belfast woman, who later bequeathed a large collection of his work to the Ulster Museum, where a generous selection was on view in an interesting exhibition of his designs in the spring of 1977. Shoesmith now and then exhibited with the Art Society, from a London address.

Most of the pictures reproduced, except the Conor drawing which had a contemporary English quality and, perhaps, the Annesley and Hunter prints, had the sense of belonging to much earlier in the century, although by 1936 Cézanne had been thirty years dead, and Cubism had been invented by Picasso and Braque a quarter of a century before.

In the years immediately preceding World War II, the illustrators of *The Tree* represented very fairly the state of art as it was generally accepted in Northern Ireland, since the younger generation typified by the short-lived Ulster Unit were appreciated only by a small circle of interested persons. Isolated and far ahead of any, Middleton, who, since he had seen Van Gogh's paintings in London in 1928, was sensitive and responsive to western European discoveries, like a veritable seismograph alert to the latest tremor, by now, was making the Surrealist vocabulary his own, and finding nurture in Miro's organic abstractions.

Then, with the outbreak of hostilities, the Art

Gallery's contents were evacuated to a safe store, a church hall in a County Antrim village where it was hoped no bombs would fall, and the entire top floor at Stranmillis was covered by a sahara of sand, to nullify any likely incendiaries. But, the concentrated air raids of 1941 over, the barrage-balloons moved eastward to more useful locations, and the sky clear of the vast but momentary hosting of American planes, the sand was brushed off the floor and the empty rooms offered exhibition-space once more.

John Luke, who had been experimenting with tempera, oil and tempera, oil and wax, stopped painting after 1939, then, with the threat of air raids, took himself to a cottage in County Armagh, on a farm belonging to a sympathetic farmer, not to take up painting again till 1943. Paul Nietsche was interned in the Isle of Man. George McCann was in Burma with the Inniskilling Fusiliers. Patric Stevenson was with the RAF. John Hunter, a Lieutenant Colonel now, was commanding the Army Cadet Corps in Belfast. In 1940 and 1941 Colin Middleton was painting Belfast street scenes in a modified impressionist manner. William Conor was an official war artist, recording troops in training and civil defence activities.

By early in 1943 it seemed safe to use those empty rooms at Stranmillis again. So Middleton, who had been working in his hut in the garden at home, accumulating a great stack of canvasses, was persuaded to provide the material for a One Man Show, his first. The exhibition consisted of 115 paintings and occupied two rooms and a corridor. In one room and the corridor were hung seventy-four items grouped in eight sections each developing an imaginative theme — Middleton frequently conceived his paintings as related, not as separate statements — one section contained *The Poet's Garden* and three other small pieces, which were later dispersed, now seem, in retrospect, one of the artist's most original and authoritative sets of images. Surrealist, Impressionist, abstract, tense with imagined lives, still as a jar on a table, the array of styles and forms was astounding; as Tom Carr remarked at the time, it was 'an amazing anthology of modern art'. More than that, it was the public's first opportunity to see our first artist move among contemporary conceptions like a scholar, in a library, choosing the volumes he needed, if only for a paragraph, or even a footnote, to yield the helpful reference, the illuminating quotation.

As Hilary Pyle wrote in *Irish Art 1990-1950* (1976) of Middleton's eclectic variety, 'His incessant experimentation with styles, themes, colours and technique has subjected him to severe criticism.' Yet such critics fail to recall that no man would ever paint a picture if he had never seen one. A man who has caught the sense of many books we call 'well read'. By analogy, Middleton's imagination might be described as 'well-pictured'. Certainly in that exhibition of 1943, the young man of thirty-three asserted his claim to be the most various, technically equipped and imaginative artist that Ulster had yet seen.

Yet all the time he was carrying on the family business of damask designing, painting in full spate at the weekends, for his father had died in 1935.

It is interesting to consider the importance of the

47 COLIN MIDDLETON
If I were a Blackbird
c1941; oil; 50.8 x 61 cms;
private collection

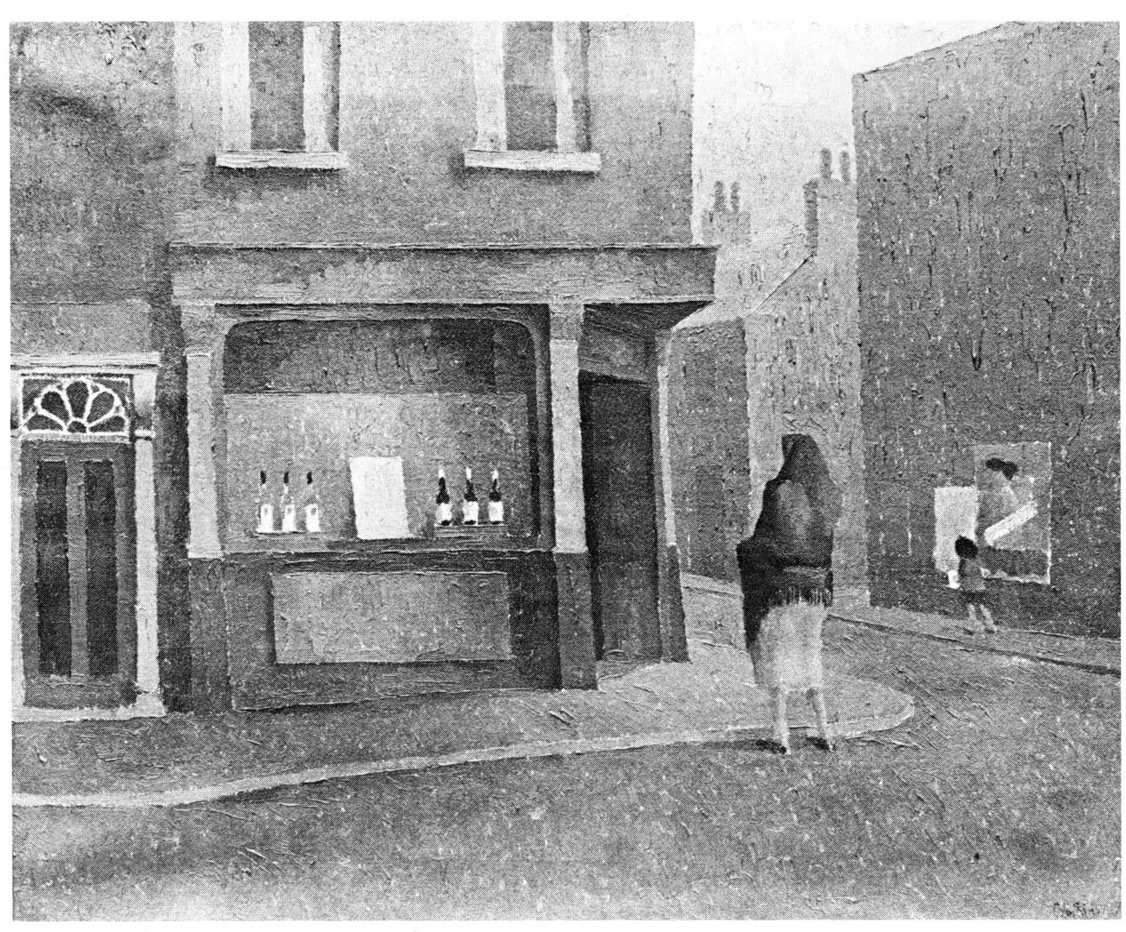

48 COLIN MIDDLETON
The Wind that Shakes the Barley
c1950; oil; 68 x 77 cms; private collection

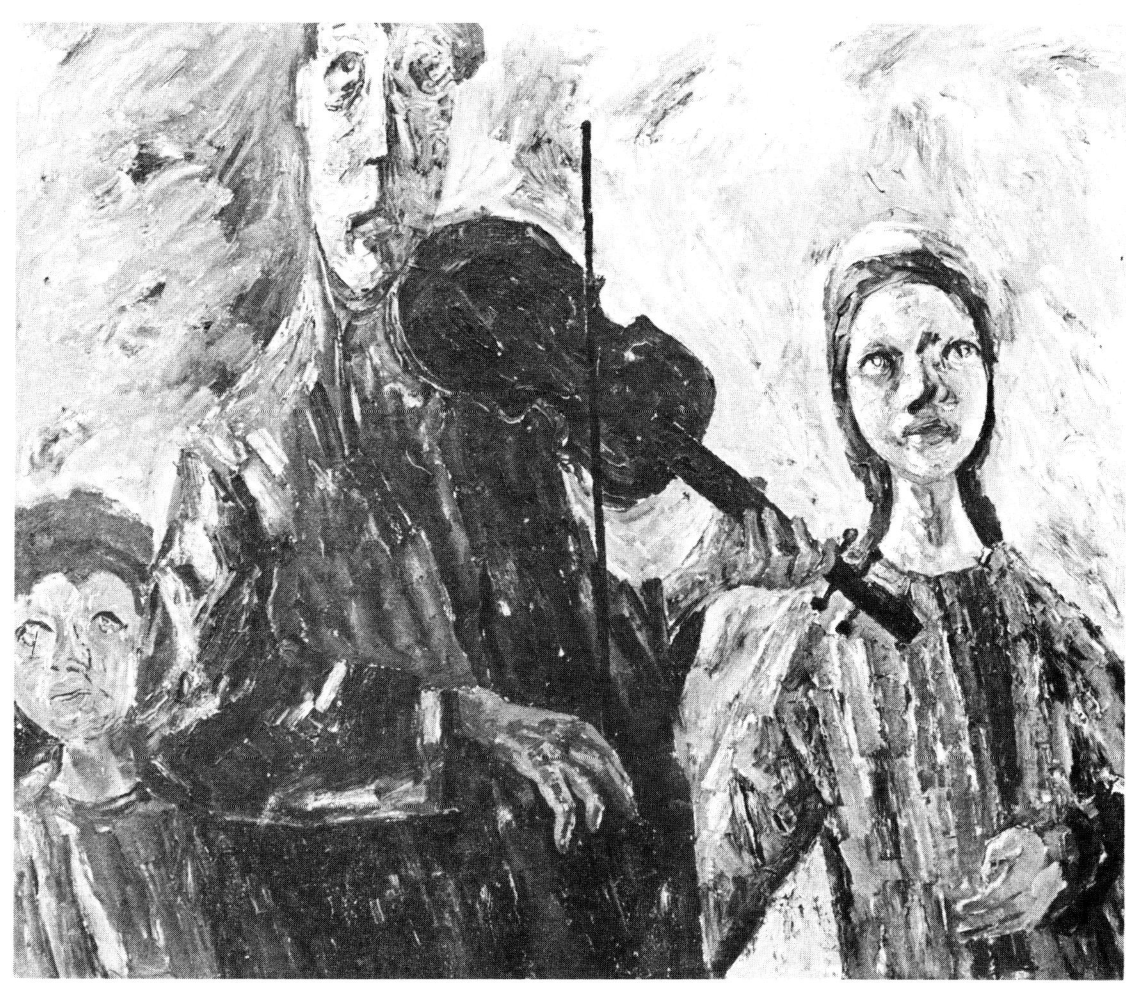

profession of damask designing in providing a prop to unrelated creative activity among Ulster artists from the first decades of the century. Run over the names of those who, in that way, earned the bread that sustained them while they painted well: Hans Iten, John McBurney, Charles Middleton, Charles Harvey, Colin Middleton, and add the names of John A McAllister, good watercolourist whose life was too short for his promise — even when he left town for Rostrevor to husband his failing strength, he still worked at his craft when he could, Sorley MacCann (Somhairle MacCana), an apprentice-designer while studying part-time at the College of Art. But after his scholarship to the RCA, he took up teaching in the Irish Free State for the rest of his days. Charles Harvey, too, turned to teaching, and Colin Middleton also, for about twenty years.

But with social, economic and technological development the significance and nature of designing altered; the swing-over to man-made fabrics was part of the change. Now as then, few artists can live entirely by the brush, and, not only in Northern Ireland but throughout these islands, in art teaching many find their necessary support.

The Municipal Art Gallery was to continue with local one man shows, but not at regular intervals. The next was not until 1945, with a memorial exhibition of the paintings and sketches by James Humbert Craig who had died the year before. With the bulk of the material from his widow, it comprised ninety-five items. With sketches from his travels abroad and other hitherto unexhibited works, it demonstrated an unexpected variety to the accepted view of his stature and significance.

CHAPTER 4

But already in 1940, the Joint Committee for Adult Education of Queen's University had received £700 from the Pilgrim Trust to promote Music for the People and Art for the People. After approaches, the Trust agreed to put up £1,500, if the Northern Ireland Government would match it with a like sum and take responsibility for the entire scheme. So the Council for the Encouragement of Music and the Arts (NI) was set up on 1 February 1943. Advisory committees were nominated, that for Art consisted of Miss Rosamond Praeger, John Hunter and seven others, of whom I was one. Our activities that first year started with a loan exhibition, *Living Irish Artists*. Of the nineteen who took part, the northerners were Kathleen Bridle, Craig, Conor, Paul Henry, Charles Lamb, Luke, Langtry Lynas and Violet McAdoo. Norah McGuinness could hardly be counted as one of them, since, though born in Londonderry in 1903, she had received her training in Dublin, London and Paris where she lived from 1925 to 1931, studying under André Lhôte. Back in London she exhibited with the London Group. Two years in the USA, she returned to Dublin in 1939, where she made her permanent home. In 1950 with Nano Reid, she represented Eire in the Venice Biennale. So, like others who, though Ulster-born, spent their working lives outside the province and whose work had little, if any, detectable influence on artists living here, she cannot be fairly claimed, any more than Sine MacKinnon, Sorley MacCann, or Muriel Brandt, though the last, like MacCann, was born in Belfast, went to the Belfast College of Art, took a scholarship to the RCA, for, again, like him, after that she settled south of the border. Only her painting, *The Battle of Scarva* [*13th July*]

(1946), now in the National Museum, Dublin, could be quoted as contrary evidence. Violet McAdoo, securely numbered with the northerners, art teacher in a Belfast girls' school, was a vigorous watercolourist.

The second CEMA Exhibition consisted of fourteen resident watercolourists, probably the best practitioners of that medium at that time. To the so-far-mentioned Bridle, Conor, Gordon, Hull, McAdoo and Toogood, were added eight others, all highly thought of locally, frequently showing with the Ulster Academy or the Arts Club, providing a full span of the generations. Of the younger men, Richard Faulkner and J D McCord who had succeeded Charles Braithwaite at Methodist College and later followed John Hunter in the Ministry's inspectorate — he had married Elizabeth Clements whose sculptures had been in The Ulster Unit — were fairly representative. Theo J Gracey, a prolific and very popular artist, and H Echlin Neill who was with David Allen's, were of the middle age-group, and George Waters, who, I believe, had been with Marcus Ward's, and David Gould, were elderly men. Gould had come to Belfast from Scotland — he kept his accent to the end — in 1891, to learn damask-designing, and became an art teacher. The influence of Trobridge, under whom he had studied at the Government School of Art, was apparent in his work. Kathleen Bridle and Violet McAdoo were joined by the sisters Marjorie and Olive Henry, the former a watercolourist only, the latter much more versatile; employed with a stained glass firm, her pictures often had strongly marked patterns.

In the catalogue foreword, under the title 'Watercolour in Ulster', I wrote of that medium: 'It is certainly well adapted to outdoor work in our climate. The magnificently unstable weather, with swiftly altering skies and the coiling protean clouds, determined by our nearness to the Atlantic here made it necessary for the landscape artist to have at his fingertips a lively and responsive implement for recording the restless panorama of hour and season.' And I summarised the exhibition in a lyrical passage:

'Here is an Ulster anthology... the brilliant leafiness of summer in the park; the quiet lapping of the calm tide; the sound and rush of swirling bog-brown water; the laughter of children at play; the breathtaking surprise of a ghostly gable caught in the headlights of a car; the absurd incongruity of the thatched cottage mobbed by the encroaching villas; the chatter and chair-scraping of tourists; the friendly whiteness of walls in strong sunlight.' And even this confusion of the seen and heard makes it clear that the exhibits were all figurative and readily comprehensible to the viewer.

In the summer of 1944, in its second year, CEMA was able to have a first showing of paintings belonging to *The Collection of Zoltan Frankl*. Mr Frankl, an Austrian refugee industrialist, had a knitwear business in Newtownards but lived in Belfast. The thirty-nine pictures included a number by British artists such as Sir George Clausen, Ethel Walker and R O Dunlop. The southern Irish artists, the late Nathaniel Hone, W J Leech, Sean Keating whose *Irish Romanesque* was one of its owner's greatest favourites, and Jack B Yeats with four, the excellent *Race in Hy Brazil*, one of them, made a strong impact; but already northern painters were finding Frankl a discriminating patron;

Conor, Iten, Carr, Lamb and Sidney Smith, with a gouache *Self Portrait*, were well represented by characteristic pieces. So was inaugurated CEMA's long indebtedness to a generous collector, always eager to share his possessions with the community, and Zoltan Frankl had at once taken his place as, perhaps, the first serious Art collector to have become resident in Ulster.

In its third year exhibitions by Conor, the first ever sent on tour of provincial centres, and by Colin Middleton — John Rothenstein, Director of the Tate Gallery, over to lecture on British Painting in the Art Gallery, visited this show, and bought a small painting — are worth noting.

The third CEMA Exhibition that year consisted of flowerpieces by Paul Nietsche, a resident foreigner. Of German family but born in Kiev, Russia, Nietsche trained at art schools in Munich and in Paris, and painted both in France and Switzerland. Becoming friendly with Dr M A O'Brien, lecturer at Queen's University, whom he met in Germany, he came to Belfast in 1929, clean-shaven then, as the tempera *Self Portrait* in the Ulster Museum shows. Like Conor, he too had made a foray in the United States, and while there sold a painting among others, called *The Philosopher*, a portrait of a friend who was, like Paul, a member of the Arts Club. Seen earlier, in Magee's shop window, it seemed his best work. In the United States he met a thrifty Texan collector who engaged him to paint a Van Gogh landscape for a reasonable sum. Returning to England, he worked in Devon and Cornwall before coming back to Belfast. The war years saw him interned on the Isle of Man with chess-playing intellectuals. Now back to his attic studio, he resumed his nocturnal habit of working, painting his still lifes and making his own frames, a patriarchal figure with a long beard, wearing a *beret* out of doors and in. Zoltan Frankl had become a great friend and staunch supporter; his collection of the previous year had had two landscapes both of local scenes and a flowerpiece, *Madonna Lilies*. Towards the close of 1945 an exhibition of the paintings of Georgina Moutray Kyle was assembled in the Art Gallery. A lively and voluble octogenarian, Miss Kyle was one of those independent ladies who had asserted a Victorian daughter's right to follow her own path, though no suffragette, since, as a vigorous Unionist, she had travelled widely in Great Britain, articulating the case against Home Rule for Ireland, in the years before the first world war. A student in Paris, she had exhibited at the Paris Salon, the Royal Scottish Academy and the Royal Institute of Oil Painters, as well as the Royal Hibernian Academy and regularly with the Ulster Academy. She had two varieties of subject-matter; still life, usually of porcelain or pottery figures, but including flowers in restrained pastel shades — she claimed a perfect sense of pitch which carried over to the other sense — and market scenes on the Continent and at home, girls at work, at fish quays, fishing-boats at anchor, doubled by their reflections, in little Dutch, Breton, Cornish or County Down harbours. Generally, her colours were quiet, their range restricted, and, in many later canvasses, the flat areas of colour were bound together by a bold linear definition, but, in landscape, with little response to textures. *The Lifting of the Fog* (1929) a study in flat pattern of the Belfast gasometers beside the Lagan, was probably her most successful painting. She could have been described as a gentle Post-Impres-

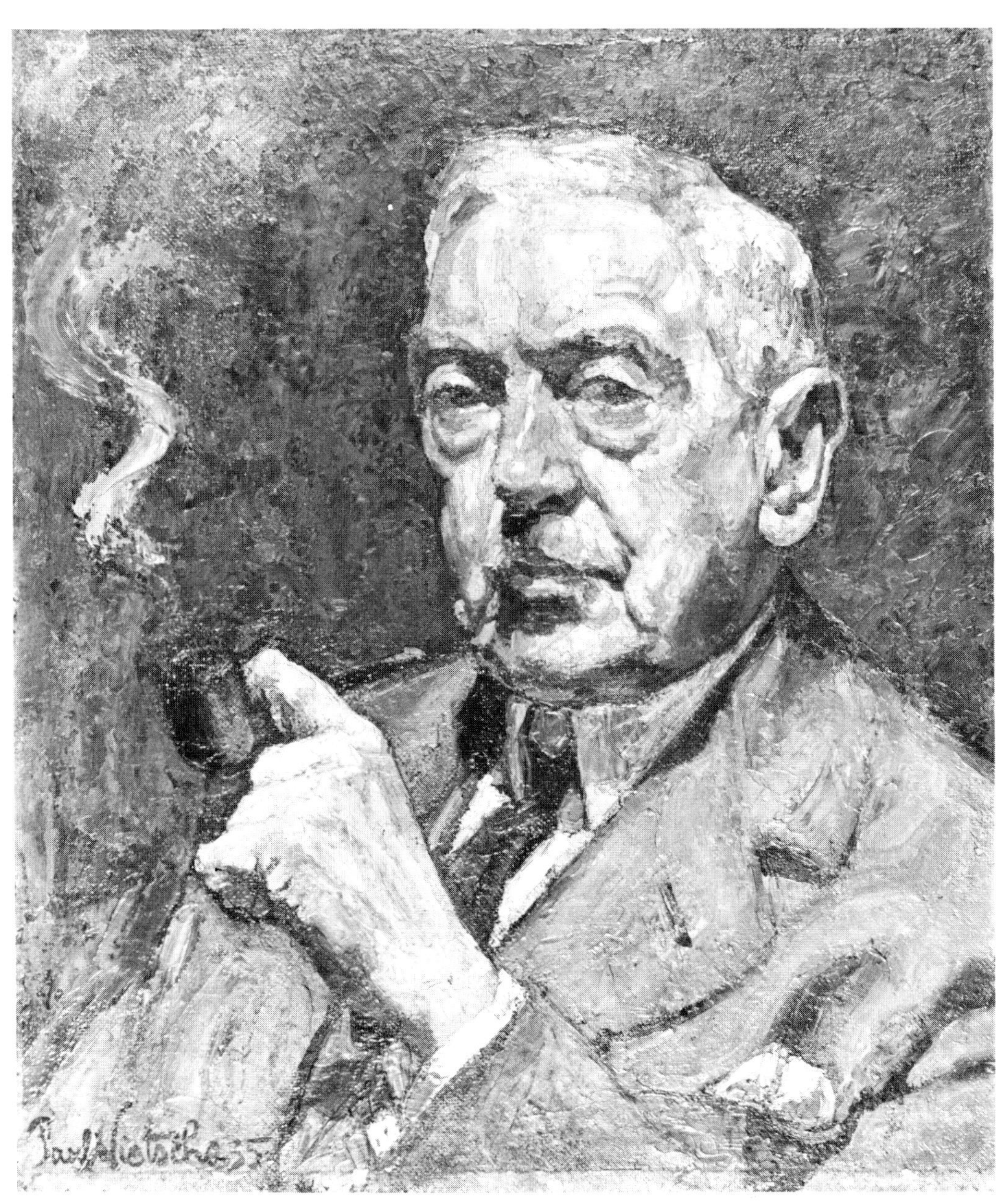

49 PAUL NIETSCHE
Portrait of Mr F W H
1935; oil; 51.8 x 45 cms;
Ulster Museum collection

V JOHN LUKE
Shaw's Bridge
1939; oil and tempera; 31 x 43 cms; private collection

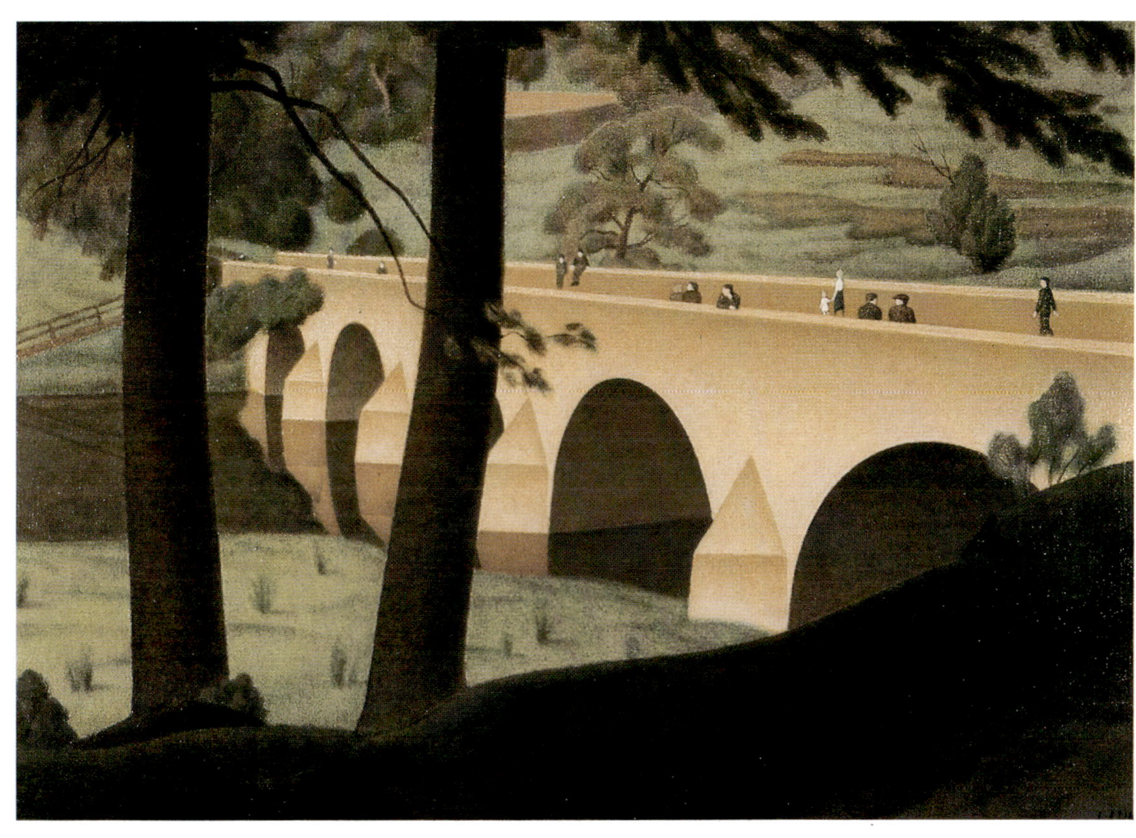

facing page 112

sionist, even if that term notoriously lacks precision.

The Art Gallery continued its series of Ulster Artists Exhibitions with a display of *The Work of John Luke* in September 1946. His first one man show at the age of forty, he was able, though never a prolific painter, to take stock, for, though he could not have known it, by that time much of his best work had been accomplished. Still at Knappagh, County Armagh, he was more deeply than ever absorbed in aesthetic theory which expanded into a philosophy for life, and in mastering neglected or forgotten techniques, unfortunately reducing the number of paintings to reach completion. But the exhibition included *The Old Callan Bridge* (1945) secured by the curator, the indefatigable George Patterson, for his Armagh County Museum.

Almost exactly a year later, the series took the form of a two-man show: *The work of W R Gordon and Morris Harding RHA*. These two had, for a long time, been co-opted members of the Committee of the City Council responsible for the Museum and Art Gallery. Gordon, in a lifetime's involvement with the arts, had been engaged in painting the decorative friezes for the Ulster Pavilion in the British Empire Exhibition of 1924, and in designing the official standard for the Governor of Northern Ireland and, with John Hunter, had been commissioned by the Haverty Trust, to carry out the mural painting *The Bronze Age in Ireland*, for one of the museum's antiquities galleries. This last, while competently executed, was not an outstanding success, the different hands of its creators failing to merge in coherent unity, so that it is easy to identify and engage in the naming of parts; while, over all, the composition reminds me, at some remove, of Leighton's once famous picture of the Phoenician traders in Cornwall.

But in this exhibition Gordon had fifteen oil-paintings and more than thirty watercolours. The paintings seldom as good as one expected from the intelligence and experience of the man, the watercolours had a much greater interest, showing a surprising topographical range from France to Ulster where he had found subjects from Carlingford to Derry, but most enduringly in Cushendun and its environs.

Morris Harding, like Gordon, in his early seventies, had come to Belfast about twenty years before, from his native England, where he had trained as a sculptor under his uncle Harry Bates ARCA, and had worked under J M Swann, RA, the leading animal sculptor and painter of the great cats of late Victorian times. He had modelled and carved memorials for Prestwold, Bisham Abbey, and Eastergate near Chichester, which figure in books on English Church Sculpture. In Belfast, the task for which he had been invited, he had been responsible for much of decorative carving of the capitals of the columns in the Cathedral. His fifty-four exhibits were largely carvings or bronzes of animal groups, polar bears or leopards at play, crouching, asleep ... within the tradition which dates from the French *animalier*, J F Barye (1796-1875) who had so deeply influenced Swan. The portrait-busts, some done from photographs, were of little interest, but the most original works of his Belfast years were the few realisations in stone of plant forms, *Benweed* being a memorable essay in organic abstraction. His chalk drawings of carnivores in the zoo, from about twenty-five

50 JOHN LUKE
Old Callan Bridge
1945; oil and tempera; 55.3 x 77.5 cms; Armagh Museum collection

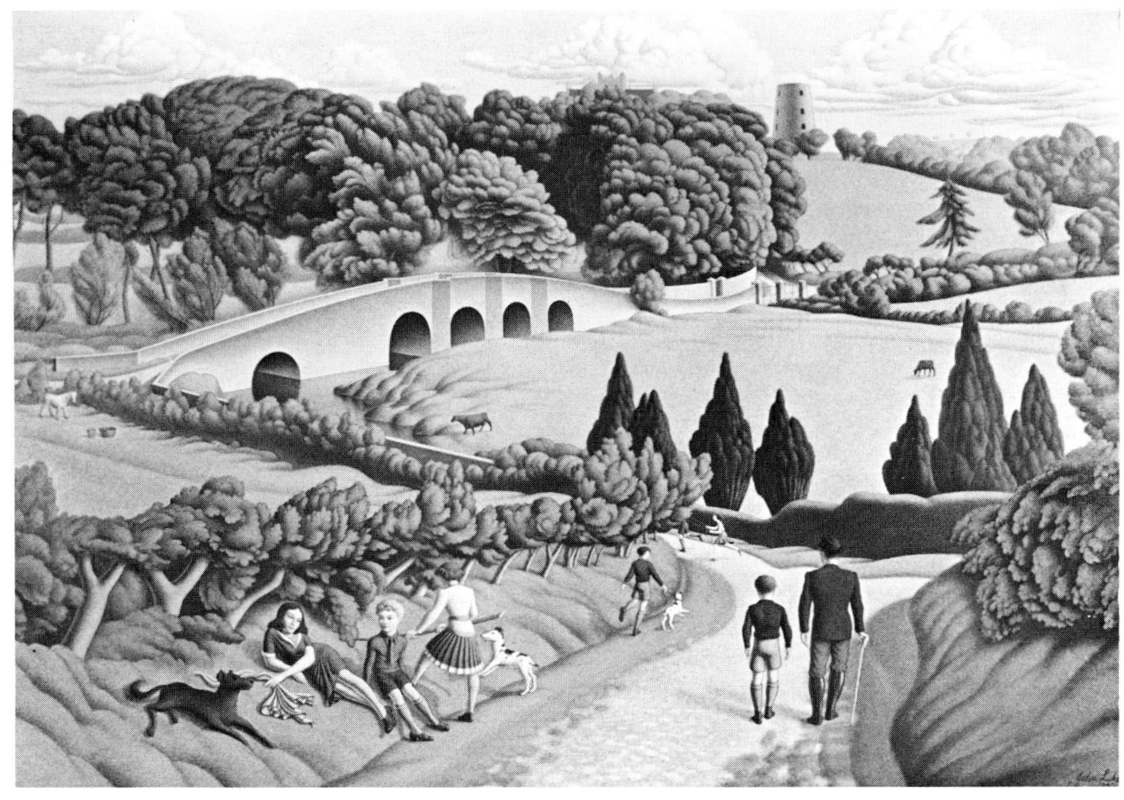

years earlier, showed where his vivid and vital talent lay.

Harding's studio was only a few doors from Miss Praeger's in Holywood, County Down, and it seemed an eccentric decision for the Local Authority to have commissioned a non-resident Englishman, L S Merrifield, to supply the town's war memorial, one of those stereotype steel-helmetted soldiers with rifle and fixed bayonet at the ready, when there were two resident sculptors at hand. Miss Praeger's bronze figure, *Johnny the Jig* perched on his rock, certainly has much more vitality, and is still one of the most satisfactory and pleasurable sculptures in the Six Counties.

But surely our most successful war memorial is, after all, by an Ulster sculptor: the *Lion* in Mourne granite, in Newcastle, County Down, by Frank Wiles. A Larne man, trained at the Dublin Metropolitan School of Art where he was a contemporary of John Hunter, the Ulster Museum has a marble figure, *The Dawn of*

51 ROSAMOND PRAEGER
The Philosopher
c1920; marble; 43.5 cms high; Ulster Museum collection

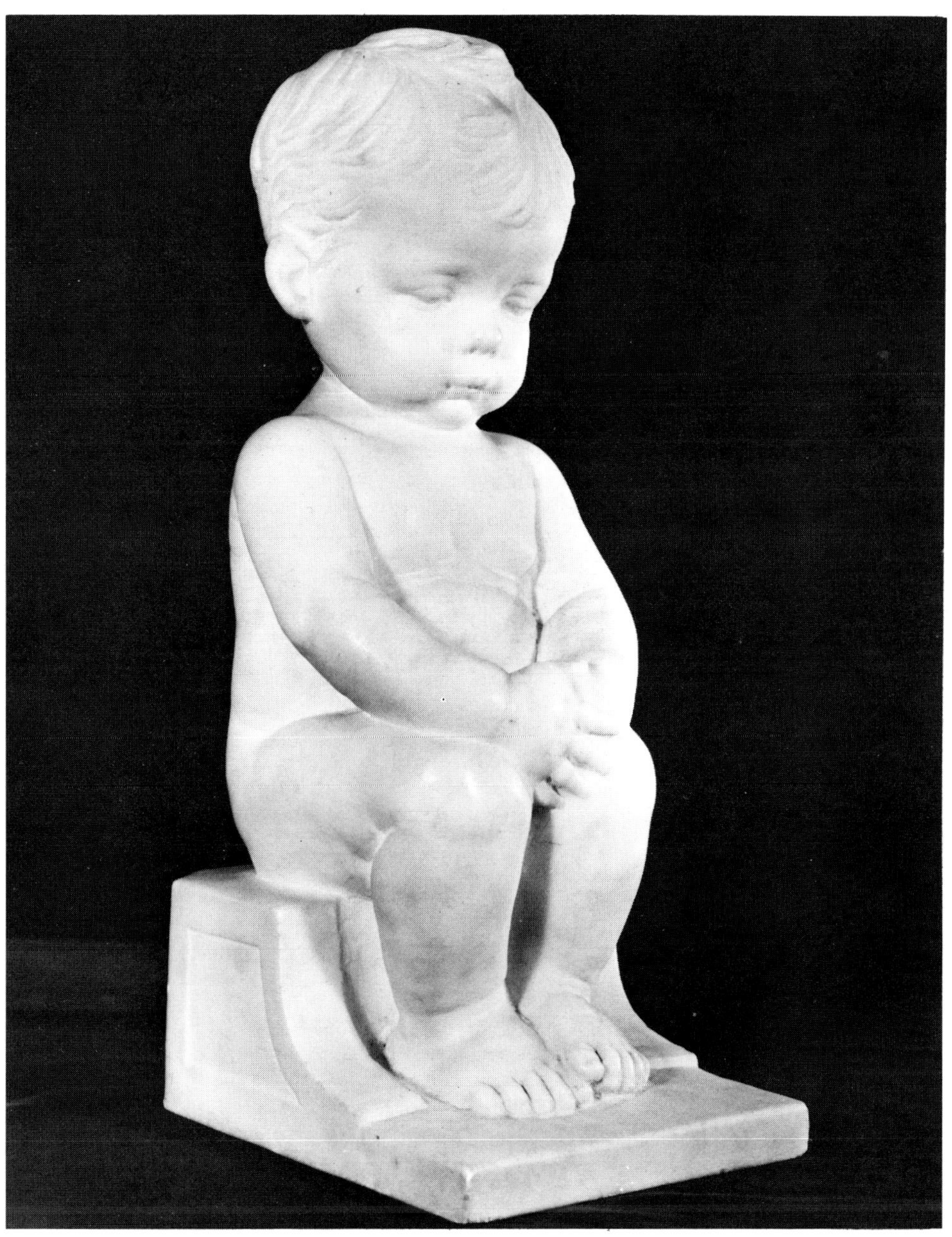

52 ROSAMOND PRAEGER
Johnny the Jig
n d; bronze; at Holywood, Co Down

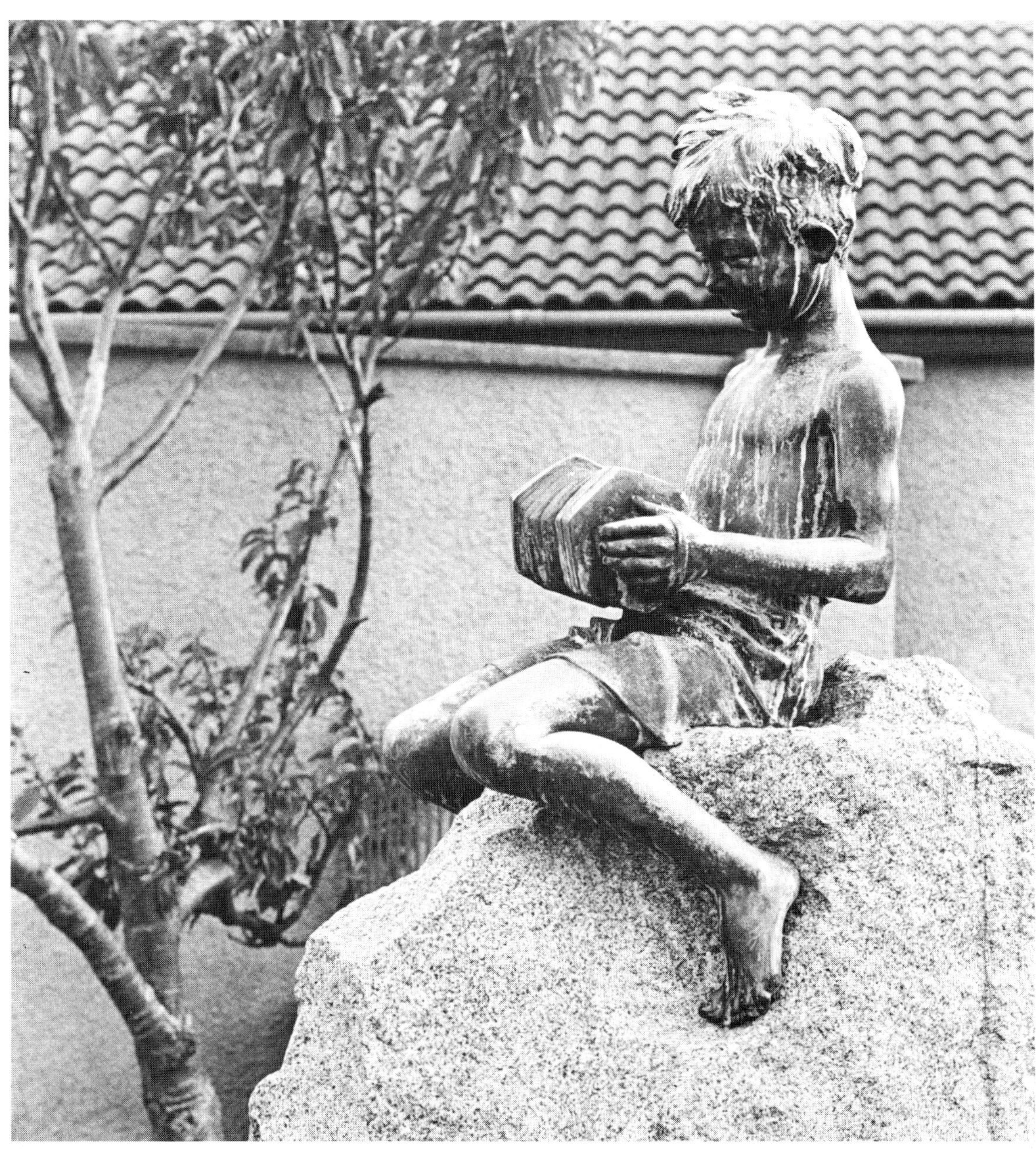

Womanhood, of a kneeling girl with hands clasped behind her head, with vague undetailed features. Never required or driven to great effort, his modelled portraits were not memorable, but *The Lion* has a sculptural presence of unexpected power. Banal in its symbolism, the creature is realised with rigid but impressive abstraction, its hard material given form, no unnecessary detail being wrenched or tortured beyond the limits of its resistant material. There is a story, likely to have been apocryphal, that the sculptor visited a local quarry to select his piece of granite, and that, after a long lapse of time, anxiously he contacted the quarry owner to enquire when it could be delivered; the reply was that the lion had been roughed out and was ready for delivery to the site. An amusing fable, it does in no way diminish the authority of that monument in its permanent equilibrium.

The Art Gallery continued with its Ulster artists series in 1948 with *The Work of Doris V Blair*. Student at the Belfast College and the RCA, during the war years she had made an extensive series of oilpaintings and watercolours illustrating the women's services in industry, the American Air Force and Red Cross. A number had been acquired by the War Artists Advisory Committee. She had also exhibited widely at the RA, the RSA, and the RHA. After the war she was able to take up a travelling scholarship long delayed, studying in New York and in Paris with Lhôte and Léger, this experience turned her to abstract and non-representational art; and the exhibition showed work before and after the deep change. Shortly after she married a Belgian and left Northern Ireland.

The work of F W Hull in 1949 gave the public an opportunity to appreciate the paintings and watercolours of this rather underexhibited artist and had an awakening effect on some of the younger men who had left, or were on the point of leaving, the College of Art. And, a year later, *The work of Kathleen Bridle* showed her to have widened her scope, extending her subject matter from her Fermanagh base to Belgium and the Mediterranean.

CEMA, too, never slackened. By agreement with the Gallery authorities, its more important loan exhibitions were shown at Stranmillis, and the use of premises in 55A Donegall Place gave a venue suitable for almost continuous displays of a less prestigious nature. The Art Advisory Committee now included W R Gordon, Zoltan Frankl, Denis Hanna the architect, and Ivor Beaumont, head of the College of Art until on his retirement he was succeeded by James Warwick the new principal. Lady Antrim, herself a sculptor and member of the Ulster Academy, A T Donald the City Schools' art advisor, and J D McCord, art inspector, also served for lengthy periods, almost giving evidence for the suggestion that there was 'an Art Establishment' which the introduction of limitations on the length of service and the holding office attempted to dispel. When I retired in 1957, I had been a member for fourteen years, the last of the original advisory committee.

In this century, for art, the generations seem to emerge about every decade, but we must be scrupulous in avoiding the term progress. In the Arts there is technical development, change of fashion, of social demand, or of aesthetics; but progress in the sense that, because something is

53 FRANK WILES
War memorial
n d; Mourne granite; at Newcastle, Co Down

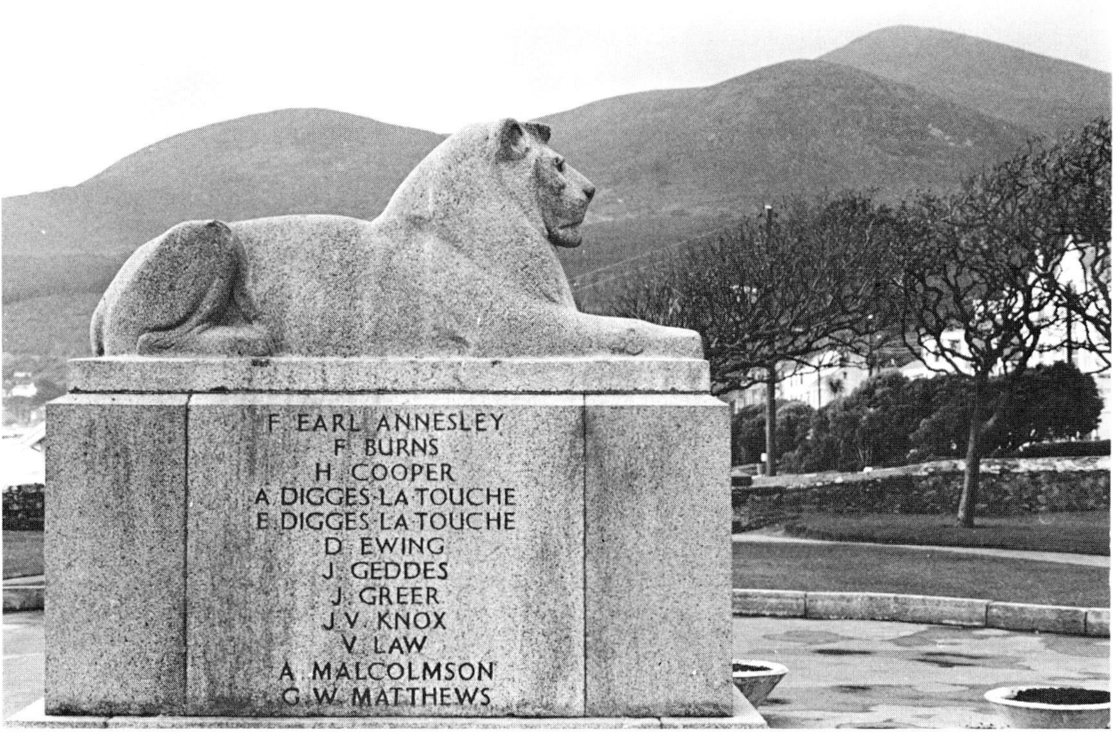

more up-to-date, it is qualitatively better not simply because it is more in keeping with contemporary ideas, is a fallacy. Batoni is not better than Giotto, because he came centuries later. Belief in Progress for its own sake was one of the most powerful and operative Myths of the Victorian Age, and still has its adherents.

At any rate, by 1944, when the generation, or wave, of the Ulster Unit, was ten years older, the ideas which had activated it had become more widely accepted; ideas of form and mass and their special relationship — Charles Harvey had declared, 'How best to represent the Form of Things is my problem', R C Toogood that 'the painter's aim... is to find in nature some sense of formal order, and to translate the same in terms of form and colour into a pattern which relates to the size and shape of his canvas'. So, while some of them became more experienced, more skilful painters, and they were reaching a greater degree of acceptance and appreciation, the wave behind them was driven by different winds.

In *Northern Harvest*, an anthology of Ulster writing, edited by Robert Greacen, which came out that year, I contributed an essay on 'Paintin Ulster'. After a brief sketch of the past, I

54 TOM CARR
Steps to the Shore
n d; oil; 61.6 x 76.8 cms;
Arts Council of Northern Ireland collection

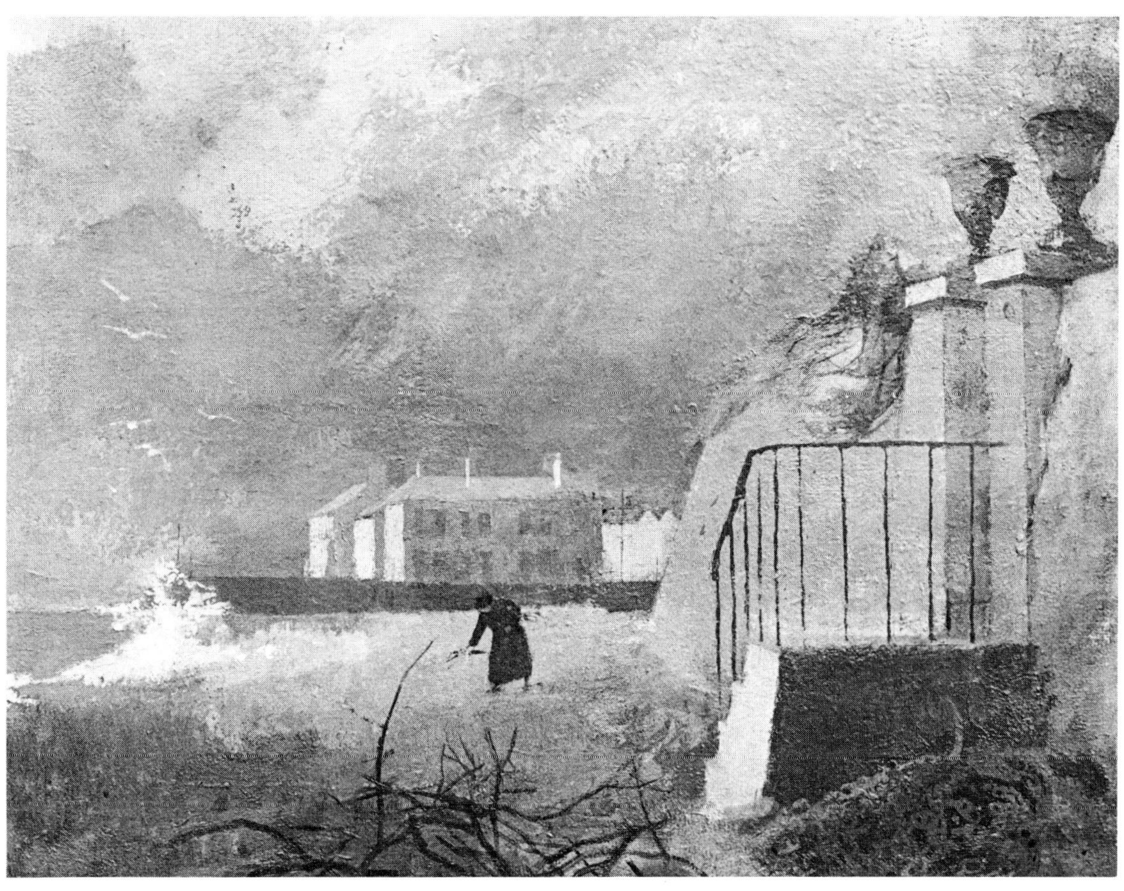

turned to the contemporary scene, to Conor, Craig, McKelvey, the watercolourists Gracey, Gordon, and Waters, then on to my own generation, to Toogood, Luke, Tom Carr, Middleton, and Sidney Smith, for these then seemed to me the front-runners of the time. Of Toogood, I wrote: 'His colour is altogether quieter than Luke's; his shapes not so sharply formalised, his vision closer to normal representation. He prefers a high skyline or none at all, and a broad landscape in which the brown ploughed fields, the dark hedges and the meadows, the slate roofs and the white-washed gables make a pleasing pattern of unemphatic but subtly related colour, organised mainly by the manipulation of diagonal tensions.' This was accurate reporting, but entirely in those terms of shape and pattern, all emotion locked away from what I should now call friendly or companionable landscapes. In my reference to Tom Carr, I permitted a little more feeling, in his 'affectionate approach to subjects of ordinary experience — a breadserver's van rattling along, children leaning on a sea-wall, a bare armed servant girl — he is kin to Bonnard and Vuillard, while a striking study of the entrance to the British Museum, its grimy columns partially obscured by steel scaffold and sandbag, somehow recalls the work of Sickert, and it is in the company of those masters of quiet acceptance that Carr finds his own climate and significance'. I have changed one word in that quotation, and it still is not the right one, for there is something elusive in Carr's work I find inexpressively moving, like the butterfly on the thumb in Colin Middleton's *Jacob and the Angel*.

The war was still on; my estimate of Sidney Smith drew upon his response to the romantic motifs 'of Breton and negro *matelot*, of coloured American soldier, and once or twice he has achieved an Ardizzone gusto... in a rowdy portrayal of an army billet loud with song and instrument. The landscapes with which he has most sympathy are of gritty suburban allotments, of city streets under snow or with tall buses swaying in the rain... balloon sites in which he has made arrangements of line and mass that, while they explicitly do not explore new areas of fantasy, deepen and enrich our contemplation of the contemporary scene.' But of these three only Carr, to my knowledge, has continued on his gentle way. Toogood gave too much to teaching, Smith left the country, and I have seen no work since.

In that same year, however, Arthur and George Campbell edited another anthology of prose and verse, *Now In Ulster* (1944), which included a batch of reproductions of paintings and drawings. These consisted of Middleton's ambiguous *Dark Tower* — though this was misdated 1945 in the catalogue of his 1976 exhibition — Luke's *Road to the West*, a watercolour, *Caravans*, by Arthur Campbell, a pastel *Portrait* of Rachel, his wife, by John Turner and a watercolour *Man and Wife* by him, too, a *Bombed Street* by Gerard Dillon, a *Harbour Scene, Dublin* and *Conlig Street* where he then lived, by Dan O'Neill, a watercolour, *Holidays at Home*, and a shadowy *Dead Street* by George Campbell.

I wrote the accompanying essay: 'Under Forty: some Ulster Artists'. Indicating that I had selected neither the artists nor the illustrations, I suggested that a comprehensive survey would have required notice of Sidney Smith, R C Toogood 'just at the age limit and not recently working in oils', Maurice Wilks and Markey Robinson, with the watercolours of Violet McAdoo and Olive Henry who, that summer, had had a joint exhibition in the Stranmillis series. Writing of Luke, I referred to the danger he ran in allowing his insistent rhythms to become over-elaborate, and commended *The Road to the West* for its return to simplicity, though the outcome of a technique of some complexity. Middleton involved me in a full page discussion of his current symbolism. For the other, younger quartette, it was the first occasion I had had to set down words.

John Turner, at the College of Art, had painted highly finished portraits which looked like Old Masters. Now returned from the Slade, it seemed as if his Oxford sojourn, to which, in wartime, the school had been evacuated, had jolted him off course. A brief engagement with *Pointillisme*

55 GEORGE CAMPBELL
Slack Day, Smithfield
n d; oil; 55.9 x 73.1 cms;
Ulster Museum collection

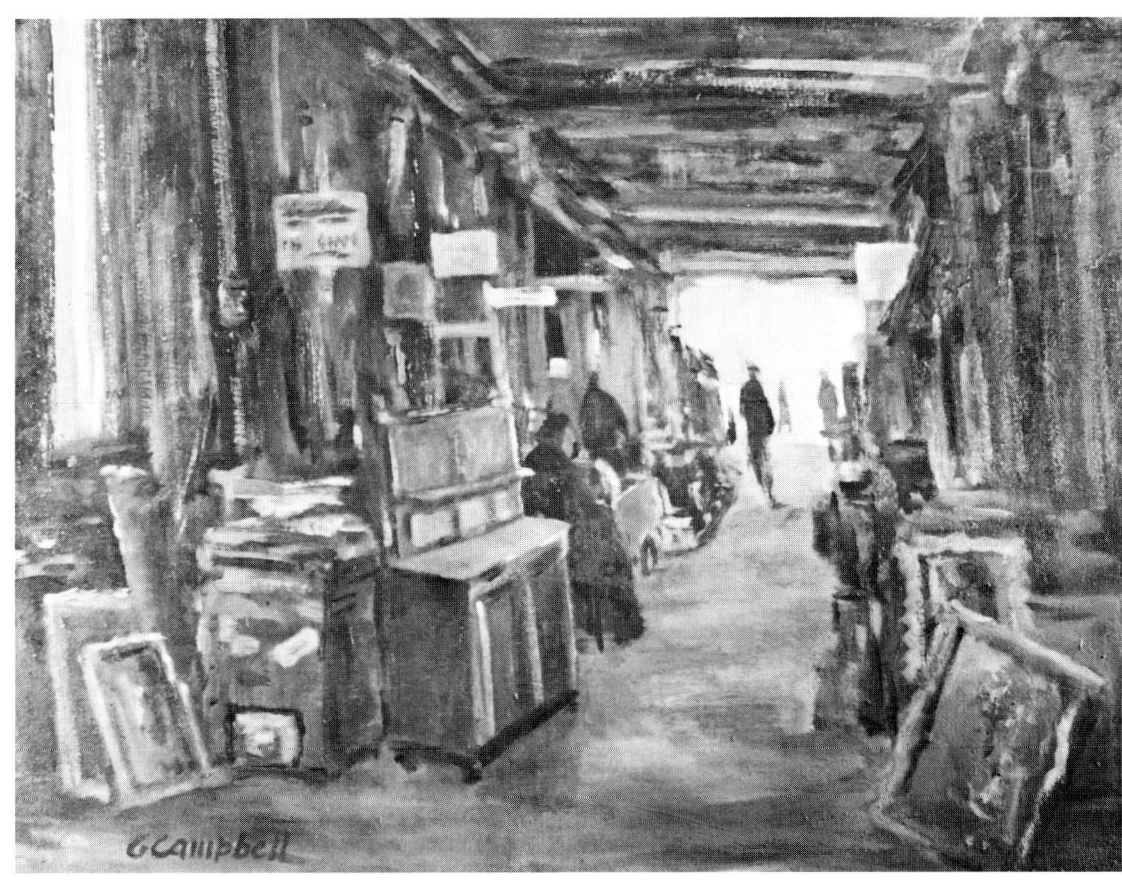

— unmixed, clean colour laid on in small touches — had lightened his palette for landscape — one of these is now in the Armagh County Museum — and the straightforward pastel and the rather caricatural *Man and Wife* reinforced this sense of lost direction. Another pastel, not illustrated, indeed, destroyed, entitled *The Holy Family*, had been highly promising. A group of father, mother and child with exaggerated limbs — hands, feet — by the emphases of their volumes, gave a sort of sculptural unity to the interlocked figures. That composition, enlarged and transposed into oilpaint, now in the Ulster Museum, lost a great deal of its compelling unity, and remains terminal to another lost direction.

But the coming together of the trio, Campbell, Dillon and O'Neill marked the striking of a new distinctive note, for *Caravans*, Arthur Campbell's watercolour, though well drawn and realised, remained safely within the canon of local work in that medium. With only the slightest contact with the orthodox training of the art school, at that time, untravelled, basically too diverse in personality to cohere in a formal group, they were to emerge in the next decades as three of the best painters in the country. Just then, I quote, 'Their subject-matter is drawn largely from the life of men in towns, the life at hand, seeking no escape into the psychological world of Middleton or the ideal world of Luke. Their techniques are means to ends — and are not often signed with evidence of the artist's affection for the stuffs of his craft.'

Late in 1943 or early in 1944, Arthur and George Campbell had brought out a booklet of drawings, *Ulster in Black and White*, their fellow-contributors being Maurice Wilks and Patricia Webb. George was represented by humorous groups of American sailors or civilian technicians and straight portrait sketches of US servicemen, at that time a conspicuous feature of Belfast night life; Arthur by landscapes in the north; Patricia Webb by magazine-type drawings of children; and Maurice Wilks by two portraits, *A Countryman*, and *Seafaring Men*, both good academic statements. I was very likely introduced to the others in some room or studio down town, which they had taken as temporary headquarters, but I had seen paintings by Dillon and O'Neill in a joint show in Dublin, when, exactly, I do not remember. I was struck by the seeming clumsiness of the little pictures, the apparent morbidity of O'Neill's dead or dying figures.

Dan O'Neill, a tall fair handsome man, was an electrician on night-work in the City Transport Department, his days free to paint. George Campbell, small, dark, worked in an aircraft factory. Gerard Dillon, small, too, a house painter by trade, had been working in London before the war, had come back to Ireland, and, now, by war-time restrictions, was stranded here.

They put on their little exhibitions wherever a place could be found. One of these was in a frame-maker's shop, and, in June 1944, in a gallery in Portadown belonging to John Lamb, brother of Charles, the artist. This consisted of paintings by Campbell and Dillon only, sixty of them, and few, if any, were sold. But by 1944/45 O'Neill, Dillon, Campbell, and Turner were included in a CEMA Exhibition of *Works by some Ulster Artists*, with Kathleen Bridle, Olive Henry, Colin Middleton, Sidney Smith, and Markey Robinson, and had, by then, entered the recognised company. With whose help I do not know, O'Neill was enabled to visit Paris and returned, suddenly a much improved painter. Dillon, at the end of the war, went back to London to be engaged in demolition work with a sympathetic employer who allowed him a couple of days a week off to paint. Victor Waddington in his Dublin Gallery proved interested, and, by 1946, both Campbell and O'Neill had successful shows with him. Dillon followed in 1950, having earlier had, as the others had too, a CEMA exhibition in Belfast. And all three took part in the annual *Irish Exhibition of Living Art*, Dillon, in 1950, being elected to the organising committee.

While each was highly individual, they had this in common, besides being close friends, that they were romantics. Though one critic has called Campbell Gothic, and another described

56 DAN O'NEILL
Flowers on the Shore
1951; oil; 40.6 x 50.8 cms;
private collection

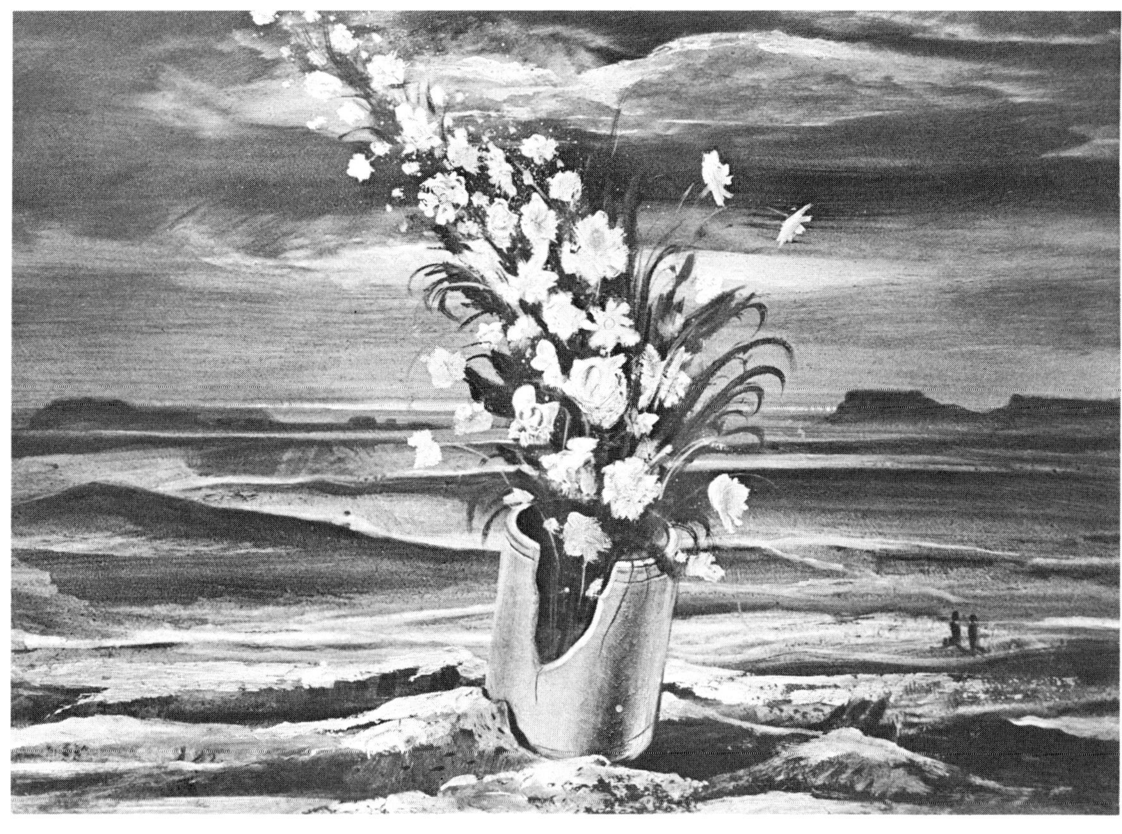

O'Neill as an Expressionist, more precise labels than 'Romantics' are impossible to affix. Campbell's swift dark smear or dash of colour, O'Neill's golden or creamy pastes, Dillon's gay patchwork are more useful indications of dominant devices, but these, at once, summon up specific pictures: the sombre interior of a stall in the covered market with its accumulated objects; the reclining woman on the couch; the map-like landscape of mountain, lake, and dry-stone wall. The drawing, by life-class standards was usually inaccurate, but the distortions demanded by the mood of the theme, for theirs was an art of feeling, of emotion symbolised, not of designed structure of thought.

Campbell, who was sometimes tempted to emotive abstraction, had to travel far to find himself, to Spain, to *A Blind Flamenco Guitarist*, to *Gypsies Moving Camp*, to the Holy Procession in the narrow street. Dillon found himself in Connemara where so many had gone for inspiration, like Paul Henry, like Charles Lamb, like Humbert Craig, when the piled rocks with

57 GERARD DILLON
Connolly's Bar
1955; oil; 38.1 x 50.8 cms; Arts Council of Northern Ireland collection

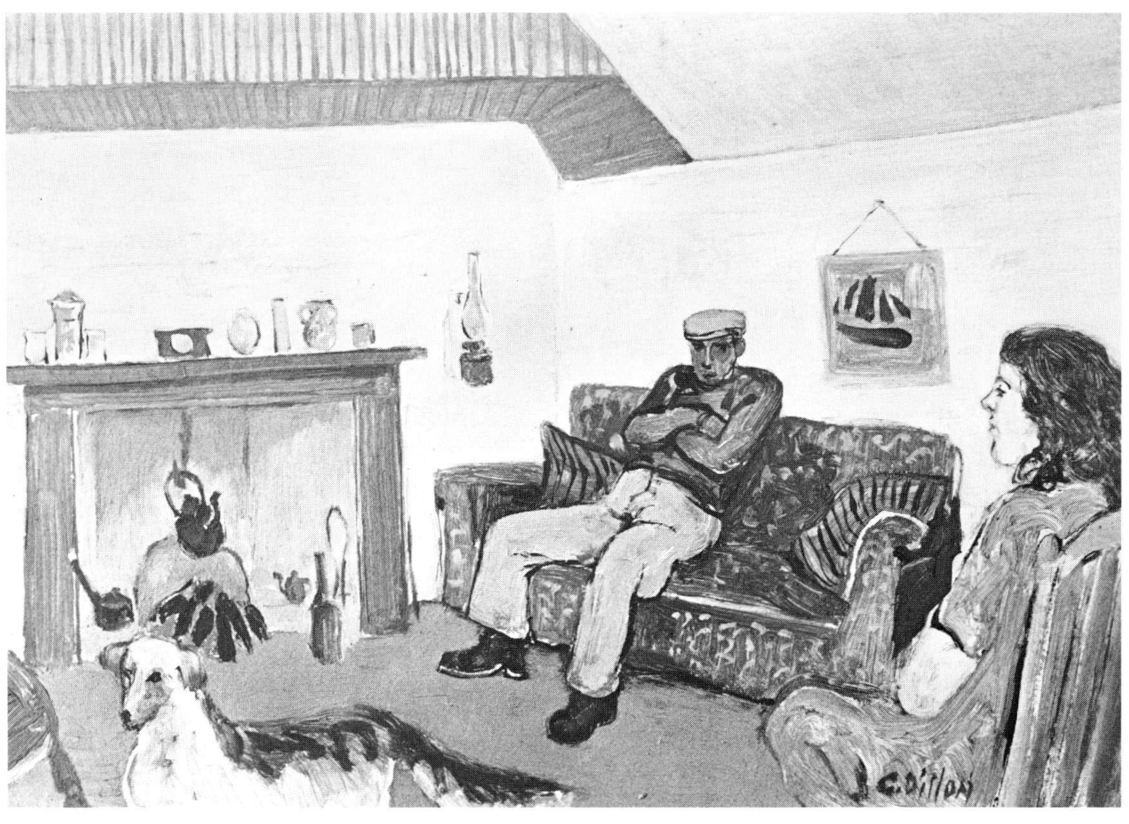

the creel-bearing boy peering over them, the country bar room with the man sitting, arms folded, on the sofa, the strand with the lads on their ponies, proved it an inhabited country. With his landscape, I recall that line from Robinson Jeffers about those Irish places 'where every stone has been handled ten thousand times'. O'Neill found himself equally, in the memory of the small boy, his back to the woman in child-bed, gazing at the basin, the kettle, and the shirt-sleeved doctor's handbag, and in the cracked jam-jar with flowers, tilted on the mysterious sea-shore, which could be any shore.

George Campbell crossed to London. Daniel O'Neill was the last to go, for with no enterprising art dealer nearer than Dublin, with only a tiny purchasing public, artists had to find markets, adding to and continuing the outflow of talent from which the arts here have always suffered.

There were, at that time, only two commercial galleries, both with limited wall space. The first

I DAN O'NEILL
irth
952; oil; 53.3 x 61 cms;
rts Council of Northern
eland

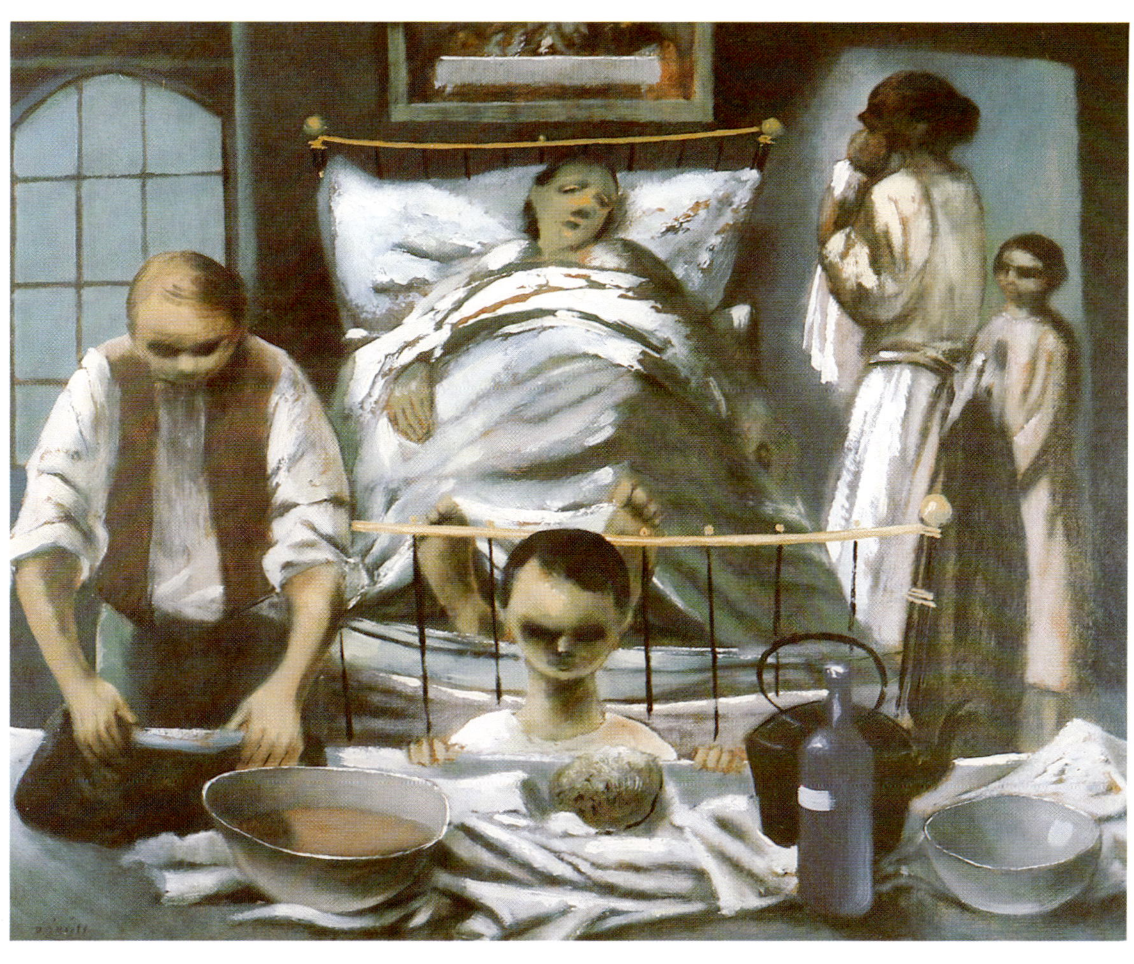

ing page 124

handled mainly pictures in gold frames acceptable to a conservative taste, a large magnifying glass always laid conveniently on a low table, the better to admire and marvel at those minute details in the foreground of the recommended canvas. The second carried Old Master reproductions, *bric-à-brac*, once in a while a Paul Henry painting, or more often, work by Frank McKelvey. So CEMA's use of the Donegall Place gallery proved of inestimable value in its work of encouraging and providing local artists with a window. CEMA also started and regularly added to its own collection, both building up a body of loan material for showing round the country, and patronising, in a minor way, the artists of the community.

The Arts Society, which had become the Ulster Academy in 1930, seeking to receive permission to use the Royal prefix, which it achieved in 1950, remained the only body of its kind in Northern Ireland, and, with annual exhibitions, provided a useful local focus for the better amateurs and those professionals who cared to support it, for regular displays no longer involved the full membership of the Arts Club as its shows so far back had done, and other societies petered out. But change of name notwithstanding, the Academy had not changed its nature, that of a local art society. Indeed, the concept of an academy was obsolete, or, at best, obsolescent. The Royal Academy in London had been an eighteenth century foundation and, after its Victorian heyday, was no longer the vital and growing end of British Art which had, by critical approval, been transferred to the dealers' galleries of the Bond Street square mile. By their established nature, academies anywhere had seldom been able to find room for younger experimental artists, or to compel the continued participation of the more mature professionally successful. Without its own premises, without endowments and property, it could not, could never achieve an authoritative position of authentic prestige, sponsoring lectures or important loan exhibitions, but it was a fact that, under one name or another, it had, for over seventy years, held a place in the life of the community for non-material values and given many occasions of pleasure to exhibition visitors and satisfaction to picture-makers that their work had been seen. Most of the artists of this century to whom reference has been made had been members of the society — Lavery, Carey, Iten, Praeger, Conor, Craig, McKelvey, Luke, Carr, Middleton, Harding, Wilks, to name a dozen.

Leafing through my newspaper cuttings, often critical of standards, I have found that a number of names have regularly recurred for commendation; A P Jury, H Echlin Neill, Olive Henry, Patric Stevenson, Padraic Woods, who supplied some sort of armature of aesthetic, if never revolutionary, integrity to the yearly displays.

Of these, Padraic Woods, while painting in Donegal or Down, by the rush-spiked water among the little hills, or the pier and the bare shore, has followed by ways not often trodden, but with a kindly unemphatic art, never dashingly adventurous nor ploddingly pedestrian, noting the red calves grazing beside the clumps of purple loosestrife, or the leisurely passage of mountainy folk up the long road and between the clustered cabins of the west, quietly romantic moments, neighbourly to communicate, honestly applied with a scarcely varying touch. Patric Stevenson, Sussex-born, came to

58 F E McWILLIAM
William Scott
1956; bronze; 66.5 cms high; Ulster Museum collection

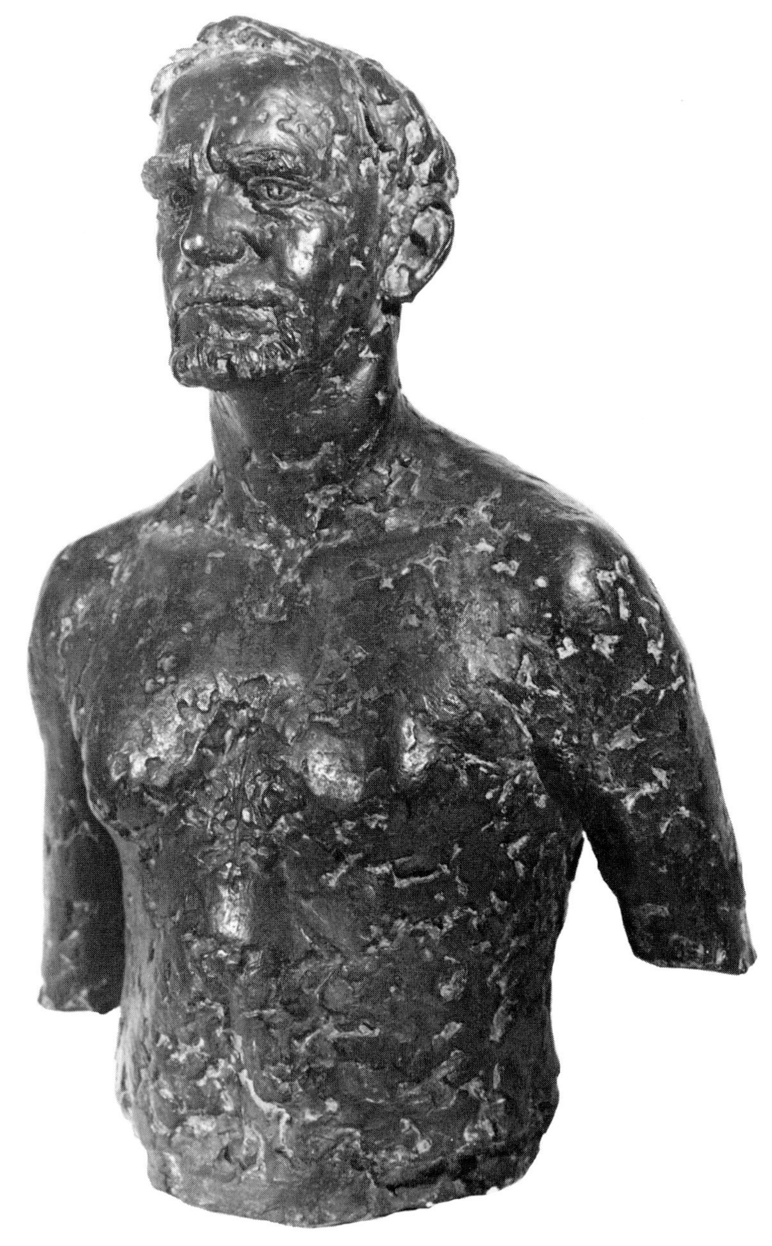

Ireland when he was ten years old, deeply interested in music, an observant nature poet, and a witty rhymer — his *Flowing Water* was published in 1945, after he had served with the RAF. Highly experimental in watercolour, using a variety of technical devices, tinted or coloured paper, loading his pigment with flour-paste to give a kind of *impasto*, challenging the flow and drag of oilpaint, his subjects remained landscape, frequently with the effect of vivid spontaneity, a search which was to lead him in the Sixties and Seventies to utilise *acrylic* for the small lyrical panels. I remember a grained watercolour by him of a great turfstack dark in the foreground with Knocklayde lighter behind, and another, of Rathlin floating offshore like a thick, cliff-sided slab of land.

In the early years of the century, when exhibitions of Irish painters' work were organised for showing outside the country, the exhibitors included artists like Gerald Kelly, Ambrose McEvoy, C H Shannon, J J Shannon, simply because their names sounded as if they were Irish, and men like Orpen and Lavery needed help to cover the walls with creditable pictures. But when, in 1950, the Cultural Relations Committee set up by the Ministry of External Affairs in Dublin arranged an exhibition of *Contemporary Irish Painting* to be shown across the Atlantic, in Rhode Island, Boston and Ottawa, of the seventy-three exhibitors, eleven were from the north, nine not counting Norah McGuinness, originally from Derry and Tom Nisbet from Belfast, for these two had lived and worked in Dublin. Paul Henry, Colin Middleton, George Campbell, Daniel O'Neill had two paintings each, and Rowel Friers, Charles Lamb, Frank McKelvey, James S Sleator, Gladys and Max MacCabe one each; and among those illustrated were Henry, McKelvey, O'Neill, and Gladys MacCabe. So we might have judged that, though not fully representative of our best, it did establish that, for the first time, taken nationally, our artists could not be overlooked.

The exhibiting artists were resident in Ireland, north or south, but nearly a decade before, William Scott had been having his own one man shows in London, and taken his place in exhibitions of *Modern British Painting* touring in Greece, Italy, France and Czecho-Slovakia, and F E McWilliam the sculptor, four years earlier than Scott, had had his first London one man show.

These two men are perhaps the most difficult to accommodate in our story, for both have spent most of their lives outside Ireland. Roland Penrose (1964) has described McWilliam as 'a Londoner for more than thirty years'. Scott has been away since he left the Belfast College of Art in 1931. Both are in the front rank of British artists, called upon for international exhibitions, their works placed in the leading galleries of Western Europe, North and South America and Australia. It can be asserted that they play in a different league. But since McWilliam was born in Banbridge, County Down, son of a local doctor, and Scott, though born at Greenock, belonged to an Enniskillen family and came to Ireland when he was eleven, and since both were students at the Belfast College of Art, it would be a failure of nerve not to claim them; we have declared an interest in British Field Marshals and American Presidents on incomparably more flimsy evidence. But it will have to be admitted that neither of them had or has had much effect on the course of either painting or sculpture here.

CHAPTER 5

Sculpture has been less important than painting in these islands. Constable and Turner both influenced the course of French painting in the nineteenth century, but until Henry Moore and Barbara Hepworth no contribution has been made to European Art. It was Flaxman's drawings, not his sculpture, which won international approval.

That even when, in remote ages, there was sculpture in this island, it was in low relief only, might be taken to support the thesis that if there is any detectable strand in the very debatable concept of 'Irishness', it has been linear rather than three dimensional in its sense of form: *The Book of Kells* contrasting with the carvings of Chartres. There is also the practical circumstance that since the statues were rallied round the City Hall, there has been little chance for any public employment of the sculptor's skill. So McWilliam's movement from those pieces built of feature-or-figure-fragments to the wirefleshed, spindly creatures and on to the crankshaft compositions, the Giacometti-like presences, and the excellent portraits, while charting a versatile and inventive development, has wakened few, if any ripples in the village pond.

It is, however, interesting to note that from the wrestling *Cain and Abel*, shown here in the CEMA *Exhibition of Sculpture* in February 1953, to the later *Cain and Abel VI* (1957) through *Aggressor* (1960) and *Aggressive figure* (1961), *Resistance* figures (1961-2) and *Animus* (1962), the theme of violence seemed to claim expression and point forward to the poigant bronzes, *Women of Belfast* (1972-3), victims of the terrorist bomb-blasts. The sculptor himself, commenting on these, wrote: 'I left Belfast when I was 18, and although I seldom return, what happens there concerns me closely... because my early roots remain unbroken... especially the roots of memory. I can recall what happened in my home town during the former "troubles", this left me with a lasting awareness and hatred of intolerance and religious bigotry.'

Since the middle of last century the north of Ireland has been prone to periodic outbreaks of sectarian and political violence; many incidents in these have passed into folklore and song, but there has been no overt expression in the visual arts; even the popular craft of processional banner painting has had no more than a symbolical or totemic import. The absence of subjects of this violence, or of the underlying social tensions, outside the political cartoon, must have been indicative of some deep failure of imaginative realisation among the artists who might have been expected to have been the more acutely sensitive.

There is a particularly pertinent passage in Roland Penrose's essay already referred to; 'His arrival in London had been his first step towards freedom. His father, a general practitioner in the town of Banbridge, between Belfast and the Ulster Border, was in no way opposed for his ambitions, but McWilliam soon found the provincial atmosphere of his home too limited. Also during that unhappy period known euphemistically as "the troubles" the intense rivalry among his own countrymen due to religious and political hatred often flared up into wild scenes of violence. As a child he was both fascinated and terrified by the riots and murder that went on around him, but he soon began to long for an atmosphere in which the Arts could have their place of honour and cease to be smothered by the ugly passions bred by intolerance. He had learnt through these scenes that tranquillity could however have a precarious existence even when surrounded by violence and fear, that at the centre of every typhoon there is an area of calm which cannot last for long but which is an essential part of the structure of the whirlwind. This discovery of the action of opposing forces was later to lead to an understanding of the tensions which were to animate his sculptures.'

Of William Scott, Ronald Alley wrote, in 1963, that the artist 'spent his youth in Enniskillen, a small town in Northern Ireland. Life there was governed by a strict Protestant code and the Scott household was one of great simplicity and austerity.' And there have been those who argued that, from this circumstance was derived the frugal nature of the subject-matter which characterised his work; the pots, the pans, the bottles, the plain table-tops. As Scott himself, said, 'The objects I painted were the symbols of the life I knew best'; and these simply led on to almost complete abstraction, as his concern with shapes and space took over. But this, coupled with an equally dominant interest in colour and the subtle sensitivity to the textures of the painted surfaces, has led critics to postulate a tension — that word which comes so glibly to anyone writing of art these days — between 'the puritan simplicity of Scott's composition' and 'that vein of sensuality which seems to give them life and excitement'. And to suggest that 'these very qualities are basic parts of Irish life, where, as in other poor countries, life itself is very simple but can be set on fire by imagination', seems a wilful exercise, at the back of it, an

59 WILLIAM SCOTT
Prisoners
Colour lithograph; illustration from *Soldiers' Verse*, chosen by Patric Dickinson, Frederick Muller, London, 1945

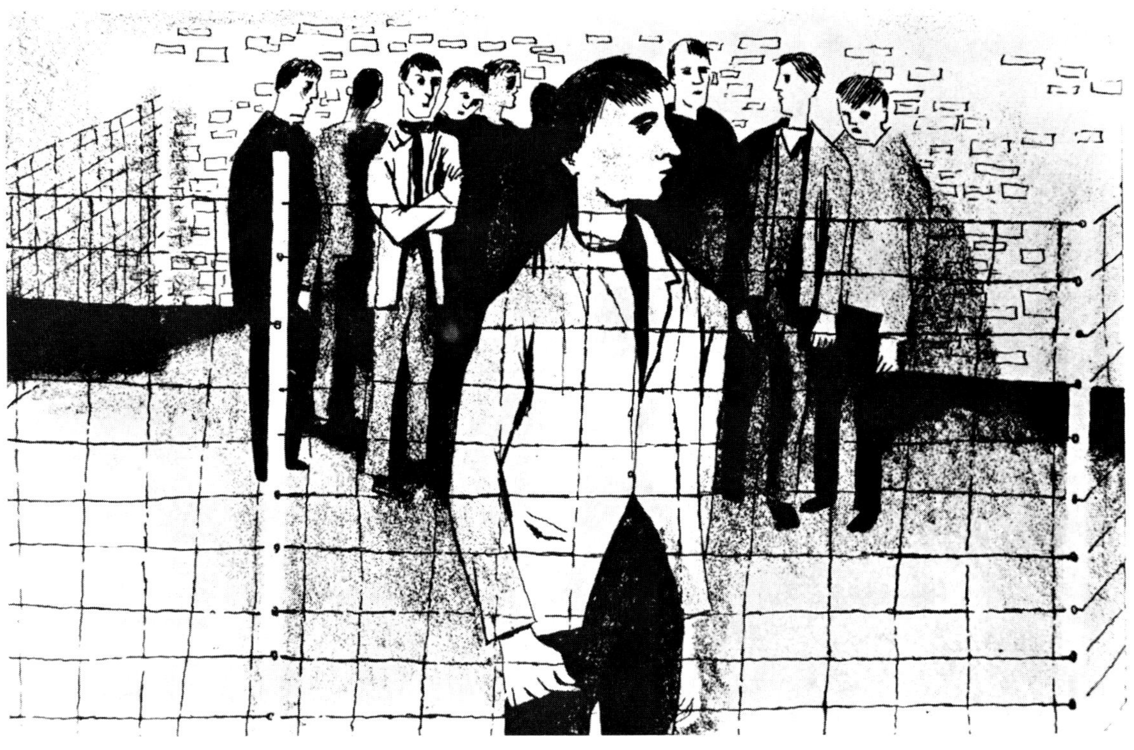

earnest desire to claim for one whose mother was Scottish, and who spent his first eleven years, those years usually thought of as formative, in her country, an unassailable Irishness of nature and sensibility. For, since his Breton period, when he painted peasants and landscapes between 1938 and the outbreak of war, Scott's elimination of detail and reduction of representational form had stripped his images of all content other than aesthetic.

Yet in the Royal Engineers for almost four years, when he only painted a few watercolours, but mastered the technique of lithography with the map-making section, he was equipped to produce the original lithographs which enhance (the editor's word) Patric Dickinson's anthology of *Soldiers' Verse* (1945), those of the sprawling corpse, the army truck travelling menacingly along the empty street, the anonymous ruins, the civilian prisoners — the men behind the wire — by their vigorous simplicity achieve a generalised validity which could be taken to apply to all wars on whatever scale, and prophetic of wars to come.

But to turn to a different matter. Alley in that essay proceeded to remark of Scott's boyhood. 'It was an unpromising environment... for a future painter. By extraordinary good fortune, however, Scott was encouraged by a girl who had recently left the Royal College of Art and who lent him books on modern French art, including the writings of Roger Fry and Clive Bell. So it happened that he was introduced to the work of Cézanne, Modigliani, Picasso and Dérain at the age of fourteen, before he knew anything about Old Master painting.' Of course, we can give that girl her name; but that contact provides a pointer to an important element in the stimulation of contemporary awareness. Miss Bridle's lending the boy those books and talking to him out of her brisk up-to-date experience, represents what was becoming more and more a shaping and determining force in the spread of theories of modern art and its practice. From the printed word and the recent reproduction, the pulsations of change succeeded each other with speed. The defensive provincialism of places once distant from the creative centres had become harder to maintain. When a small boy, in 1927, in a little town on the western edge of Europe, heard of Picasso, he had become an inhabitant of 'the global village'.

But though McWilliam and Scott had physically been absent for so long, drawings by both of them and sculptures by the first had been shown in CEMA exhibitions, and an unusual chance resulted in their being given a presence in Ulster. With the building of a new hospital at Altnagelvin, Londonderry, the architects, in 1957, commissioned a sculpture by McWilliam and a large mural by Scott for the site, the local authorities approved, and the north received its first modern works of art outside the Ulster Museum, since George MacCann's panels were put up in the Londonderry Guildhall.

Of the members of the Ulster Unit of 1934, a few withdrew from exhibiting, and most of the rest, involved in art teaching, remained within the Six Counties, but of the Campbell, Dillon, O'Neill coterie, the principals departed, leaving, for a year or two, their younger friends, Arthur Armstrong and James MacIntyre to maintain the individual expression of the non-systematically trained, the first with his paintings of still life with an almost cubist-rectilinear rigidity and pale pleasant colour, the second with landscapes of buildings and rural figures described with flat passages of colour and pen drawings expressed in sinuous unshaded unbroken line. Subsequently these two also left for London, MacIntyre to follow the craft of commercial illustration, Armstrong, after a spell in the capital, crossed back to Dublin where he evolved his technique of weighting his forms with plaster to gain recession and depth from his undulant contoured surfaces. John Turner who had been briefly an associate, on the strength of his fine early portrait of his father which passed into the CEMA Collection, found some demand for his skill in that field, once or twice being called upon for a mayoral portrait; but since he was qualified by his Slade experience, he was able to find employment as a teacher.

The Festival of Britain, 1951, was not taken as an opportunity for the participation of a representative group of Ulster artists, the then Minister of Education at Stormont, denying any sense of regional identity and insisting that Northern Ireland was as much a part of Britain as the Yorkshire ridings. However, the City Art Gallery seized the chance to stage a comprehensive

60 JAMES MACINTYRE
County Down Farmyard
n d; oil; 30.5 x 38.7 cms;
private collection

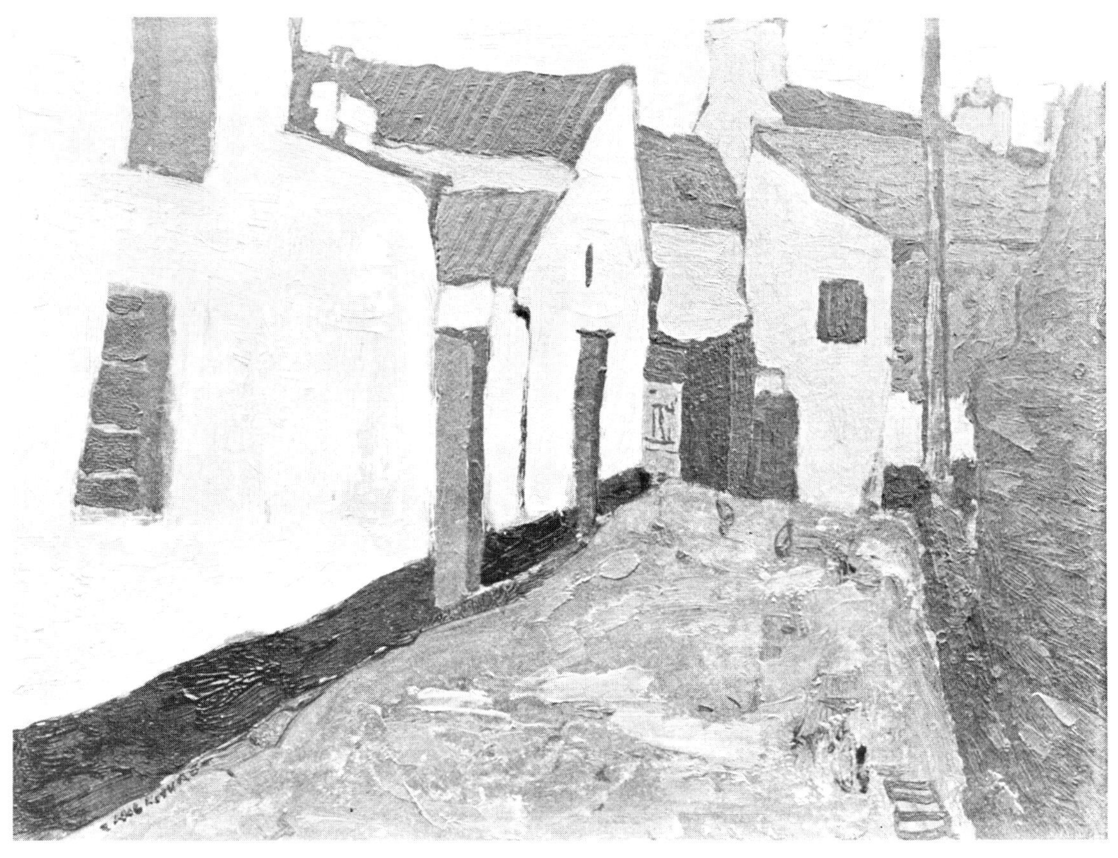

Lavery Exhibition with fine paintings from Glasgow, and the artist's family, added to its own collection.

CEMA made a lasting contribution by commissioning a symposium on *The Arts in Ulster* the first volume ever to be devoted to the full range of achievement in our cultural history, by engaging George MacCann to make two relief sculptures for the Guildhall, Londonderry, and John Luke a large mural in the Belfast City Hall.

George Galway MacCann, one of the Ulster Unit generation, besides painting and stage-design, was the only sculptor in the modern idiom in the north. His two panels, *Saint Columba*, and *The Four Just Men* of the London Guilds, were, of course, related to Derry's history, and were realised somewhat in the manner of a robust Eric Gill. MacCann had, in 1942, published a little book of stories, *Sparrows Round My Brow*, illustrated by his wife, Mercy Hunter, with several whimsical line-drawings. She had studied under

61 GEORGE MacCANN
St Columba
1951; stone relief sculpture; at the Guildhall, Londonderry.

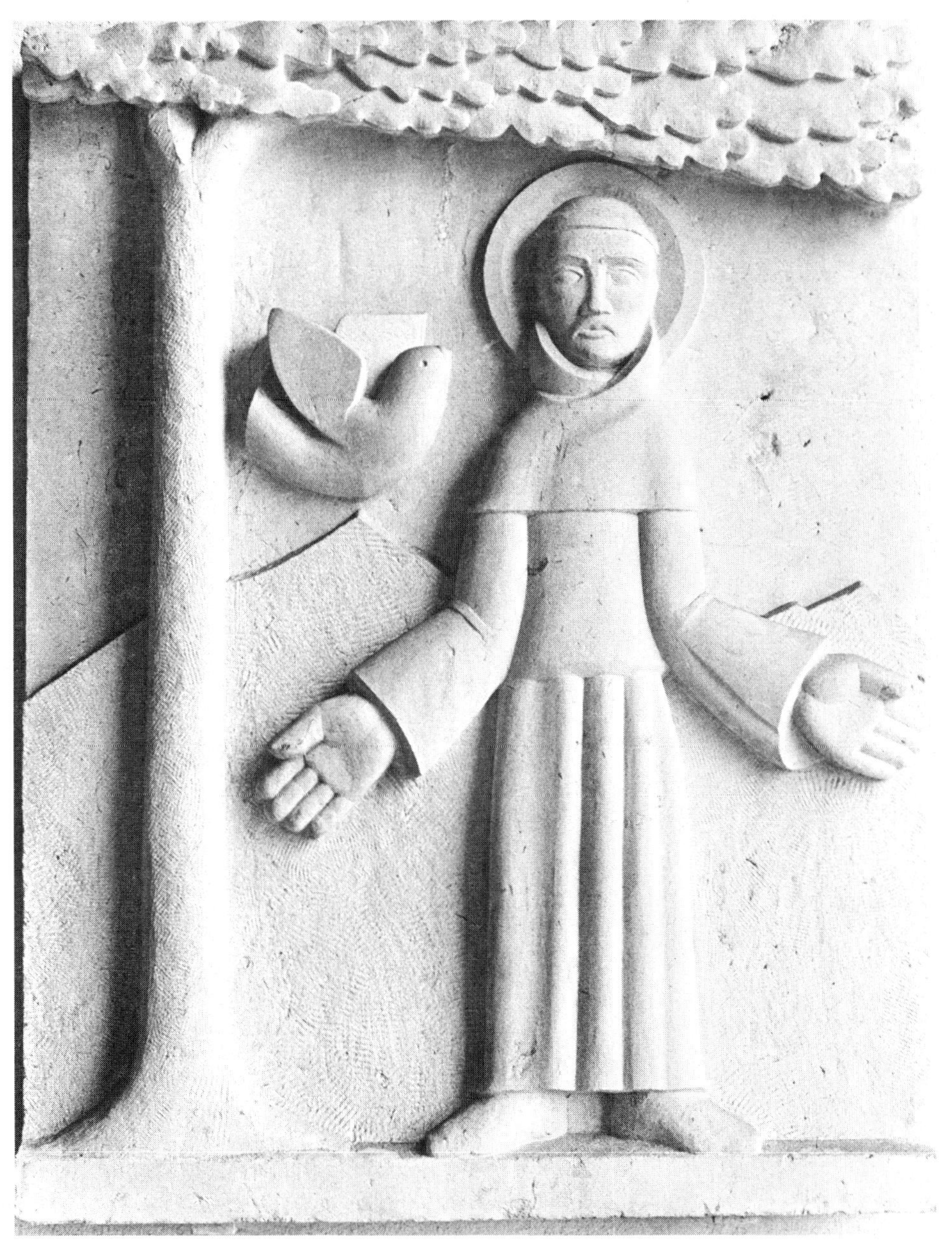

the great calligrapher Edward Johnston at the RCA and was noted for her figure and portrait pencil studies which demonstrated her controlled and skilful handling.

John Luke's mural represented, with a decorative but cavalier attitude to history, the *Reading of the Town's First Charter 1613* by a bearded Jacobean gentleman to a scattered gathering of handloom weavers, rope-makers, and builders of a wooden ship; a true *mural* painted on the wall surface, unlike those by Conor and Gordon and Hunter in the City Museum at Stranmillis. This was followed by a commission for a *Building of the Temple* (1955) for the Provincial Lodge Room in the Masonic Hall, Rosemary Street, Belfast, and another which the artist's irresolution never permitted him to finish. Now teaching at the College of Art, and carving emblematic panels for Government House at Hillsborough, Luke's last significant easel painting was *Madonna and Child*, commissioned by a County Armagh Catholic priest in 1948, when he was living at Knappagh; a man obsessed and brought to a halt by the convolutions of his thought.

Another Festival show, that arranged by the Royal Society of Ulster Artists' Design Group of whom Denis Hanna was a member, took over a bombed-out corner of Castle Street, with a display of architectural photographs, a *patio* garden and a living room with specially designed furniture and a few sympathetic paintings by William Scott and sculptures by George MacCann and F E McWilliam whose concrete *Man and Wife*, a close-wrought composite figure topped by two masks, afterward passed into the Art Gallery's collection, where it was subsequently joined by his bronze portrait of William Scott.

In 1947 Colin Middleton with his wife and family joined Middleton Murry's community-farm project at Thelnetham, East Anglia. He stayed a year, painting, I believe, only one canvas of that flat Constable landscape. Settling in County Down, he was given a contract by Victor Waddington and had a highly successful Dublin show, *Paintings 1942-49*, which placed him firmly among the artists of the whole country. These thirty pictures included townscapes like *Nelson Street*, country themes like *Glenwherry*, but also *Columbus* (1947) with the tilted boat stranded on the bare sand's edge, the still life group of the mandolin and the sheets of music, while an almost transparent female nude half-materialises from the even expanse of sky; *Elijah* (1948) with the beautifully modelled madonna with strange accessories and the duplicated prophet in two sizes, but most memorable of all, *Jacob wrestling with the Angel* (1948), the sloping-shouldered patriarch standing with the butterfly resting on his coarse thumb.

In May 1951 Waddington arranged for a team of artists under his sponsorship, to be shown in the Arthur Tooth Gallery in the Bond Street acre, under the title of *Five Irish Painters*, two of whom need hardly concern us, Thurloe Connolly, a Dublin artist and Nevill Johnson who, though English, had spent some years in Belfast before settling in Dublin. The other three were Gerard Dillon, Dan O'Neill, and Colin Middleton. That show included Dillon's *Lonely Boy*, an urchin squatting on a tombstone inside a roofless Irish Romanesque ruin, O'Neill's *Gamekeeper*, a man with a stick in the foreground of a low landscape with houses and a swirling sky above, and Middleton's *Halloween*, one of his groups of moonfaced figures against a night-town background, illustrated in the catalogue. Tooths were hosts also to a further Middleton exhibition, *Paintings 1947-52* in October of the last year. Among the twenty-seven canvasses *Point of Phenick* (c 1950), one of his best seascapes, with the moving sculpture of the great waves and the flat-topped tocks, *Give me to Drink* (1949) of Christ and the woman of Samaria, purchased by the Contemporary Art Society, now in the Ulster Museum, and *Girl with an Owl* (1951), one of the artist's own favourites.

Four years before the first exhibition at Tooths, CEMA had been called upon to arrange a representative, if small, show at the newly acquired home of the London Office of the Northern Ireland Government. This consisted of five paintings by William Conor, by now a member of the RHA, five landscapes by Frank McKelvey, five, from several periods, by Colin Middleton, three by John Luke, two townscapes of Derry by John Hunter, two by Rowel Friers becoming better known as a caricaturist in humorous journals, and a solitary canvas by Sidney Smith. But it received little notice in the metropolitan press. The foreword to the catalogue attempted to explain and justify the variety and disparity of styles in even so small a selection of work. It suggested that Ulster artists may sincerely and strenuously devote their lives to working in modes of expression which have long been superseded in the places of their origin. With the acceleration in the communication and the diffusion of ideas brought about by modern agencies, this time-lag has, in recent years, been considerably shortened, so that the variety and contrast in styles is more and more apparent. It went on to consider the question that for whatever reason, historical, sociological, with us, circumstances have so far not favoured the formation of groups bound together by acceptance of common ideas and engaged upon co-operative effort in any of the arts. An artist, insisting upon his individuality, may follow his craft completely uninfluenced by the aims and practices of his fellows. Craig, among our stronger painters, was alone in having many following his practice. Middleton, by contrast, though he derived aesthetic nourishment from many elsewhere, was the head of no school or group. Luke, another lonely figure among the Ulster painters, seemed to have attacted no more than momentary imitation. The paramount reason in this may have been that these two were superlative technicians, too skilled easily to emulate. But a practical factor may well have been that landscape based upon certain aspects of the northern Irish countryside provided themes and a more readily assimilable style which had proved popular with the local picture-buying public.

When, in 1951, the organiser of the Scottish Committee of the Arts Council selected the material for an exhibition of *Contemporary Ulster Paintings* for showing in Edinburgh in return for the Scottish Exhibition shown here at the invitation of CEMA, two years earlier, it was drawn, with four exceptions, from the Lewinter Frankl collection. This exercise of an outside independent judgment was indeed a tribute to the quality of that collection, and the four excepted works, from the City Art Gallery and from CEMA itself, were by artists who were also among those with paintings lent by Anny and Zoltan Lewinter Frankl.

Certainly, most of the painters whose pictures had been chosen by the Scottish organiser were those one should have expected: Campbell, Carr, Conor, Craig, Dillon, Hunter, Middleton, O'Neill, the last two with five each, being best represented. However, the inclusion of Paul Nietsche, Nevill Johnston and H E Broderick might have seemed anomalous to a selector aware of the inherent difficulties in defining the characteristics of those who best fitted the designation of 'Ulster Artist', for none of these three was native to this island. If Broderick, an Englishman, had made any relevant contribution to local art, it had surely been in the handful of colour-linocuts of Derry. But the choosing of Alicia Boyle and Markey Robinson was, indeed, a welcome affirmation. Born in Siam, of an Ulster family long resident in north Antrim, Alicia Boyle had spent much of her childhood in the country round Limavady and Magilligan. Trained at the Byam Shaw School of Art, she had exhibited in London, and taught in various English towns, but, since 1945 had spent her holidays painting in West Donegal, Londonderry and the Glens of Antrim. Her distinctive style of subtle colour and bold outline gave her subjects, drawn from the rural scene, from country folk at their work, in byre, in barn, at the fair or the *ceilidh*, an unusual intensity of feeling which carried them over into the terrain of myth, archetypal, emblematic. The self-taught Belfast-man, Markey Robinson had been a shipyard worker, a boxer, toy maker, decorator of glasses, turning his hands and wits to many tasks. His work had been first seen in the *Civil Defence Arts and Crafts Exhibition* in the spring of 1944 when his paintings bore such titles as *Shipyard*, *The Fleet at Bangor*, and the *Minister of Public Security inspecting NFS.* Handling gouache with great verve, his more successful landscapes had a vivid starkness of cottage gable and bare-branched tree, and, after a visit to Paris, his street scenes showed more than a hint of Utrillo's influence. It was Markey who provided the basis of the character of the painter Lukey Malquin in F L Green's Belfast novel, *Odd Man Out* (1945). Mr Green repaid the debt in part by purchasing his *Portrait of May*, an oilpainting of the artist's wife, its composition and surface recalling O'Neill and Modigliani, the best of Robinson's few essays in actual portraiture, though he used figures to some effect in other compositions. Primitive painting and drawing had, of course, occurred before. William Miller of Lurgan has already been mentioned, the first of whom we have record; and, in the Armagh County Museum, there is a large complicated pen and ink drawing by Robert Donnolly, whose *Poems on Various Subjects, Moral, Religious and Satirical* was published in Portadown in 1852. This, centred on the buildings and vehicles involved in the activities of the Railway Station, aligns the people, carts and carriages round the margins in a continuous flow regardless of perspective. And, throughout the province in working-class districts, the gable paintings illustrating political events or persons prominently associated with them, were primitive too, but usually conceived within the strict limits of an

62 ALICIA BOYLE
The White Horse
n d; oil; 76 x 100 cms; Arts Council of Northern Ireland collection

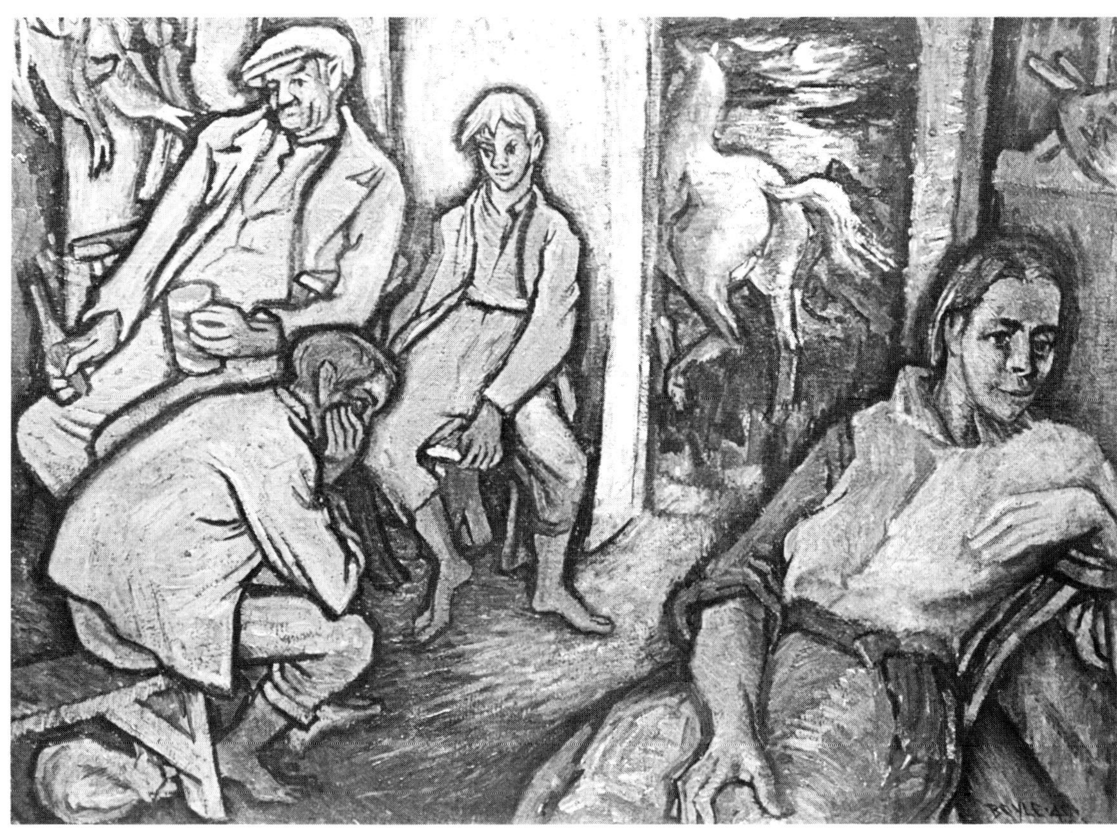

accepted convention which eliminated the quirks and quiddities of individual expression. Oddly enough, I recall John Luke telling me that in his boyhood he had painted a gable in the approved manner.

But it was not until 1955 that opportunity arose for us to see the work of Gretta Bowen, an old lady of seventy-three, mother of Arthur and George Campbell, who had taken to painting and drawing four years earlier. A genuine primitive of the Grandma Moses kind, she used chalk, wax crayons, gouache and oil paints, prefering the last, as, she said, 'richer looking', not mixing her colours but taking them straight out of the tube. Her innocent practice was to begin at the top of the picture, as, by leaning forward over a 'wet' passage of pigment, 'you may get paint on your clothes'. With no preliminary sketch, she drew directly with the brush in full colour. Her subjects, taken from memory, the memories of a long life, memories of girlhood, of a photograph in a newspaper seen only the day before, reminding her of a childhood incident; and these memories were preponderatingly happy, of merry activities, of places pleasant to a child, of festive occasions, military bands and marquees, swathes of bunting, flowerbeds in parks, yachts, cats, and little houses, typical among the coruscations of her imagination. Her figures were never intended as portraits; they were people engaged with life, nuns, coming back from church, walking past a lopsided fountain's jet, a woman in a kitchen cleaning fish, with a basket of washing on the floor, and a white-whiskered cat patiently waiting.

Another interesting primitive had come to notice just a year earlier, with the annual Exhibition of the Coleraine Art Society. An elderly Scottish engineer, Andrew Foyer by name, had, in his retirement, taken up painting. Sometimes transposing from postcard views, he also arranged still life groups and painted them. For one of these, *Primroses in a Japanese Jar* (1954) he spent the winter on the complicated detail of the highly decorative receptacle before the primroses were out; these, in due season, he recorded in leaf and bud, in full bloom, in full face and in profile, giving, as an interested botanist remarked, 'all the information you'd need about the Primrose'. Examined carefully, the rim of the lip can just be detected, slightly raised, beneath the painted petals, proving that the jar was completed, ready for the flowers to come. Primitive paintings can often be naive, sometimes clumsy, often incompetent, but never dull or empty of feeling.

Of the same generation as the Campbell, Dillon, O'Neill trio, often exhibiting with them in mixed shows, but not closely associated, the MacCabes, Gladys and Max, came to notice about the same time in the nineteen forties. They took part in that exhibition of *Contemporary Irish Painting* sent out from Dublin to America in 1950, and, besides, unlike the three, being members of the Ulster Academy, had their own joint shows in Dublin and London — in one of the latter, Max received enthusiastic commendation for one particular painting of fishes, from Percy Wyndham Lewis, then art-critic of *The Listener* — though there was an inevitable kinship apparent in general colour and handling, with Max, his subjects, frequently of fishes or of imaginary landscape, seemed, by inhabiting an enclosed or private world, to be more introverted, Gladys, more extrovert, and with more bravura, seemed to have wider sensory awareness, with a marked gusto for the public occasions, highly crowded activities, race-meetings, regattas — I recollect one pen and wash drawing of men digging up a city road, brisk notation indicating men, watchman's hut and background buildings in a summary fashion — and in the contrasting textures of still life.

In 1951 the MacCabes exhibiting in the first show of the Contemporary Ulster Group, had, among their fellow exhibitors Angela Antrim and Kathleen Bridle but the Group was short-lived.

That year, which began the second half of the twentieth century, saw also in the very next month the first exhibition of *Oil Paintings* by Deborah Brown, a young woman of twenty-four. She had had lessons from Sidney Smith, attended the Belfast College of Art, the National College of Art, Dublin, and spent some time in Paris. The thirty-five paintings of which it consisted were very largely of landscape, woodland and river — October evening on the Seine, of Dublin and the country of the Middle Glens of Antrim — her parents had long had a pleasant house at Cushendun — but, though some early pieces showed a very natural indebtedness to Craig who had been a friend of her father, she had a predilection for the subtleties of winter rather than the summer lushness, the textures of treebole and branch rather than the burden of heavy foliage. Then, in 1956, she was given an exhibition in the City Art Gallery which comprised thirty-six paintings of a very different kind carried out in a broad forceful expressionist manner in non-naturalistic colour. These fell into several groups, those consisting of single figures, those of single figures in little crowds, and, thirdly, in larger decoratively organised panels clustering round the ancient Irish *Legend of the Three Cows*, vividly evoked in flowing pigment, or dealing with religious themes, such as *Procession to the Altar in the Woods* and, in the latest works, moving towards a greater and greater degree of abstraction, always with the same breadth of handling and the same painterly gestures.

The most memorable local show in 1952 was the exhibition, sponsored by CEMA and held at Stranmillis, of forty-five paintings by Dan O'Neill, chosen from his work from 1944 to that date. Here was the impact of a thoroughgoing romantic, his subjects, often of a single figure, compacted of layers of association, emotional, or of form, which represented, in the mind of the viewer, whole clusters of feelings, of memories drawn from his or her culturally-conditioned imaginings. So, one painting, *Young Man with a Rose*, to one viewer, seemed sentimental, yet was also 'Dowson remembering Cynara, Yeats and his Secret Rose, Rilke and his destiny, Narcissus, the contemplator and the object contemplated fused in a unity-of-contemplation'. The only other Ulster painter who could present images of such ambiguity and intensity in a single thrust, was, of course, Middleton, but if, for O'Neill, the painting seems to demand the formulation of its verbal equivalent, for Middleton the greater complexity of the image and the more resourceful the technique he brings to bear, make this an even more difficult effort.

Sculpture had always been something of a minority art and interest. In mixed exhibitions by local societies, it resolved into a couple of modelled heads on pedestals in the corners, and a few small figurines on a baize-covered table. So, a trifle belatedly, in the early spring of 1953, CEMA, in an attempt to draw attention to the state of the art locally, in Ireland, and in Great Britain, where, following the break-through of Moore and Hepworth, a vigorous school of young sculptors was emerging, calling upon the help of the British Arts Council, of the very few collectors in the north, and of individual artists, organised a very miscellaneous show. The display of sixty-nine pieces included Moore's *Family Group* and *Rocking Chair*, Epstein's *George Bernard Shaw* and three other busts borrowed from the Lewinter-Frankl collection, and another bronze by him lent by Miss Helen Campbell, a Robert Adams, a Lynn Chadwick and an Uli Nimptsch from the Arts Council. F E McWilliam had a *Seated Figure* and an early *Cain and Abel*.

Three items from Oisin Kelly brought in the best of Irish sculptors.

Rosamund Praeger, with her well loved *Philo-osopher*, Morris Harding, with leopards and a tiger, Frank Wiles, with a *Negro* head and a display-tailed *Turkey*, and Anne Acheson, Ulster-born but long working in London, were our accepted figures. A bust of *Denis Ireland* by John Langtry Lynas brought to mind that versatile, if eccentric, little man. John Luke with two stone carvings and the plaster *St Patrick*, George MacCann and Elizabeth McCord with works in wood, brass and pottery recalled the Ulster Unit group of almost twenty years before. Angela Antrim, with three heads by herself, and the *Portrait of Gandhi* by Clare Sheridan, which she owned, reminded us that *Gandhi* had been last seen with the Contemporary Ulster Group in 1951, when Clare Sheridan, now living in Galway, and Lady Antrim had been the sculptors. The latter had exhibited at the RA from the age of seventeen, and, more recently, at the RHA and in the Irish Exhibition of Living Art, her most attractive work the boldly modelled Daumieresque figures.

There were about twenty other pieces which would now have little interest, but reference should be made to the four wood exhibits by Ian Friers, whose skill in adapting pieces of tree-trunks or timber to anthropomorphic shapes, among the local work, struck a witty note in the general cacophony.

In the same year, in the gallery, 55A Donegall Place, Rowel Friers, Ian's younger but much better known brother, was given his first one man show. This consisted of twenty paintings, and a host of drawings, cartoons and illustrations, and, measured by the attendance of visitors, was the most popular of the one man exhibitions of the past years. The most versatile of his generation, Friers had produced a steady flow of book illustrations, book plates, caricatures and cartoons, designs ranging from Christmas cards to stage-sets, and oil paintings. The paintings, in the manipulation of pigment, placed him with John Luke and Colin Middleton, rather than with the majority of his less dexterous contemporaries. But, as his interest was emphatically figurative, and so much of his craftsmanship involved in the interpretation of human character and behaviour, his paintings were descriptive of mood or event, never moving out of the area of illustration into the abstract, non-representational, and, by the use of humorous detail or exaggeration, were doubly debarred from the approval of the *avant-garde* aesthetician.

Very likely the most accomplished of Ulster draughtsmen, Hugh Thomson and George Morrow, though different in range and intention, both had, to achieve fulfillment of their talents, to seek employment outside their native province. So, too, with David Wilson. But the prosperous years in the life of the humorous journal *Dublin Opinion* gave some of their successors in the field of black and white illustration the chance to see their work published in their own country. W H Conn limited himself to painstakingly detailed evocation of rather sentimental occasions, demonstrating a firm persistence in a kind of vision which seemed stubbornly anachronistic; in this an example of that 'time-lag', which, for so long determined style and technique in the arts and much else, of Ulster.

Rowel Friers, on the other hand, well-informed in the current practice on both sides of the Atlantic, was able to place his work in *Punch, London Opinion* and other metropolitan journals, without any fear of provinciality, while remaining on his native ground. In the years before the temper of the time drove him into the area of political comment, when he became a pertinent social critic with deep liberal sympathies, it was fair to assert — I quote from the foreword to his book of cartoons, *Wholly Friers* (1948).

> 'His is a broad world and a friendly world, not a narrow sector of eccentricity... A merry world which gently mocks our pretentious planning and our monstrous materialism, our too-readily-accepted conventions, for it admits the train without tracks, the forgetful elephant, and the bugle in the back street. Friers' pirates are genial ruffians who knit socks and slip little schooners into bottles. His highwaymen have a quiet dignity. His assassins carry rubber daggers. His ghosts are good spirits. His travellers declare their innocence.'

Kenneth Mahood who began as a promising draughtsman and a painter more in tune with recent aesthetic formulations than Friers, when he too turned to humorous drawings, proved himself technically equipped, but without any reference to, or overt evidence of, his native *milieu* when he made his career outside.

But Elizabeth Shaw travelled farther. Born in York Street, Belfast, where her father was manager of a bank, educated at the Belfast Royal Academy when A R Foster was headmaster, she left in her teens for England, studied graphics in London, married a refugee German sculptor, and, after the war, went to live in East Berlin, where she is now recognised as a leading graphic artist in the German Democratic Republic. Her collaboration with a woman poet has taken her over most of eastern Europe and into Asia, their journeys recounted in vivid drawings and amusing verses. It is, perhaps, in Bertolt Brecht's *Ein Kinderbuch*, that a first-rate example of her direct but thoughtful, good humour can most readily be appreciated.

If, as has been suggested, the visual genius of this island is not three dimensional but linear, then, perhaps, this little company, from Hugh Thomson to Elizabeth Shaw, can be taken as true exponents of a natural trait, even though their individual impacts upon us have been diverse and disparate, and not easily to be resolved into a coherent convention.

When Richard Hayward, that energetic man, embarked upon his shelf of books about Ireland the choice of an illustrator was close to his purpose. For the first and best known, *In Praise of Ulster* (1938), James Humbert Craig supplied the wash drawings. But this artist could only express his vision in colour, his drawings lacked authority or conviction, as if he did not much care for what he was being asked to do. For *In the Kingdom of Kerry* (1946) Hayward brought in Theo J Gracey. His drawings, expressed with a firm line of unvarying strength, had the effect of unfocussed monotony; the outline of a cloud as harsh as the edge of a mountain; foreground and background a palimpsest of strokes. So *Leinster and the City of Dublin* (1949) was first of

63 ROWEL FRIERS
Illustration from *This Happy Morning* by Janet McNeill, Faber and Faber, London, 1959

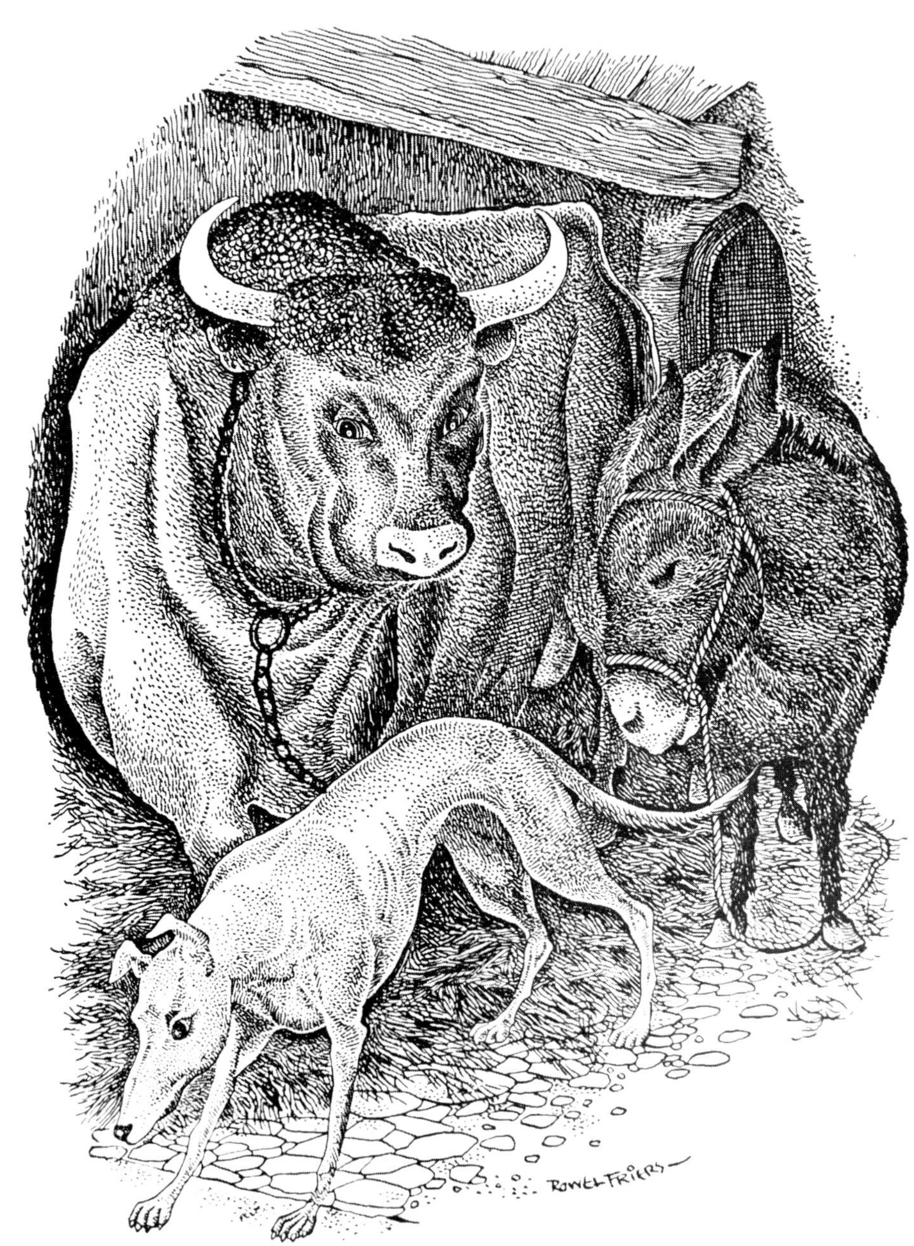

64 ELIZABETH SHAW
Illustration from *Ein Kinderbuch* by Bertolt Brecht, Der Kinderbuchverlag, Berlin, n d

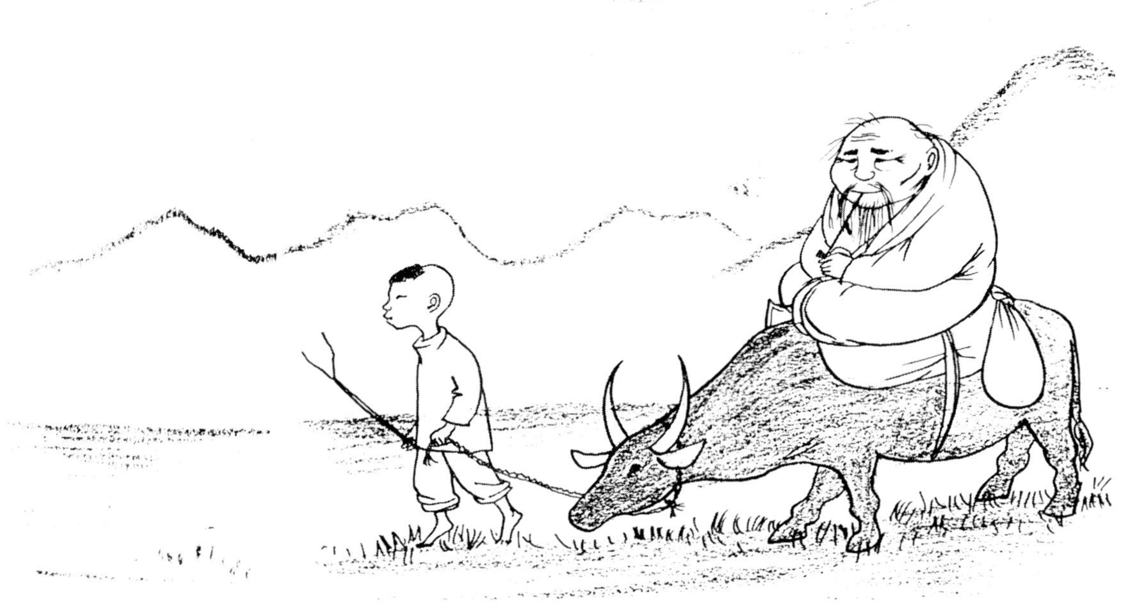

Raymond Piper's collaborations with the author. At once it was apparent that the young artist's accurate pencil with its well modulated range of tone lay on the page alongside the printed words in an effective harmony. When he was bidden again to illustrate *Connacht and the City of Galway* (1952), his even skill was shown in sketch of ruined abbey or castle, in city lane, or in the reliefs on a high cross, for Piper was a very experienced descriptive draughtsman, what was before him he could record without fumbling or hesitation. But when, in 1957, he supplied only the coloured book jacket to *Border Foray* by the same author, his hand faltered. It became a scramble of little not very original humorous groups, a marked failure of imagination. He could have drawn a black pig rooting in the ground, but not the Black Pig of legend. Still, a man should be grateful for his gift. In May 1953, CEMA had given him his first one man show which, oddly enough, did not include any of his recent topographical drawings. Instead it presented him as a portraitist in oil and in pastel. The paintings were mostly of known public persons seen in their rôles. *The Playwright, The Actor, The Coroner, The Connoisseur* — this last, Zoltan Lewinter Frankl — but at that time, he had not grown to control and enjoy the brush so much as he did the pencil, and their interest now is that these were the apprentice efforts of the older man who came to monopolise the Mayoral portraits in the Belfast City Hall and other borough offices. The pastels, largely of children, were happier, and the couple of pencil drawings of old corners of Belfast, commissioned for the Gallery's local collection, showed him in secure familiar vein.

By 1954, a decade after the coming of Campbell, Dillon and O'Neill, none of whom had stayed long enough at the College of Art to be shaped by the experience, a wave of younger artists began piling-up, when students who had taken advantage of the full College course began exhibiting. In the month of February, Robert Linton, painter and sculptor, who had also attended the Central School, London, and Martin McKeown, painter, had their first one man shows, and were followed by three painters together, Wilfred Stewart, Terence P Flanagan, and Lewis Logan, in the down town gallery, 55A Donegall Place. Then, in February 1955, Basil Blackshaw, whose work had been seen in mixed exhibitions for the past few years, had his first one man show in the same gallery. With these, public awareness of the emergence of a new, vigorous and varied generation of schooled artists was evident. And when, next year, the Lewinter-Frankl collection of *Contemporary Irish Drawings* was exhibited at Stranmillis in the summer, three of the College's recent pupils, Blackshaw, Flanagan, and Cherith Boyd, were included, that perceptive patron already alert to their promise.

But these artists, all being under thirty years of age, have their place in a later story; that is, those among them who continued as exhibiting painters and did not become immersed in teaching, or found other channels for their talents. Of course, this attempt to fix a rigid time-grid on an endless flow creates many difficulties which, it could be argued, invalidate any strict systematisation. For example, James MacIntyre and Deborah Brown were both within a year or two of, say, Cherith Boyd and Terence Flanagan, but, for various reasons, were not closely associated with the College, and, anyhow, had begun exhibiting before 1954, and their individual styles evidenced no marked affinity to each other or to the rest. Kenneth Mahood, largely self-taught, also stood apart, though of the same age-group, perhaps, alone in his essays in abstraction, a pictorial mode to which Blackshaw and his fellows were temperamentally averse, considering it 'empty'.

There had never been at any time enough work in the north to engage more than a small handful of artists and yield them a living by the practice of their skill and craft. So the steady outward flow of native talent to other market places was a regular phenomenon, from Hugh Thomson to Kenneth Mahood. Often their some way distant success was a matter of pride to those who were left, but, just as often, the work accomplished failed to have any influence on those active in the arts at home.

Portraiture, an obvious stand-by once, did not promise a consistent demand since the middle of last century, when even Hooke, who painted nothing else, in the end married a wealthy widow and left for Manchester. And since then, as photography, cheaper and more convenient, has rendered likeness-catching in paint obsolete, their need diminished. The social function of the prestige-portrait which recorded or celebrated the rôle of the sitter, certifying his or her place in the class structure has withered away. Even miniatures, so popular at the beginning of the nineteenth century, and much less ostentatious than the easel-painting, have all but disappeared. The main field of the artists' activity was and has largely remained, the landscape in oil or, more often, in watercolour.

Yet even in this, to take the three most interesting watercolourists of Victorian times, Andrew Nicholl moved for periods of varying duration to London, to Dublin as promise of work appeared; James Moore, a busy doctor and useful committeeman could only afford to take his paintbox and brushes when he went on holiday; Howard Burgess took private pupils in Donegall Place, and, when chance offered, accepted any commission Marcus Ward's gave. That firm, during the years of its prosperity, provided employment, and for the younger folk, training which was not wholly at odds with their personal interests. J W Carey, with a long career as a prolific and prosperous watercolourist, carried out murals on historical subjects for the Ulster Hall, and used, from time to time, to decorate or illuminate official presentation addresses, a craft which he had learned from Vinycomb. Later, David Allen's gave work and training to many. Teaching drawing in schools served men like Joseph Molloy, W R Gordon and Charles Braithwaite, but such posts were rare, and not until the College of Art was able to provide courses to qualify students to become teachers in state-provided schools, designing for the textile industry was a means of support, so that John McBurney, John A MacAllister, and Charles Harvey and Colin Middleton, till they moved into teaching, leaned upon it. For, from about 1930, it was teaching in the College or in the schools, which, with their long vacations, made possible most of the creditable work which has appeared, a circumstance not in any way unique to Northern Ireland.

Throughout this discursive narrative it must have been apparent that the suggestion or implication that anyone named should necessarily have been considered an Ulster artist, has been put forward without dogmatism. Being born here is not in itself enough. John B Yeats, painter of so many interesting portraits of Irishmen and women of his time, was born at Tullylish, County Down, but it would be absurd to claim him. Oliver Sheppard, born at Cookstown, County Tyrone, was taken to Dublin as an infant and achieved his reputation as a sculptor there. He is, of course, best known for that bronze statue of the *Dying Cúchullain* which stands in the Dublin GPO, a national monument. Yet, oddly enough, the head of that ambiguous hero was modelled from the sculptor's friend, James S Sleator, of Armagh. But even that does not invalidate his exclusion. However, this is not only an Ulster-Irish phenomenon: Epstein was born in New York, but that did not make him an American sculptor, any more than the circumstance that Jack B Yeats, John B's son, was born in London made him an English painter.

When Conor Cruise O'Brien, reviewing an anthology of Irish verse, set himself to consider the question of Irishness, he decided that 'the thing can be done, I believe, if we adopt a historical rather than a geographical point of view. Irishness is not primarily a question of birth or blood or language; it is the condition of being involved in the Irish situation, and usually of being mauled by it.' If we can, for a moment, thrust aside the harsh reality of that last consequential clause, we could well rewrite the sentence to read, 'being an Ulster artist is not *primarily* a question of birth, of blood or accent; it is the condition of being involved in Ulster life and Irish landscape, and finding therein the material for his art'; and that is as near a definition as we shall ever reach. For, though history has dealt differently with the north-eastern counties and left the majority of their people with another ancestry and faith, they are, irrevocably, inhabitants of the same island within the British archipelago, and all that that implies.

To select any particular date as marking the end of a period during a continuing process must always be an arbitrary decision, like ending a financial year on 31st March. Yet to close the narrative here has a certain logic, apart from the fact that I was no longer professionally involved in what was happening to art in Ulster. For, in 1958, the gallery at 55A Donegall Place was to become no longer available to CEMA which had to spend some time in finding a replacement. It had been the utilisation of that bare room for repeated exhibitions, which, reinforced by the City Art Gallery's series of local one man shows, created an unprecedented opportunity for the artists and art societies in the area to display their works, familiarising the interested public with the habit of easy exhibition-visiting and presenting them with the ready possibility of making purchases. In that place, in one short span of weeks, Rowel Friers, William Conor, and the MacCabes had each attracted over 2,000 visitors.

The post-war years, too, had been those in which our first serious Art collector had set an impressive example to the community, culminating in the exhibition of the *Lewinter-Frankl Collection* in the City Art Gallery in March 1958, including, with English, Scottish, Continental painters, particularly rich in works by Jack B Yeats and Stanley Spencer, paintings and drawings by a score of northerners from the seventy-seven year old Conor to Blackshaw who was twenty-six.

By this time, too, many senior artists had died or were soon to die; Nietsche, Hunter, Gordon, Praeger, Hull, Lynas, Gould. The youngest apprentice of Marcus Ward's had gone; nor could one readily name any surviving student of the old Government School of Art.

CEMA, with its own collection, had been as generous in patronage as its funds permitted; when, in 1955, an Exhibition of *Modern Ulster Paintings* was specially selected for showing in Londonderry, twenty items were lent by the Belfast City Art Gallery, and sixteen came from CEMA's own holding. As part of its policy, CEMA, with its awards of frugal travelling scholarships, had attempted to widen the horizons of the younger artists of promise, and to educate the general public also by bringing works not readily accessible to local notice, contemporary Italian, Australian, Dutch, Scottish, to recall the best. But soon CEMA was to shed its chrysalis and become the Arts Council of Northern Ireland, developing a more professional expertise, with a more liberal budget. For, in 1957 also, Captain Terence O'Neill became Minister of Finance in the Stormont Administration, and, in this office and later as Prime Minister, saw the admirable re-housing of the Public Records Office, the establishment of the Ulster Folk Museum at Cultra, the beginning of the re-organisation and completion of what was to be renamed the Ulster Museum at Stranmillis, and, a minor but no less praiseworthy gesture, the granting of the first civil list pensions to a brace of elderly artists, all, as it were, suggesting the emergence of a cultural regional consciousness.

BIOGRAPHIES

LADY MABEL ANNESLEY 1881-1959
Wood engraver of landscapes and watercolourist

Born 25 February 1881, daughter of Hugh, fifth Earl Annesley, of Castlewellan, Co Down. In 1895 studied art at the Frank Calderon School of Animal Painting. The Belfast Art Society received her into membership in 1899. Studied wood engraving at the Central School of Arts and Design under Noel Rooke, 1920-1921, and was elected a member of the Society of Wood Engravers in 1924. She illustrated two Duckworth books by Richard Rowley, *Apollo in Mourne*, a play, and *County Down Songs*. A commission followed to decorate the limited edition of *Songs from Robert Burns* for the Golden Cockerel Press, then run by an Irishman, Robert Gibbings (1889-1955). An active member of the Belfast Art Society, she lectured on 'Wood Engraving' at 12 Lombard Street, Belfast. Later at the same address, also in 1925, she exhibited her collection of engravings. In 1933 she had a one woman show at the Batsford Gallery, London, and also exhibited in Dublin. In 1938 she showed with the Dublin Painters, and in the following year she generously presented Belfast Museum and Art Gallery with one hundred contemporary wood engravings, including some of her own. The British Museum also holds her work. During the Second World War Lady Mabel, who suffered from severe arthritis, especially in her hands which made woodcutting difficult, left her home at 44 University Road, Belfast, settling in New Zealand, near Nelson. Returning to England about 1953, she died at Clare, Sudbury, Suffolk, on 19 June 1959. A memorial exhibition of the work of three of the earliest members of the Society of Wood Engravers — Mabel Annesley, Robert Gibbings and Gwen Raverat — took place at the Whitworth Art Gallery, Manchester, 1960. An unfinished autobiography, *As the Sight is Bent*, edited by Constance Malleson, appeared in 1964.

ARTHUR ARMSTRONG 1924-
Landscape painter

Born in Carrickfergus, he was sketching by the age of four. Allowing for half a year at the Belfast College of Art, he was practically self-taught. Soon after he began to work professionally, the Walsh Studio in Dublin published *Eight Reproductions by two Irish Artists, George Campbell and Arthur Armstrong* (1947). Armstrong was also a contemporary in Belfast of Gerard Dillon (q v) and Daniel O'Neill (q v). In later years, after moving from London to Dublin in 1962, he shared a house with Dillon in Ranelagh. In 1957 he won a travel scholarship from CEMA and visited Spain. In recent years he has held one man exhibitions at two leading Madrid galleries. CEMA in 1961 and the Arts Council of Northern Ireland in 1966 also staged one man shows. Winner of the President Hyde gold medal at the Oireachtas exhibition in 1968, the following year he became an Associate of the Royal Hibernian Academy; in 1972, a Member. His paintings have also been shown at the Irish Exhibition of Living Art. At Belmont House School, Londonderry, there is a play sculpture which he constructed in connection with the Arts Council of Northern Ireland's Art in Context scheme. Inspiration for many of his landscapes emanated in the West of Ireland. Arthur Armstrong is represented in practically all the Irish collections, including those of the Arts Councils, Belfast and Dublin, and the Ulster Museum.

JAMES ATKINS 1799-1833
Painter of portraits and figure subjects

Born in Belfast, James Atkins was the son of a Scotsman, James Atkins, who came from Stranraer. At Back Lane, off Prince's Street, Belfast, the father carried on business as a 'house, sign, and coach-painter' (1819 Belfast Directory). The son assisted his father in heraldic painting and when he was about fifteen he was sent to the drawing class at the Belfast Academical Institution under the Italian, Gaetano Fabbrini (q v). After studying there for four years he gained a prize medal. Following the midsummer examinations at the school in 1818, this notice was published in the *Belfast News-Letter*: 'Mr James Atkins, junr., a pupil in the drawing school of the Academical Institution, gained the prize medal for oil portrait painting. His performances do this young man much honour, and they remain at the Institution for the inspection of the public.' Thanks to the financial aid of patrons, the Marquis of Downshire, the Marquis of Londonderry and a Mrs Batt of Purdysburn, Atkins visited Italy in 1819. 'He who improvises can never fashion a perfect line of poetry,' declared Titian, but Atkins spent thirteen years studying and copying the Old Masters in Rome, Florence and Venice. Fortunately, he copied Titian's 'St Peter Martyr', destroyed by fire 1867. Atkins' copy is at Queen's University, Belfast. In 1831 and 1833 he showed portraits at the Royal Academy, London. In December, 1832, he had travelled from Rome to Constantinople to paint the Sultan. His health became impaired and he removed to Malta, where he died at Valetta in December, 1833. More than a year after his death an advertisement appeared in a Belfast newspaper: 'The late Mr Atkins' Paintings. To be sold by auction at No 8 Donegall Place on Tuesday, 31 March, 1835, at 12 o'clock noon, the entire paintings of the late Mr James Atkins, a native of this town, but latterly residing at Rome... Admittance sixpence. Catalogues to be had of George C Hyndman, 7 Castle Place, Belfast.' The Ulster Museum has three works by Atkins, including a copy of Titian's Portrait of Lavinia, his daughter.

JAMES BLACK fl 1810-1829
Painter of landscape, portrait and inn signs

Apart from the material evidence in Armagh County Museum, where there is a large oil painting of the city of Armagh, and two drawings, not much is known about James Black, who painted some local celebrity portraits. The 'City of Armagh' painting was presented by Thomas Dobbin in 1870 to the Armagh Town Commissioners. Black is credited with painting 'most of the signs' of a dozen Armagh Inns which were in existence in 1819. Black's murder in English Street is mentioned in the *Belfast News-Letter* of 10 February, 1829, but contains no reference to an altercation or interference. The following letter appeared in *The Armagh Guardian*, 16 December 1870, signed by the rather inappropriate pseudonym of 'Civis':- 'A few facts regarding the Painting of Armagh, presented to the inhabitants of this city, by Mr Dobbin, may be interesting to your readers. The oil-painting is dated 1810, and gives a very good view of the city of Armagh, crowned by the old Cathedral, with the lofty spire which used to top the venerable edifice. Black, the artist, wished to part with the picture, and offered it by raffle. There were 30 subscribers at £1 each, and the picture was won by Robert Steen, a tanner, who used to live in the house occupied by Mr McClelland. Reverses came over Mr Steen, and the picture ultimately passed into the hands of Mr Dobbin. A word as to Black. In 1829, he was returning home one night, and on passing the house of a butcher named Fealey, he heard an altercation going on between the butcher and his wife. He interfered, and was struck with a cleaver on the head, and died a few days later.'

GRETTA BOWEN 1880-
Primitive painter

Harbour House, North Circular Road, Dublin was the birthplace on New Year's Day, 1880, of Margretta Bowen, daughter of Samuel Arthur Bowen, a Midland Great Western Railway official. She married, in Dublin, Matthew Campbell, who moved North in 1921 to start a catering business. He was a native of Caledon, Co Tyrone. In 1925 he died and his widow took in boarders to support herself and her three sons, Arthur, Stanley and George (q v), all of whom later painted. A few weeks before her seventieth birthday Gretta Bowen, untutored, began to paint herself. In 1955 CEMA arranged in Belfast a one woman show. In the same year an article about her appeared in *The Times* of London. She has exhibited in several group exhibitions, at home and abroad. In Dublin her works have been seen at the Irish Exhibition of Living Art, the Royal Hibernian Academy, and the Oireachtas. Her sons Arthur and George have exhibited with her at the Oireachtas and the Royal Hibernian Academy. Other one woman exhibitions in Belfast were: 1965 Bell Gallery; 1970 and 1976 Tom Caldwell Gallery. An Arts Council of Northern Ireland poster print in 1974 of her painting 'Rustic Sports' proved very popular. A portrait of Gretta Bowen by her son George was commissioned in 1975 by the Arts Council of Northern Ireland, and appeared in the 'Women of Ulster' exhibition. She is represented at the Ulster Museum.

ALICIA BOYLE 1908-
Painter of landscapes and figure subjects

Alice Louisa Letitia Boyle, daughter of B P Boyle, MIEE, was born in Bangkok, Siam, on 1 August 1908. Her father was the second son of Major Alexander Boyle of Bridge Hill, Limavady, Co Derry. Her father had to relinquish his post with the British Dock Company in Siam because of the climate, and the family returned to Limavady in 1909. When she was aged twelve the family moved to London, and she received her education at Clapham High School, subsequently attending Clapham Art Training College and the Byam Shaw School where she won two scholarships. Since then her life has been filled with part-time teaching in several schools, lecturing and painting. In 1939 she received an invitation from the Greek Government to be guest artist at the School of Fine Art, Mykonos, Greece. Peter Jones Gallery, London, staged her first one woman exhibition in 1945. She still retained her Irish links and in 1947, for example, was painting in Co Derry and Co Donegal. In 1950 and 1952 CEMA arranged exhibitions in Belfast. In 1951, ninety works were shown at Northampton Art Gallery. In the 1950s she also exhibited at the Irish Exhibition of Living Art, Dublin; studied lithography at the Central School of Arts and Crafts, London, and painted in France, Mallorca and Spain. In 1959 she showed at the Belfast Museum and Art Gallery, again under CEMA auspices. Alicia Boyle won first prize in the 1962 CEMA open painting competition, Northern Ireland category, and the following year the Arts Council of Northern Ireland arranged a touring exhibition. In 1967 she again exhibited at the Arts Council gallery; also at the North-West Arts Festival. Since 1971 she has been living in Co Cork, exhibiting in Dublin and Cork galleries. She has also exhibited at the Oireachtas exhibition. Work is in the collections of the Arts Council of Northern Ireland, North-West Art Trust, Ulster Museum, An Chomhairle Ealáion, Dublin; Cork Municipal Art Gallery.

CHARLES BRAITHWAITE 1876-1941
Painter of landscape and craftsman

Born in Lisburn, he studied at the Government School of Design, Belfast, where he was awarded a scholarship to the Royal College of Art, London, and became skilled, under Professor W R Lethaby (1857-1931), in the applied arts of illumination, jewellery and leatherwork, examples of which he displayed at many important exhibitions in such centres as Paris, Berlin and Weimar. As a landscape painter he exhibited in the Royal Hibernian Academy, Dublin, becoming an Associate in 1914. He also exhibited with the Belfast Art Society, and at a meeting in 1912 held at the Scottish Provident Buildings he delivered a lecture on 'Illuminated Manuscripts'. In 1925 he was mentioned in *La Revue Moderne*. Charles ('Baldy') Braithwaite was on the Methodist College staff from 1909 until his death. The first ten years were in a part-time capacity as drawing master, and thereafter he became full-time and head of the newly-created department of art. He was responsible for Methody's first war memorial (1923), an example of his skill in lettering and Celtic ornament, now in the entrance foyer; the illuminated scroll at Downey House (1933) which records the school motto; and he also designed the memorial door (1936) to Mrs J W Henderson, wife of the headmaster. He died at his home, 165 Cliftonpark Avenue, Belfast, on the anniversary of his birth, 25 February 1941. The Ulster Museum has an illumination by him of W B Yeats' poem 'The Lake Isle of Innisfree.'

KATHLEEN BRIDLE 1897-
Landscape and still life painter

Kathleen Bridle's father, who was reared in Ireland, was a coastguard officer and she was born at Swalecliff, Kent, on 19 November 1897. In 1915 she went to Dublin to attend the Metropolitan School of Art and remained there until 1921, winning two silver medals and, from the Royal Dublin Society, the Taylor Art scholarship. Later she attended the Royal College of Art, London, where she was awarded a continuation scholarship and the George Clausen prize. A teacher all her life, it was in 1926 that she went to Enniskillen after spending a few months at the Harry Clarke Stained Glass Studios, Dublin. At Enniskillen, she taught at

Portora Royal School; the Convent Grammar School, Mount Lourdes; the Technical School, day and night, and, full-time, the Collegiate School, retiring from there in 1963. She taught T P Flanagan and William Scott (q v), and in 1973, under the auspices of the Arts Council of Northern Ireland, a 'Teacher and Two Pupils' exhibition was held at the gallery in Belfast and then at Enniskillen Collegiate School. Prior to that event, she had rarely exhibited in Belfast: certainly at Magee's Gallery in 1936 and at the Belfast Museum and Art Gallery in 1950. She has painted often on the Continent. An honorary academician of the Royal Ulster Academy, Kathleen Bridle has also exhibited in Dublin at the Royal Hibernian Academy, the Irish Exhibition of Living Art and the Oireachtas. Collections include Arts Council of Northern Ireland and Ulster Museum.

DEBORAH BROWN 1927-

Constructor in fibreglass and painter of abstracts

Deborah Brown, daughter of Austin Brown, estate agent, who also painted, was born in Belfast but received her first unofficial lessons in painting from J Humbert Craig (q v) in Cushendun. In 1944-1945 she attended classes held in the Belfast studio of Sidney Smith (q v). She spent some months in the Belfast College of Art, but decided on study at the National College of Art, Dublin, and was there from 1947 to 1950, moving on to Paris where she made her first contact with modern abstract art. The gallery at 55a Donegall Place, Belfast, administered by CEMA, housed her first one woman show in 1951, and four years later she had her first exhibition outside Ireland, at the British Council Rooms in Glasgow. Then in 1956 she was honoured at the Belfast Museum and Art Gallery. A member of the Women's International Art Club, London, and the Free Painters and Sculptors, London, she exhibited at the New Vision Art Centre in London in 1959 and 1964. One woman shows were held at the Arts Council of Northern Ireland Gallery in 1962 and 1969; and at the New Gallery, Belfast in 1964. Deborah Brown's work is familiar in Dublin, where she has exhibited at the David Hendriks Gallery as well as in the group exhibitions, Irish Exhibition of Living Art and the Oireachtas. In 1965 Ferranti Limited commissioned her to paint a series of eight canvases for the interior of their new building at Hollinwood, Manchester. At the Irish Exhibition of Living Art in 1970 she won the Carroll £400 open award with a fibreglass form. Collections include the Arts Councils, Belfast and Dublin; the Hugh Lane Municipal Gallery of Modern Art, Dublin, and the Ulster Museum.

ALBERT BRUCE-JOY 1842-1924

Sculptor

Son of Dr W Bruce-Joy of Belfast, Dublin and London, he was born in Dublin. Descended from an old Huguenot family which settled in Antrim in 1612 and founded the Ulster branch of the Joy family, an ancestor, Francis Joy, founded the *Belfast News-Letter*. Albert was a brother of George William Joy (1844-1925), historical and portrait painter, known in his youth as 'gentle Georgie'. The sculptor-to-be was educated at Becker's School, Offenbach; in Paris, and at King's College, London. A student at South Kensington and the Royal Academy Schools of Art, he became a pupil of the Dublin-born J H Foley (1818-1874) for four years and studied in Rome for three. Twice he visited and travelled extensively in the United States of America, and many of his statues are there and in English provincial cities. At the Paris International Exhibition of 1878 he was awarded one of three medals given to British sculptors, and other awards followed. In 1893 he was appointed a Member of the Royal Hibernian Academy. His works, many of which are colossal — he was known as 'ardent Albert' in his youth — include statues of W E Gladstone, Lord Frederick Cavendish and John Bright. Nearer home, he was responsible for the figure of Lord Kelvin in the Botanic Gardens, Belfast, and that of the recumbent Bishop Berkeley in Cloyne Cathedral. He modelled a bust of King Edward VII (Royal Academy, 1911) and was responsible for the death mask. Medallions, including one of his father and Sir G Gabriel Stokes, FRS, were also modelled, and he is represented in this medium at the Hugh Lane Municipal Gallery of Modern Art, Dublin. Work on a larger scale is at the Belfast Harbour Office and the Ulster Museum. Representation in England includes the National Portrait Gallery, the British Museum, and the Walker Art Gallery, Liverpool. He died on 22 July 1924, after a long illness, at Bramshott Chase, near Hindhead, Surrey.

JAMES HOWARD BURGESS c 1817-1890

Painter of landscapes and miniatures

He practised for many years in Belfast, the Carrickfergus area and Dublin. When he exhibited for the first time at the Royal Hibernian Academy in 1830 (presumably aged about thirteen) his address in Dublin was given in the catalogue as 11 Digges Street but this is believed to have been an accommodation address. James Howard Burgess contributed twenty-five illustrations to Halls' *Ireland, its Scenery, Character*, published in 1841. Marcus Ward, Belfast, published without a date *Illustrations of the North of Ireland*, with a guide to the Giant's Causeway, 'from drawings made expressly for the work by J Howard Burgess'. From London appeared *Burgess' Sketches from Nature in Ireland*, featured in Friedel's Drawing Book. He was living in or near Carrickfergus in 1846 when he was awarded a prize of ten pounds by the Royal Irish Art Union for a lithograph. Lamont Brothers of Belfast published a lithograph of his drawing of the opening in 1849 of the New Channel (Twin Islands). He also painted in England and Scotland, but a fair proportion of his work was associated with Irish coastal scenes. Henderson's Belfast Directory for 1850 lists J Howard Burgess' drawing academy at 16 Donegall Place, Belfast. The National Gallery of Ireland, Dublin, has watercolours of Dunluce Castle and the Giant's Causeway. The Ulster Museum collection includes an oil of Dundrum Bay; Armagh County Museum has a pencil drawing of Carlingford Lough; Belfast Harbour Office has an oil painting of Queen's Bridge, 1858; and there are lithographs at the Linen Hall Library, Belfast. In the National Library of Ireland, Dublin, there is a pencil drawing of 'Carrickfergus Castle from Innisglass Cottage, Green Island'. He died in Belfast on 9 November 1890, at the Royal Hospital, as stated in the newspaper death notice. The general register office in Belfast does not record a relevant entry.

GEORGE CAMPBELL 1917-
Painter of landscapes, figure subjects and abstracts

Born in Arklow, Co Wicklow, son of Gretta Bowen (q v), he received his schooling in Dublin. His maternal grandfather was an amateur woodcarver. The family moved from Dublin to Belfast, where he worked in various jobs but eventually decided to make a break from commercial life for full-time painting. Virtually self-taught, he struggled financially in his early painting years with Gerard Dillon (q v) and Dan O'Neill (q v). Much of his painting time was spent with Dillon in Connemara, and when they later lived in London he exhibited with him at the Piccadilly Gallery. Campbell has also exhibited in Canada, Gibraltar, Holland, Spain, South Africa and the USA. For the past twenty-five years he has been living part of the year in Malaga, Spain, where he attained proficiency as a Flamenco guitarist. In 1943 he and his artist brother Arthur published *Ulster in Black and White*. The following year was also a memorable one as they exhibited together at the Mol Gallery, Belfast, and published yet again in war-time: *Now in Ulster*. George's first one man show was at the Victor Waddington Galleries, Dublin, 1946. CEMA arranged one man exhibitions in Belfast in 1949, 1952 and 1960, followed by two under the auspices of the Arts Council of Northern Ireland: in 1966 and 1972. The Walsh Studio, Dublin, published in 1967 *Eight Reproductions by two Irish Artists, George Campbell, RHA, and Arthur Armstrong*. In 1962 George Campbell was the winner of a £500 prize in an open painting competition sponsored by CEMA. In the same year he won an award in an exhibition of modern church art held by An Chomhairle Ealáion, Dublin. In 1964 he became a full member of the Royal Hibernian Academy. Two years later he won the Douglas Hyde gold medal award at the Oireachtas exhibition, Dublin. He has also exhibited at the Irish Exhibition of Living Art, Dublin. In addition to painting, he has shown his versatility designing stained glass windows, notably for Galway Cathedral, and has written on art, in particular a series for *Artists International*. He has also broadcast, devised settings for the theatre, and illustrated the *Guide to the National Monuments in the Republic of Ireland* (1970) by Peter Harbinson. He is represented in practically all the Irish collections, from as far west as the Sligo County Library and Art Gallery to Cork Municipal Art Gallery in the South.

JOHN P CAMPBELL 1883-1962
Black and white decorative illustrator

John Patrick Campbell was born in Belfast, 7 March 1883, son of William Henry Campbell. Early training consisted of 'sheer hard study and some experience in the local school of art'. When a schoolboy he was called on to draw posters advertising school events. Some of his earliest illustrations appeared in Irish text publications of the Gaelic League. As an illustrator of ancient Celtic romance, the name Seaghan MacCathmhaoil became familiar, but among his friends in the Ulster Literary Theatre — he designed costumes as well as acted — he was known as John Patrick Campbell. His work also appeared in *Ulad* (1904-1905), a short-lived literary quarterly, and in *The Shanachie*, 1906. Most important of all were his illustrations for the second edition of Mary A Hutton's *The Táin*, retold in verse, which appeared in 1907. At the centenary exhibition in 1910 of the birth of Sir Samuel Ferguson (q v), held at the Central Public Library, Belfast, a portrait by Campbell, a study from an earlier portrait of the poet, was published as a souvenir. Copies were available from print-sellers or the artist himself at 43 Chichester Street, Belfast. The Belfast Directory for 1911 describes him as a 'rent agent'. About 1911 he emigrated to the USA. After his death in New York on 19 August 1962, the poet, Padraic Colum (1881-1972), wrote in a letter from the USA, 'He illustrated many books when he came to New

York, but his main interest was the stage and the pageant field. His great achievement was the memorable Irish pageant produced in the Armory, Thirty-first Street, New York.'

JOSEPH W CAREY 1859-1937
Painter of landscapes and seascapes

Son of the Rev J W Carey, he received his early training in the firm of Marcus Ward & Co, Belfast, and was subsequently in a business partnership with Richard Thomson. Carey and Thomson's offices were at Rea's Building, 142 Royal Avenue, Belfast. This was the firm which produced the presentation album (1915) containing an illuminated address which is in the Armagh County Museum; watercolour sketches by J W Carey. The list of members of the Belfast Ramblers' Sketching Club for 1886 shows his address as 11 Claremont Street, the same as his brother John, who also painted. Joe, as he was affectionately known, was also an active member of the Belfast Art Society and in 1898 gave a talk on 'Aerial Perspective', but by 1927 he was partially back to earth with a talk entitled 'By Sea and Land'. When the Ulster Academy of Arts, of which he became an Academician, was founded three years later he was the only surviving member, at its meeting, of the Art Society. He favoured marine subjects and appropriately his 'Sailing Ships off Blackhead, Co Antrim' (1912) is in the Belfast Harbour Office, and 'British Fleet Anchored in Bangor Bay, 1914-1918 War' in the Town Hall, Bangor. He is also represented in the Ulster Folk and Transport Museum, Cultra; and in Belfast at the Ulster Museum, the Linen Hall Library, by murals (1903) in the Ulster Hall; and the Ulster Medical Society has an illuminated address. Died on 28 May 1937, at his home, 31 Knockdene Park, Belfast.

TOM CARR 1909-
Painter of landscapes and figure subjects

Thomas Carr was born in Belfast, 21 September 1909, son of a stockbroker, Thomas James Carr. His grandfather, John Hughes Workman, was a watercolourist. After studying at the Slade School, he lived for six months in Italy. In 1933 he first exhibited in London, with a group of artists calling themselves 'Objective Abstractionists'. Victor Pasmore and Ceri Richards were two of the group. Later he became associated with the Euston Road Group. Carr also exhibited in London with the New English Art Club, London Group and at the Royal Academy; also at the Redfern, Leicester and Wildenstein Galleries. In 1938 he returned permanently to his native city, spending much of his painting time in the Newcastle area. He has had one man shows in Belfast under the auspices of CEMA and the Arts Council of Northern Ireland; also at the Tom Caldwell Gallery in Belfast and the David Hendriks Gallery in Dublin, where his work has also been hung in the Oireachtas and Royal Hibernian Academy exhibitions. A member of the Royal Society of Watercolour Painters, his pictures, under their auspices, have been shown in the USA and Japan. In collaboration with Robert McKinstry, the architect, he opened the Piccolo Gallery, Wellington Street, Belfast, in 1957. In 1970 one of his paintings was reproduced on a postage stamp for the Ulster '71 celebrations. An Academician of the Royal Ulster Academy, he won the gold medal in 1973 and the Conor award in 1976, in which year he also received the Oireachtas award in Dublin for landscape. A commission of note was a series of four watercolours of the family seat in Stewartstown, Co Tyrone, painted for the Earl of Castlestewart. In 1975 he was commissioned by the Arts Council of Northern Ireland for a portrait of Hilda Hawnt which appeared in the 'Women of Ulster' exhibition. His pictures have been purchased by the Arts Council and the Ulster Museum, and he is also represented in the collection of Her Majesty the Queen Mother. The Tate Gallery, London, has a lithograph.

WILLIAM H CONN 1895-1973
Illustrator in black and white and cartoonist

His father was William Conn, a Belfast lithographer, and is probably the artist of that name who exhibited in the Belfast Ramblers' Sketching Club exhibition, 1890. When son Billy was at Ulster Provincial School (now Friends' School, Lisburn) his talent was already pronounced — he was in keen demand as a contributor to autograph albums. W & G Baird Limited employed him as a commercial artist in 1921. In 1936 he was appointed staff artist on the *Belfast Telegraph* and *Ireland's Saturday Night*, remaining in that work until his retirement in 1962. His best known contribution as a newspaper artist was his regular cartoon 'The Doings of Larry O'Hooligan' in *Ireland's Saturday Night*. He also contributed a full-page black and white drawing to the *Dublin Opinion* every month, and exhibited occasionally in the Royal Hibernian Academy. A member of the Ulster Arts Club and the Royal Ulster Academy, the Arts Club held a memorial exhibition. After being in the Belfast City Hospital for three years, he died there on 25 August 1973. Represented in the Ulster Museum.

WILLIAM CONOR 1881-1968
Figure and portrait painter

Born in Fortingale Street, Belfast, on 6 May 1881, he was the son of a gasfitter and attended Cliftonpark Central National School, Avoca Street, followed by the Government School of Design, after which he became an apprentice poster designer at David Allen & Son, Ltd, Corporation Street, at 4s 6d per week. By 1912, Conor was in Paris; he exhibited later at the Paris Salon. During the First World War he was appointed by the Government to make official records of soldiers and munition workers. When peace came he lived for a few years in London, off the Tottenham Court Road, becoming acquainted with Sir John Lavery (q v), Augustus John (1878-1961) and the Café Royal circle. He was a member of the Chelsea Arts Club. In 1921 he painted the official opening of the Northern Ireland Parliament by the King and Queen. The Goupil Gallery, London, showed an exhibition in 1923. Another exhibition landmark was his show two years later at 7 St Stephen's Green, Dublin. By 1926 Conor was in New York where he painted portraits and exhibited at the Babcock Galleries. In the 1920s his studio was at 7 Chichester Street, Belfast, and he then moved to 1 Wellington Place. In 1932 he made designs for some of the principals in a pageant of St Patrick at Castleward, Co Down. In the same year his mural on the growth and history of Ulster was unveiled at the Belfast Museum and Art Gallery. He also became the first Irish member of the Royal Institute of Oil Painters, also exhibiting at the Royal Academy, and in exhibitions of the Royal Portrait Society and the Society of Portrait Painters. Illustrations by Conor were used in *Ballygullion Ballads* by Lynn Doyle (Leslie A Montgomery) and *The Ballygullion Bus*. In the Second World War he was again an official artist, some of his work being shown at an exhibition of war artists at the National Gallery, London. Appointed an Associate of the Royal Hibernian Academy, Dublin, in 1938, he became a full member in 1946. He also exhibited in Dublin at the Oireachtas. *The Irish Scene* (Derrick MacCord, Belfast) appeared in 1944 with coloured reproductions of his work. CEMA honoured him in 1945 with a one man show at Tyrone House, Belfast, and it became the first one man exhibition to tour the Province; catalogues, one penny each. In 1948 he exhibited at the Victor Waddington Galleries, Dublin. Lynn Doyle appeared in Belfast in 1950 to open a Conor exhibition at 55a Donegall Place, Belfast, organised by CEMA. Two years later he received the OBE and when another CEMA show was held in 1954 the attendance exceeded 2,800. The year 1957 was an eventful one: CEMA organised a retrospective exhibition at the Belfast Museum and Art Gallery; he was elected president of the Royal Ulster Academy (holding office until 1964); and he received an honorary Master of Arts degree from Queen's University, Belfast. A Civil Pension was awarded in 1959. In the following year he decided to close his studio at 11a Stranmillis Road, Belfast, where he had worked for two decades. The Bell Gallery in Belfast held exhibitions in 1964, 1966 and 1967. Few of his formal portraits appeared in exhibitions. Among the notable people who sat for him were Dr Douglas Hyde, Most Rev Dr D'Arcy, Sir William Moore, Lord Chief Justice of Northern Ireland, and the Marquess of Londonderry. His painting of Major-General Sir Oliver Nugent is in the City Hall, Belfast. His work, principally in watercolour and crayon, is in practically all the Irish collections of note. There is a Conor room at the Ulster Folk and Transport Museum, Cultra, and the Linen Hall Library, Belfast, has a collection of his works. Also represented in the Armagh County Museum, the Arts Council of Northern Ireland collection, the New University of Ulster, Coleraine, and by a large collection at the Ulster Museum. His work is also in the Imperial War Museum, London. He died on 5 February 1968, at his home, 107 Salisbury Avenue, Belfast, and was buried at Carnmoney churchyard. As a memorial tribute, the Arts Council of Northern Ireland held an exhibition which then toured the Province.

J HUMBERT CRAIG 1878-1944
Painter of landscapes

Born in Belfast, he spent his youth at Ballyholme, Co Down, where he was educated at a private school. In his boyhood he had always drawn and painted. His father was Alexander Craig, a wholesale tea merchant, and he had married Miss Juanita Metysaen, a native of Lausanne with a painting tradition in the family. 'Jimmy' spent some time in his father's business, but left and an unsettled period followed. Practically a self-taught artist, he failed to see a term through at the Belfast School of Art. The Glens of Antrim was a favourite spot for painting; he lived at Tornamona Cottage, Cushendun. His other address was Dunedin, Antrim Road, Belfast. Donegal and Connemara were other favourite areas for painting. Several visits were made to the Continent and he painted in Switzerland, South of France and Northern Spain. In 1925 he was appointed an Associate of the Royal Hibernian Academy and in 1928 a Member. He was also an Academician of the Royal Ulster Academy. When the Fine Art Society held a group exhibition of Irish artists' work in their London gallery in 1928 he exhibited along with Paul Henry (q v). The Royal Academy and the Glasgow Institute also showed his landscapes. J Humbert Craig, RHA, illustrated Richard Hayward's *In Praise of Ulster* (Mullan, Belfast,

1938). Working up to the time of his death, he died on 12 June 1944, at Cushendun and was buried at Cushendall. The following year a memorial exhibition was held at the Belfast Museum and Art Gallery. In her will his widow, Mrs Annie S L Craig, bequeathed a dozen paintings to Bangor Borough Council and there is a Craig Room at the Town Hall. A portrait of the artist by Paul Nietsche (q v) is in the Ulster Museum, where Craig is represented. His work is also in the collections of the Arts Council of Northern Ireland, the Armagh County Museum, in Dublin at the Hugh Lane Municipal Gallery of Modern Art, and the National Gallery of Ireland as well as other Irish collections.

EBENEZER CRAWFORD 1830-1874
Painter of domestic subjects

Born 1830 in Belfast. After studying at the Belfast School of Design, he went to London and became a pupil of the historical painter, E M Ward, RA (1816-1879), giving promise of talent as a subject and portrait painter. In Algernon Graves' *Dictionary of Artists 1760-1893* his speciality is described as 'Domestic'. He exhibited about a dozen pictures at the Royal Academy from 1859 to 1873, including 'The Smithy, Red Bay Cave, Co Antrim' (1861), 'A capricious customer' (1871) and 'The doctor's visit' (1872). In 1873 the catalogue gave his address as 4 Foxley Road, Kensington. Crawford also exhibited at the British Institution. A portrait by him of 'J Scott Porter' was engraved in mezzotint by R Josey. The Ulster Museum has a sketch by Crawford for 'An Incident in the Great Plague of London'. He died in 1874.

NICHOLAS J CROWLEY 1819-1857
Painter of portraits and domestic subjects

Born in Dublin, he was the third son of Peter Crowley, 'a gentleman of some property'. The Dublin Society's School admitted him as a pupil in 1827, and in 1832 he became a student at the Royal Hibernian Academy, exhibiting a portrait at the age of thirteen at the annual exhibition. Next year he contributed six portraits and became a regular exhibitor until his death. In 1835 and 1836 he was residing in Belfast, and painted portraits. The RHA catalogue for 1835 lists his address as 1 Fisherwick Place, Belfast. Algernon Graves in his *Dictionary of Artists 1760-1893* gives 1835-1858 as the first and last year of exhibiting in important exhibitions in London. His 'town' is shown as Belfast and during the period mentioned he showed forty-seven pictures at the Royal Academy. Crowley was elected an Associate of the Royal Hibernian Academy in 1836, and a Member in 1837. He was one of the original members of the Belfast Association of Artists when it was founded in 1836. About 1837 he made his home in London — much of his time, however, continued to be spent in Ireland — and from 1843 until his death his address was 13 Upper Fitzroy Street, where he died on 4 November 1857. He is represented in the British Museum. The Ulster Museum has a self-portrait. In the 'Pictures from Ulster Houses' exhibition at the Belfast Museum and Art Gallery in 1961, Nicholas J Crowley's 'Tyrone Power at the Theatre Royal, Haymarket, in the character of Connor O'Gorman in "The Groves of Blarney"' was lent by his great grandson, Sir Tyrone Guthrie.

E M O'RORKE DICKEY 1894-1977
Painter and wood engraver of landscapes

Born 1 July 1894, son of a Belfast solicitor, Edward O'Rorke Dickey, he was educated at Wellington College and Trinity College, Cambridge, studying art at Westminster School of Art, London. From a studio in London he exhibited with the London Group, New English Art Club and Royal Academy. Deciding to take up art teaching, in the middle of the 1920s, he became art master at Oundle School. Shortly after the First World War he was living in Antrim. An original member of the Society of Wood Engravers, his woodcuts illustrated Richard Rowley's book of poems *Workers* (Duckworth, 1923). E M O'R Dickey was the author of *A Picture-Book of British Art* (Bell, 1931). In 1923 the Leicester Galleries, London held a two man exhibition at which drawings and paintings by Vincent van Gogh were shown. *The Studio*, London, critique said, 'Among the works of van Gogh there were a few which gave some hint of the power with which he has been credited by his followers, but as a whole the show was certainly unconvincing. Mr Dickey, however, made an excellent impression as an artist...' Professor of fine art and director of King Edward VII School of Art, King's College, University of Durham, 1926-1931, he then served for twenty-six years as staff inspector of art, Ministry of Education. He was awarded the CBE and his last address was Turvey, Bedford. He died on 12 August 1977. In Irish collections, his work is in the Ulster Museum, the Hugh Lane Municipal Gallery of Modern Art, Dublin; and the Cork and Limerick Municipal Art Galleries. He is also represented in the British Museum, London.

GERARD DILLON 1916-1971
Painter of townscapes, landscapes and imaginary figure subjects

Born at 26 Lower Clonard Street, off Falls Road, Belfast, the youngest of eight children, his father, Joseph Henry Dillon, was a postman. Left school at fourteen and became a house-painter with the firm of Maurice Sullivan, 41 Falls Road, but after seven years he attended Belfast College of Art, for only three months. Lived in London 1934-1939 when he worked in odd jobs to make a living. The war years found him in Ireland and his first one man show was held in 1942 at the Country Shop, Dublin. Much of his painting time was spent in Connemara with George Campbell (q v), resulting in lively contributions, either by prose or illustration, to the magazine *Ireland of the Welcomes*. Dillon first exhibited with the Irish Exhibition of Living Art in Dublin in 1943, becoming a regular exhibitor and a valued committee member, although from 1945 until 1968 he lived most of the time in London. CEMA gave him one man shows in Belfast in 1946 and 1950. In later years he was to have two one man shows in Dublin at the Victor Waddington Galleries and several at the Dawson Gallery between 1957 and 1971. Apart from painting, he was commissioned by Dublin Tourism for a wall hanging and he helped to provide set and costume designs for an Abbey Theatre play, also a poster. His work appeared in several exhibitions of international importance, notably the 1958 Pittsburgh International, 1958 and 1960 Guggenheim International, and the 1961 and 1963 Marzotto International, Rome. The links with Belfast and Dublin remained strong and in 1966 came a one man show at the Arts Council of Northern Ireland Gallery. His painting, 'Black Lake' was reproduced on a postage stamp issued from Dublin, where he had a spell of lecturing two years before his death. He resided at 28 Chelmsford Avenue, Ranelagh, Dublin, and died at the Adelaide Hospital, Dublin, on 14 June 1971. His work appears in practically all the principal Irish collections; the National Gallery of Ireland, Dublin, has a self-portrait. A retrospective exhibition was held in 1972 at the Ulster Museum and the Arts Council of Northern Ireland Gallery, moving from Belfast to the Municipal Gallery of Modern Art, Dublin.

LORD DUFFERIN 1826-1902
Illustrator

Born at Florence, 21 June 1826, he was a descendant of Richard Brinsley Sheridan (1751-1816) and a son of Helen, Lady Dufferin, spending his formative years at Clandeboye, Co Down, where he died. When the Belfast School of Design opened in 1849 he was invited to become president and proved a good friend of the school in many ways. In 1856, soon after beginning his career as a diplomat, he established himself as a writer with his *Letters from High Latitudes*, being an account of a voyage in a schooner yacht to Iceland and other places. In the dramatis personae at the front of the book, which he illustrated, he describes himself as 'Navigator, Sagaman, Artist.' When Governor-General of India, a member of the Council, Sir Edwin Collen, wrote of him: '... if things were going just as he wished them, he would sketch types of beauty in a masterly way, and I often longed to annexe the sketches after Council.' A portrait of Lord Dufferin by G F Watts (1817-1904) is in the National Portrait Gallery, London. The inscription on the bronze statue by F W Pomeroy, RA (1856-1924) on the west side of the City Hall, Belfast, reads:- 'To the illustrious memory of Frederick Temple, 1st Marquess of Dufferin and Ava, KP, 1826-1902, Governor-General of Canada, Viceroy of India, Ambassador of St Petersburg, Constaninople, Rome and Paris. HM Lieutenant of the County of Down and Freeman of the City of Belfast. This memorial of a great Irishman is erected by his countrymen and by his many friends throughout the world.'

GAETANO FABBRINI fl 1816-1845
Portrait and subject painter

A native of Florence, he was appointed drawing master and teacher of Italian at the Belfast Academical Institution about 1816. In the drawing school was taught 'figure drawing, ornamental drawing, and oil portrait painting on Grecian models and in the style of the Florentine Academy...' From the first, relations between Fabbrini and the other masters were strained; anything they proposed, he opposed. Matters reached a crisis in 1820, when Fabbrini refused any longer to attend the meetings of the board of masters, or even to conduct his school. The Italian was dismissed, but that was not the end of the matter. He made various claims for sums alleged to be due to him, and for many years these claims were kept up. During this period and after he practised as a portrait painter in Belfast. He was an honorary member of the Belfast Association of Artists, established in 1836. In 1834, when he exhibited at the Royal Hibernian Academy, Dublin his address was 3 Little May Street, Belfast. In 1835 and 1845 he again exhibited at the RHA. Martin's Belfast Directory for 1840-1841 contains an advertisement: 'The Belfast Italian Drawing Academy, 21 Little May Street. Conducted by Signior Gaetano Fabbrini, native of Florence, and member of the Florentine Royal Academy. In the above mentioned Academy, Figure and Architectural Drawing are chiefly taught on the most approved principles; the subordinate branches are also taught if required. It is opened three days in the week, for Ladies and Gentlemen, at different hours. Terms — One Guinea and a-half per quarter.' But in the 1843-1844 directory issued by the Post Office, Belfast, he is described as a 'teacher of dancing' at 29 Little May Street.

SAMUEL FERGUSON 1810-1886
Architectural draughtsman and sketcher of nature

Youngest child of John Ferguson who married a daughter of John Knox, watchmaker, he was born in Belfast in the house of his maternal grandparents in Belfast, which, on the occasion of the centenary celebrations of his birth was stated to be occupied by John S Shaw, hatter, 21-23 High Street. In 1929 the Ulster Tourist Development Association erected a sign at the premises: 'Sir Samuel Ferguson, Poet and Antiquary, was born in this house 10th March, 1810...' A son of the Plantation, his forebears came from Scotland to settle on lands in the valley of the Six-Mile-Water in County Antrim. Educated at the Belfast Academy, the Belfast Academical Institution and Trinity College, Dublin, he was called to the Bar 1838, retiring from practice 1867 to take up the post of Deputy Keeper of the Records in Ireland. Although art played only a minor part in a distinguished career, he drew and etched with accuracy. Indifferent health sent him on a tour of the Continent 1845-46 where he made many sketches. His notebooks included studies of cathedrals, and churches dedicated to Irish saints. In Italy he studied painting and sculpture. In 1867 he delivered an important lecture entitled 'Our Architecture' at the Museum of Industry, St Stephen's Green, Dublin. A long and intimate friendship with Sir Frederick W Burton, RHA (1816-1900), a mutual friend of George Petrie (1789-1866), strenghtened his interest in art. Some of his sketches are in the Linen Hall Library, Belfast. He died at Howth, 9 August 1886, and was interred at Donegore, Co Antrim.

THOMAS FITZPATRICK fl 1857-1868
Sculptor

An early student at the Belfast School of Design, founded in 1850, Thomas with his brother William and a younger brother Michael all gave generous financial support to the school. Later the Fitzpatrick brothers contributed to the running of the Government School of Design which opened in 1870. Thomas Fitzpatrick, probably assisted by William, executed the carving on the pediment of the Custom House (1857) with Britannia and others looking seaward, having been designed by their fellow student at the School of Design, W H Lynn (q v). Thomas Fitzpatrick is also credited with the carved stonework at the Ulster Bank (1860), Waring Street, where Britannia also appears on high with other figures. The Fitzpatrick brothers also carved the heads on the building at the corner of Donegall Square South and Linen Hall Street. The 1860-61 Belfast Directory lists at 6½ Wellington Place: Thomas and William Fitzpatrick, marble and stone yard. William, marble carver, lived at Ballynafeigh. About 1868 John Lytle and Sons, wholesale grocers, seed merchants and starch manufacturers, went into occupation of 34 Victoria Street; and Samuel McCausland, wholesale grocer, seed merchant and shipowner took over no 36, where Fitzpatrick's heads now adorn an empty building. No 34 is less ornate but at the side of the building in Marlborough Street is a Chinaman whose helmet may well be needed once demolition begins.

WILLIAM FOY 1791-c 1861
Portrait painter

Born in Londonderry in 1791, he was a pupil of the Rev James Knox who was master of the Free School of Derry from 1794 to 1814 and headmaster of the New Free School (later called Foyle College) from 1814 to 1834. This association between the artist and Knox provides evidence today of Foy's connection with Londonderry. A head and shoulders portrait of Knox by Foy is in the Foyle and Londonderry College, and it is thought this was given to the school by the artist. Another painting of Knox by Foy, full length, was painted in 1844 when the sitter was in his 88th year and is referred to in the *Londonderry Sentinel*, 24 September 1844. The portrait was in the possession of the Young family of Culdaff when their house was burned down by the IRA in 1922 and destroyed. The painting had been, however, lithographed by G Foggo, and one of the prints is in the school at Springtown along with the original work. Foy trained as an artist in the Dublin Society's School in Hawkins Street, winning a medal in 1808, but for the next two decades little is known about him although he may have painted portraits in his native town. He appears to have established a good practice as a portraitist, exhibiting at the principal exhibitions in London between 1828 and 1861. A portrait of General Hart, MP, Governor of Londonderry, was shown at the Royal Academy in 1829, and that of the Hon Richard Ponsonby, Bishop of

Derry, at the RA in 1833. Returning from London to Dublin in 1836, he made his initial appearance at the Royal Hibernian Academy that year, showing no fewer than five portraits, but appears to have been back in London in 1838 and 1839. In 1841 he resumed contributing to the Royal Hibernian Academy and from that year until 1859 was a fairly regular exhibitor. The 1853 RHA catalogue gives his address as 19 Upper Merrion Street, Dublin. Probably he revisited Londonderry for short periods. Foy exhibited at the British Institution in 1861 and his address was then 201 Piccadilly, London. The date of his death is not known by the Royal Academy, London.

HUGH FRAZER fl 1813-1861
Landscape and portrait painter

A native of Dromore, Co Down, he was admitted as a pupil in the drawing school of the Dublin Society in 1812, about four years after the departure of William Foy (q v). Frazer, whose name is sometimes spelt Fraser, wrote *Essay on Painting* which was published by M Jellett, Belfast, and by James Burnside, Capel Street, Dublin, and printed by Alexander Mackay, junr, 1825. Frazer began to exhibit in the Royal Hibernian Academy, Dublin, in 1826 and was a regular contributor to 1861. At the 1835 exhibition his address in the catalogue was Dromore and 12 Capel Street, Dublin, but he also lived for a time in Belfast. In 1834 he exhibited in the Commercial News-Room, Commercial Buildings, Waring Street, Belfast 'A View of Belfast, taken from the Curator's House in the Botanic Gardens', and in the same year he painted 'River Lagan from Stranmillis', now in the Belfast Harbour Office, where there are other works, including 'Ruins of Old Priory Church, Holywood'. Elected an Associate of the Royal Hibernian Academy in 1830, he became a Member in 1837. Martin's Belfast Directory for 1842-1843 lists Hugh Frazer, artist, 7 Hamilton Street. President of the Association of Artists founded in Belfast in 1836, he wrote the preface to the catalogue of the inaugural exhibition in that year. In the period 1832-1841 he occasionally exhibited in London. Two works in the Ulster Museum collection bear the titles 'River Lagan with Barge' and 'View of Cave Hill from the Lagan'. Frazer somewhat mysteriously resigned his membership of the Royal Hibernian Academy 'owing to future absence from Dublin and perhaps from Ireland'.

ROWEL FRIERS 1920-
Cartoonist and illustrator

Born 1920 in Belfast, Rowel Boyd Friers was the son of William Friers, cashier, and was educated at Park Parade Intermediate School, Ravenhill Road, where in later years he painted a large mural on the theme of horses charging. Early in his career he served as an apprentice lithographer with S C Allen & Co Ltd, Corporation Street, being released for study at the Belfast College of Art for certain days; he also attended at night. In 1953 CEMA organised an exhibition where he showed paintings, drawings, cartoons and illustrations at 55a Donegall Place, Belfast. In addition to his television work for the BBC and Ulster Television — illustrating for schools and cartooning — he has illustrated more than thirty books, notably *Irish Folk Tales* edited by W B Yeats, issued in 1973 by the Limited Editions Club, Avon, Connecticut. Designing sets for the Lyric Theatre and grand opera in Belfast has also added variety to his work. Blackstaff Press, Belfast, has published four books of Friers' cartoons: *Riotious Living* (1971), *Pig in the Parlour* (1972), *The Book of Friers* (1973) and *The Revolting Irish* (1974). *Mainly Spanish* (H R Carter Publications, Belfast) appeared in 1951, and *Wholly Friers* (Lisnagarvey Press, Lisburn) in 1950. Cartoons have also appeared in several magazines, including *Dublin Opinion, London Opinion* and *Punch*. An Academician of the Royal Ulster Academy, he has also exhibited at the Royal Hibernian Academy, Dublin. In 1977 he was awarded the MBE for 'contributions to journalism and broadcasting'. Represented in the collections of the Arts Council of Northern Ireland, Ulster Folk and Transport Museum, Cultra, and the Ulster Museum.

WILHELMINA GEDDES 1888-1955
Stained glass artist

Born in Leitrim and educated at Methodist College, Belfast (1898-1902) she studied at the Belfast School of Art and under Sir William Orpen (1878-1931) at the Metropolitan School of Art, Dublin. Rosamond Praeger (q v) recognised her talent early on, taking some of her watercolours to an exhibition in Dublin which drew the attention of Sarah Purser (1848-1943), who employed her at An Tur Gloine ('The Tower of Glass') at 24 Upper Pembroke Street, Dublin. From about 1911 until 1922 Wilhelmina worked in 'The Shop', a nickname she and other employees had for 'The Tower'. At the Arts and Crafts Society of Ireland's exhibition, Metropolitan School of Art, 1921, her needlework pictures attracted attention. Three years later she had a joint exhibition with Rosamond Praeger in Belfast when she showed, among other works, linocuts. Moving to London in 1925 she opened a studio at 11 Lettice Street, Fulham, and it was at the kiln there that Evie Hone (1894-1955) converted her — Evie's — designs into stained glass. Notable among the Belfast woman's principal works is the Duke of Connaught's war memorial window at St Bartholomew's Church, Ottawa, and a window in Ypres Cathedral in memory of King Albert of the Belgians. 'The Children of Lir' at the Ulster Museum was an official purchase. Two windows at Rosemary Street Presbyterian Church in Belfast were destroyed in the 1941 air raids. A window in the Presbyterian Assembly Hall, Belfast, was damaged by bomb blast. Among other windows in Ulster are: Townsend Street Presbyterian Church, Belfast; St John's Church, Malone Road, Belfast; Inver Church, near Larne; and a third Church of Ireland church at Money, County Fermanagh. Stained glass by Wilhelmina Geddes is on view at the Hugh Lane Municipal Gallery of Modern Art, Dublin, and more than thirty designs for stained glass windows are in the National Gallery of Ireland, Dublin. Also represented in the Victoria and Albert Museum, London. In poor health for many years, she died in London, 10 August 1955.

W R GORDON 1872-1955

Landscape and banner painter

Born at Moira, Co Down, on 18 August 1872, he studied in his spare time at the Laird School of Art, Birkenhead, when working in the Port Sunlight Soap Factory. He also laboured at the Belfast shipyards and studied at the School of Design under George Trobridge (q v). In 1901 he was appointed art master at the Royal Belfast Academical Institution and was there for forty-five years, acquiring the nickname of 'Daddy'. Always willing to help in the organisation of cultural events, he was honorary secretary in 1902 of a sketching club and a founder member of the Ulster Arts Club, for which he was the first secretary. As a means of augmenting his income, he painted banners for both Orange and Hibernian lodges; and for many years he cycled from his home at 33 Glendower Street, off Cregagh Road, to take evening classes at Newtownards Technical School. A foundation member of the Ulster Literary Theatre, he was prominently identified with the amateur theatrical movement. In 1934 he was commissioned with John F Hunter (q v) to paint a mural in the Belfast Museum and Art Gallery, 'The Bronze Age in Ireland'. An honorary member of the Royal Ulster Academy, he also exhibited at the Royal Hibernian Academy, Dublin. W R Gordon served on the committee of CEMA. His work, which was on exhibition at 55a Donegall Place, Belfast the year before his death, is also in the collections of the Arts Council of Northern Ireland and the Armagh County Museum. Died on 23 February 1955, at his home, 9 Sicily Park, Belfast.

MORRIS HARDING 1874-1964

Sculptor

Born at Stevenage, Herts, on 29 April 1874, Morris Harding taught sculpture and life drawing at the London County Council Technical Institute. He was trained in the studio of his uncle, Harry Bates, ARA (1850-1899) and worked under J M Swan, RA (1847-1910). He was a member of the Royal Society of British Sculptors and the Society of Animal Painters. He exhibited at the Royal Academy and the Glasgow Institute. The major work of his career was on Belfast Cathedral, and in 1925 he came to the Province from London on the invitation of the Cathedral architect, Sir Charles Nicholson. Rosamond Praeger (q v) was responsible for him settling in Holywood, Co Down, and they used St Brigid's Studios. He rented a flat on the ground floor. He spent at least twelve years working on the nave columns and corbels of St Anne's. Each column's capital is devoted to a theme and these include agriculture, art, womanhood and shipbuilding. He also undertook a series of portraits of dignitaries of the Irish Church in corbels above the pillars; and there are groups in the portals of the west front. The cathedral was said to be the only one in which all the sculptural work was done by one man but this is incorrect. Rosamond Praeger was responsible for the justice pillar and for other work. In Belfast, Morris Harding also carved the font in St Peter's Church, Antrim Road; the Royal Coat of Arms at Telephone House; the Civil Service War Memorial in the old Parliament Buildings; and work at Queen's University. Coats of Arms at the old Government House, Hillsborough, for the Duke of Abercorn and Earl Granville, were by him. In 1932 he was appointed an Associate of the Royal Hibernian Academy, Dublin, and in the same year a full Member. He was also an Academician of the Royal Ulster Academy and held the office of president for several years. In 1938 he was responsible for a 150 ft long frieze, 4 ft deep with fifteen panels, for the Ulster Government's pavilion at the Glasgow Empire Exhibition, and was assisted by Poppy Mollan and John Luke (q v). Harding was represented in an exhibition of sculpture held at the Belfast Museum and Art Gallery in 1953 and organised by CEMA. Awarded the OBE in 1950, he received an honorary Master of Arts degree from Queen's University in 1958 but was too frail to attend the ceremony. He died on 15 January 1964, at his home, Church Road, Holywood. His work is in the Ulster Museum collection.

CHARLES W HARVEY 1895-1970
Landscape and still life painter

Born in London, his father was a map-maker in Ordnance Survey and his home town was Brentwood, Essex. The Harveys arrived in Belfast in 1906 and always lived in the Antrim Road area. Charles Harvey studied at the Belfast School of Art with John McAllister (q v). He won a gold medal in the National Competition for design. In 1914 he attended the summer term at the Metropolitan School of Art, Dublin. Training as a damask designer, he became friendly with Hans Iten (q v), and on one occasion gave an illustrated lecture at the Belfast Museum and Art Gallery on 'Linen Damask'. Harvey had wide interests and was very knowledgeable about antique furniture. Teaching in Belfast began at St Mary's Training College, in a part-time capacity, from 1932-1936. From 1936-1960 he was a full-time lecturer, retiring as head of the art department. In a busy professional life he exhibited at the Ulster Arts Club, rarely elsewhere. He was included in 'The Ulster Unit: Exhibition of Contemporary Art' in the Locksley Hall, The Carlton, Belfast 1934. Landscape painting was generally in Connemara, Donegal or County Down. In the 1930s he painted in Brittany with Padraic Woods (q v). He died on 26 June 1970, at his home, 124 Somerton Road, Belfast. A retrospective exhibition was held in 1976 at the Arts Council of Northern Ireland Gallery.

SAMUEL HAWKSETT 1776-1851
Portrait Painter

Practised in Belfast where he was the principal portrait painter of his time. The Ulster Museum holds portraits of David McTear, Robert Langtry and Thomas Mulholland. At the Belfast Harbour Office is a portrait of John Dunn. Hawksett exhibited portraits in the Royal Hibernian Academy, Dublin, from 1826 to 1834; his address in the catalogue fro the 1831 exhibition was 2 Fountain Street, Belfast. According to a writer in the Royal Belfast Academical Institution centenary volume, 1810-1910: 'In November, 1831, in response to a request from the Earl of Belfast, His Majesty King William IV was graciously pleased to signify his assent to the change of the title of the Institution to "The Royal Belfast Academical Institution". To commemorate this event the boards commissioned a Mr Hawksett to paint a portrait of His Majesty, who granted the artist special sittings for this purpose, and the portrait was hung in the boardroom in October 1835.' This portrait is no longer in the boardroom. In 1836 he was appointed the first treasurer of the Belfast Association of Artists. Hawksett's portraits also included one of the Marchioness of Donegall, shown at the Royal Hibernian Academy, 1826. That of the Rev Hugh McNeill, Dean of Ripon, was engraved in mezzotint by T Lupton, and published by S Hawksett at 39 Great Edward Street, Belfast, 1845. He died in 1851.

OLIVE HENRY 1902-
stained glass artist and genre painter

Born in Belfast, daughter of George Adams Henry, tea merchant, and educated at Mountpottinger National School and Victoria College, Belfast, Olive Henry became probably the only woman stained glass artist in Ulster. When attending evening classes at the Belfast School of Art she was attracted to stained glass and when her teacher heard that the firm of W F Clokey & Co Limited, King Street, was looking for an apprentice he recommended her. She obtained the job, remaining there all her working life. Academician of the Royal Ulster Academy, she has also exhibited in Dublin: Royal Hibernian Academy, Irish Exhibition of Living Art, Oireachtas and the Watercolour Society of Ireland. In 1944 she showed with Violet McAdoo at the Belfast Museum and Art Gallery. In 1957 she had a one-woman show under the auspicies of CEMA at 55a Donegall Place, Belfast. She has also exhibited in England. A founder member of the Ulster Society of Women Artists, she is represented in the Ulster Museum collection. A stained glass window is at Sullivan Upper School, Holywood.

PAUL HENRY 1877-1958
Landscape and portrait painter

Born 11 April 1877 in Belfast, son of the Rev R M Henry, University Road, the minister of Great Victoria Street Baptist Church, who later joined the Plymouth Brethren. He died when Paul was aged fifteen. The boy was educated at the Royal Belfast Academical Institution, where he made friends with Robert Lynd (1879-1949). Outside of school, Thomas Bond Walker gave drawing lessons. On leaving 'Inst' he entered the Broadway Damask Co as an apprentice designer but stayed only a year, moving to the Government School of Design where he met William Conor (q v). A cousin, later Sir John McFarland, Chancellor of Melbourne University, helped him to go to Paris and survive financially for about a year. Henry frequented Julian's studio, then one opened by Whistler. From Paris he moved to London, where his old friend Lynd joined him in accommodation. They lived together until 1912 when Henry left their home, then near Guildford, Surrey, for a holiday in Achill Island. In London, he had contributed illustrations to several magazines, including *The Graphic, The Lady* and *Black and White*. Illustrations were also done for John Lane of the Bodley Head. He painted occasional portraits and had a show of charcoal drawings at the Goupil Galleries. He was on the hanging committee of the Allied Artists Association first show in 1910. In 1908 he had exhibited at the Ulster Arts Club, Belfast. The visit to the west of Ireland was the turning point in his career; he stayed on Achill for about seven years, 1912-1919. Moving to Dublin, he became a founder member of the Dublin Painters. He exhibited regularly with his wife, Grace. As from 1920 he had red-green colour blindness. Paris saw his work in 1921 and again in 1922 when the French Government purchased 'A West of Ireland Village' for the Luxembourg Gallery. The following year he exhibited at Magee's Gallery, Belfast. In 1925 the London, Midland and Scottish Railway issued their 'Connemara' poster which became a familar one in railway stations at home and abroad. In 1925 he held an exhibition at his studio, 13a Merrion Row, Dublin. The next year he was appointed an Associate of the Royal Hibernian Academy; in 1929 a full Member. Between 1930 and 1950 he lived in County Wicklow, in a cottage overlooking Enniskerry. Outside of Ireland, his work was exhibited in Brussels, Boston and New York, London and Toronto. In addition to the Royal Hibernian Academy exhibitions, he also showed in Dublin at the Oireachtas; at Combridge's galleries, in particular; and the Victor Waddington Galleries. About 1945 he had a nervous breakdown which destroyed his sight. In 1957 a retrospective exhibition was held at the Ritchie Hendriks Gallery, Dublin, and at the Belfast Museum and Art Gallery. *An Irish Portrait* (Batsford, 1951) by Paul Henry was followed in 1973 by an addendum to that autobiography, *Further Reminiscences* (Blackstaff Press). Grace Henry died in 1953. At the time of his death, 24 August 1958, he was living with his second wife, Mabel Young, also an artist, at 1 Sidmonton Square, Bray. He was buried at St Patrick's Church, Enniskerry. Represented in practically all the principal Irish collections, notably the Ulster Museum and the Hugh Lane Municipal Gallery of Modern Art, Dublin. Also represented at the Victoria and Albert Museum, London.

RICHARD HOOKE c 1822-1887
Portrait painter

Born in County Down about 1822, he was originally a carpenter, and showing a gift for painting was induced by Andrew Ferguson, manager of the Sion Flax-Spinning Mills, to begin portrait painting. Ferguson taught him photography, which he used in his portrait painting. When Hooke went to Belfast he had a considerable local practice, painting many of the principal merchants there and in the neighbourhood. The Belfast Harbour Office has two portraits; one is of William Herdman (1777-1855), a Belfast merchant and shipowner, who also appears in the Ulster Museum's collection of seven portraits. At the City Hall, Belfast, the years of office for three portraits of Mayors indicate Hooke's popularity over thirty years: Sir William G Johnston (1849), Samuel McCausland (1868) and John Browne, JP (1879-1880). This artist exhibited at the Royal Hibernian Academy from 1850 to 1856, and from 1873 to 1887. In 1852 the RHA catalogue gave his address as 17 Chichester Street, Belfast; in 1881 it was 41 Donegall Place. Hooke also lived in Manchester where he married a lady of some means, and when he showed his portrait of the Marquess of Downshire, his patron, at the Royal Academy in 1872 his address was given as 18 Exchange Street, Manchester.

FRED W HULL 1867-1953
Landscape painter

Born in Drogheda, he became a Belfast businessman who lived at 8 Ireton Street for more than half a century. When about thirty years of age he took up painting as a hobby, attending evening classes at the Government School of Design under George Trobridge (q v), and having lessons in outdoor sketching with David Gould, a watercolourist. Elected a member of the Belfast Art Society in 1902, he also sent his pictures to exhibitions at the Ulster Arts Club, Belfast, of which he was a foundation member and later president. For about ten years up until the First World War he exhibited at the Royal Hibernian Academy, Dublin. In 1924 his work was on view at the British Empire Exhibition, London. He also exhibited at one of the annual exhibitions at the Walker Art Gallery, Liverpool. The Lagan Valley was a favourite painting area: Barnett's Park, Edenderry and Shaw's Bridge scenes all appearing on canvas. He died on 21 April 1953 at the Royal Victoria Hospital, Belfast. His portrait by Paul Nietsche (q v) is in the Ulster Museum, where he is represented.

JOHN F HUNTER 1893-1951
Wood engraver and landscape painter

Born in Manchuria, where his father, Rev William Hunter, of Doagh, Co Antrim, was an Irish Presbyterian Church missionary. Brother of Mercy Hunter (q v), he was educated at Trinity College, Dublin, and the Royal College of Art. In 1923 he became inspector of art to the Ministry of Education, Northern Ireland. He gave a lecture in 1931 at the Belfast Museum and Art Gallery on 'The Making of Prints from Woodcuts and Linoleum Blocks'. In 1934 he completed with W R Gordon (q v) the large mural 'The Bronze Age in Ireland' at the Belfast Museum and Art Gallery, presented by the Haverty Trust, Dublin. An Academician of the Ulster Academy of Arts, he was also president. Much of his spare time was taken up in an administrative capacity; he was chairman of the art committee of CEMA, 1944-1949. He served in both World Wars. In 1951 Lieut Col John F Hunter ARCA, senior art inspector, was awarded the OBE. He died at his home, 132 Merville Garden Village, Whitehouse, on 23 October 1951. The Arts Council of Northern Ireland and the Ulster Museum hold his work. In 1952 CEMA organised a memorial exhibition at 55a Donegall Place, Belfast.

MERCY HUNTER 1910-
Calligraphist and draughtswoman

Born in Belfast, at the age of four travelled to China by the Trans-Siberian Railway and spent her childhood in Manchuria where her father, Rev William Hunter of Doagh, Co Antrim, was an Irish Presbyterian Church missionary. Toronto and the Belfast Royal Academy provided her secondary education. Studied at Belfast College of Art 1927-1929, and subsequently on a scholarship at the Royal College of Art, London, 1930-1933. In London she formed one of a colony of Ulster art students which included William Scott (q v) and F E McWilliam (q v). Her special subject at the Royal College was calligraphy under Edward Johnston (1872-1944). In 1937 she returned to Northern Ireland and married the sculptor, George MacCann (q v). Her career was devoted to grammar school teaching — Dungannon High School for Girls, Banbridge Academy, Armagh High School and Victoria College, Belfast, where she was head of the art department from 1947 until her retirement in 1970. In addition to illuminated addresses and other lettering and calligraphic commissions, she has lectured and broadcast extensively on art; designed costumes for the theatre, grand opera and ballet; and illustrated books. Academician of the Royal Ulster Academy, she has also served as president and is founder member and past president of the Ulster Society of Women Artists. In 1970 she was awarded the MBE for services to education and art, and in 1975 an honorary degree of Master of Arts was conferred on her by Queen's University, Belfast. Represented in the Ulster Museum collection.

ROBERT HUNTER fl 1750-1803
Portrait painter

A native of Ulster, but of his early years nothing is known. From about 1750 until the arrival in Dublin in 1779 of the Englishman, Robert Home (1752-1834), who attracted the leaders of fashion, Hunter was the principal portrait painter in Ireland. 'He modelled his tone of colouring on the painting of the old masters,' says the *Dictionary of National Biography*. 'His portraits were excellent likenesses, if not of the first rank in painting.' Hunter took a prominent part in the foundation of the Society of Artists in Dublin, and regularly contributed to its exhibitions down to 1777, and again, for the last time, in 1800. Indeed in 1765 his thirteen year old daughter, Mary Anne, exhibited, 'being her first attempt in colours'. Among her father's portraits was one of Arthur Dobbs (1689-1765), MP for Carrickfergus. When the 'Pictures from Ulster Houses' exhibition was held at the Belfast Museum and Art Gallery in 1961 there was a painting by Hunter of General James Gisborne, MP for Lisburn, painted in 1771. Many of his portraits were engraved. He was living in 1803 but the date of his death has not been established. In Dublin, the National Gallery of Ireland has five oil paintings; three are portraits and the others are 'Gentleman with gun and dog' and 'Gentleman and boy in library.'

HANS ITEN 1874-1930
Landscape and flower painter

Born in Zurich, 10 March 1874, he studied art at the School of Art, St Gall, Switzerland, and later in Paris. In 1904 he arrived in Belfast to take up an appointment as a damask designer with McCrum, Watson and Mercer Ltd, linen manufacturers, Linen Hall Street, and resided most of his life in Belfast at 18 South Parade. A favourite haunt for painting was Belvoir Park, but he also painted elsewhere in Co Down and Co Donegal. He shared a studio at 20 Rosemary Street and took an active part in the affairs of the Belfast Art Society; a lecture on 'Vincent van Gogh' was given in 1924.

He retained his links with the continent, going there on holiday. He exhibited at the Society of French Artists exhibitions, the Paris Salon, the Glasgow Institute, the Royal Institute of Fine Arts and latterly at the Royal Academy. In Ireland, he exhibited in 1926 at Rodman's Gallery, Belfast, and he also sent works to the Royal Hibernian Academy, Dublin. Known as John Iten to his contemporaries in Ulster, he died in August 1930 at Bulach, Switzerland. The Ulster Museum, Armagh County Museum and the Hugh Lane Municipal Gallery of Modern Art, Dublin, hold his work. A portrait of him by Pierre Montezin (1874-1946) was presented to the Belfast Museum and Art Gallery (now Ulster Museum) by his widow, Mrs Frieda Iten. In 1971 the Arts Council of Northern Ireland in collaboration with the Ulster Arts Club, of which Iten was vice-president, presented an exhibition of his works at the Arts Council Gallery.

ALBERT BRUCE JOY

See Bruce-Joy

ANNE P JURY 1907-

Lanscape, flowerpiece and animal painter

Born at Dunmurry, she lived for many years at Brooklands Cottage, Upper Dunmurry Lane, which was designed by her father, Percy Morgan Jury, architect, of Blackwood and Jury, Belfast. Studied art at the Belfast School of Art and in England, France and Switzerland. The first painting she sold was in an exhibition of the Royal Hibernian Academy, Dublin. An Associate of the Royal Ulster Academy in 1933, she became an Academician in 1976. In 1969 she won the RUA Conor award. Outside of the Royal Ulster Academy shows, her exhibitions have not been many despite a long painting career. She has had one woman shows in Belfast at Rodman's Gallery and Magee's Gallery, and also at the Victor Waddington Galleries, Dublin. She has also exhibited in Edinburgh and London. Represented in Limerick Municipal Art Gallery collection.

GEORGE MacD KANE 1890-1954

Sculptor and portrait painter

Born in Belfast, son of William Kane, plasterwork designer and contractor, he attended Belfast Mercantile Academy ('Pyper's Academy'), Glenravel Street, and was later associated with the Ulster Literary Theatre. Deciding on architecture as a profession, he was with the firm of Blackwood and Jury. He then took up art, attending the Belfast School of Art and winning the Dunville scholarship to the Metropolitan School of Art, Dublin. After teaching art for a short time at the Royal Belfast Academical Institution, George MacDowell Kane left for Edinburgh to assist James Pittendrigh MacGillivray, RSA (1856-1938) with work on the grandiose Gladstone Memorial, St Andrew Square, sculpting the minor figures. The monument was unveiled in 1917. On returning to Belfast, he devoted most of his time to portrait drawings, often in pencil or conté crayon; some studies were done of actors and actresses preparing for performance. He painted a mural in the kitchen of the family house at 8 Dunluce Avenue, Belfast. In the Ulster Museum there is a bronze bust of John Whaley, modelled in 1912, and a drawing of Hans Iten (q v), 1913. Kane died at Purdysburn Hospital, Belfast, 5 March 1954.

G MOUTRAY KYLE 1865-1950

Landscape and genre painter

Born Craigavad, Co Down, she was the daughter of G W Kyle, and was educated at home by governess and tutors. She attended the Colarossi Studio, Paris, and travelled widely, exhibiting in the Paris Salon, Royal Institute of Oil Painters, Royal Scottish Academy, Glasgow Institute, and Walker Art Gallery, Liverpool. Her work was also in the 1924 Wembley exhibition. An Academician of the Ulster Academy of Arts, of which she was for many years a leading member, as far back as 1902 she was active in the running of the Belfast Art Society life class. In addition to exhibiting regularly in Belfast, she also exhibited at the Royal Hibernian Academy, Dublin. She appears to have occasionally signed — a letter — Georgina M Kyle. Her work is in the collection of the Ulster Museum, including oil paintings of 'The Street Market, Concarneau' and 'The Lifting of the Fog at the Gasworks, Belfast'. Also represented at the Armagh County Museum, Bangor Town Hall and Queen's University, Belfast.

CHARLES LAMB 1893-1964

Landscape, portrait and figure painter

Born 30 August 1893 at Portadown, he was the eldest of seven children of John Lamb, a painter and decorator in Bridge Street. At fourteen years he attended Portadown

Technical School and in 1913 won a gold medal for being the best apprentice house painter of the year. Attended Belfast School of Art in the evenings, arriving back at midnight at his Portadown home. Winning a scholarship to the Metropolitan School of Art, Dublin, in 1917, he studied there for four years, then went to Carraroe, a remote part of Connemara where he had a cottage. At this period he painted in many parts of Ireland. In 1922, the year he was appointed an Associate, he began to show at the Royal Hibernian Academy, Dublin, and thereafter exhibited regularly. One of his earliest one man shows was at Magee's Gallery, Belfast, 1924. In 1926 and 1927 he was in Brittany, the following year in Aran in a horse-drawn caravan. In the period 1928-1934 he exhibited in Boston, New York, London, Los Angeles (Olympic Art Exhibition, 1932) and Chicago. He was an Academician of the Ulster Academy of Arts. In 1935 Lamb built a house at Carraroe and started an annual exhibition and summer school there. In 1938, the year he exhibited at the Royal Academy, London, he was elected a Member of the Royal Hibernian Academy. In the period 1941-1954 he spent much more time painting in the North — on the Bann and in Rostrevor. CEMA arranged an exhibition in Belfast in 1947. Portadown Borough Council, in 1956, commissioned a painting of his native town. The fee was fixed at £250 but later the commission was withdrawn, after lively controversy, on the grounds that it was too much money to spend on one painting. He died at Carraroe, 15 December 1964. His widow, Katharine, is a great grand-daughter of Ford Madox Brown (1821-1893). In Ulster, Charles Lamb is represented in the Armagh County Museum and Ulster Museum; and in practically all other Irish collections. A memorial exhibition was held in 1969 at the Municipal Gallery of Modern Art, Dublin; the oldest painting 'Country People at Prayer', had been painted half a century earlier.

ELISH LAMONT (or LA MONTE) c1800-1870
Miniature painter

Born in Belfast about 1800, she was self-taught as an artist and was for many years a successful miniature painter in Belfast. Titled people were among her patrons. When she exhibited at exhibitions she became Miss Elish La Monte. The Belfast Directory for 1852 shows Surgeon AE Lamont at 3 Castle Street, also Miss Lamont, artist. In the 1856 issue Aeneas Lamont, MD, surgeon, was residing at 8 Chichester Street and Miss Lamont, miniature painter, lived there too. Dr James Moore (q v) was at No 7 Chichester Street. Charles Dickens (1812-1870), who gave readings in Belfast, knew Moore and when Elish Lamont was in England she was also acquainted with Dickens; she may have met him in 1858, the first of his three reading visits to Belfast. She was an exhibitor at the Royal Hibernian Academy, Dublin, from 1842 to 1857. In 1846 *Christmas Rhymes, Three Nights' Revelry* was published by Lamont Brothers, Belfast, with ballads, or rhymes, by Elish and her sister Frances, and drawings by Elish. The book was dedicated, by permission, to the Right Honourable The Lady Dufferin and Clandeboye '... noble alike in mind and station, the descendant and inheritress of genius this trifle is offered by the Christmas Rhymers'. When Elish La Monte exhibited at the Royal Academy, London, in 1856 she showed miniatures of Lady Dufferin and the late Earl of Belfast. In 1857 at the RA she gave her address as 14 Clare Street, Dublin, and among her miniatures was one of Miss Agnew of Cairn Castle. Towards the end of her life she settled in England where she knew the Irish artist, Daniel Maclise (1806-1870). She died at Rochester on 3 July 1870. A miniature of an unknown lady is in the Ulster Museum.

SIR JOHN LAVERY 1856-1941
Portrait and landscape painter

Born in Belfast, 26 March 1856, son of a wine merchant, Henry Lavery, the place of John Lavery's birth was 47 North Queen Street, his father presumably trading under 'Richard Lavery', spirit store at that address. He was baptised at St Patrick's Catholic Church, Donegall Street. In the baptismal register is recorded: 'Mary Donnelly, mother; names of sponsors, Richard Lavery, Ellen Dornan'. Left an orphan at the age of three, he was sent to the farm of his uncle, Edward Lavery, situated between Soldierstown and Moira, and known then as 'The Back of the Wood' but subsequently, in due recognition of the advent of trains, renamed 'Train View Moira'. He attended Magheralin National School and at the age of ten moved on to another relative, described by his aunt as 'very rich', at Saltcoats, Ayrshire, where there were solid golden balls over the front door. Unhappy as the 'wee pawn man', he ran away to Glasgow where he was found, impoverished, brought back to Saltcoats and then 'returned' to Ulster and his uncle's farm, helping to herd the cows. Returning to Glasgow, he found an uncongenial job at 7s 6d per week with the mineral department of the Glasgow and South-Western Railway, but soon left to have a short spell at another pawnbroking business, this time in Hamilton. After experiencing a doss house in Glasgow, he returned to Saltcoats where he began to draw, being fascinated by the grocer 'because he drew profiles in pencil that held enormous interest for me'. Shortly afterwards he became indentured to a Glasgow 'artist and photographer', touching up negatives and colouring prints. He was now able to attend the Glasgow School of Art and in 1876 he painted his first picture. After his three years' apprenticeship was up — as a miniature painter over photographs — he carried on as a free-lance artist with his own studio. In 1879 the studio was gutted by fire. The £300 insurance money provided Lavery with the means of studying in both London — for a year at Heatherley's Art School — and Paris, where he became a student at the Academie Julian. A small student work 'Les Deux Pecheurs' was hung at the 1882 Salon next to 'A Bar at the Folies-Bergère' by Edouard Manet (1832-1883). Lavery painted at the village of Grès-sur-Loigne before returning with the Scotsman Alexander Roche (1861-1921) to join his friends in Glasgow, achieving recognition as a member of the 'Glasgow School'. In 1888 he was commissioned to paint 'Queen Victoria's Visit to Glasgow Exhibition'. This mammoth painting began the development of his career as an international society portrait painter complete with a London address at 5 Cromwell Place and a house and studio in Tangiers. The clientèle included, as one writer remarked, 'the ultimate in glamour — the stars of Hollywood in the 1930s'. His portraits found places in the leading galleries at home and abroad, and near the end of the day he had acquired among other honours: Member of the Royal Academy, the Royal Scottish Academy and the Royal Hibernian Academy; also of the Royal Academies of Rome, Antwerp, Milan, Brussels and Stockholm. Member of the Sécessions of Berlin, Munich and Vienna. Knighted in 1918. Chevalier of the Crown of Italy and of Leopold of Belgium. Hon Ll D of Queen's University, Belfast, 1935; and Trinity College, Dublin, 1936; and a freeman of both cities. On the occasion of the opening of the new Belfast Museum and Art Gallery, Sir John donated more than thirty paintings, among them 'The Bridge at Grés', and portraits, including Cardinal Logue, the Marquess of Londonderry and Viscount Craigavon. The 'Hazel Lavery Memorial Collection' is in the Hugh Lane Municipal Gallery of Modern Art, Dublin. A drawing of Hazel, his second wife, was reproduced on the Irish bank note, 1923. A triptych, 'The Madonna of the Lakes' (1919) is in St Patrick's Catholic Church, Belfast. His autobiography, *The Life of a Painter* (Cassell, London) was published in 1940.

JOHN LUKE 1906-1975
Painter of landscape and figure subjects and sculptor

Born in Belfast 16 January 1906, he was the son of James Luke, boilerman, formerly of Ahoghill, Co Antrim. After attending Hillman Street National School, he became a riveter's boy at the shipyards. He then worked in the York Street Flax Spinning Co Ltd and, when there, heard about the School of Art. He attended evening classes, obtaining the Sorella scholarship for day classes. The Dunville award in 1927 took him to London where he studied at the Slade School under Professor Henry Tonks (1862-1937). He won the Robert Ross scholarship. Ulster artists Tom Carr (q v) and F E McWilliam (q v) were at the Slade with him. In 1930 he exhibited at the Redfern Galleries, London. During 1931 he stayed in London, occasionally working at the Westminster School of Art, under Walter Bayes (1869-1956); at the end of the year he returned to Belfast. Within a few years he was exhibiting at the Royal Hibernian Academy, Dublin, and Magee's Gallery, Belfast. In 1938 he assisted Morris Harding (q v) in the 150 ft frieze for the Northern Ireland Government's pavilion at the Glasgow Empire Exhibition. After the air raids on Belfast in 1941, he left the city with his mother to stay at a farm, Knappagh House, Killylea, Co Armagh. Then he obtained a post as art teacher at the Manor House School, Milford. In 1946 a one man exhibition was held at the Belfast Museum and Art Gallery, and two years later CEMA staged an exhibition at 55a Donegall Place, Belfast. Luke was responsible for the large mural painting in the dome of the City Hall, Belfast, representing the life and history of the city. This work was commissioned by CEMA to commemorate the Festival of Britain, 1951. Another mural is in the Masonic Hall in Rosemary Street, Belfast. A mural at the Millfield extension of the College of Technology, representing building and engineering, was not completed after more than ten years of intermittent work. In 1953 he was represented in an exhibition of sculpture at the Belfast Museum and Art Gallery arranged by CEMA. He was a Member of the Royal Ulster Academy. His representation at the Ulster Museum includes a portrait of Dr Alexander Irvine (1863-1941) and a self-portrait, 1928, when he was at the Slade. At the Armagh County Museum there is an oil, 'The Old Callan Bridge', which was painted for Armagh County Council in 1945. He also carved relief coats of arms for two Governors of Northern Ireland, Lord Wakehurst and Lord Erskine of Rerrick. Both stone carvings are at Hillsborough. He lived in a flat at 240 Duncairn Gardens, Belfast, and died in hospital, 4 February 1975.

J LANGTRY LYNAS 1879-1956
Portrait painter and sculptor

Born of Ulster parents at Greenock, 10 April 1879, the family came to Belfast when he was about three years old.

Throughout his life economic necessity meant a search for regular employment to support a wife and family, and he was a signwriter in the Belfast Corporation at the time of his retirement. At one period he was a contractor in building, painting and general jobbing. At the age of twenty-five he gave up a business career and with ten shillings in his pocket began a trip through Europe. He spent a short time at the Belfast School of Art. He had an interest in the Belfast Art Society. In 1927, when living at 33 Bridge End, he was represented in the Belfast Museum and Art Gallery's exhibition, 'Irish Portraits by Ulster Artists' in which one of his exhibits was 'The Artist as a Young Man'. In 1928 there appeared *Psychological Satyr or The Hounds of Hell* by J Langtry-Lynas, first edition limited to 200 copies and apparently published by a London firm with the name of Simpkin, Marshall, Hamilton, Kent & Co Ltd. However, the book, which had ample illustrations by the author, was printed by David Allen & Sons Ltd of Corporation Street, Belfast. A dealer in fine art, jewellery and stamps, T W Reid, 29 Wellington Place, provided space for an exhibition in 1931. *Why* (W & G Baird Ltd, Belfast) appeared in 1935 with more imaginative drawings, also reproductions of his works. Four years later he held an exhibition of sculpture, paintings, and drawings at Magee's Gallery, Belfast; he was then living at 12 Bloomfield Gardens. CEMA gave him an exhibition at 55a Donegall Place in 1952. In the following year he was represented in an exhibition of sculpture at the Belfast Museum and Art Gallery, organised by CEMA. He died on 26 August 1956, at Massereene Hospital, Antrim. A self-portrait is in the Ulster Museum; at the Armagh County Museum is a pastel, 'Creation of Man'. He is also represented at the Walker Art Gallery, Liverpool.

S F LYNN 1834-1876
Sculptor

Born 29 October 1834, at Fethard, Co Wexford, Samuel Ferres Lynn was the son of Lieut Henry Lynn, RN, and a brother of the architect, William H Lynn (1829-1915). Early in his career he studied architecture in his brother's Belfast office; he also attended classes at the Belfast School of Design. When there, modelling so interested him, and the winning of prizes so encouraged him, that he decided to become a sculptor. In 1854 he went to London, entered the Royal Academy as a student in 1855, winning two silver and one gold medal. He exhibited for the first time at the Royal Academy in 1856 and for the last time in 1875 with 'Master McGrath' (Lord Lurgan's greyhound). In 1861 he had been elected a member of the Institute of Sculptors. Lynn resided most of the time in London, and when he exhibited in 1873 at the Royal Hibernian Academy, Dublin, his address was given as 152 Buckingham Palace Road, London. He was made an Associate of the RHA in 1872. For some years he worked in the London studio of the Dublin-born sculptor, J H Foley, RA (1818-1874). He was much employed in sculpture for public buildings in Dublin, London and elsewhere. In Belfast, before he left architecture behind, he designed the figures on the east front of the Custom House, 1855, and he also designed the sculpture for the tympanum facing Donegall Quay. By his own hand there is his statue of Dr Henry Cooke, 'The Black Man', with his back to 'Inst'; Prince Albert on the Albert Memorial clock, and the busts of John Clarke and John Lytle in the Harbour Office. At Hillsborough, there is the bronze statue of the Marquess of Downshire. Apparently he contracted an illness when he was on the continent from which he died soon after his arrival back at his brother's residence, on the Crumlin Road, 3 Crumlin Terrace, on 5 April 1876. In 1916 an exhibition of works by W H Lynn, RHA, and S F Lynn, ARHA, was held at the Museum and Art Gallery, Free Public Library, Belfast.

JOHN A McALLISTER 1896-1925
Painter and etcher of landscape and figure subjects

Born in 1896, he attended the Belfast School of Art and was a contemporary and friend there of Charles Harvey (q v). Another fellow student, William J Coombes, whose portrait by McAllister is in the Ulster Museum, is still alive. He says: 'McAllister's work was very refined. He had a beautiful colour sense and his favourite medium was pastel. With other students we went to the Metropolitan School of Art, Dublin, for the summer term, 1914 (travelling by boat, five shillings each way). Sir William Orpen was the Professor for the course and we learnt a great deal under him. All our spare time was spent in the National Gallery. We came home inspired. (Remember, none of us had been away from home before).' Early in his short career McAllister worked as a designer for W J Jenkins and Co (Belfast) Ltd, Linen Hall Street West, where his work attracted the attention of the linen trade. Then he started business on his own account — he had an office at 7 College Street, Belfast — and was rapidly building for himself a reputation as one of the most promising men in the profession. Painting in the Glens of Antrim and elsewhere in Ireland, including Dublin, he exhibited at the Ulster Arts Club exhibitions, and was preparing for an exhibition at a London gallery when death intervened. He had been spending a couple of months in Rostrevor in the summer of 1925 to try and restore his health, but died at his home, 18 Amcomri Street, Belfast, on 17 October 1925. Hans Iten (q v) wrote about him after his death: 'He was a great artist and one of nature's gentlemen. To the inner artistic and intellectual coterie of Belfast he was known as one of the most brilliant of young men that Ulster has produced.' An exhibition of his watercolours and pastels was held after his death at the Ulster Arts Club premises, 11 College Square North. Represented in the Ulster Museum; and in the Town Hall, Bangor by 'Early Dawn' and 'The Source'.

JOHN McBURNEY 1877-1917
Landscape painter and illustrator

Born 14 May 1877, in Belfast, he attended the Government School of Design and entered some damask designs in a competition promoted by John S Brown & Sons of 12 Bedford Street, and won prizes valued £10.00 and £5.00. Referring to the National Competition of 1898, *The Studio* of London commented: 'For semi-naturalistic decoration the wild rose as treated by John McBurney (Belfast) is first rate.' At the end of his five years' study in Belfast he was awarded an exhibition to South Kensington for two years, after which he came back and settled in Belfast, where he spent the remaining years of his life. He was advised by his doctor to go abroad but preferred to remain in his native land. In 1902 he becamed associated with the Belfast Art Society. He was actively involved in the affairs of the Ulster Literary Theatre and was a close friend of W R Gordon (q v). He was president and exhibited in Ulster Arts Club exhibitions and was a member of the joint arts committee of Belfast Corporation. As an embroidery designer, he had an office at 1 Bankmore Street, Belfast. In the year of his death, Talbot Press, Dublin, published *Unknown Immortals* by Herbert Moore Pim, illustrated by John McBurney. He died 1 December 1917, at his father's residence, 31 Glandore Avenue, Belfast. His work is in the Ulster Museum, where there is a self-portrait.

GLADYS MACCABE 1918-
Landscape and genre painter

Born 5 June 1918, at Randalstown, daughter of George Chalmers, she received her education at Brookvale Collegiate School and studied sculpture and commercial art at Belfast College of Art, 1934-1938. A Member of the Royal Institute of Oil Painters, she has also exhibited in London in Artists of Fame and Promise at the Leicester Galleries, where her husband Max (b 16 August 1917, Belfast), who also paints, showed with her. Both artists, who have lectured on art, also exhibited together at the Watercolour Society of Ireland exhibitions, Dublin. Gladys Maccabe, an Academician of the Royal Ulster Academy, has also shown at the Royal Scottish Academy, and again in Dublin at the Royal Hibernian Academy, the Irish Exhibition of Living Art and the Oireachtas. She was a foundation member of the Ulster Society of Women Artists, 1957, and its first president. Represented in the Arts Council collections in Belfast and Dublin, as well as the Ulster Museum, a portrait by her of William Conor (q v) is in the Ulster Folk and Transport Museum, Cultra.

GEORGE MacCANN 1909-1967
Sculptor and stage-designer

Born in Belfast, 14 February 1909, son of David MacCann, monumental sculptor, George Galway MacCann spent six years at the Royal Belfast Academical Institution before entering the Belfast School of Art in 1926 to study sculpture under Seamus Stoupe (q v), and it was there he met his wife to be, Mercy Hunter (q v). Winning a major scholarship in 1929 to the Royal College of Art, London, he graduated in 1932 and was awarded a special prize largely on the commendation of Henry Moore, then a lecturer at the college. Among an Ulster contingent at the RCA were Romeo Toogood (q v) and a cousin of George's, Crawford Mitchell (q v). Returning to Ulster he taught art at the Royal School, Armagh, then Portadown College, and in 1938-1939 he lectured in sculpture at the Belfast College of Art. During the war he was a captain in the Royal Inniskilling Fusiliers, and when he was in Burma the Mourne Press, Newcastle, published his short stories, *Sparrows Round My Brow* (1942) by George Galway. On returning to Northern Ireland he taught art for a short time at Sullivan Upper School, Holywood. CEMA, in connection with the Festival of Britain 1951, commissioned two sculptures, 'The Four Just Men' and 'St Columba' for the Guildhall, Londonderry. He also painted murals for the Northern Ireland section of the Festival of Britain in London and also for the exhibition of Castlereagh, Belfast. As for sculpture in Belfast, there is an angel at Avoniel Primary School (1935). He was represented at CEMA's exhibition of sculpture at the Belfast Museum and Art Gallery in 1953. Two years later he became a freelance designer and painter, working for the Group Theatre and Lyric Theatre and painting murals for public houses. In 1963 he made the death mask of his friend the poet, Louis MacNeice. In 1965 a one man show was held at the New

Gallery, Belfast, and the following year he was elected an Associate of the Royal Ulster Academy. He also exhibited at the Irish Exhibition of Living Art, Dublin. He died in Belfast on 4 November 1967, and a memorial exhibition of paintings, drawings and sculpture was held in Belfast at Queen's University, 1968. Represented in the Arts Council of Northern Ireland and Armagh County Museum collections.

SOMHAIRLE MacCANN 1901-1975
Painter of landscape and figure subjects

Son of J P MacCann, cabinetmaker, he was born in Belfast and educated at Christian Brothers' School. In 1915 he was appointed as a textile designer to Joseph Mathers Ltd, damask and linen manufacturers, 9 Upper Queen Street, Belfast, and attended Belfast School of Art in his spare time, studying damask and embroidery designing. In 1921 he was sentenced to death by British court martial. Winning the Sorella art scholarship in 1923, the following year he taught at the School of Art. In 1925 he won the Dunville scholarship, enabling him to study at the Royal College of Art, London, for three years. On returning as an ARCA to Ireland, he became art master at Galway Technical School, 1929-1935, a post which was followed by art inspector in the Department of Education, Dublin, 1935-1937. He became principal of the Crawford Municipal School of Art, Cork, in 1937 and stayed in that post until retirement. Apart from exhibitions in Munster, he exhibited at the Royal Hibernian Academy, Dublin, and his work also appeared occasionally as book illustration. He died in Cork in 1975. He is represented in the Cork Municipal Art Gallery.

SEAGHAN MacCATHMHAOIL

See John P Campbell

SAMUEL McCLOY 1831-1904
Figure and genre painter

Born in Lisburn, 13 March 1831, he was apprenticed as a lad to the firm of engravers J and T Smyth, who had a considerable reputation and an address in the 1850s at 25 Castle Street, Belfast. Whilst serving his time there, he studied art at the old School of Design, 1850-51, where he gained an exhibition and several prizes. Subsequently he continued his studies at South Kensington. About 1853 he was appointed master of the Waterford School of Art, which he held for several years, and when he exhibited at the Royal Hibernian Academy exhibition in Dublin in 1862 he gave the school as his address. He continued to exhibit occasionally at the RHA until 1882. He had returned to Belfast in 1875, finding an address at 9 Magdala Street and remained in the city until 1881 when he crossed to London. His work had been seen there occasionally since 1859, especially in the exhibitions of the Society of British Artists. Algernon Graves in his *Dictionary of Artists* gives his speciality as landscape; 1891 was his last exhibiting year in London. McCloy was still a member of the Belfast Art Society in 1895. His wife was a Miss E L Harris of Waterford, also a painter. He died at 117 Fernlea Road, Balham, on 4 October 1904. Represented in the Victoria and Albert Museum, London, and at the Ulster Museum, where there are four oils, notably 'Where the White Foam Kissed my Feet', not to be confused with 'Waterworks, Antrim Road' at the same address.

A D McCORMICK 1860-1943
Seascape, figure painter and illustrator

Arthur David McCormick, son of Arthur McCormick, was born on 14 October 1860 in Coleraine. After school in Coleraine, McCormick studied at the Government School of Design, Belfast. In 1883 he went to South Kensington, London, travelling over with Albert Morrow (q v) and Hugh Thomson (q v). McCormick studied for three years and worked for the *English Illustrated Magazine*. The Royal Academy showed his work in 1889 and he exhibited there for another thirty years. In 1902 he had one picture at the RA: 'Night scene — Central Africa: crocodiles feeding on dead hippo.' Accompanying Sir Martin Conway as artist on his expedition to Karakoram, Himalayas, 1892-1893, and with Clinton T Dent to Central Caucasus, 1895, his illustrations appeared in Conway's *Climbing and Exploration in the Himalayas*, 1894, and in the following year appeared in his own book, *An Artist in the Himalayas*. He worked in many other parts of the world, illustrations decorating the pages of books on Africa, New Zealand, the Netherlands, Norway and India. He was a Fellow of the Royal Geographical Society. As well as the Royal Academy, his works were hung in the exhibitions of the Royal Institute of Painters in Watercolours and the Royal Institute of Oil Painters; he was an RI (1906). He also exhibited at the Royal Hibernian Academy, Dublin. An exhibition of his Alpine views was held at the Alpine Club Gallery, London, in 1904. Later in life he became involved in design, and in 1927 the tobacco manufacturers, John Player

& Son commissioned him to paint what was to become the well-known sailor's head and shoulders on their cigarette packets. His recreations in *Who's Who* were given as mountaineering and yachting; his address was 53 Colet Gardens, Barons Court, London, W 14. He died on 12 March 1943. He is represented in the Victoria and Albert Museum, London. An oil painting, 'His Old Ship', in the Coleraine Town Hall, was loaned by John Player & Son, Nottingham. In 1973 the Central Library in Belfast arranged a display of paintings and book illustrations by A D McCormick.

PATRICK MacDOWELL 1799-1870
Sculptor

Born in Belfast 12 August 1799, he was the son of a tradesman whose heavy losses in business caused ruin. An early death left a widow and only child almost without provision. The sculptor to be was sent to a school which was run by a man called Gordon who combined the trade of an engraver with the profession of a schoolmaster; probably Hugh Gordon, engraver, of 24 Church Lane. 'When his school duties were over for the day, the child of eight years of age was wont to amuse himself by making copies from the collection of prints in the possession of the preceptor.' (*Dublin University Magazine*, November, 1851). When he was about twelve, his mother left Ireland and settled in England where she had friends. Patrick was apprenticed to a London coachbuilder who became bankrupt. Lodging in the house of Peter Francis Chenu (1760-c 1834), a sculptor, of 23 Charles Street, Middlesex Hospital, he began to sketch from casts, and applied himself to drawing and modelling. In 1822 he made his first appearance at the Royal Academy with a posthumous bust of 'J Andrews, Esq', and soon became a regular exhibitor until 1870. Having obtained entrance to the Royal Academy Schools on the recommendation of John Constable, RA (1776-1837), he was also fortunate in his early days to have the good offices of Sir James Emerson Tennent (1804-1869), who was elected MP for Belfast in 1832. A marble bust of Tennent by MacDowell is in the City Hall, Belfast. He was elected an Associate of the Royal Academy in 1841. Thanks to the help of a patron, he visited Italy. In 1846 he was elected an RA. Between 1843 and 1847 he exhibited at the Royal Hibernian Academy, Dublin. In the article in the *Dublin University Magazine* in 1851 the writer also said: '... he is of the middle-size, and slight, with looks silent and dignified; his manners are mild and unassuming, with a winning gentleness which bespeaks the kindliness of his nature.' Such was his fame that a monument to Admiral Lord Exmouth by him was voted by Parliament. A celebrated memorial to the Earl of Belfast (1827-1853), a marble group, is in the Belfast Castle chapel. He also sculpted the statue (1855) of Lord Belfast, in bronze, which is now in the City Hall but was erected by public subscription amounting to £1,500 and placed in front of the Royal Belfast Academical Institution: the original 'Black Man'. MacDowell was one of the sculptors engaged on the Albert Memorial in London and was responsible for the Europe group. He died in London on 9 December 1870. Also represented in the Victoria and Albert Museum, London.

AMBROSE McEVOY 1878-1927
Painter of portraits, figure subjects and landscapes

Born 12 August 1878, at Crudwell, Wiltshire, his father, Captain Ambrose McEvoy, was an Irish soldier of fortune who won a reputation in the American Civil War (1861-1865) and became friendly with Dr Whistler, brother of the artist, J A McN Whistler (1834-1903), who took a lively interest in Ambrose. His father died when he was little more than a boy. On Whistler's advice, he entered the Slade School when aged fifteen, becoming friendly with Augustus John (1878-1961). In 1902 McEvoy married Mary Spencer Edwards. In 1905 he was commissioned to paint three large pictures for the Long Tower Church, Londonderry. Part of the agreement was that he should also supply eighteen pictures (later increased to twenty-two) which were to be copies of Old Masters and portray incidents in the Life of Christ. In this task he was assisted by his wife and for two years they laboured on the stipulated copper panels, which remain today. McEvoy exhibited at the New English Art Club, in the International Society of Painters, Sculptors, and Gravers exhibitions and also at the Royal Academy, becoming a leading society painter, particularly of women, and among his numerous portraits was one of Lady Lavery, wife of Sir John Lavery (q v). He became an Associate of the Royal Academy in 1924 and died in London on 4 January 1927. Represented in many of the principal collections in England, including, in London, the Tate Gallery and the National Portrait Gallery. His work is also in the Ulster Museum. At the City Hall, Belfast, is a portrait of Field Marshal Earl Roberts, after C W Furse (1868-1904). The National Gallery of Ireland, Dublin, has a portrait of the artist's brother, Charles McEvoy (1879-1929), dramatist, and he is also represented in the Cork Municipal Art Gallery. An exhibition of his work was held at the Ulster Museum in 1968.

NORAH McGUINNESS 1903-
Landscape painter and book illustrator

Born 7 November 1903, in Londonderry, her father, Joseph Allison McGuinness, was a coal merchant and shipowner. The family lived at Lawrence Hill and she attended Victoria High School under Misses MacKillip. In 1921 she entered the Metropolitan School of Art, Dublin, studying later at the Chelsea Polytechnic, London, and then under André Lhôte in Paris, 1929-1931. After Paris she went to India to stay with her sister, then returned to London where she became principally engaged in book illustration. In 1937 she went to New York and created window displays for a store in Fifth Avenue, and also held exhibitions. After returning to Dublin in 1939 she eventually continued her window display work and was closely connected with the foundation of the Irish Exhibition of Living Art in 1943, being president for several years. In 1959 an exhibition of her works was jointly sponsored by CEMA and the Belfast Museum and Art Gallery, and held at Stranmillis. In 1968 a retrospective exhibition of paintings, drawings, theatrical designs and book illustrations was held at Trinity College, Dublin; in the following year a selection of the works was shown at the Brooke Park Gallery, Londonderry. Appointed an honorary member of the Royal Hibernian Academy, she later resigned. She has held many Dublin exhibitions in the Victor Waddington Galleries and then in the Dawson Gallery. She returned to her native city in 1976 for an exhibition at the Keys Gallery. Represented in nearly all the Irish collections, including the Ulster Museum and the Hugh Lane Municipal Gallery of Modern Art, Dublin. Two Abbey Theatre designs are in the Victoria and Albert Museum, London.

JAMES MacINTYRE 1926-
Painter of landscape and figure subjects and book illustrator

Born in Coleraine, son of a policeman, James MacIntyre, he attended Woodvale Public Elementary School, Belfast. A self-taught artist, an early exhibition was in 1948, when he was one of nine Ulster painters who showed in the gallery at 55a Donegall Place, Belfast. Included in that group were Arthur Armstrong (q v), George Campbell (q v), and Daniel O'Neill (q v). In 1952 he had a one man show at the same gallery, and three years later he won a CEMA travel scholarship which took him to Paris. London claimed him for six years, principally as a book illustrator, and he had the gigantic task of supplying about 500 illustrations for the two volumes of *Europe and World History* (Edward Arnold (Publishers) Ltd, 1967). CEMA organised shows at their gallery in Chichester Street in 1960 and, when he was in London, 1969, and on each occasion he also exhibited at the Piccadilly Gallery, London. Paintings have also been shown at the Reese Palley Gallery, New Jersey, USA. In recent years he was involved in a poster design for the Arts Council of Northern Ireland and has had one man shows at the Bell Gallery, Belfast, in which paintings of West of Ireland subjects have been prominent. The Trustee Savings Bank commissioned MacIntyre murals for the Mountpottinger branch, Albert Bridge Road, Belfast, and for the Portadown office, the themes being the Shipyards and County Armagh respectively. In addition to exhibiting at the Royal Ulster Academy, of which he is an Associate, he has also shown in Dublin at the Irish Exhibition of Living Art and at the Royal Hibernian Academy; also at the Royal Academy, London. Represented in the collections of the Arts Council of Northern Ireland and the Ulster Museum.

FRANK McKELVEY 1895-1974
Landscape and portrait painter

Born 3 June 1895, in Belfast, son of a painter and decorator, William McKelvey, he worked as a poster designer before entering the Belfast School of Art, where he won the Sir Charles Brett prize for figure drawing (1911-12), the Fitzpatrick prize for figure drawing (1913-14), and a bronze medal (Irish art competition, 1917). In the early part of his career he was commissioned by Thomas McGowan to paint pictures of Old Belfast, or to copy old pictures, and this collection is in the Ulster Museum. In 1923 he became an Associate of the Royal Hibernian Academy, Dublin, and seven years later an RHA. He was represented at the 'Irish Portraits by Ulster Artists' exhibition at the Belfast Museum and Art Gallery, 1927. By the early 1930s he had a studio at Rea's Buildings, 142 Royal Avenue, the same building as Carey and Thomson (see Joseph W Carey) had their business. On 18 July 1933, he was in Londonderry painting a picture of the Lord Mayor of London, Sir Percy Greenaway, Bart, and his Sheriffs, on the occasion of the opening of the Craigavon Bridge. Subsequently this painting was presented to Derry Corporation by Thomas McGowan. One of his rare one man shows was held at Locksley Hall, Fountain Street, Belfast, in 1936, the year that three of his landscapes were purchased as a wedding present for Princess Juliana from Dutch people residing in Ireland. In the following year he had his first one man show in Dublin, at the Victor Waddington Galleries. Throughout his professional life he was a regular exhibitor in Dublin at the Royal Hibernian Academy; he also exhibited at the Oireachtas. He was an Academician of the Royal Ulster

Academy. McKelvey painted the first Governor of Northern Ireland, the Duke of Abercorn (1869-1953), and among his other portraits were: Professor Sir William Thomson (Queen's University, Belfast), Sir Kenneth Sinclair (Belfast Harbour Office), Thos G Henderson (City Hall, Belfast), Sir William Whitla (Ulster Medical Society, Belfast), Charles F Milligan (Town Hall, Bangor). He died on 30 June 1974, at hospital. Represented in the Ulster Museum and other Irish collections, including those of the Cork, Limerick and Waterford municipal galleries.

W G MacKENZIE 1857-1924
Portrait painter

Born in Belfast, he received his early training in the Government School of Design under T M Lindsay, winning the national scholarship and subsequently studying under Sir Edward Poynter, RA (1836-1919) and at Julian's, Paris. In the 1890s he exhibited at the Royal Academy London. He was associated with the Belfast Ramblers' Sketching Club. An active member of the new Belfast Art Society, he showed at their exhibition in 1895, giving his address as Fulham Studios, 452 Fulham Road, London. In Ulster, he became the foremost portrait painter, and MacKenzie (as signed) portraits were hanging on the walls of the Ulster Reform Club, Belfast. A presentation portrait of Sir Crawford McCullagh (1868-1948) was hung in the Royal Hibernian Academy, Dublin. Probably the most difficult task of his painting career was the completion of a large commemoration picture, the proclamation of King Edward VII, from the front of the Old Town Hall, 1901. This picture was begun by Ernest E Taylor (1863-1907) and was uncompleted by the time of his unexpected death from a chill, contracted when arranging for his father's funeral at Bournemouth. MacKenzie was a bachelor and rather a recluse, who, it was said, 'shrank from the economic side of his profession'. He had a studio at 10 Clarence Place, May Street, Belfast. He was an Associate of the Royal Hibernian Academy, who recorded his Christian names as William George, but the death notice inserted by his family refers to 'W Gibbes Mackenzie'. He died on 23 October 1924, at the Royal Victoria Hospital. In the Bangor Town Hall is a portrait of Lady Bangor. Ulster Museum representation includes a portrait of William Gray, MRIA (1830-1917) and a painting which was hung at the Royal Academy, London, in 1894: 'My new shoes!'.

F E McWILLIAM 1909-
Sculptor

Frederick Edward McWilliam was born in Banbridge 30 April 1909, son of Dr W N McWilliam, and was educated at Campbell College, Belfast. In 1926 he entered the Belfast School of Art and two years later the Slade School, London, where he studied under Henry Tonks (1862-1937) and Randolph Schwabe (1885-1948). Tom Carr (q v) and John Luke (q v) were fellow students there. In 1931 he won a leaving scholarship from the Slade which took him to Paris for a year, and when he returned, London became his home. In 1933 he started sculpture, by definition a 'sculptor in stone, wood, terra-cotta, concrete and bronze'. Exhibiting with the British Surrealist Group in 1938, the following year he had his first one man show, at a London gallery, and then war intervened. From 1940-1945 he served in the Far East as Intelligence Officer with the RAF. After the war he taught for a short period at Chelsea School of Art and was also a lecturer at the Slade School. His spell at the Slade ran from 1946-1968. He had joined the London Group in 1949 and in 1951 the committee of the Irish Exhibition of Living Art invited him as a guest artist to their annual exhibition in Dublin. Before the end of the decade he was credited with a number of important commissions, notably, Festival of Britain 'The Four Seasons' (1951); Harlow New Town, 'Elizabeth Frink' (1956); and Altnagelvin Hospital, Londonderry, 'Princess Macha' (1957). In 1959 he became an Associate of the Royal Academy but later resigned. When the international exhibition of sculpture was held in the Municipal Gallery of Modern Art, Dublin, in 1959, McWilliam's 'Study for Princess Macha' was on view. In Belfast, he was one of the artists represented in CEMA's exhibition of sculpture at the Belfast Museum and Art Galler, 1953. In 1960 he had a one man show at Queen's University, Belfast, and he was included in the International Museum of Sculpture exhibition at the Belfast Museum and Art Gallery. His work was now internationally known and in 1963, for example, he was represented in the 7th International Sculpture Exhibition, Japan; International Open Air Sculpture Exhibition, Battersea Park, London; and a one man show at the Felix Landau Gallery, Los Angeles, USA. The year 1961 saw the first of a series of one man shows at the Waddington Galleries, London. Alec Tiranti published in 1964 a book on the artist by Roland Penrose with many illustrations. McWilliam was awarded the CBE in 1966. Winner of the Oireachtas gold medal in Dublin for sculpture in 1971, he was the principal exhibitor at the opening in the same year of the Hillsborough Art Centre, Co Down. In 1973 McClelland Galleries International, Belfast, staged the 'Women of Belfast' exhibition after it had been shown at the Dawson Gallery, Dublin. In

1977 the Bell Gallery, Belfast, had a one man show, and he also exhibited in the Oireachtas again after a two year interval. The Ulster Museum has in its collection one of the 'Women of Belfast' bronzes, also the first cast of 'Head of William Scott' (q v), the second of which is in the Tate Gallery, London along with McWilliam's 'Mary Scott', the painter's wife. He is also represented at Queen's University, Belfast: 'Reclining Figure' (1963). His work is also in the collections of the Arts Council of Northern Ireland, the Victoria and Albert Museum, London, and at the National Portrait Gallery, London, 'Dame Ninette de Valois'.

W HENRY MAGUIRE fl c 1830-1840
Landscape painter

William Henry Maguire was an artist painting in Belfast from about 1830 to 1840, but after that period his whereabouts is unknown. He was one of two associate members of the Association of Artists founded in Belfast in 1836. In 1835 he had painted a picture which showed the rare combined views of the old 'Long Bridge' and the 'halfpenny' or toll bridge, opened in November of the same year. 'View of Belfast' was painted in 1838.

PADRAIG MARRINAN 1906-1973
Painter of landscape and figure subjects

Born in Belfast on 10 December 1906, he was the son of James Marrinan, Royal Irish Constabulary, who was born in County Louth. At the age of five he contracted infantile paralysis, and owing to this disability he was educated privately. He was practically self-taught at art. Antrim, Kerry, Connemara and Donegal were favourite places for painting landscapes. He was also interested in subjects of Celtic mythology and in religious art. He painted Stations of the Cross for the Church of the Good Shepherd, Churchtown, Co Dublin, and for St Colman's Church, Lambeg, Co Antrim. 'Our Lady of Belfast' is in Holy Cross Church, Ardoyne, Belfast. 'The Madonna and Child of Loreto' is at the convent school, Omagh. Member of the Royal Ulster Academy, he exhibited regularly in their exhibitions. In 1951 he had an exhibition at 55a Donegall Place, Belfast. A charcoal drawing in 1934 of the Northern Fenian, Robert Johnston, who died three years later, is in the National Gallery of Ireland, Dublin. He was to have held an exhibition at the Irish Club, London in 1974 but died at Tyrone County Hospital on 25 October 1973; his home address was James Street, Omagh.

CHARLES MIDDLETON 1878-1935
Marine landscape painter

Charles Collins Middleton, the father of Colin Middleton (q v), was born in Manchester, 1878. He attended Manchester College of Art and by profession was a cotton damask designer. After visiting Northern Ireland on his summer holidays, he thought it so beautiful that he decided to stay, obtaining work with William Moyes, damask designer, 35 Royal Avenue, Belfast. In 1899, the year he came to Northern Ireland, he was living at Wellington Street, Belfast. A founder member of the Ulster Arts Club, he was a close friend of his fellow designer and artist, Hans Iten (q v). In 1902 Charles C Middleton, 28 Marsden Gardens, was elected a member of the Belfast Art Society. He formed a damask designing partnership with Hugh Page, who had an office at 7 Adelaide Street. In 1931 he visited Belgium and painted in Bruges. As his health deteriorated, he had a spacious hut erected in the garden of his Chichester Avenue house, no 28, where he continued his design work. He died in 1935. A painting 'Off Dover' is in the Ulster Museum; his easel is still used by his son, Colin Middleton.

COLIN MIDDLETON 1910-
Painter of landscape and figure subjects

Born at 48 Victoria Gardens, Belfast, 29 January 1910, the son of Charles C Middleton (q v). After attending the Belfast Royal Academy for nine years, he left in 1927. His father was a damask designer with indifferent health and Colin joined the firm as an apprentice. He entered the Belfast School of Art for evening and morning classes, principally studying design under Newtown Penprase (q v). In the year 1935 that he became an Associate of the Royal Ulster Academy (later he was appointed an RUA) his father died and the responsibility of running the business fell on his shoulders. In 1941 he showed for the first time at the Royal Hibernian Academy, Dublin, and in 1970 he became an RHA. Belfast Museum and Art Gallery having decided to stage exhibitions of the works of individual Ulster artists, Middleton was the first on the list and the exhibition in 1943 was the largest one man show held at Stranmillis. The following year he had a one man show at the Grafton Gallery, Dublin and in 1945 he exhibited for the first time at the Irish Exhibition of

Living Art. His first exhibition at the Victor Waddington Galleries was in 1949, and subsequently, mainly under that Dublin gallery's motivation, his work was exhibited abroad. Two years after the exhibition at Stranmillis, CEMA organised a show at Tyrone House, Ormeau Avenue, Belfast and others (1954 and 1961) were to follow elsewhere. After spending about a year with his wife Kate and family at the Middleton Murry community in England, they returned in 1948, making their home at Ardglass, Co Down. The following year he exhibited for the first time at the Oireachtas, Dublin, and in 1950 he was represented in the New Irish Painters exhibition, Institute of Contemporary Art, Boston, USA, a tour following. The work of Thurloe Conolly, Gerard Dillon (q v), Nevill Johnson and Daniel O'Neill (q v) was also in that American tour and these were the artists represented in 'Five Irish Painters' at the Tooth Galleries, London, 1951. Middleton's first one man show in London was at Tooth's in 1952. In 1953 the Middleton family moved from Ardglass to Bangor, and in 1954 there began a sixteen year period as a teacher of art — first, part-time, at the Belfast College of Art, 1954-1955, and from 1955-1961 at Coleraine Technical School. From 1961-1970, he was head of the art department at Friends' School, living in Lisburn and then Belfast, but eventually returning to Bangor. During this teaching period he continued to exhibit at group shows in Belfast, Dublin and London (Royal Academy, 1955). In 1955 he had a one man show at Hynes Gallery, Bangor; and in that year the Victor Waddington Galleries staged a retrospective, 1939-1954. In 1958 came the first of three solo shows at the Ritchie Hendriks Gallery, Dublin. Middleton also exhibited at Studio 25, Belfast, in 1962; and again in Belfast at the Magee Gallery in 1962, 1963 and 1964. In 1964, through Arts Council of Northern Ireland auspices, he showed at Armagh County Museum. The Bell Gallery (1965) and New Gallery (1966) had other one man exhibitions in Belfast, and at Coventry in 1968 he exhibited at the Herbert Art Gallery and Museum with T P Flanagan. On a bigger scale were the exhibitions under Arts Council of Northern Ireland auspices in 1965, 1967, 1970 and 1972, notably that for 1970, a retrospective for the period 1960-1970 which was also shown at the Brooke Park Gallery, Londonderry; Edinburgh and Glasgow. The year 1970 saw the first of three shows at the David Hendriks Gallery, Dublin, and the first of five at the Tom Caldwell Gallery, Belfast. In 1968 he was commissioned by the Arts Council of Northern Ireland for a poster design; and he was a prizewinner in the Arts Council's open painting competition. In 1969 he was awarded the MBE. In 1970 he was again commissioned by the Arts Council, for a portrait of J Kenneth Jamison. In 1970, too, he was granted a major subsistence award by the Arts Council, and in connection with the Ulster '71 festivities, one of his paintings was reproduced on a postage stamp and he was commissioned for a mural of County Down. An honorary MA degree was conferred on him by Queen's University, Belfast, in 1972, and in that year he and his wife went on an extensive tour, visiting Australia. An exhibition of Australian watercolours was held at McClelland Galleries International, Belfast, 1973, and the Wilderness Series, Southern Hemisphere and Barcelona 1972-1974 at the Caldwell Gallery, Belfast, 1974. The major exhibition was the retrospective one in 1976 organised by the Arts Council of Northern Ireland and An Chomhairle Ealáion, consisting of nearly 300 works, and held at the Ulster Museum and the Hugh Lane Municipal Gallery of Modern Art, Dublin. In association with this exhibition, the Arts Councils published *Colin Middleton* by John Hewitt. Middleton is represented in practically all the Irish collections, including both Arts Councils, the New University of Ulster, Coleraine; the Ulster Museum and the Hugh Lane Municipal Gallery of Modern Art, Dublin. Representation outside Ireland includes the National Gallery of Victoria, Melbourne.

JOHN W MILLER c 1810-1876
Architectural draughtsman

John Miller's name as an artist first came to light as a member of the Belfast Association of Artists established in 1836, but he was a local architect who designed, when still a student, Third Presbyterian Church in Rosemary Street, Belfast, which was completed in 1831 and destroyed by the 'blitz' in 1941. Miller emigrated to New Zealand, then to Australia, and then to New Zealand again where he died in 1876.

WILLIAM MILLER fl 1762-1778
Portrait and flower painter

William Miller, of Knocknashane and the Montiaghs, near Lurgan, was the son of William Miller (d 1756). He married Sarah Hoope of Hoope Hill, Lurgan, in 1760. The Hoopes were a prominent Quaker family in the town. Writing in the *Ulster Journal of Archaeology*, July, 1906, William Jackson Pigott, a great grandson of this unusual man, referred to him as the constructor of the speaking clock and then stated in part: 'He also painted on glass likenesses of himself and his wife and friends. He made a very extraordinary picture of George Whitefield preaching in a timber yard in Lurgan, the multitude of eager faces around him said to be likenesses of the Lurgan people of that day — amongst others, a well-known idiot woman is easily distinguished. The faces and figures are all cut out and placed in a frame; the text from which he preached being printed; altogether forming a very remarkable picture.' On 3 November 1969 this picture was sold at Sotheby's and bought by the Ulster Museum. Sotheby's stated in their catalogue it was 'The Property of a Lady' and then said: 'Methodists. The Rev. Mr. George Whitefield preaching in a Timber-Yard at Lurgan, Friday, July 12, 1751, a contemporary gouache drawing of Whitefield preaching to a large crowd against a landscape, the figures partly cut out to give a three-dimensional effect, with angels above holding clouds on which blank verse is inscribed...' In the same note in the *Ulster Journal of Archaeology*, W J Pigott added: '... one of his daughters remembers spending an evening alone with him when he was in declining health, and she a little girl seven years old, and watching him painting a picture of flowers on glass... I have a miniature on glass, and set in jewellers' gold, of my grandmother Sarah Jackson, as a baby, in the arms of her mother, Sarah Miller, née Hoope, painted by my great-grandfather, William Miller; and I am under the impression that his portrait is still in the possession of the members of the Druitt family, formerly of Corkraine, Portadown, now residing in England. He was, so far as I have been able to ascertain, a cambric manufacturer...' Evidence concerning a picture credited to William Miller in the first Methodist Chapel in Lurgan, 1778, is contained in a memoir of Margaret Malcomson, by her brother John Malcomson, in the *Methodist Magazine* 1827: 'In this good work they were greatly assisted by Mr. Miller, a respectable woollen draper, although he was not a Methodist. This gentleman was a curious artist, and painted an angel, pointing to Rev. 22, verse 17: "The Spirit and the bride say Come, and whosoever will, let him come, and take of the water of life freely." This picture was placed above the pulpit. Some account of this very ingenious man, and of a speaking statue formed by him, is given by Mr. Wesley in his Journal.' John Malcomson was present as a boy of ten at the opening of the chapel. Miller, the inventor, is mentioned in *The Journal of John Wesley*, 26 April 1762: 'In the evening I preached to a large congregation in the market house at Lurgan. I now embraced the opportunity which I had long desired, of talking with Mr. Miller, the contriver of that statue which was in Lurgan when I was there before. It was the figure of an old man standing in a case, with a curtain drawn before him, over against a clock which stood on the other side of the room. Every time the clock struck he opened the door with one hand, drew back the curtain with the other, turned his head as if looking round on the company, and then said with a loud, clear, articulate voice: "Past one, two, three", and so on. But so many came to see this (the like of which all allowed was not to be seen in Europe) that Mr. Miller was in danger of being ruined, not having time to attend his own business; so, as none offered to purchase it or reward him for his pains, he took the whole machine in pieces; nor has he any thought of ever making anything of the kind again.' However, Wesley records for 14 June 1773: 'After preaching at Lurgan, I inquired of Mr. Miller whether he had any thoughts of perfecting his speaking statue, which had so lain by. He said he had altered his design; that he intended, if he had life and health, to make two, which would not only speak, but sing hymns alternately with an articulate voice; that he had made a trial, and it answered well. But he could not tell when he should finish it, as he had much business of other kinds...' In James Stuart's *Historical Memoirs of the City of Armagh* (1819) there is also a reference to Miller's 'speaking figure, which may possibly yet be in the possession of his son, Joseph Miller, of Lurgan, Esq., M.D.' Stuart goes on to say that the 'mock-man used to call the hour — "Past twelve o'clock — O how the time runs on!"'

CRAWFORD MITCHELL 1908-1976
Linocut and wood engraver

Born in Belfast, son of Joseph Mitchell, confectioner, 222 Grosvenor Road, he attended the Belfast Model School, Falls Road, and from there won the Dunville scholarship to Belfast School of Art, where he studied for three years, winning a scholarship to the Royal College of Art, London, where he worked for a further three years as a contemporary of Mercy Hunter (q v), and George MacCann (q v), his cousin. In 1935 he returned to Northern Ireland and taught part-time at Rainey Endowed School, Magherafelt, and also at Lurgan College and Portadown College. In 1950 he became head of the art department of the newly founded Grosvenor High School, which was then in Roden Street, close to where he had lived as a boy. Remaining at Grosvenor until his retirement in 1970, subsequently he taught part-time at the Rupert Stanley College of Further Education, Belfast, and devoted much of his spare time to printmaking. In 1975 he won the silver medal of the Royal Ulster Academy and in the same year became an Associate. His work is in the Victoria and Albert Museum, London.

JOSEPH MOLLOY 1798-1877
Landscape painter

Born in 1798, Joseph Molloy was appointed art master of the Belfast Academy, Academy Street, in 1828, and in 1830 was elected as master of the Belfast Academical Institution, which position he held for forty years, retiring in 1870. He was a member of the Association of Artists founded in Belfast in 1836. In 1906 the Belfast Museum and Art Gallery exhibited twenty-three sepia drawings by Molloy, sketches of the leading residences in the vicinity of Belfast. These sketches were made during 1828 and 1829 as illustrations for E K Proctor's *Belfast Scenery* published in 1832. Proctor in fact engraved thirty views in aquatint and published in London — in Belfast through Morgan Jellett, 27 Bridge Street. In the Ulster Museum are two seascapes, 'Folkestone, Kent' and 'Tilbury Fort', and a third oil painting, a portrait of Robert Williamson of Lambeg. Residing late in life at Hazlefield Cottage, Molloy died in Belfast in 1877.

JAMES MOORE 1819-1883
Landscape and topographical painter

Born March, 1819, the son of Dr David Moore, a naval surgeon who later settled in Belfast, he enrolled as a medical student at Edinburgh University and obtained his degree of MD in 1842. He was a pupil of James Syme and provided illustrations for *Principles of Surgery* (1842). When in Edinburgh he became acquainted with a number of artists, notably Sam Bough (1822-1878), who encouraged him to draw and paint in watercolours. In 1842 he sketched the embarkation of Queen Victoria viewed from the beach near Granton, Edinburgh. When he returned to Belfast he soon became interested in the affairs of the School of Design. A consultant surgeon at the Belfast Royal Hospital, he made frequent visits to Scotland and England, mainly connected with his practice, acquiring the habit of carrying his 'colour box and sketch block' wherever he travelled. He was particularly keen on sketching ancient buildings and ruins. In the period 1845-1867 he visited France, Holland, Belgium, Germany and the Channel Islands, and he also sketched in Donegal, Dublin and Waterford. He was a member of the Royal Irish Academy, and exhibited at the Royal Hibernian Academy, Dublin, being made an honorary member in 1868. Moore knew Charles Dickens (1812-70), who visited Belfast in 1858, 1867 and 1869 for readings. Moore also exhibited at the Royal Scottish Academy. He died on 28 October 1883, at his residence, 7 Chichester Street, Belfast. He is represented at the National Gallery of Scotland. The Ulster Museum has about 400 of his drawings, one-third of which were exhibited at Stranmillis in 1973 with works by Andrew Nicholl (q v), a special catalogue appearing for each artist. This exhibition was later shown at the National Gallery of Ireland, Dublin.

THE MORROWS
Illustrators

Albert, Edwin, George, Jack and Norman Morrow were five of the eight sons of George Morrow, painter and decorator, of Hanover House, Clifton Street, Belfast. Albert (1863-1927) was born in Comber but left at an early age, attended the Government School of Design in Belfast and won a scholarship to South Kensington School of Art, later becoming a book and magazine illustrator in London with a high reputation as a theatrical poster designer; he is represented in London at the British Museum and the Victoria and Albert Museum. Edwin, who was born in 1877, also attended the School of Design in Belfast and he too won a scholarship to South Kensington where he was one of few to be trained in fresco, becoming a portrait and landscape painter and black and white artist; he is represented in Ulster Museum. George Morrow (1870-1955) was the best known of the family and also attended the School of Design, exhibiting later at the Royal Academy and the Royal Society of British Artists. In 1906 he began to contribute to *Punch*, and after contributing for some eighteen years he joined the staff in 1924, becoming art editor in 1932 and holding that post for five years. He illustrated many books and collaborated in a series with E V Lucas (1868-1938); Methuen published *George Morrow: his book* (1920), *More Morrow* (1921) and *Some More* (1928). He is represented in the Ulster Museum, the Linen Hall Library, Belfast, and the British Museum, London. Jack Morrow (1872-1926) was, like other members of the family, connected with the Ulster Literary Theatre, but was Nationalist in outlook. He was in a painting and decorating business at 15 D'Olier Street, Dublin, and had a spell teaching in the Metropolitan School of Art. A landscape painter and a political cartoonist, he is represented in the National Gallery of Ireland, Dublin. Norman Morrow (1879-1917) also attended the Government School of Design and in London became noted for his weekly theatrical sketches in the *Bystander*; he was also responsible for some posters. His work is in the Ulster Museum.

H ECHLIN NEILL 1888-
Landscape painter

Born 39 Lower Frank Street, Belfast, 14 August 1888, son of Henry James Neill, telegraphist overseer. Harry Neill attended Willowfield National School, Woodstock Road, where his services were much in demand for posters. He studied at the Belfast School of Art and by profession became a lithographic artist, serving his time with McCaw, Stevenson & Orr, Ltd, Castlereagh Road, and later joining S C Allen & Co Ltd, Corporation Street, He became a member of the Belfast Art Society in 1912, and has been exhibiting regularly since then, being made an honorary academician of the Royal Ulster Academy. He has also exhibited at the Royal Hibernian Academy, Dublin. At the age of eighty-nine, he has been conducting an art class in Belfast. Represented in the Ulster Museum.

ANDREW NICHOLL 1804-1886
Landscape painter

Son of Henry Nicholl, bootmaker of Church Lane, Belfast, he was born there on 4 April 1804, and was apprenticed as a compositor with the Belfast printer, Francis Dalzell Finlay, who in 1824 started the *The Northern Whig*, Nicholl working on the newspaper. Drawing and painting, however, were his chief interests, and he probably received encouragement from his elder brother, William Nicholl (q v). A comprehensive series of watercolours of the Antrim coast, and some other views, were painted before he left for London about 1830. In that year he published there 'Dunluce Castle', engraved by J Gleadah. By 1832 he had moved to Dublin where he contributed for the first time to the Royal Hibernian Academy (Associate, 1837; Member, 1860) and to the Royal Academy, sending to the London exhibition until 1854 and other exhibitions there until 1867. Some of his drawings, tending to have a topographical and antiquarian interest, were engraved for the *Dublin Penny Journal* from its first number in July, 1832, and he was one of the artists selected to illustrate *Halls' Ireland: its scenery, character* (1841-43). Then there was a series, published in 1834, of thirteen colour prints, *Views of the Dublin and Kingstown Railway*, engraved by Robert Clayton and published by P Dixon Hardy. When he exhibited at the Royal Hibernian Academy in 1835 he gave his address as 27 College Street, Belfast, and 4 Church Lane, College Green, Dublin. In 1835 there appeared *Fourteen Views in the County of Wicklow*, in collaboration with Henry O'Neill (1798-1880); published by W F Wakeman, Dublin; Ackermann, London. Wakeman was also associated in 1835 with *Picturesque sketches of some of the finest landscape and coast scenery of Ireland* from drawings by George Petrie, RHA, A Nicholl and H O'Neill. *The Northern Coast of Ireland*, a series of twelve lithographs was published by himself at 27 College Street, Belfast, and by Ackermann, London. In 1840 Nicholl took up residence in London where he must have continued his part-time teaching, for he was appointed by the Government as a teacher of painting and drawing at Colombo Academy. In 1846 he travelled to Ceylon, where his friend, Sir James Emerson Tennent (1804-1869), of Belfast, was the Colonial Secretary (see also Patrick MacDowell). In 1848 Nicholl accompanied Tennent on an official tour of the island — a five-week sketching vacation for the artist, who wrote a lengthy account for the *Dublin University Magazine*, November and December issues, 1852 (his 'Sketches from Nature' had appeared in the October 1843 issue). On his return to Europe he lived in London, then Dublin, followed by Belfast where he continued to teach landscape drawing. He died at 7 Camberwell Grove, London, 16 April 1886. A large exhibition of his work was held at 55 Donegall Place, Belfast, in May, 1886. Represented in London at the British Museum and the Victoria and Albert Museum, his work is also in the Linen Hall Library, Belfast; the National Library of Ireland, Dublin; and most important of all, the Ulster Museum. In 1973 the Ulster Museum, in conjunction with an exhibition of the works of Dr James Moore (q v), showed sixty-nine of Nicholl's drawings, practically all watercolours, the separate catalogue also listing the works, again from the permanent collection, not exhibited. This exhibition was later shown at the National Gallery of Ireland, Dublin.

WILLIAM NICHOLL 1794-1840
Landscape painter

Born 11 December 1794, he was the son of Henry Nicholl, a bootmaker of Church Lane, Belfast, and the elder brother of Andrew Nicholl (q v). He was in business as a ship's chandler and flax merchant in Belfast. In 1832 he exhibited at the Royal Hibernian Academy along with his brother Andrew, who moved in that year to Dublin, their name being spelt 'Nichols' in the RHA catalogue. William is believed to have encouraged Andrew to take up painting as a career. He appears to have painted extensively in the neighbourhood of Knock where he lived. He died in April, 1840, and was buried in Knock graveyard. Like his brother, he favoured watercolour, and among the drawings in the Ulster Museum collection are: 'Knock, near Belfast'; 'Cave Hill from Strandtown'; 'The Throne, Cave Hill'; and 'Borthwick Castle'.

Also represented at the British Museum and the Victoria and Albert Museum, London.

PAUL NIETSCHE 1885-1950
Landscape, flower and portrait painter

Born in Kiev of German parents, and educated in Odessa, Paul Nietsche spelt his name differently from his brother Eugen Nitsche, who lived in Greece. Something of a wanderer, he was said to have studied in Berlin, at the Munich Royal Academy and Paris, but it was not until the 1920s that he arrived in England and exhibited in London. About 1926 he travelled to Ulster where he was impressed with the scenery, paying for his accommodation by gifts of paintings, and by same token to his dentist. In 1930 he was living at 411 Lisburn Road, Belfast, and before long he was away to the South of France, Switzerland and Cornwall (1933). Then in 1936 he had a long visit to the USA and Canada. Because of his German parentage, he was interned in the Isle of Man during the War, when he made crayon studies of other internees. On his return to Northern Ireland he had a number of exhibitions in the 1940s at the CEMA gallery at 55a Donegall Place, Belfast, one of which was opened by the novelist, F L Green (1902-1953). At this time Nietsche was residing at 76 Dublin Road. He died at the City Hospital Belfast, 4 October 1950. Represented in the Arts Council of Northern Ireland collection; among his works at the Ulster Museum is a self-portrait. In 1964 a small group, representative of Ulster's artistic and theatrical life, gathered at his graveside to mark the fourteenth anniversary of his death. Photographs of the informal ceremony were taken to West Berlin by Prof J L Montrose, who was the executor of the artist's will, and given to Paul's only surviving brother, Hugo.

JOHN NIXON c 1750-1818
Landscape painter and caricaturist

Although W G Strickland in his *Dictionary of Irish Artists* (1913) states that John Nixon 'appears to have belonged to Belfast', his place of birth still remains uncertain. He was in business with his brother Richard in London as an Irish merchant — probably in Basinghall Street — and managed to combine the duties of secretary of the Beefsteak Club with having the time available to use his talents as an amateur artist; some of his caricatures he etched himself. He was a frequent exhibitor at the Royal Academy from 1784 to 1815. Nixon contributed a number of views of the seats of nobility in Ireland as well as England, and these were engraved for a series published by William Watts, the engraver. He visited Ireland on several occasions in the 1780s and 1790s, also managing a tour of the Netherlands in 1784. 'Dunluce Castle', drawn by him, was engraved in Volume II of *Antiquities of Ireland* by, in part, Francis Grose (1731-1791), appearing in 1796. In the *Copper Plate Magazine* (1792-1802) there are plates after his drawings: 'Belfast', Blarney Castle', 'Carrickfergus Castle' and 'Londonderry'. In Paul Sandby's *The Virtuosi's Museum* (1778) there are illustrations of Dunluce Castle, Shane's Castle and the Cave Hill. Nixon provided drawings for Thomas Pennant's *Journey from London to the Isle of Wight* (1801), and died at Ryde, 1818. The Belfast Harbour Office has a watercolour of High Street, Belfast, 1786. The National Library of Ireland, Dublin, has a watercolour of Dunluce Castle. He is represented in London at the British Museum and the Victoria and Albert Museum. Also at the National Museum of Wales and Carisbrooke Castle.

JOHN O'CONNOR 1830-1889
Scenepainter and architectural draughtsman

Born Co Londonderry 12 August 1830, he was the son of Francis O'Connor. Left an orphan at the age of twelve, he attended a school run in Dublin by the Church of Ireland Education Society and then came to Belfast where a maternal uncle gave him a job as a call-boy at the Belfast theatre and also as an assistant in scenepainting. For a short time he worked in the Dublin theatre and in 1845 joined a travelling company as scenepainter, but as the tour was unprofitable he was reduced, in order to get back to Dublin, to making silhouettes with the pantograph. In 1848 he was in London and found employment at Drury Lane Theatre. Later in the year he joined the Haymarket Theatre staff, eventually becoming principal scenepainter. In 1849 he was in Ireland and painted a 'Diorama of the Queen's Visit' which was exhibited in London at the Chinese Gallery, in which O'Connor is said to have lived for more than a year until the close of the exhibition. Still pursuing his calling as a scenepainter he took up landscape painting and made many architectural drawings, visiting Italy, France and Spain. He contributed to several London exhibitions, including the Royal Academy, between 1853 and 1888. In 1855 he was appointed drawing-master to the London and South-Western Literary and Scientific Institution for three years. He contributed to the Royal Hibernian Academy, Dublin, from 1875 onwards and was elected an Associate in 1883. Drawings were made of many important

Court ceremonials. He painted the scenery for the Shakespeare tercentenary performances at Stratford-on-Avon, 1864; and found time to decorate a whole room for the Duke of Westminster at Eaton Hall with large pictures in oil, and a second room with sets of drawings. Died at Yateley, Hampshire, 23 May 1889. The Ulster Museum has an oil painting, 'The Market Place, Vicenza'. Also represented at the National Gallery of Ireland, Dublin; Walker Art Gallery, Liverpool; and British Museum, London.

DANIEL O'NEILL 1920-1974
Landscape and figure painter

Born in Belfast, 21 January 1920, he was the son of a Belfast electrician, Frank O'Neill, of 4 Dimsdale Street, Belfast, and was educated at St John's Public Elementary School, Colinward Street. Spending only a brief period at the Belfast College of Art, he worked for a short time at the studio of Sidney Smith (q v) in Howard Street. In 1940, one year after he began to paint, he exhibited in a group show at the Mol Gallery, Belfast. In 1943 he exhibited with Gerard Dillon (q v) at the Contemporary Picture Galleries, Dublin. As an electrician in the Belfast Corporation Transport Department he worked on the night shift so that he could paint at home during the day; changing his job to the shipyards the same pattern remained. About 1945, after four years, he decided he could not stand any longer the 'double life', and having received encouragement from the Dublin dealer, Victor Waddington, he had a one man show at his galleries in 1946. He exhibited regularly at the Victor Waddington Galleries until 1955, and during this period he showed regularly in Dublin at the Irish Exhibition of Living Art; works also appeared in Royal Hibernian Academy exhibitions and at the Oireachtas. After the 1946 Waddington exhibition, O'Neill's work began to appear in London and abroad. As for London, his work was in a group show of religious paintings at the Ashley Gallery, 1950; Five Irish Painters, Tooth Galleries, 1951; and with Colin Middleton (q v) at the Tooth Galleries, 1954. Biggest event of all was the loan exhibition of paintings 1944-1952 organised by CEMA and held at the Belfast Museum and Art Gallery in 1952 when more than 4,000 people attended. At this time he was living at 4 Hall Street, Conlig, Co Down, a village in which George Campbell (q v) and Dillon also painted. In 1958 he left Ireland for London and lived in Holland Road, W 14, subsequently showing in Dublin at the Dawson Gallery and in Montreal at the Waddington Galleries. In 1970 he exhibited at the McClelland Galleries, Belfast, his first exhibition in his native city for eighteen years. In 1971 he returned to live in Belfast and died at the City Hospital on 9 March 1974. Represented in most of the Irish collections including both Arts Councils, Ulster Museum, Queen's University, Belfast; and Hugh Lane Municipal Gallery of Modern Art, Dublin. Also in the National Gallery of Victoria, Melbourne, Australia, and the Bishop Suter Gallery, Nelson, New Zealand.

ANTHONY PASQUIN

See John Williams

NEWTON PENPRASE 1888-
Landscape, figure painter and sculptor

Born 24 March 1888, at Redruth, Cornwall, his father was an interior decorator whose work involved the maintenance and restoration of church interiors, and he was sometimes accompanied by his son, who, in 1903, entered Redruth School of Mines and Art. When still a student — he was just seventeen — he had nine sheets of drawings and studies purchased by the Victoria and Albert Museum, London, and some of these were of drawings of woodwork in Cornish churches. October 1st, 1911, proved an eventful day for Newton Penprase — he began teaching on the top floor of the College of Technology, College Square, Belfast. He retired forty-two years later, having acquired the nickname 'Pen'. He exhibited at the Royal Ulster Academy and at the Ulster Arts Club, of which he was president. In 1936 he began the huge task of building in concrete 'Bendhu House' at Ballintoy, Co Antrim; it is still unfinished. His remarkable inventive powers were employed to the full on the house, plus relief and sculptural forms, painted ceilings and stained glass inserts in windows. In 1977 an exhibition, compiled by Roy Johnston, was held at the Arts Council of Northern Ireland Gallery, composed of drawings and studies, paintings, sculpture, and trophies — including one for Ballintoy Regatta. Some of the works were lent by other members of the family, who spelt the name 'Penpraze'.

RAYMOND PIPER 1923-
Portrait painter and illustrator

Born in London 6 April 1923, the son of Frank Piper, he came to Belfast at the age of six. Studied at night at the Belfast College of Art for only a year, he eventually gave up his job in Belfast to teach for a short time at Royal School, Dungannon. Became a professional painter in 1948. Two years later he was awarded a travel scholarship by CEMA, which organisation provided 55a Donegall Place, Belfast, for his first one man show in 1953. In 1957 he was among the CEMA scholarship holders who exhibited there. So much of his time has been spent on portrait commissions in Northern Ireland and England that exhibitions have been few. When he held his first one man show in London in 1961 it was opened by one of his sitters, the former Lord Mayor, Sir Bernard Waley-Cohen. In 1962 at Queen's University he held an exhibition. Within the next few years his portraits were of such diverse people as Eoin ('Pope') O'Mahony and Sir Charles Dodds, president of the Royal College of Physicians, London. Brown Thomas Little Theatre staged an exhibition in 1965, his first 'one man' in Dublin, although he had already exhibited at the Royal Hibernian Academy. An exhibition of his portraits was shown at the Bell Gallery, Belfast, and in 1969 he exhibited at Kenny's Art Gallery, Galway. He has also exhibited at the Royal Ulster Academy, of which he is an Academician. He has illustrated several books written by Richard Hayward, for example: *Ulster and the City of Belfast* (Barker, London, 1950) and *Munster and the City of Cork* (Dent, London, 1964). For several years he worked on a sketch book of ballet and then on illustrations of Irish orchids. An exhibition of the flower drawings was held at the Ulster Museum in 1975, and at the Royal Dublin Society in 1976, followed by the Wexford Festival. In 1974 he was awarded the John Lindley Medal of the Royal Horticultural Society, London, for his illustrations of Irish orchids, and the botanical aspect of his work admitted him to a Fellowship of the Linnaean Society, London. Represented in the Ulster Museum, where there is a portrait of William Conor (q v); the Armagh County Museum; and at the City Hall, Belfast, where there are portraits of former Lord Mayors, Sir William Geddis, Sir Cecil McKee, Sir William Jenkins, Sir Joseph Cairns and Sir Myles Humphreys.

S ROSAMOND PRAEGER 1867-1954
Sculptor

Born in Holywood in 1867, Sophia Rosamond Praeger was the daughter of a linen merchant, William E Praeger, a native of the Hague who came to Belfast as a boy. Educated at Sullivan Upper School 1879-1882, she attended the Government School of Art in Belfast under George Trobridge (q v), and studied also at the Slade School, London, under Alphonse Legros (1837-1911), winning the silver medal for drawing. On returning to Holywood, where she lived all her life, she became a member of the Belfast Ramblers' Sketching Club, and when she exhibited with the Belfast Art Society in 1895 her studio was at 1 Donegall Square West, Belfast, but later she transferred to Holywood: St Brigid's Studio. Early in the century, as her work on sculpture was not bringing in an income, she illustrated at least fifteen children's books, many of which were written by herself. One of the earliest was *Child's Picture Grammar* (Allen, 1900). An early commission for sculpture was 'Literature' (1909), a figure, Carnegie Branch Library, Falls Road, Belfast. She showed at the Irish Decorative Art Association's annual exhibition at Portrush, 1913. In 1920 her most famous piece, 'The Philosopher' was exhibited at the Belfast Art Society (a copy was donated by her to the Belfast Museum and Art Gallery in 1929). The original was bought at the Royal Academy, London, by an American collector, but hundreds of copies were sold all over the world; from the proceeds she built the studio in Holywood. In 1924 she had a joint exhibition in Belfast with her friend, Wilhelmina M Geddes (q v). As well as exhibiting in Belfast and London, she also showed in Dublin and was an honorary member of the Royal Hibernian Academy. She was an Academician of the Ulster Academy of Arts and served as president. In 1938 Queen's University, Belfast, conferred an honorary Master of Arts degree; in 1939 she was awarded the OBE. In 1952, when living at Rock Cottages, Craigavad she decided to give up her Holywood studio. She presented four of her works to Holywood Urban District Council, including a bronze bust of Sir Robert Patterson (1836-1906) and in the same year, 1953, the Praeger Memorial Committee established 'Johnny-The-Jig' in bronze at the children's playground, Holywood. The original of this work is believed to be at the Town Hall, Bangor. The original of 'The Fairy Fountain' is at the Ulster Museum; a copy is at the preparatory department of Sullivan Upper School, Holywood, and there are two plaques by her at the school. Some of her work is in Belfast Cathedral, notably in the baptistry; also a plaque of Lord Carson. She was responsible for a relief (1933) in the entrance hall of the Royal Maternity Hospital; also for a font at Stormont Presbyterian Church, Belfast. In the National Gallery of Ireland, Dublin, is a bronze bust by her of her brother, Robert Lloyd Praeger (1865-1953). She died 17 April 1954. In 1976 the Holywood Business and Professional Women's Club held a memorial exhibition in Holywood.

A MARJORIE ROBINSON 1858-1924
Miniature portrait painter

Born in Belfast 15 August 1858, Marjorie Robinson's earliest evidence of her bent towards art occurred in her schooldays, as a girl of twelve. She was accustomed after finishing her homework to working out an ornamental border around the exercise, consisting of a rustic design of twigs and flowers. The teacher introduced her to Vere Foster (1819-1900), who in turn placed her under the tuition of John Vinycomb (q v), head of the art department at Marcus Ward's, where she became skilled in illuminating. She attended the Government School of Design where she gained several prizes and an exhibition of three years free tuition for proficiency in drawing. For some time she worked at illuminating on her own account, frequently being called upon to insert vignettes, portraits and views in the borders. In 1907 she decided to take up portraiture in London, where she received tuition from Alyn Williams (1865-1955) of the Royal Society of Miniature Painters. She also studied modelling in London, remaining there until the outbreak of War when she returned to Belfast. In 1912 she was elected an AR Min Soc and in 1917 an Associate of the Society of Women Artists. She exhibited in these societies' exhibitions as well as the Royal Academy, but rarely at the Royal Hibernian Academy, Dublin. She was an active member of the Belfast Art Society. In 1922 she contributed at the request of Princess Marie Louise a miniature painted colleen to the Queen's Doll's House. Marjorie Robinson, who lived at 139 Antrim Road, died in Belfast, 22 October 1924, and her brother, John B Robinson, presented as a memorial a collection of twenty-two miniatures to the Belfast Museum and Art Gallery, where she is also represented by sculpture, watercolours, a self-portrait in oil, and the triptych 'St Brigid'. A miniature, presented by her brother, is in the National Gallery of Ireland, Dublin.

MARKEY ROBINSON 1918-
Landscape painter and sculptor

Born in Belfast in 1918, son of a housepainter, he attended Perth Street Public Elementary School, studied for a time at the Belfast College of Art and visited Paris, to which city he has returned on several occasions. His work was in the Northern Ireland Civil Defence Art Exhibitions of 1943 and 1944, held at the Belfast Museum and Art Gallery. He received encouragement from the Rev Dr A L Agnew, who opened several of his exhibitions, and from the collector, Zoltan Lewinter-Frankl, whose collection was shown at the Belfast Museum and Art Gallery in 1958 and work by Markey Robinson was included. As for exhibitions in Belfast, the 1950s was the busiest period, beginning with a one man show at the Cottar's Kitchen, Donegall Square South, in 1950. He also exhibited at 55a Donegall Place and at the McNeice Gallery, 27 Chichester Street. In 1956, at the Robinson and Cleaver Gallery, nets and model boats made by the artist were used as decorative units. His work found a place in the sculpture exhibition at the Belfast Museum and Art Gallery, 1953. In 1961 he showed at the Piccolo Gallery, Wellington Street. A small studio which he used in Lyle Street, Crumlin Road was destroyed in the current troubles. His primitive paintings have appeared in Dublin at the Royal Hibernian Academy exhibitions, and in 1977 he had a one man show at the Oriel Gallery, followed by another at the Sligo Art Gallery. He signs his work 'Markey'. Represented in the collections of the Arts Council of Northern Ireland and the Ulster Museum.

THOMAS ROBINSON fl 1790-1810
Portrait painter

Born in Westmoreland, he early displayed a talent for art and studied for a time under the famous portraitist, George Romney (1734-1802). After leaving Romney, he went to Ireland, and practised for a short time as a portrait painter in Dublin, where wealth and fashion gathered. An advertisement in the *Dublin Chronicle*, 21 August 1790, issued by him from 32 William Street, refers to the short time he had been in Ireland. In his boyhood at Kendal he may have known Dr Thomas Percy (1728-1811), later Bishop of Dromore, and shortly after his eldest son's birth (1793) in Dublin, he decided to go North, probably with the intention of prospering under the patronage of Dr Percy, who lived in a large mansion outside Dromore, Co Down. Robinson lived at Laurencetown, about ten miles from Dromore, and then the family moved to Lisburn, where he painted 'The Battle of Ballynahinch' (1798), exhibited in November with other pictures at the Exchange Rooms in Belfast, admission 'one British Shilling'. The painting was disposed of in December by raffle and won by the Marquess of Hertford. It is now in the National Gallery of Ireland, Dublin, on loan from Aras an Uachtarian. Moving in 1801 to Belfast, Robinson painted there his most important work, 'The Entry of Lord Hardwick into Belfast as Lord Lieutenant', 27 August 1804, but also called 'A Military Procession in honour of Lord Nelson' or even 'Parade of Ulster Volunteers in Castle Place'. Whatever its name, there is no doubt that it contains portraits of many of the prominent citizens of Belfast, and hangs in the Belfast Harbour Office. In 1949 the Belfast Museum and Art Gallery secured a portrait by Thomas Robinson of Rev Dr James Armstrong (1780-1839), a teacher in the Belfast Academy who figures in the assembly of spectators in the Harbour Office painting and was the favourite tutor of Thomas

Romney Robinson, son of the artist and the school's most precocious pupil. It was the son, astronomer and mathematician, who presented the painting to the Harbour Commissioners in 1852. Robinson, the artist, left Belfast in 1808 and settled in Dublin, where he exhibited in 1809 and 1810, at the Society of Artists, a number of portraits. He died at his home, 7 Jervis Street, on 27 July 1810. In the Ulster Museum's collection are also portraits of Col William Sharman, Dr William Gamble and two of William Ritchie. Also represented at the City Art Museum of St Louis, Missouri, USA by a portrait (1792) of Barry Yelverton, second Viscount Avonmore. In the 'Pictures from Ulster Houses' exhibition held at Stranmillis in 1961, a portrait of Agnes Traill, wife of Rev Anthony Traill, Archdeacon of Connor, was signed: 'Robinson of Wyndemere pinxt. 1795'.

RICHARD ROTHWELL 1800-1868
Portrait and genre painter

Born in Athlone, 20 November 1800, he entered the Royal Dublin Society's Schools at the age of fourteen, and in 1820 was awarded a silver medal for his studies in oil from the antique. That period was the most settled of his life. The surprising thing is that he was not called 'Roving' Richard Rothwell. After the foundation of the Royal Hibernian Academy, Dublin, he was elected in 1824 an Associate and in 1826 a Member (he later resigned twice and was made an honorary member). He contributed portraits to the RHA exhibitions from 1826 to 1829, including one of 'Lord and Lady Dufferin' at the 1828 hanging. In 1829 he went to London where he became the chief assistant of Sir Thomas Lawrence (1769-1830). On the death of Lawrence, Rothwell was entrusted with the completion of his commissions; he himself had many portraits requested. From 1830 to 1862 he exhibited seventy-two pictures at the Royal Academy, made up of portraits and fancy subjects. During this time, however, he was on the move. In 1831 he visited Italy and stayed about three years. In 1842 he married Rosa, daughter of Dr Andrew Marshall, a Belfast physician, whom he painted. About 1847, now somewhat depressed by lack of patronage, he left London and settled at Rathfarnham, Co Dublin. Leaving Rathfarnham after a few years, he returned to London; then twice he visited America, apparently leaving his wife and family with her friends in Belfast. But accompanied by his wife and children he went to Rome, where he remained a year and a half; and on his return to England in 1858 he took a house in Leamington, which he left in 1862, and after a short stay in Belfast, where he left his wife and family, he went abroad. Showing some of his works in Paris and Brussels, he then went to Rome and died there, 13 September 1868. Among his portraits at the Ulster Museum are: Frederick Richard, First Earl of Belfast; John Lawless, Marcus Ward, Rev John Scott Porter, Miss Knowles, daughter of Sheridan Knowles; and a self-portrait. At the National Gallery of Ireland, Dublin the works include: 'Calisto' (said by the artist to be his masterpiece); a self-portrait; 'The Young Mother's Pastime'. Also represented at the National Portrait Gallery, London, and the Victoria and Albert Museum, London.

GEORGE W RUSSELL (AE) 1867-1935
Painter of landscapes and inner visions

Born 10 April 1867, at William Street, Lurgan, his father was Thomas Elias Russell, a bookkeeper. He attended the Model School in 1871 and was there with his brother and sister. In 1878 the family moved when his father changed employment for Dublin, where George attended Dr Power's school in Harrington Street and, with an ambition to become an artisit, evening classes at the Metropolitan School of Art in 1880. Entering Rathmines School in 1882, he left two years later and there followed some intermittent employment until he entered the drapery store of Pim's, 1 August 1890, becoming an efficient cashier capable of drawing humorous sketches of members of staff. After a break attending the School of Art, he resumed in 1883, stayed for two years and then enrolled for evening classes at the school attached to the Royal Hibernian Academy. He became a close friend of the sculptor, John Hughes (1865-1941) and the poet, W B Yeats (1865-1939). On becoming involved with the Theosophical Society at Upper Ely Place, he painted mystical murals on the walls. His first exhibition was in 1903 when he showed with the Count Markievicz and his wife at the Leinster Lecture Hall, Molesworth Street, and in 1906 he exhibited at the Royal Hibernian Academy. He was a founder member of the United Arts Club in 1905, and from 1911-33 his home at 17 Rathgar Avenue was one of the centres of Dublin cultural life. Busiest of men, he was the chief exponent of agricultural co-operation and edited, 1905-23, *Irish Homestead*, organ of the Irish Agricultural Organisation Society, at the same time following fervently the arts of painting and poetry — painting in Donegal, often near Dunfanaghy, on his annual holiday. Early in life he spent holidays in Armagh with an aunt. From 1923-30 he edited *The Irish Statesman*. His first visit to America was in 1928. He died at a Bournemouth nursing home, 17 July 1935. He is represented in nearly all the Irish collections. 'The River in the Sand' was given by him to the Belfast Museum and Art Gallery, 'as an Ulsterman in token of my friendship for Ulster'. In the Armagh County Museum there is a self-portrait and other works. A 1903 portrait drawing of W B Yeats by Russell is in the National Gallery of Ireland, Dublin, where there is also a portrait of Russell painted in the same year by Yeats' father, John Butler Yeats (1839-1922). A memorial exhibition was held at the Daniel Egan Gallery, Dublin, 1936. A centenary exhibition in 1967 was held in the Municipal Gallery of Modern Art, Dublin. A biography, *That Myriad Minded Man* (Colin Smythe Ltd) by Henry Summerfield was published in 1975.

WILLIAM SCOTT 1913-
Painter of abstracts and still life

Born on 15 February 1913, at Greenock, Scotland, the family moved to Enniskillen when he was eleven. On 1 September 1924, he enrolled at the Model School. His father, a house-painter and decorator, was tragically killed in a fire in the town a few years later. His mother, left to bring up a large family of eleven young children, did not find life easy. They moved from Forthill Road to Queen Street to Sedan Terrace. After leaving the Model School, William began the Technical School night classes under his mentor, Kathleen Bridle (q v). Moving on to the Belfast College of Art in 1928, he was there for three years, won a scholarship to the Royal Academy Schools, London, and there won a silver medal for sculpture and became a Landseer scholar in painting. In 1935 he was awarded a Leverhulme scholarship, and the following year had his first painting exhibited at the Royal Academy. In 1937 he married Mary Lucas, a sculptress and fellow student at the Royal Academy Schools, and until the outbreak of War they lived on the Continent, helping to run an art school at Pont-Aven in Brittany in the summer months. In 1938 came the first of many honours, Sociétaire du Salon d'Automne. At the outbreak of war he went to Dublin, then London, and from 1942-46 served with the Royal Engineers, learning lithography in the map-making section. In 1942 he had his first one man exhibition in London. In 1945 he exhibited for the first time at the Irish Exhibition of Living Art, Dublin. From 1946-56 he taught at Bath Academy of Art, but in the summer of 1953 he was guest instructor at Alberta University's Banff School of Fine Arts and afterwards visited the USA where he met several of the leading artists. Exhibitions abroad now almost matched the number at home, although he was a regular exhibitor at the Hanover Gallery, London. In 1953 and 1961 he was represented at the Bienal, Sao Paulo, Brazil; 1958, Biennale, Venice. At private galleries abroad his work was shown in the USA, Italy, Switzerland, West Germany, France, Canada and Australia. Nearer home, he executed a mural 46 ft long by 9 ft high for Altnagelvin Hospital, Londonderry, 1961; in 1963 the Ulster Museum held a retrospective exhibition; and in 1972 the Tate Gallery, London, held a retrospective 1938-71. The Arts Council of Northern Ireland held the 'Teacher and Two Pupils' exhibition at their gallery in 1973 with the works of Kathleen Bridle, William Scott and T P Flanagan; later it was shown at Enniskillen Collegiate School. Two publications are of particular interest: *Soldiers Verse* (Muller, London, 1945) by Patric Dickinson; lithographs by William Scott; and *William Scott* (Methuen, London, 1963) by Ronald Alley. Recent honours are: 1966, CBE; 1975, Honorary Doctor, Royal College of Art, London; 1976, Hon D Litt, Queen's University, Belfast; 1977, Hon D Litt, Trinity College, Dublin. Scott is represented in more collections at home and abroad than any other artist with Irish connections. His work is in the collections of the Arts Council of Northern Ireland, Belfast Education and Library Board, Hugh Lane Municipal Gallery of Modern Art, Dublin; Trinity College, Dublin, Gallery; Ulster Museum. Among many others might be mentioned: Tate Gallery, London; Musée National d'art Moderne, Paris; Museum of Modern Art, New York; Galleria Nazionale d'Arte Moderna, Rome.

ELIZABETH SHAW 1920-
Illustrator

Born in Belfast 4 May 1920, Elizabeth Shaw was the daughter of a bank manager in York Street and was educated at the Belfast Royal Academy. The family left Belfast in 1933 to live in Bedford, where Betty went to the High School, finishing in December, 1937. In 1938 she entered Chelsea School of Art where she studied illustration under Graham Sutherland. Because of the war the art school was closed down in 1940 and she was directed into industry. In 1944 she married Rene Graetz, the German sculptor, who was a refugee from the Nazi regime. After the war she became a freelance illustrator in London, contributing to *Lilliput* and other journals. Moving to Berlin in 1946 with her husband, she made her home there. She quickly built up a secure reputation for her drawings and lithographs, and for her popular series of travel sketches publicised in *Das Magazin*, which took her across Europe. She also illustrated many books, including some children's stories written by herself. In 1958 she was represented in an exhibition of sculpture and graphic work from the German Democratic Republic, held in London. An extensive exhibition of her work, including forty-three sets of drawings made on her travels, was held in 1964 at the Herbert Art Gallery and Museum, Coventry, organised by the director, an Ulsterman, John Hewitt.

JAMES SLEATOR 1889-1950
Painter of portraits and still life

James Sinton Sleator was born in County Armagh in June, 1889, son of William Slator (different spelling), who taught at Derryvane National School, near Portadown, and was later principal of Strandtown National School, Belfast. The son studied at Belfast School of Art and in 1910 secured a scholarship for study at the Metropolitan School of Art, Dublin, where he was under Sir William Orpen (1878-1931) and won several prizes. Continuing his studies at the Slade School, London, from there he went to Paris. He returned to Dublin in 1915 to become a teacher at the Metropolitan. Elected an Associate of the Royal Hibernian Academy in 1917, he became a Member in the same year. Five years later he went to Florence where he painted portraits and landscapes, finally returning to London where he set up a studio (1927) as a portrait painter and where he was closely associated with Sir William Orpen. Sleator was a member of the Chelsea Arts Club and exhibited at the Royal Academy and with the Royal Society of Portrait Painters. He taught painting to Winston Churchill, taking over the job from Orpen. In 1935 he was made an honorary member of the Ulster Arts Club, Belfast. He kept in touch with his sister Ethel Slator in Belfast and visited her and his friends. He returned from London to Dublin in 1941 and, apart from an occasional journey abroad, remained there until his death. Among his principal portraits were those of Sir John Lavery (q v), Sir William Orpen, Dermod O'Brien, Lennox Robinson, Jack B Yeats and Rutherford Mayne. He became president of the Royal Hibernian Academy in 1945 and held this office until his death at Academy House, Ely Place, Dublin, on 19 January 1950. In the Ulster Museum is a portrait of Forrest Reid; the Armagh County Museum and the National Gallery of Ireland, Dublin, have self-portraits. In 1951 a memorial exhibition at the Victor Waddington Galleries, Dublin, was opened by the Ulster playwright, Rutherford Mayne (1879-1967).

SIDNEY SMITH 1912-
Mural painter

Born in 1912 in Belfast, son of a businessman, Alexander Smith, he received his education at Royal Belfast Academical Institution. Attending evening classes at the Belfast College of Art, he met Daniel O'Neill (q v). Under the private tuition of R Boyd Morrison (1896-1969), during which he spent months drawing, he was eventually allowed to paint his first picture — and sold it at the Royal Hibernian Academy, Dublin. Initially he painted landscapes with occasional portraits — one was a drawing of the poet W R Rodgers (1909-1969). When living at 50 Landscape Terrace, Belfast, in 1939, he had two paintings exhibited by the Royal Society of British Artists. In his studio at 20 Howard Street, he helped Daniel O'Neill, and worked locally himself on Belfast scenes; eight drawings of air raid subjects are in the Ulster Museum. Portraits of American Army officers proved lucrative. During the War, too, he gave talks on art in country towns and in Belfast factories, all under the auspices of CEMA. He also exhibited at the Ulster Academy of Arts. The first mural he ever painted was at the British Restaurant in Victoria Street, Belfast, and in 1948 he went to live in London where he became fully occupied with this medium. In 1951 his large painting 'The Flight of the Huguenots' was shown in the Ulster Farm and Factory Exhibition at Castlereagh, Belfast; this painting is now in the Town Hall, Bangor. In 1958 he returned to Belfast to paint murals in the new Union-Castle liner *Pendennis Castle*, at Queen's Island. He also painted murals in the Canadian Pacific liner *Empress of Britain*, and on five Clan Line ships. By 1960 he estimated that he had covered more than 100,000 square feet since he concentrated on murals. One of his biggest tasks was completed in 1966: a large and complex mural, measuring 48 feet by 12 feet with many life-size figures, commissioned by Lord and Lady Beaverbrook for the new Playhouse Theatre at Fredericton, New Brunswick. Sidney Smith has travelled all over the world, from China to South America, but is not now climbing so many ladders. Also represented in the Arts Council of Northern Ireland and Armagh County Museum collections.

A C STANNUS fl 1851-1909
Marine and landscape painter

Anthony Carey Stannus was said to be one of the most versatile artists of the early students of 1850-54 at the Belfast School of Design, but a watercolour by him (a copy?) at the Belfast Harbour Office of High Street, Belfast, 1835, does not help the archivist! Further confusion arises from a note on the back of a watercolour at the Bangor Town Hall: 'Born about 1835 ... died about 1890'. However, the *Dictionary of British Watercolour Artists up to 1920* says: '... lived in London and exhibited from 1862 to 1909. He painted landscapes and marine subjects, often from the Cornish coasts, as well as architectural, figure and genre subjects. He also painted in Ireland and Belgium.' No doubt the Anthony Carey Stannus who exhibited at the Royal Academy from 1863-1903 was a Belfast Stannus because 'Evening on the

Dogger bank', shown in the 1902 exhibition, was presented by the artist to the Belfast Museum and Art Gallery. In 1903 he was living at 39 Westbourne Park Road, London. As for his early days in Belfast, the Harbour Office has a watercolour, 'Launch at the Queen's Island', 1858. In 1860 he was living at 13 Donegall Place, Belfast, the same address as Marcus Ward & Co, the printers and stationers. In 1882 he was living at 11 Chichester Street, Belfast, when he exhibited at the exhibition of Irish Arts and Manufactures at the Rotunda, Dublin; and also in 1883, the Cork Industrial Exhibition. He was president of the Belfast Ramblers' Sketching Club and by 1895 he was an honorary member of the Belfast Art Society and living at Tudor House, Holywood. He is represented at the Victoria and Albert Museum, London. One London source quotes his 'dates' as 1830-1919 (!) but alas the origin of this information is unknown.

PATRIC STEVENSON 1909-
Landscape painter

Born 5 September 1909, at Wadhurst, Sussex, Patric Stevenson is the son of a former Dean of Waterford, Very Rev Leslie Creery Stevenson. Educated at Methodist College, Belfast, he studied at Belfast School of Art (1926-28), moving on to the Slade School, London. In 1936 he exhibited at the Robinson & Cleaver gallery, Belfast; the following year at Magee's Gallery. From 1940-45 he served in the RAF as a radar mechanic, and from 1946-50 he was arts assistant at Pendley Adult Education Centre, Tring, Herts, where he lectured on art and music. A painting of Marsworth Churchyard, Herts, was bought by the Duke of Edinburgh in 1949. The next year he returned to Northern Ireland. In 1953 he was appointed as Associate of the Royal Ulster Academy; in 1959 a full member. He has also exhibited at the Royal Hibernian Academy, Dublin, and in London at exhibitions of the New English Art Club and the Royal Institute of Painters in Watercolours. The 1950s saw exhibitions at 55a Donegall Place, Belfast, and the Grafton Gallery, Dublin; also he personally pioneered open-air exhibitions during the summer at Rostrevor, 1951-1954; and at The Shambles, Hillsborough, 1955-1968. In 1961 he had an exhibition in Belfast at the CEMA gallery, 7 Chichester Street. He was director of the Hillsborough Art Centre which opened in 1971 but had to close because of the troubles. In recent years, too, he has served as the Royal Ulster Academy's secretary-administrator and then its president. Represented in the Ulster Museum, Ulster Folk and Transport Museum, Cultra; and Waterford Municipal Art Gallery.

SEAMUS STOUPE 1872-1949
Sculptor

Born 27 October 1872, in Belfast, James Stoupe was the son of John Stoupe, carpenter. Educated at the Belfast Model School, he presumably attended the old Government School of Design. He entered the Belfast School of Art as modelling master on 1 October 1904, and remained until 1938. In 1894, when living at 55 Hanover Street, Belfast, he was elected a member of the Belfast Art Society. He was also a painter and had an interest in lithography, attending a course of lectures on the subject at the Metropolitan School of Art, Dublin, 1915. In 1921 he was president of the Ulster Arts Club and it was at that year's exhibition he showed the portrait of Councillor (later Alderman) James A Doran. This portrait bust was shown at the 1927 exhibition of 'Irish portraits by Ulster artists' at the Belfast Museum and Art Gallery together with one of William Gray, MRIA. He exhibited at the Royal Hibernian Academy, Dublin. Died on 20 May 1949. Represented in the Ulster Museum by a self-portrait drawing and among oil paintings are: 'Portrait of William Gray' and 'French Barque in York Dock', 1912.

T C THOMPSON c 1778-1857
Portrait painter

Thomas Clement Thompson was born about 1778, probably a native of Belfast. Admitted to the Dublin Society's drawing schools in 1796, on leaving he became a miniature painter in Belfast and Dublin. An advertisement in *Saunders' Newsletter* in October 1802 said 'Mr. Thompson, miniature painter, having returned from the north, informs his friends and the public that he is now ready to attend their commands as usual.' In 1803 he was back in Belfast, but when next he exhibited in Dublin in 1809 he sent, from Belfast, a portrait in oil to the exhibition in Hawkins Street, having apparently abandoned miniature painting. In 1810 he settled in Dublin and soon had a flourishing practice, painting many persons of distinction. At the exhibition in Hawkins Street in 1816 he contributed no fewer than fifteen portraits. In 1817 he left for London and did not return to Ireland except for occasional visits. During the period 1816-1857 he showed nearly 150 paintings at leading exhibitions in London, principally the Royal Academy. In addition to portraits, he also painted genre, biblical subjects, scenes from Shakespeare, and landscape. On the foundation of the Royal Hibernian Academy in 1823 he was elected one of the original Members, and contributed occasionally to its exhibitions down to 1854. When he exhibited at the 1826 exhibition his address was 13 Henrietta Street, Cavendish Square, London. About 1853 he went to Cheltenham and in 1856 resigned his membership of the RHA and was made an honorary member. He died at his residence, 18 Cambray Place, Cheltenham, on 11 February 1857. Included in the Ulster Museum's collection is 'Searching the Scriptures' and a portrait of Francis Johnston. The Linen Hall Library, Belfast, has a portrait of its president, 1798-1817, Rev William Bruce, DD. Among the paintings at the National Gallery of Ireland, Dublin are: Portrait of John Thomas Troy (1739-1823), Archbishop of Dublin, painted in 1821; self-portrait; and 'Our Lord in the House of Martha and Mary'. At the Royal Dublin Society: 'Embarkation of George IV from Kingstown' (1821), painted 1821-26, containing numerous portraits.

HUGH THOMSON 1860-1920
Illustrator

Born 1 June 1860, at 9 Church Street, Coleraine, he was forever sketching as a schoolboy 'with many a lesson book suffering grieviously'. Employed in the office of the firm of E Gribbon & Sons Ltd, linen manufacturers, Coleraine, it was soon obvious he was unsuited for the world of commerce. Thanks to the firm's proprietor, Henry A Gribbon, Thomson secured in 1877 an apprenticeship in Marcus Ward's in Belfast, on especially favourable terms, and John Vinycomb (q v), the head of the artist department, took him under his care. Vinycomb said later that he was the most outstanding original draughtsman they had ever had. Thomson, who would sometimes rise at 5 o'clock in the summer to sketch in the fields in the vicinity of Ballynafeigh, was one of the staff of artists of the Royal Ulster Works (Marcus Ward's) who formed 'The Belfast Ramblers' Sketching Club'. In 1883 he decided on London in the hope of becoming a book illustrator, but found employment in this line very difficult. Largely through the goodwill of Comyns Carr he secured employment on the staff of *The English Illustrated Magazine*. This proved to be the foundation of his success as a book illustrator, and he was responsible for the illustrations for more than sixty books, principally classics and many published by Macmillan. The first appeared in 1886: *Days with Sir Roger de Coverley*. In 1879 the Fine Art Society arranged a joint exhibition of drawings by Linley Sambourne and Hugh Thomson. In 1895, when living at Seaford, Sussex, he was an honorary member of the Belfast Art Society. *The Vicar of Wakefield* (1890) and *Cranford* (1891) were the next Macmillan publications. He kept in touch with his homeland and wrote weekly letters to his father in Kilrea, Co Derry. In 1906 he held in Belfast an exhibition at the Ulster Arts Club. He was a member of the Royal Institute of Water Colour Painters, and illustrated for Macmillan's 'Highways and Byways' series. By 1919, when he toured the Severn Valley on a bicycle in search of sketches, his life's work was virtually over. He died on 7 May 1920, at his home at Wandsworth Common. In 1931 appeared: *Hugh Thomson: His art, his letters, his humour and his charm* (Black, London) by M H Spielmann and Walter Jerrold. In 1935 the Belfast Museum and Art Gallery arranged an exhibition of his works. Among the drawings at the Ulster Museum are: 'The same kind of delicate flattery'; 'Delighted in his dry bon-mots'; and a caricature of Harry Lauder. Also represented at the Ulster Folk and Transport Museum, Cultra; and in London at the British Museum, Imperial War Museum and Victoria and Albert Museum.

ROMEO TOOGOOD 1902-1966
Landscape painter

Born 6 May 1902, in Belfast, Romeo Charles Toogood attended Hillman Street Public Elementary School and began his career as a painter and decorator. Later he went to the Belfast School of Art, where he taught part-time before attending the Royal College of Art, London. On returning to Northern Ireland he began his teaching career at Larne Technical School, then he moved to Dungannon Technical School, Down High School and Friends' School, Lisburn. On 1 August 1949, be became painting and drawing master at the Belfast College of Art, and among his pupils there were Basil Blackshaw, Terry Flanagan and Cherith Boyd (now McKinstry). When he found time to paint, he often favoured the Lagan Valley or the Cushendun area. He was an Associate of the Royal Ulster Academy. Exhibiting at the Royal Hibernian Academy, Dublin, was rare. When he showed at the Piccolo Gallery, Belfast, 1958, it was under the auspices of CEMA. He also exhibited at the Magee Gallery, Belfast, 1964. He died 11 August 1966, in hospital. Represented in Arts Council of Northern Ireland collection and the Ulster Museum's, which includes 'Dan Nancy's, Cushendun'.

GEORGE TROBRIDGE 1851-1909
Landscape painter

Born at Exeter in 1851, he studied in the National Art Training School in London from 1875 to 1880, winning a gold medal for painting and other honours. He was an

ARCA. In 1880 he was appointed headmaster of the Government School of Design in Belfast, where he remained until 1901, when the school was taken over by the Corporation. However, the Belfast School of Art staff records show that as a teacher he began on 17 September 1901, and finished November, 1906. He exhibited in the British Institution in 1884 and 1889, also in other English exhibitions; and at the Belfast Ramblers' Sketching Club exhibition in 1888. He was in the list of members of the Belfast Art Society in 1895 with an address at 2 Mount Pleasant, Belfast. His work was also shown in Dublin at the Royal Hibernian Academy where appreciation — judging by sales — was much more apparent than in Belfast. Trobridge was the author of *The Principles of Perspective as applied to Model Drawing and Sketching from Nature* (London, 1884). His name was also associated with the *'Grosvenor' Freehand Drawing Cards* (Charles & Dible, London, 1907). He also wrote *Swedenborg, his life, teachings and influence* (Warne, London, 1907) and *The Foundations of Philosophy* (Speirs, London, 1904), a novel, and contributed to journals and newspapers. In a letter in the *Northern Whig*, 19 March 1908, on the progress of art in Belfast, he said: 'I do not disparage our local Art Society and the Ulster Arts Club, but the former is chiefly composed of amateurs, and the latter is a social club.' About 1908 he left Belfast to reside in England and died at Gloucester, 1909. Represented at the Ulster Museum.

JOHN TURNER 1916-
Portrait painter

Born in 1916 in Percy Street, Belfast, his father was a blacksmith. He attended Belfast College of Art from 1935-38 and the Slade School, London, 1938-41. On returning to Northern Ireland he taught art at Coleraine Technical School and Coleraine High School, 1942-43. In 1948, under the auspices of CEMA, he held a one man exhibition of portraits at 55a Donegall Place, Belfast. It was this aspect of painting that he concentrated on and at the same time he was interested in the revival of old techniques in painting. In 1955 he was teaching part-time at Down High School, Downpatrick, and Ballynahinch Technical School. His work was included in the Lewinter-Frankl Collection exhibition held at the Belfast Museum and Art Gallery, 1958. He joined the part-time staff at the Belfast College of Art in 1960 and in 1964 became full-time. An Academician of the Royal Ulster Academy, in 1975 he was commissioned by the Arts Council of Northern Ireland for a portrait of Elizabeth Begley; subsequently this painting was exhibited in the 'Women of Ulster' exhibition. In the City Hall, Belfast, there are portraits of three Lord Mayors: Sir Percival Brown, Sir William Coates and Sir James Norritt. A portrait (1947) of Rev George Woodburn was hung in Magee University College, Londonderry. Also represented at Armagh County Museum, Ulster Museum and in the collection of the Arts Council of Northern Ireland.

PETER TURNERELLI 1774-1839
Sculptor

Born in Belfast in 1774, his father was James Tognarelli, the son of an Italian refugee, and worked as a statuary in Belfast, and afterwards, from 1787, in Dublin. He transformed his name to 'Turnerelli'. Peter entered a seminary in Dublin, and was intended for the priesthood. In 1792 his mother died and the rest of the family left Dublin and settled in London. In 1793 he gave up his studies for the church and went to England too. In London, he became a pupil of the sculptor, Peter Francis Chenu (1760-c1834), who later befriended Patrick MacDowell (q v). He also joined the Royal Academy Schools, where his name in the admission book was spelt 'Taguarelli', and distinguished himself there as a student. In 1797 he was recommended as a teacher of modelling to the young Princesses. He held the appointment for three years, and during that time executed busts of all the members of the Royal Family. On the termination of his engagement he was appointed Sculptor-in-Ordinary to the Royal Family, and was offered a knighthood by George III (reigned 1760-1820), which he declined. Apart from the English Royal Family, he had many other distinguished clients, notably Louis XVIII. In 1802 he made his first appearance as an exhibitor at the Royal Academy; thereafter his works appeared frequently until 1838, and during that period he showed more than one hundred. In 1812 Turnerelli visited Ireland, and among the many commissions he obtained was one of Henry Grattan (1746-1820), now in the National Gallery of Ireland, Dublin, and said to have been made in eleven hours. In 1828, 1829 and 1830 he was again in Ireland, and modelled a bust (1829) of Daniel O'Connell, of which, it is also said, at least 10,000 copies were made. Turnerelli exhibited in the Royal Hibernian Academy in 1828, 1829 and 1830; and again in 1834 and 1835. In addition to his portrait busts, he did some important monuments, for example, the national one to the memory of Robert Burns at Dumfries. He died at his home in Newman Street, London, 20 March 1839. Also represented: National Portrait Gallery, London; Scottish National Portrait Gallery, Edinburgh.

JOHN VINYCOMB 1833-1928
Illuminator and heraldic artist

Born 1833 in Newcastle-on-Tyne, John Vinycomb was the son of Andrew Vinycomb of an old Devonshire family. John studied art at the School of Design, Newcastle-on-Tyne. In 1855 he entered as an engraver the art department of Marcus Ward & Co, Belfast, and rose to head of the department, remaining until the break-up of the firm in 1899, after which he occupied himself as an artist, designer and illuminator. In 1900 some of his old friends, on hearing of the likelihood of his soon leaving Belfast for London, presented him with a purse containing 100 guineas, and to Mrs Vinycomb two silver candelabra. The Vinycombs, however, did not leave Belfast until 1909, by which time, when he was living at The Scriptorium, Riverside, Holywood, he was a member of the Royal Irish Academy; vice-president of the Royal Society of Antiquaries of Ireland and vice-president of the Ex-libris Society of London (he had an international reputation for his bookplate designs); one of the founders and past president of the Belfast Art Society, and of the Ulster Arts Club; past president of Belfast Naturalists' Field Club. Vinycomb was a recognised authority on heraldry and illuminating, and the publisher and author of various books, notably on bookplates. At the age of ninety-four he was still active in his work. He died in London, 1928. At the City Hall, Belfast, is a scroll for Mrs W J Pirrie, first Lady Burgess. Also represented at the Belfast Harbour Office and the Victoria and Albert Museum, London. In the Ulster Museum is a portrait of John Vinycomb, MRIA, by Ernest E Taylor (1863-1907).

JOHN WARD 1832-1912
Landscape painter

Born in Belfast 7 August 1832, he was the son by the second wife of the famous Marcus Ward of Marcus Ward and Co, printers and publishers. He attended the Royal Belfast Academical Institution, and was one of the first pupils of the Belfast School of Design in the north wing of that building. Ward's artistic gifts were early manifest. First intended for the architect's profession, his life plans underwent alteration on the death of his father in 1847 and he soon entered the business. A writer in the *Northern Whig*, 12 November 1931 stated: 'The Belfast Art Society was born, cradled and nurtured in the artists' department of the great printing works of Marcus Ward & Co, of which Mr John Ward was the driving power. He was a watercolour painter himself, and exhibited in the art gallery in connection with the firm under the name of "Bonnington Smith" and gave every encouragement to the artists on the staff to exhibit their work. These exhibitions were held in the magnificent premises in Donegall Place, where the retail fancy business was carried on, with the late William Rodman as manager ... John Ward also started a drawing class after hours in one of the rooms of the works with John Vinycomb as superintendent.' The Belfast Ramblers' Sketching Club was founded in 1879 and changed its name to the Belfast Art Society at a meeting in November, 1890. Ward, an Egyptologist, wintered in Egypt and Sicily, where he indulged in his favourite hobby of sketching and also found ample material for the exercise of his literary gifts. He was an enthusiastic collector of Greek coins and Egyptian scarabs. From 1876 to 1890 he was the honorary editor of Sir E J Poynter's *South Kensington Drawing Book* and in 1890 he published *A selection from the Liber Studiorum of J M W Turner as a Drawing-book for students of Landscape Art*. He was the author of other books, including *Pyramids and Progress: Sketches from Egypt*, published in 1900. When he left Belfast to live in England he had been residing at Lennoxvale. He died on 17 February 1912, at The Mount, Farningham, Kent.

ROBERT WARRINGTON fl 1831-1839
Portrait and landscape painter

In his *Dictionary of Irish Artists* (1913), W G Strickland states that Warrington 'lived and practised in Belfast for many years'. The date of his birth and death is still unknown. In 1831 he sent to the Royal Hibernian Academy in Dublin portraits of William Tennent, Belfast, and J Sheridan Knowles; his address in the catalogue was 28 Castle Street, Belfast. He was a member of the Association of Artists on its establishment in Belfast in 1836. As he had worked in England, he may eventually have decided to reside there: for Mr John Cunningham, of Macedon, Belfast, he made a number of copies of the principal pictures in the Dulwich College Picture Gallery. Judging by the title, a 'Portrait of James French, Chronometer Maker, London, a native of Randalstown', shown in Belfast in 1888, might have been painted in London. He also painted 'Launch of the Aurora, the first passenger steamer built in Belfast, 1839'.

GEORGE WATERS 1863-1947
Landscape painter

Born in 1863 in Holywood, he was the son of Austin Waters, Town Clerk of that town for many years. He studied at the

Government School of Design in Belfast and won prizes. He spent a great part of his life as a lithographic artist with David Allen & Sons. His work was in the Belfast Ramblers' Sketching Club exhibition, 1890, and he was a founder member of the Belfast Art Society. He painted most of his watercolours in Counties Antrim, Donegal, Dublin and Wicklow, exhibiting occasionally at Magee's Gallery, Belfast. He formed, along with several of his contemporaries, including William Conor (q v) and Frank McKelvey (q v), the Ulster Society of Painters. Waters was also a member of the Ulster Arts Club. He died 28 March 1947, at his home, 11 Ophir Gardens, Belfast. Represented at the Ulster Museum by 'On the Dodder' and 'Spring's advent, Belvoir Park'; also at the Linen Hall Library, Belfast, and Limerick Municipal Art Gallery.

FRANK WILES 1889-1956
Sculptor

Francis Wiles was born at The Crannie, Larne, on 7 January 1889. His father, David N Wiles, was a Petty Sessions clerk in Larne. His mother, Margaret, was a woodcarver of ability. A sister of Frank's said that he became a sculptor when he was ten years of age — he set out to collect fishing bait in the harbour and returned carrying a handful of clay, from which he modelled a bunch of grapes. Educated at Larne Grammar School, close to his home, he studied sculpture at Belfast School of Art under Seamus Stoupe (q v) and won a travel scholarship to Paris. Later he attended the Metropolitan School of Art, Dublin, where he worked under Oliver Sheppard (1865-1941) and was a friend of James Sleator (q v). In the National Competition of Schools of Art he won in 1914 a gold medal for a modelled figure of a kneeling girl. After leaving the Dublin art school, he lived and worked for several years in that city. At the Royal Academy, London, 1918, he showed a carved figure of a kneeling girl in marble which had been done for the Dowager Lady Smiley, Park Street, Park Lane, London. Wiles modelled a figure of a boy for a war memorial library at St Columba's College, Rathfarnham, Dublin. A figure in Irish limestone of Saint Finbarre is at St Finbarre's Cathedral, Cork. Exhibiting with the Belfast Art Society, he later became an Academician of the Royal Ulster Academy. He showed also at the Royal Hibernian Academy, Dublin, often attending the annual exhibitions. In 1927 at the 'Irish Portraits by Ulster Artists' exhibition arranged by the Belfast Museum and Art Gallery, Wiles showed a bronze portrait relief of Judge J Creed Meredith of Dublin. He was the sculptor responsible for the Newcastle, Co Down, war memorial, and was included in the exhibition of sculpture at the Belfast Museum and Art Gallery in 1953. At the Moyle Hospital, Larne, John Moore Killen, MD, is commemorated by a bronze plaque by Wiles. He died at The Cottage Hospital, Larne, 20 September 1956. Represented in the Ulster Museum. In 1958 the Royal Ulster Academy arranged a memorial exhibition at the Old Museum building, Belfast, possibly the first one man exhibition of sculpture ever held in the Province.

MAURICE WILKS 1910-
Landscape and portrait painter

Born 25 November 1910, in Belfast, the son of Randal Wilks, linen designer, he was educated at Malone Public Elementary School, Belfast, and then attended night classes at the Belfast School of Art, winning the Dunville scholarship to the day school. When aged nineteen, he exhibited at the Royal Hibernian Academy, Dublin, and in the 1940s had several one man shows at the Victor Waddington Galleries, Dublin. He has also shown in Dublin at the Oireachtas. In the 1950s he had one man shows, mainly at the Anderson & McAuley gallery, Belfast, where, on one occasion, some Dutch landscapes were on view. In the 1960s one man shows were held in Canada, at Toronto and Montreal; and he also exhibited at Boston, Mass, USA. An Academician of the Royal Ulster Academy, in recent years he has also held exhibitions at the Walker Art Gallery, Coleraine. Represented at the Ulster Museum, Armagh County Museum and the Ulster Folk and Transport Museum, Cultra; also Belfast Harbour Office. At the Town Hall, Bangor, is a portrait of J Humbert Craig (q v).

JOHN WILLIAMS 1761-1818
Portrait and genre painter

Born in London, 28 April 1761, John Williams was better known as a writer than a painter, as Anthony Pasquin. At the age of seventeen he was apprenticed to Matthew Darly, the engraver and caricaturist in the Strand, but abandoned art, at least temporarily, to become an author and translator. In the period 1770-1775 he exhibited in London, but if the date of his birth is correct, from the *Dictionary of National Biography*, this would mean he exhibited when nine years of age. About 1780 he crossed to Ireland, where he appears to have practised as an itinerant painter. He was in Belfast in 1783 and painted there a large picture of the 'Adelphi Club', a group which included portraits of Andrew Cherry, actor; Michael Atkins, owner and manager of the Belfast Theatre; Amyas Griffith, excise surveyor of Carrickfergus; James Pinkerton, merchant; and the painter himself. This painting is mentioned in *A Dictionary of Irish Artists* (1913) by W G Strickland who stated it was owned by J C Pinkerton of Fernville, Jordanstown. Publishing trouble over an attack on the Government in the *Volunteers' Journal*, which he edited in Dublin, led him to decamp to England in 1784. There is no record of his having returned to Ireland but it is odd that twelve years should elapse before there appeared in London under his name: *An Authentic History of the Professors of Painting, Sculpture, and Architecture, who have practised in Ireland*, 'involving original letters from Sir Joshua Reynolds, which prove him to have been illiterate; to which are added Memoirs of the Royal Academicians'. Wherever he went, Williams, a satirist, was unpopular, and Lord Kenyon in a court case (1797) said of Williams, the plaintiff: 'I do most earnestly wish and hope that some method will ere long be fallen upon to prevent all such unprincipled and mercenary wretches from going about unbridled in society to the great annoyance and disquietude of the public.' In addition, he was noted for the dirt and slovenliness of his person and dress. He died of typhus fever at Brooklyn, New York, 3 November 1818.

DAVID WILSON 1873-1935
Caricaturist, landscape and flower painter

Son of the Rev A J Wilson, DD, of Minterburn, Co Tyrone, and later of Malone Presbyterian Church, Belfast, he was born at Minterburn Manse, 4 July 1873, and when he was about ten years of age the family moved to Belfast. After completing his education at the Royal Belfast Academical Institution, he entered the head office of the Northern Bank in Belfast, but spent his evenings drawing at the Government School of Design, where his gift for caricature began to develop. The urge to become an artist was so strong that he eventually went to London, but after lean years he became recognised in Fleet Street as one of the leading black and white artists. In 1896 at a meeting of the Belfast Art Society he read a paper on 'Illustrators'. For several years he was cartoonist to the *Daily Chronicle* and he also worked for the magazines *London Opinion* and *The Passing Show*. He was intimately connected with the poster and decorative work of the Apollo Theatre. To most people he was known by his brilliant cartoons and caricatures of famous politicians and many other notable figures in contemporary affairs, to others as a painter of flowers and landscapes. An exhibition of his caricatures was held at the Burlington Gallery, London, in 1921 but three years later at another gallery he showed flower paintings and landscapes. A member of the Royal Society of British Artists and the Royal Institute of Painters in Water Colour, he also exhibited at the Royal Academy and the Paris Salon. He died on 2 January 1935, in London. In 1938 the Belfast Museum and Art Gallery held an exhibition of his watercolours, and in the following year displayed his caricatures. In 1939, too, there was an exhibition of landscapes and flower studies at Rodman's Gallery, Belfast. Wilson is represented at the Ulster Museum and the Victoria and Albert Museum, London. At the National Gallery of Ireland, Dublin, there is a caricature of Sir John Lavery (q v).

J GLEN WILSON fl 1851-1855
Marine painter

So little is known about this artist in Irish records — he does not appear in W G Strickland's 1913 *Dictionary of Irish Artists* — that it may be assumed, on the evidence of his available paintings in Belfast, that the city was something of a 'port of call'. The National Maritime Museum at Greenwich rather substantiates this theory in that they have an engraving by J Glen Wilson of HMS *Herald*, May, 1855, which would appear to indicate, judging by the inscription, that he was associated with this survey vessel, which was stationed at the Fiji Islands in 1855. The Belfast Harbour Office has an oil painting 'Belfast Harbour Ferry Steps, Donegall Quay', 1851, and the oil paintings in the Ulster Museum are: 'Belfast Quay', 1851; 'Emigrant Ship Leaving Belfast'.

JOSEPH WILSON (or WILLSON) fl 1770-1793
Portrait painter

The earliest artist of note in Belfast, of whom there is any record, Joseph Wilson practised also in Dublin, and his widow Jane died there in 1804. The *Belfast News-Letter* for 28 June-2 July 1782, contains a notice, dated 26 June 1782, which refers to a painting of 'Daniel interpreting to Belshazzar the Writing on the Wall' which was to be raffled on 9 July 'at the Exhibition-Room of Mr. Joseph Willson, Portrait-Painter, Warren-Street, near the Exchange'. In the same year, he had a notice dated 'Belfast, September 8, 1782' in the *Dublin Evening Post* in October, 'not so much for emolument he may gain by it, as for the establishment of his name, publishing of a print of a gentleman executed in London after the Original full-length Picture and most striking Likeness which may now be seen at Wilson's Exhibition-room, in Waring Street ...' W G Strickland of *Dictionary of Irish Artists* (1913) fame had a written annotation in his copy stating that Wilson painted in 1784 a portrait of 'William Ware, organist of St. Anne's, for which he was paid 2 guineas Irish'. A volume of *Miscellaneous Tracts* by Amyas Griffith, the deformed and wittily malicious excise surveyor of Carrickfergus, published in Dublin in 1788, has an engraved portrait of the author as frontispiece, 'J. Wilson Pixt'. This is apparently the engraving advertised in the *Belfast Mercury or Freeman's Chronicle*, 13 January 1786, as 'From the original Drawing by Joseph Wilson of Belfast, Portrait Painter', and 'sold by all the Booksellers in Belfast, Lisburn, Newry, Armagh, Strabane, Derry, Coleraine and Downpatrick'. Joseph Wilson's death is given in the *Belfast News-Letter* for Tuesday, 12 March-Friday, 15 March 1793: 'On Wednesday at Ech i ville [?], Mr. Joseph Wilson; long a Portrait and Landscape Painter in this town; and a very worthy honest man.' It is assumed that the word has missing letters and should be Echlinville (House), which was near Kircubbin, Co Down. When Irish portraits by Ulster artists were shown at the Belfast Museum and Art Gallery in 1927 these included, by Wilson, Mrs Margaret McTear and Mrs David McTear, her daughter-in-law, the latter dated 1789; also a portrait of David Manson, a famous Belfast schoolmaster. The Ulster Museum also has in its collection portraits of John Magee, William Magee, and Mrs William Magee. Strickland in his 1913 dictionary stated that a 'Portrait of a Lady' belonged to Dr Hyndman. An Ulster Museum acquisition a few years ago was of 'Lieutenant Hyndman' in the uniform of Belfast 3rd Volunteer Union Company, established in 1778; this portrait is attributed to Wilson. The Armagh County Museum has an oil painting of Alexander Stewart of Acton, Co Armagh, 1789, and a pastel portrait of Mrs Stewart, Acton, c 1789.

SHAKSPERE WOOD 1827-1886
Sculptor

Born in Manchester, 13 November 1827, he was the son of Hamilton Wood of the firm of Wood, Rowell & Co, smallware manufacturers, Manchester. On the break-up of the business the Wood family moved to London, where the father was connected with the Wood Carving Company. Shakspere received part of his education as a sculptor in the schools of the Royal Academy, and about 1851 he visited Rome for further study. For some years he worked hard, and exhibited five sculptures at the Royal Academy between 1868 and 1871, giving his address as 'Rome'. In 1870 he lectured under the auspices of the Belfast Natural History and Philosophical Society on 'Ancient Sculpture and Modern Students', with a view to assisting the new Government School of Design. He appears, however, to have been working in Belfast prior to the lecture as there were several examples of his work at this time: a marble bust in the Ulster Museum of Henry MacCormac, MD (1800-1886), father of Sir William MacCormac (1836-1901), has the date 1869, and so, too, has one of Lady MacCormac (1835-1923). A bust of Sir William is also at Stranmillis together with one of John Charters, father of Lady MacCormac. Another local work was the bust of Alexander Mitchell (1780-1868), the blind Belfast engineer; this bust was presented in 1907 to the Museum and Art Gallery by his granddaughter, Mrs Mary Garrett, and the museum's quarterly notes for spring, 1924, also state: 'In the examination hall of the Queen's University, Belfast, there is a marble bust by Wood executed in 1871 of George Little Craik, LL.D (1798-1866) who was Professor of History and English Literature in Queen's College from 1849 until his death in 1866. There are three busts by him at Merville, Whitehouse: Sir Edward and Lady Coey, 1867, and Rev. Dr. Cooke, 1869.' But to return to Rome, where Wood took a keen interest in art and antiquity, these subjects engrossing more and more of his time and attention: he delivered lectures to English visitors, and eventually became an accredited representative of *The Times*. He died in Rome in February, 1886. Also represented at the Armagh County Museum: a white marble bust of Coventry Patmore (1823-1896), Rome, 1865. At the Royal Dublin Society, Ballsbridge, is a bust of Rt Hon Francis Blackburne (1782-1867), Lord Chancellor, 'Romae, 1865'.

PADRAIC WOODS 1898-
Landscape and portrait painter

Born in Newry, son of Peter Woods, baker, he left County Down at the age of six to live in Belfast, where he attended St Joseph's National School, Slate Street, and at the age of fifteen evening classes at the Belfast School of Art. He became a teacher at Holy Family School, Newington Avenue, but retired early in 1942 in order to have more time for painting. Locksley Hall, Fountain Street, had provided accommodation for an exhibition in 1936 when Swiss landscapes were among the exhibits. In 1940 he had received what was to be his most important portrait commission: Prof D L Savory, Professor of French, Queen's University, on the occasion of his retirement. He has also painted in France, especially Brittany; Italy and Holland. In 1948 he exhibited at the Dublin Painters' Gallery and an exhibition there in 1954 was opened by Siobhan McKenna, the actress. In the

1950s he had two exhibitions at 55a Donegall Place, Belfast. He was appointed a governor of the Belfast College of Art in 1964. He had an exhibition at Queen's University, Belfast, 1968. An Academician of the Royal Ulster Academy, he has also shown in Dublin at the Royal Hibernian Academy and the Oireachtas, and in London at the Wimbledon Gallery. He is a former president of the Ulster Arts Club. Also represented at the National Museum of Ireland, Dublin.

BIBLIOGRAPHY

It would have been tedious to list the titles of all the catalogues which were used in the compilation of this narrative; a number of the earliest are to be found in the Linen Hall Library, the others are in my own collection. I mention only those which are excellent reference items for their own subjects, and the admirable Ulster Museum publications on *Andrew Nicholl* and *Dr James Moore*.

In the field of books, *Strickland* is, of course, the basis of all work up to the date of its appearance. *Arnold* sketches the Irish background briskly, and the relevant chapters in *The Arts in Ulster* (1951) and *Causeway* (1971) are useful surveys involving local knowledge not presented elsewhere. But this present volume, given substance and authority by Theo Snoddy's biographical notes, for the first time assembles the necessary information for any further work which may be undertaken on its subject.

Though this is the first considered word on the course of the Art in Ulster it will not be the last. More thorough research will likely amplify the story, correct my mistakes, and set my opinions in their proper historical perspective as those of an elderly man writing in the idiom and with the prejudices of his period. But the biographical notes will, I believe, stand up better to the scrutiny of time, for they have been composed with a care and resolution beyond my scope or temper.

GENERAL SURVEYS

A Dictionary of Irish Artists, by W G Strickland (London/Dublin, 1913).

A Concise History of Irish Art, by Bruce Arnold (London, 1969).

The Arts in Ulster, edited by Sam Hanna Bell, etc (London 1951) (Chapter on Painting and Sculpture in Ulster, by John Hewitt).

Causeway: The Arts in Ulster, edited by Michael Longley (Arts Council of Northern Ireland and Gill and Macmillan, Dublin, 1971) (Chapter on Painting and Sculpture, by Kenneth Jamison).

CATALOGUES AND MONOGRAPHS

Irish Houses and Landscapes: Catalogue of exhibition, Dublin and Belfast, 1963.
Irish Portraits 1660-1860: Catalogue of exhibition, Dublin, London and Belfast, 1969.
The Irish Imagination 1959-1971: Catalogue of exhibition in Dublin 1971 in association with Rosc '71.
Irish Art 1900-1950: Catalogue of exhibition in Cork 1975 in association with Rosc Teoranta.
James Moore 1819-1883: Publication No 189, Ulster Museum, 1973.
Andrew Nicholl 1804-1886: Publication No 190, Ulster Museum, 1973.

BACKGROUND

Science and Art in Belfast, by William Gray (Belfast, 1904).
The Buildings of Belfast, by C E B Brett (London, 1967).
Irish Church Monuments, by Homer Potterton (Ulster Architectural Heritage Society, 1975).
Vere Foster 1819-1900 An Irish Benefactor, by Mary McNeill (Newtownabbot, 1971).

INDIVIDUAL ARTISTS

The Life of a Painter, by Sir John Lavery (London, 1940).
An Irish Portrait, by Paul Henry (London, n d [1951]).
Further Reminiscences, by Paul Henry (Belfast, 1976).
MacWilliam, introduction by Roland Penrose (London, 1964).
Colin Middleton, by John Hewitt (Arts Council of Northern Ireland, 1976).
Hugh Thomson, his art, etc: by M H Spielmann and W Jerrold (London, 1931).
William Scott, by Ronald Alley (London, 1963).

INDEX

Page numbers in italics denote illustrations, and the biographical accounts of the artists are indicated by the abbreviation 'biog'.